VULTURE
CAPITALI$M

VULTURE CAPITALI$M

Corporate Crimes, Backdoor Bailouts,
and the Death of Freedom

GRACE BLAKELEY

ATRIA BOOKS

New York London Toronto Sydney New Delhi

ATRIA
BOOKS

An Imprint of Simon & Schuster, LLC
1230 Avenue of the Americas
New York, NY 10020

First Atria Books hardcover edition March 2024

ATRIA BOOKS and colophon are trademarks of Simon & Schuster, LLC

Simon & Schuster: Celebrating 100 Years of Publishing in 2024

For information about special discounts for bulk purchases, please contact Simon & Schuster Special Sales at 1-866-506-1949 or business@simonandschuster.com.

The Simon & Schuster Speakers Bureau can bring authors to your live event. For more information or to book an event, contact the Simon & Schuster Speakers Bureau at 1-866-248-3049 or visit our website at www.simonspeakers.com.

Interior design by Silverglass

Manufactured in the United States of America

1 3 5 7 9 10 8 6 4 2

Library of Congress Cataloging-in-Publication Data

Names: Blakeley, Grace, author.
Title: Vulture capitalism : corporate crimes, backdoor bailouts, and the death of freedom / by Grace Blakeley.
Description: New York : Atria Books, 2024. | Includes bibliographical references and index.
Identifiers: LCCN 2023035159 (print) | LCCN 2023035160 (ebook) | ISBN 9781982180850 (hardcover) | ISBN 9781982180867 (trade paperback) | ISBN 9781982180874 (ebook)
Subjects: LCSH: Capitalism--Moral and ethical aspects. | Corporations--Corrupt practices. | Income distribution. | Bailouts (Government policy) | Social responsibility of business.
Classification: LCC HB501 .B614 2024 (print) | LCC HB501 (ebook) | DDC 364.16/8--dc23/eng/20230913
LC record available at https://lccn.loc.gov/2023035159
LC ebook record available at https://lccn.loc.gov/2023035160

ISBN 978-1-9821-8085-0
ISBN 978-1-9821-8087-4 (ebook)

Contents

Introduction vii

PART I: CAPITALISM AND FREEDOM

1

How to Get Away with Murder 3
Capitalism Isn't What You Think It Is 11

2

The United States of Fordlândia 19
The Ungovernable Society 26
The Neoliberal Lie 31

3

Disaster Capitalism 41
AIG: American Insurance Grifters 48
Making a Killing for McKinsey 53
The Cost-of-Greed Crisis 61
Out of the Frying Pan and into the Fire 66

PART II: THE PLANNERS

4

American-Made Sweatshops: How Big Business Plans 75
Black Box Businesses 81
Chemical Imbalances 90
Government 4 Sale 101

5

Buying Time: How Big Banks Plan 109

Dr. Debt 114

Bernie's Bros 119

The King's Coin 124

BlackRock's Black Ops 132

6

Capital's Cronies: How States Plan 139

The Highway Code 143

Shilling for Greensill 153

Nudged over the Edge 162

Ever-planned 167

7

Money at Six Percent: How Empires Plan 173

Pacifying the Natives 179

Banana Republics 186

The People versus Chevron 194

The Human Right to Capital Flight 202

PART III: DEMOCRATIC PLANNING

8

The Architect and the Bee: How to Plan Democratically 215

Lord of the Lies 222

People-Powered Planning 226

9

Taking Back Control: Democratic Planning at Scale 241

Making Capital Scream 247

Democratizing the Future 264

Conclusion 267

Notes 273

Index 343

Introduction

Probably it is true enough that the great majority are rarely capable of
thinking independently, that on most questions they accept views which
they find ready-made, and that they will be equally content if born or
coaxed into one set of beliefs or another. In any society freedom of
thought will probably be of direct significance only for a small minority.

—F. A. Hayek, *The Road to Serfdom*

A spider conducts operations that resemble those of a weaver, and a bee
puts to shame many an architect in the construction of her cells. But what
distinguishes the worst architect from the best of bees is this, that the
architect raises his structure in imagination before he erects it in reality.

—Karl Marx, *Capital, Volume 1*

When you wake up in the morning, the first thing you do is probably pick up your phone. That phone is made of rare earth metals,
which were likely extracted from a country like the Democratic Republic
of the Congo, where rebel groups use the revenues from mining these minerals to purchase weapons.[1] But that fact will be far from your mind as
you check social media, eking out a little "you time" before the day begins.
In doing so, you are surrendering information about the most intimate
parts of your life to companies like Facebook, which has been accused of
promoting far-right extremism, facilitating child sexual exploitation, and
interfering with the outcomes of democratic elections, or Twitter, recently
purchased by an egomaniacal, union-busting billionaire who fires the platform's employees when his tweets don't receive enough likes.[2]

You roll out of bed and pull on some clothes, manufactured by a multinational corporation that outsources production to Bangladesh. After

thousands of their peers were crushed to death when a garment factory collapsed in Dhaka, the workers who made those clothes organized themselves into a union, but they're still paid poverty wages.[3] You see an old piece of clothing on the floor that doesn't spark joy, so you remind yourself to take it to a charity recycling bin. The item of clothing may then continue its journey to a huge dump in Kenya, where impoverished children pick through the waste to find a few items of resalable quality.[4]

You rush out into the brisk, cold air, which is mercifully slightly warmer than the air in your house. Much as they have utterly failed to deal with the housing crisis that forces you to pay two-thirds of your income in rent, your government has failed to insulate people from rising energy costs too.[5] You guiltily jump into your car, knowing that your decision to drive yourself to work is part of a problem that's causing global temperatures to rise at an unprecedented rate. But you might console yourself with the knowledge that your car runs on gasoline, given Volkswagen's record of lying to the world about the impact of its diesel engines on the environment and your lungs.[6]

By the time the day ends, you're exhausted—physically and emotionally. You open a food delivery app, and when the delivery driver arrives, you give him a small tip. He's very grateful for the extra cash, because his motorcycle is on its last legs and he's being faced with a choice between taking out a high-interest payday loan to fix it or using his bicycle instead, which will mean more work and far fewer deliveries.[7] As you drift off to sleep, you plug in the cell phone manufactured in a warehouse in China where nets have been installed to catch workers who have tried to throw themselves out the window.[8]

This may or may not be an accurate depiction of your life. Perhaps you're reading this book in a home that is now entirely your own, having left your days of drudgery and toil behind you. But you may also be dimly aware that your children seem pathologically incapable of saving the amount of money required to purchase their own homes, let alone enough to retire as comfortably as you have. Or perhaps you are one of those lucky people who really, genuinely enjoys their job, loves their coworkers, and believes they're really contributing something to society. But maybe you also struggle to escape the sense that something isn't quite right in the world around you, even though you feel entirely unable to do anything about it—other than purchase products marketed to you as "green" and "ethical."

Elements of this story will resonate with everyone because it describes what it is like to interact with the systems that govern our society and over which most of us have little control. The luckiest among us might be able to insulate ourselves from some of them, but no one can entirely extricate themselves from the webs of labor, production, and consumption that underpin modern capitalism. And, as a result, most of us at some point in our lives will feel a little powerless. Many people will spend nearly every waking moment being controlled by these systems. And for some, that feeling of alienation drives them into a deep sense of despair.

Most of us are trying to do what is best most of the time, yet so many of our decisions don't feel like decisions at all. There is a deep contradiction between the belief that we are free and the reality of living under capitalism—a system of pervasive *un*freedom.

This sense of unfreedom is grounded in the deep disparities of power that exist within capitalist societies—many of which are completely invisible. Most people are denied autonomy over their lives, yet we are consistently told that we are free to choose how we live. Life under capitalism means life under a system in which decisions about how we work, how we live, and what we buy have already been made by someone else. Life under capitalism means living in a planned economy, while being told that you are free.

For a long time, planning and capitalism have been thought of as opposites. Either one lives in a free-market capitalist society, in which no single actor controls the production and allocation of resources, or one lives in a centrally planned economy, in which one institution—generally the state—decides everything. Many people reading this book will have grown up during the Cold War, when the miracle of free-market US capitalism was counterposed with the sclerotic and oppressive centralized planning practiced in the USSR. But while these two systems differed in many ways, they had one important thing in common: both contained elements of centralized planning.

The confusion results from the fact that most people think of free markets and capitalism as synonymous. In fact, actually existing capitalist economies are hybrid systems, based on a careful balance between markets and planning. This is not a glitch resulting from the incomplete implementation of capitalism, or its corruption by an evil, all-powerful elite. It is simply the way capitalism works.

While markets may be an inescapable part of any capitalist society, capitalism is not defined by the free market. Capitalism is defined by the class division between owners and workers, between those who own all the stuff needed to produce commodities and those forced to work to produce those commodities.[9] And the people who own all the stuff are capable, to a greater or lesser extent, of making decisions that have huge implications for everyone else. They are capable of planning.

All capitalist societies contain institutions capable of planning— from large corporations to financial institutions to states. At the global level too, the most powerful states and the institutions they control have some power to plan. This power is never total. Capitalist societies, and the world economy of which they are a part, are immensely complex systems that can never be fully controlled by any one actor or group of actors. But some individuals and institutions are better able to determine who gets what than others. This observation holds even in the most competitive capitalist economies, albeit to a lesser extent.

The question we should ask ourselves, then, is not whether planning is possible in a capitalist economy. Instead, we should ask where planning is taking place, how it is being executed, and whose interests it is serving.

One answer to these questions is to suggest that only states have the power to plan—and they tend to do so in the interests of politicians and bureaucrats rather than in the general interest. While markets may not be perfect, they are rigorous enough over the long run to ensure that no private actor is able to dominate them for too long. The state, on the other hand, with its monopoly over the legitimate use of force, is able to bend other actions to its will. And this power, some have argued, can be very dangerous if left unchecked.

Friedrich A. Hayek, Austrian economist and one of the fathers of what came to be known as *neoliberalism*, was deeply suspicious of the overt exercise of state power in capitalist societies. Without intervention to curb state power, thinkers like Hayek claimed that "socialist policies" like health care, public housing, and nationalization would transform even the most liberal economy into a totalitarian nightmare.[10]

Hayek's views were formulated in opposition to those of another economist, one whose work dominated the global economy after the Second World War. John Maynard Keynes's magnum opus—*The General Theory of Employment, Interest and Money*—was slightly less snappily named than Hayek's, but during their lifetimes it was by far the more influential of the two.[11]

Keynes believed that a level of state planning was necessary in all free-market economies because of the irrationalities that emerged from the normal operation of the market system. For example, when lots of investors felt pessimistic about the future, they would stop investing, and in doing so they would create the very conditions they had most feared. In such a context, the state could step in and act as a backstop to private demand, investing and employing workers where others would not.

After the Second World War, governments from all around the world adopted Keynes's ideas as a way of taming the irrationalities of the free market—irrationalities that had become obvious in the midst of the Wall Street crash of 1929. Unionists and socialists also eagerly took up his theories, which provided the intellectual foundations for the collective provision of services that would improve the lives of working people everywhere.

As neoliberal economists articulated during the now infamous meetings that took place in the Swiss town of Mont-Pèlerin throughout the mid-twentieth century, their project was to put an end to this wave of "Marxian and Keynesian planning sweeping the globe."[12] Neoliberals like Hayek spent the early postwar years developing a scathing critique of the kind of planning seen around the world in the aftermath of the Second World War. The toxic melding of the power of the state with that of workers, they contended, was compromising human liberty and leading us all—in Hayek's words—down the "road to serfdom."[13]

In a story with which you may already be familiar, the neoliberals won. They supported the election of politicians who crushed the formerly powerful labor movement, privatized public companies, and marketized the welfare state.[14] And they did all this in the name of "freedom."

But things didn't quite turn out the way the neoliberals promised. We live in societies that are just as tightly regulated, surveilled, and controlled as those of several decades ago.[15] Public spending has not fallen, it has simply been redistributed. Rather than spending on welfare and public services, deemed an inefficient use of resources by neoliberals, states now spend billions on supporting big business and the wealthy with subsidies, tax breaks, and bailouts.[16] And sprawling corporations have unprecedented control over many areas of our lives.[17] What happened to Hayek's dream of freedom?

Hayek was onto something when he posited that societies are far too complex to yield to any centralized authority without unintended consequences. The problem isn't that this thesis was wrong, it is that he stopped short of taking it to its logical conclusion. If centralized planning tends to lead to tyranny, then why shouldn't we be just as concerned about corporate planning as we are about state planning? Any institution capable of wielding largely unaccountable power within an allegedly democratic society should, at the very least, be subject to critical analysis.

The question that animates this book might, then, be framed in the following way: What if we were to take Hayek seriously? To do so, we must analyze actually existing capitalism by returning to our original questions: Where is planning taking place? How is it being executed? Whose interests is it serving?

The capitalist state is one source of semiaccountable authority and centralized planning within nominally free-market societies, but it is far from the only one. Corporations, for example, are able to plan investment and employment decisions—decisions that have significant implications not only for the lives of most people but also for the structure of our society.[18] And they are unaccountable to those most affected by their decisions.

Neoliberals might argue that the power of the firm is limited by the operation of the market. A manager can plan, but only within certain parameters set out by the competitive environment. If he messes up, the business will fail. States, on the other hand, are not so constrained by market forces. In fact, states are often in a position to dominate the market in a way that, according to the mainstream economist, most firms are not. State agents are therefore free to make decisions—to develop and implement plans—in a way that corporate managers aren't.

But this is true only when the market actually functions in the way it is imagined to in economics textbooks. As soon as we leave the world of small businesses competing with one another for market share and enter the reality of capitalism—one in which vast, sprawling enterprises cooperate with one another and with states as much as they compete—we enter a world of pervasive private planning. Large firms are able, to a significant extent, to ignore the pressure exerted by the market and instead act to shape market conditions themselves. As one author puts it, "The free market is a smokescreen, behind which lies the brutal, despotic power of corporations."[19]

A large employer has the power to set wages and conditions without much reference to the competition. A sufficiently large producer can set the prices it pays to suppliers, and those it charges to consumers, without much pressure from the market. A sufficiently large financial institution has the power to direct investment into certain technologies and therefore to determine which futures are available and which ones are foreclosed. And all these firms can consolidate their power by buying up competitors, erecting barriers to entry, and crushing workers' attempts to organize, further insulating them from competitive pressure and giving them significant authority both within their domains and over society as a whole.

But isn't there a fundamental difference between state planning and corporate planning? To return to our original questions, isn't private planning undertaken in service of different interests than planning undertaken by a central state?

States, you might think, plan only in the interests of unaccountable bureaucrats and greedy politicians. Corporations, meanwhile, plan in the interests of shareholders, and, so the argument goes, what benefits shareholders benefits all of us. The point of a corporation is to maximize its profits—and when corporations maximize profits, they create jobs and products that benefit everyone. States tend to get in the way of corporate planning through taxes, regulation, and other unwarranted interference with the operation of the free market.

The first problem with this argument is that, in the largely *unfree* markets that exist within all modern capitalist societies, profit maximization does not lead to outcomes that are beneficial to everyone else. Without the competitive pressure to invest or pay decent wages, profits are simply distributed to the wealthy while workers face lower wages and higher prices. A world of pervasive corporate power is one characterized by low investment, low productivity, low wages, and high inequality.[20]

And even the very limited view of freedom held by the neoliberals is not safeguarded under the capitalist monster they have created. Neoliberalism was supposed to guarantee consumers' freedom of choice, yet, as one keen observer has pointed out: "[i]nstead of having infinite choice, as we thought, we are really presented with a wall of standard-issue cans and pouches that are distinguished only by the words and colours on their labels. The secret ingredient of US capitalism . . . could have been cooked up in the Soviet Union."

But, perhaps more importantly, the idea that corporate and state planning act in service of fundamentally different interests rests on a clean distinction between political and economic power that cannot be sustained in practice. Corporations are political institutions as much as they are economic ones.[21] Many corporations prioritize growing their political power—their corporate sovereignty (a concept we'll come to in chapter 4)—over short-term profitability.[22]

Equally, the state is not a neutral entity floating on top of society, existing solely to empower those lucky enough to govern it. Politicians and bureaucrats tend to implement regulation in the interests of those best able to influence them—and powerful corporations and the wealthy individuals that run them are those that spend the most time and effort on this influencing. As anyone with some familiarity with the events leading up to the financial crisis of 2008 could attest, this means that laws are often made in the interests of powerful private actors.[23] State policy is, in other words, shaped by the balance of power within society.

As a result, the interests of politicians and corporate executives are not as different as you might expect. In fact, contrary to perceived wisdom, firms and states are not enemies in the "free market" game—more often than not they are powerful allies.

But what about democracy? Shouldn't this provide a check on the unaccountable exercise of private power—both within formal state institutions and outside them?

Capitalist democracies provide the electorate with limited freedom to shape the operation of state power and zero freedom to shape economic institutions. This is no coincidence. Without democracy in the realm of production, large corporations and financial institutions are able to wield unaccountable power of the kind that would be the envy of even the most authoritarian state. This creates a curious kind of "unfreedom" that pervades even nominally democratic societies. While citizens are assumed to be capable of voting in democratic elections, when they arrive at work they become the "subjects of a despotic corporate government"[24]—and the only alternative to obedience is destitution.

While some may argue that they are constrained by democratic processes, today's megacorporations are in fact extremely well placed to overcome these pressures and influence state policy in their favor. As Thorstein Veblen observed decades ago, the competitive process naturally creates incentives to try to change the rules to one's own advantage.[25] So, over time, the rules of the market game we're all supposed to be playing come to favor the interests of the powerful.

The next question on your lips might be "So what?" Why should anyone care about these abstract arguments about planning and markets, politics and economics? What real-world implications do these debates actually have?

The problem with our inability to understand the ways in which capitalist planning functions is that it closes off potential alternatives to the current system. When politicians mess up, we're told that the state has grown too big, so we should cut public spending and hand more power to unaccountable corporations. And when corporations abuse their power, we're told that the solution is to give more power to the politicians who are funded by those corporations. Power remains concentrated at the top of the same institutions, even as politicians lose elections and corporate executives are replaced.

This elite carousel gives many people a deep sense of hopelessness. No matter who you vote for, no matter what products you buy, no matter where you work, it doesn't seem to make a difference. Yet we're supposed to live in a free-market democracy. We're supposed to be free.

Neoliberals like Hayek promised that policies like deregulation and privatization would promote human freedom. The removal of barriers to entrepreneurship and the end to the toxic obsession with equality would allow the most capable human beings to flourish, creating wealth and prosperity for all. But as the quote at the start of this introduction illustrates, Hayek did not believe that the vast majority of people would be capable of making use of this freedom. He believed that "the cognitive capacity of the masses was . . . trivial compared with the intellectual influence of the elites."[26] The masses were destined to spend the rest of their lives taking orders from someone else.

Yet the only alternative with which we are presented—Keynes's regulated market—suffers from some deep flaws too. Keynes's ambivalence toward the freedom and autonomy of the masses is evident throughout his writing. He believed that the socially necessary role of constraining the market should be played by an enlightened class of politicians and bureaucrats who could rescue people from the consequences of their own actions. In doing so, they would be working to save capitalism from itself—to protect Western civilization and the freedoms that it supposedly guaranteed.[27]

The battle that has been raging in our politics for so long is between Hayek and Keynes—a battle between a very limited view of freedom as personal sovereignty and a conservative view of freedom as submission to the rule of enlightened bureaucrats. Both men shared a belief that most people could not be trusted to make any real decisions about the nature of society.

In the absence of any serious alternatives to the status quo, many people fall prey to conspiracy theories, which suggest that the entire world economy is being run behind closed doors by a secretive, all-powerful—and often racialized—elite. Such perspectives fail to understand the nature of capitalist planning, which exists on the knife edge between competition and control. Capitalist planning is never total; no one institution can ever become powerful enough to completely dominate its competitors. Whether you're a president or a CEO, you're always going to have to deal with competing interests and unanticipated challenges. You can use your power to plan what to do in response, but you can't control the outcome.

As Hayek observed, economies are complex systems that never completely submit to centralized control.[28] Capitalist societies are based on a dialectic—a creative tension—between planning and competition, control and anarchy. This tension is what makes these societies both so adaptable and so unchanging—institutions can be reorganized, elites can be reshuffled, ideologies can shift without fundamentally altering the structure of the society. The centralization of power in our world doesn't result from the schemes of a few individuals—it results from the class structure of capitalism.

Far before Keynes and Hayek, Karl Marx saw that capitalist societies tended to become more centralized over time. The advantages of scale, combined with the cooperation that takes place between capitalists, financiers, and states, ensure that capitalist industries become more concentrated, and a small number of powerful people are able to decide what we produce and how our societies are governed. Centralization, in other words, goes hand in hand with the development of capitalism.

Some argued that this process would bring about world peace and economic stability, as private corporations and state bureaucracies melded into one super-institution capable of planning on a world scale. But Marx saw from the outset that centralization would instead lead to an increase in "the mass of misery, oppression, slavery, degradation, exploitation" in a capitalist society, with working people suffering the consequences.[29]

More planning does not, then, equal less capitalism. The only way to get less capitalism is to constrain the power of capital—the people who own all the stuff. You can't do this by giving more power to politicians, because unless we have real economic democracy, the wealthy will simply use their influence to buy them off. Nor can we expect giant private corporations to act on behalf of the general interest simply out of their own benevolence. The way out runs through the democratization of our society—redistributing political and economic power, rather than handing it all to a different set of people and expecting them to make good decisions on everyone else's behalf.

We don't have to accept a politics that can be reduced to "more or less state," in which everything changes so that everything can stay the same. We don't have to accept the flourishing of extremist fringe groups that prey on those who, often rightly, feel hopeless and powerless. We don't have to live in a society in which only some people can be free. There is another way.

To Hayek, the worker was a bee: their role was to make the honey, not design the hive. But to Marx, the worker was at heart an architect. They yearned to create new worlds in their heads and bring those worlds into being with their hands. This view of freedom—the socialist view—is one in which each and every one of us has genuine power and autonomy over not only our own lives but over the progression of the societies in which we live. It is a conception of freedom that recognizes our mutual interdependence, while honoring the choices of the individual. It is an idea of freedom that hinges on our capacity to build and maintain *democratic* structures to govern the world.

In the current system, workers are alienated from their creative power in a society in which imagination is the prerogative of capital. Bosses decide business plans and managers implement them—considering only their personal power and the profits of the corporation. Politicians decide the rules and bureaucrats implement them—considering only their own personal power and that of the state. Workers are left to compete with one another in a game that has been designed to ensure they lose.

Marxist theorist Ellen Meiksins Wood argued that the "separation of the economic and the political" was one of the defining features of capitalist ideology.[30] Democracy is permitted in the political realm (within formal state institutions) while it is strictly limited within the economy (within the corporation and the market). Yet the designation of the corporation as an "economic" institution disguises the forms of "private government" that obtain within the firm.[31] And the understanding of the state as a political institution insulated from "the economy" obscures how the exercise of state power is shaped by a process of social struggle in which capital dominates.[32] The fusion of political and economic power in capitalist societies means, Meiksins Wood argues, that democracy "has become synonymous with socialism."[33]

To understand socialism in this way, we must accept that the divide between capitalism and socialism is not defined by technical questions like the operation of the price mechanism, the extent of planning or markets, or even the balance between the public and private sector. These factors are all important in shaping the way socialist and capitalist societies function, but the difference between the two is far simpler. A capitalist society is a class-divided society in which power is monopolized by capitalists and their allies. A socialist society is a classless society in which power is shared and decisions are made collectively. A socialist society is, then, a true democracy.

Most people respond to this idea with a similar attitude: "It sounds nice in theory, but how would it work in practice?" As I will illustrate, history has provided us with many examples of what happens when working people are able to take control over society's political and economic institutions. Experiments in democratic planning and worker control show beyond doubt the human capacity for cooperation, collective decision-making, and, above all, imagination. From the Lucas Plan, which saw workers develop proposals to transform a multinational arms manufacturer into a worker-owned social enterprise, to the participatory budgeting movement, in which citizens have taken control of government spending with astonishing results, the evidence is clear: when you give people real power, they use it to build socialism.

Hayek was right to begin his analysis with the question of freedom. The freedom to live as one wants is, after all, a big part of what makes us human. But under capitalism this freedom is, as Hayek acknowledged, available only to "a small minority."

Under socialism, the freedom offered to all is the freedom of the architect—the power to create worlds. Naturally, this is not a power that can be exercised by any one individual alone. It is a freedom that lies at the intersection between the individual and the collective—it is, in other words, a social freedom; a freedom that recognizes and upholds human beings' interdependence, with one another and with nature.

Over the course of this book I will seek to show how capitalist planning works and how we can start to resist it. I'll discuss what capitalism actually is, how it has changed over time, and why centralized planning is one feature that has remained constant. Then I'll look at the major institutions capable of planning within capitalist societies—firms, financial institutions, states, and empires. Finally, I'll outline how we can start to replace the current system of oligarchic capitalist planning with democratic socialist planning.

Most of the ideas I discuss in the book are not new. My argument is constructed based on an analysis of the work of well-known political economists, with which academic readers will already be familiar. Nevertheless, I felt that it was important to draw these ideas together into a compelling and simple argument that will, hopefully, be of interest to most people. Because, while academics have already spent a great deal of time debating these ideas, their debates have not filtered down into mass politics. As a result, most political discourse around the world is still stuck in the sterile Keynesian-Hayekian division that has predominated since the Second World War.

As someone whose job it is to engage in these debates, I find this immensely frustrating. When COVID-19 forced governments everywhere to increase spending in order to protect capital and shore up their legitimacy in the face of mounting deaths, commentators across the political spectrum were quick to describe the resulting avalanche of public cash as "socialism." It seemed that anything the capitalist state did could be described as "socialist"—even if it was dishing out billions to corporations and landlords. In early 2020, I felt like I was spending most of my energy explaining to people what socialism was and what it was not.[34]

I soon realized that these questions concerning the nature of socialism related to a much deeper misunderstanding of the nature of capitalism. Perhaps because of the legacy of the Cold War, many people believed that centralized planning was the *opposite* of capitalism. Free markets seemed so anarchic and chaotic that it would be absurd to suggest they are planned by anyone. Politicians plan, corporations respond.

But, as I will show in the following chapters, corporations and financial institutions are capable of planning on their own account. Furthermore, public and private actors often work together to plan state policy. Capitalist planning is alive and well, even after the alleged triumph of the "free market."

By the time you finish this book, it is my hope that you will be convinced that markets and states are not separate domains of power; that capitalism is not defined by the presence of free markets, but by the rule of capital; and that socialism is not defined by the dominance of the state over all areas of life, but by true democracy. More than anything, I hope that by the time you finish reading you will be convinced that you have the power to change the way the world works. Because there are a lot of very powerful people out there who want you to believe that you don't.

PART I

CAPITALISM AND FREEDOM

1

How to Get Away with Murder

On October 29, 2018, Lion Air Flight 610—a Boeing 737 MAX plane—disappeared from the sky. Thirteen minutes after the flight took off from Jakarta International Airport, air traffic control lost communication with the pilot.[1] At 7:30 a.m. authorities revealed that the plane had crashed into the sea a few miles off the Indonesian coastline.[2] It took two days to identify the first victim, and the search-and-rescue operation eventually determined that every single one of the 189 people on board, as well as six cabin crew and two pilots, had died in the crash.[3] The plane had been intact when it fell out of the sky but was decimated upon impact, with even the strongest parts of the aircraft obliterated by the extraordinary force with which the plane hit the ocean.

Investigators later discovered that the problem lay with the aircraft's angle-of-attack (AoA) sensor. For some reason, the malfunctioning sensor had caused the plane to nose-dive four times during the previous flight—and several more times during the subsequent flight, ultimately leading to the fatal crash on October 29.[4] Every time the plane nose-dived the pilot had tried to pull it back up, but the plane's power overcame his efforts. Boeing tried to blame the crew for failing to understand the systems that would have allowed them to correct the error.[5]

In the meantime, another plane—Ethiopian Airlines Flight 302, also a 737 MAX—had suffered the same fate as Lion Air 610. Flight 302 took off from Addis Ababa Bole International Airport at 8:38 a.m. on March 10, 2019, and within two minutes, the pilot had contacted air traffic control to report a "flight error."[6] The plane's nose had begun to tilt downward, sending the aircraft plunging out of the sky.[7] The pilots struggled to control the plane, trying to drag the nose back up manually.[8] At 8:44 a.m., air traffic control lost contact with the crew.[9] Ethiopian Airlines Flight 302 had plummeted out of the sky and hit the ground at a speed of 700 miles per hour.[10] Wreckage from the flight was driven thirty feet into the surrounding earth, and the impact crater was 90 feet wide and 120 feet long.[11] All 157 people on board the plane died instantly.

A year after the crash, the Ethiopian Civil Aviation Authority released an interim report detailing the results of its investigations. It found that the angle-of-attack sensors on the plane had malfunctioned, delivering different readings for each wing, which had activated a system—the MCAS—that caused the plane's nose to dive down.[12] The report confirmed that the crew and pilots had followed all the correct procedures but had been unable to prevent the catastrophe.

The 737 MAX disasters came at a bad time for Boeing, which was literally putting out fires everywhere. The company's previous plane, the 787 Dreamliner, was not only delivered extremely late and over-budget, it was also beset with technical and design flaws. One such flaw resulted in the plane's batteries catching on fire, a fault that ultimately forced the entire fleet to be grounded.[13]

The faults with the Dreamliner could be traced back to a culture of cost-cutting and corner-cutting that had set in at Boeing over the previous several decades.[14] Harry Stonecipher, the former CEO of the defunct aviation business McDonnell Douglas (a failed firm that merged with Boeing with the help of the American state, as we'll see later), became CEO of Boeing in 2003. Stonecipher was the protégé of Jack Welch, former CEO of General Electric, who financialized the firm almost beyond recognition, leading to a culture of "corner-cutting" that culminated in scandals like GE's dumping toxic chemicals into the Hudson River.[15] Stonecipher was ultimately forced to leave Boeing—and his wife left him—after it was revealed that he had been having an affair with another Boeing executive.[16]

Stonecipher's strategy for Boeing, developed alongside Welch, was simple. He'd allow problems to build and then exploit the chaos to implement what he referred to as a "cultural revolution."[17] He sought to denigrate engineering expertise, up to that point prized by the company, and instead lionize senior management to allow them to implement a radical cost-cutting agenda.[18] Previously, many positions at

Boeing had been unionized, but Stonecipher made it his mission to undermine the unions and employ contractors in their place.[19] When developing the 787 Dreamliner, Stonecipher issued an ultimatum: "[d]evelop the plane for less than 40 percent of what the 777 had cost to develop 13 years earlier, and build each plane out of the gate for less than 60 percent of the 777's unit costs in 2003."[20]

This bid to boost returns was what lay behind the 737 MAX disasters. Without push back from the regulator, the FAA, "Boeing's management prioritized the company's profitability and stock price over everything else, including passenger safety."[21] One of the surest ways to cut costs for the operators of a plane, and therefore sell more planes and boost profits, is to reduce seat mile costs—the cost of a flight per passenger per mile.[22] And one of the easiest ways to cut these costs is to make a plane's engines bigger, allowing the plane to fly longer distances with more passengers.

The only problem with larger engines is that they leave less room between the plane and the ground during takeoff and landing; the engines on the 737 MAX were huge, making this problem critical.[23] As a result, the engines were moved forward, in front of the wing. But this created another problem: "when the pilots applied power to the engine, the aircraft would have a significant propensity to 'pitch up,' or raise its nose." And when the plane's nose pitched up in this way, it would frequently stall.[24]

In essence, Boeing had created a "dynamically unstable" plane: as soon as the plane's nose started to tilt up, features of the plane's design would cause it to tilt up *even more*.[25] As aeronautical expert Gregory Travis explains, the only other dynamically unstable planes are fighter jets, "and they are fitted with ejection seats."[26]

Rather than solving this problem by changing the plane's design, which would have been expensive, Boeing crafted a software fix. The company was intent on making the 737 MAX appear as similar to the 737 as possible to honor preexisting agreements with the airlines.[27] Boeing's clients wanted to limit modifications to the plane to ensure they didn't have to retrain their pilots. And Boeing was only too happy to oblige. The company agreed to rebate Southwest $1 million for every plane the company purchased if the airline had to retrain its pilots.[28]

The hack software engineers designed was the MCAS, or Maneuvering Characteristics Augmentation System. The MCAS interacts with the plane's angle-of-attack sensors to automatically push the plane's nose down whenever the sensors detect a stall—this was supposed to solve the problem of "dynamic instability" caused by the engine placement.[29] Contrary to Boeing's former pilot-first philosophy—another casualty of Stonecipher's leadership—the system was automatic.[30] This meant there was no way for the pilot to correct the error manually—the controls would be pushed downward when the MCAS determined they should be, and the pilot would have had to use an inhuman amount of force to pull the controls back up manually.[31]

A further issue was that the MCAS was linked only to one of two angle-of-attack sensors. If both sensors had been hooked up to it, they could have disagreed with each other, an issue that would have required human intervention to remedy, and therefore would have required more pilot training.[32] The solution to this problem was to link the MCAS to just one of the two AoA sensors, meaning that if one was faulty, the plane would nose-dive out of the sky. The pilots weren't told about the software fix; the explanation of how the MCAS worked was even deleted from the pilot manual of the new machine.[33]

Ultimately, Boeing managed to create the "world's first self-hijacking plane."[34] If there was an error with only one of the angle-of-attack sensors, the plane would nose-dive into the ground with such force that it was all but impossible for the pilots to jerk the controls back up. Three hundred and forty-six people died in two horrifying plane crashes as a result of this negligence. Between 2010 and 2020, while this slow-motion disaster took place, Boeing distributed $24.6 billion in dividends to shareholders—many of whom were executives within the company—and bought back $43.4 billion worth of shares, becoming a darling of Wall Street.[35]

Boeing's employees were aware of the problems with the 737 MAX. Peter Robison, author of *Flying Blind*, details many examples of perspicacious warnings about the development and certification of the plane, which engineers blamed on the company's senior management and corporate culture, as well as shoddy regulation by the FAA. Chillingly, one of the firm's managers reportedly remarked to an employee that "[p]eople will have to die before Boeing will change things."[36]

Where was the regulator during this debacle? The FAA had cleared the plane in under a year, allowing Boeing to deliver the 737 MAX early.[37]

Yet today it has become clear that the regulator certified the plane despite concluding that it did not meet existing safety standards (not, as it happens, as a result of the MCAS but of another dodgy piece of engineering).[38] In fact, "no one at the FAA wanted to work on the Max certification."[39] No one wanted to stand in Boeing's way. Why?

Over previous decades, the FAA had been stripped down to its bones; salaries were slashed and most expert engineers ended up working for the plane manufacturers. By the time the crashes took place, the FAA—like many other agencies, including, of course, financial regulators—was being run based on a philosophy of "self-regulation." Since 2005, much of the regulation of Boeing took place "within a company unit inside Boeing," whose workers are paid by Boeing.[40] One report ultimately found that the structure of the regulation to which Boeing was subjected created "inherent conflicts of interest that have jeopardized the safety of the flying public."[41]

Just four weeks before the Lion Air crash, and after Boeing had spent $15 million lobbying Congress, another round of deregulation had been introduced. The justification, as one Republican congressman explained, was that "we are seeing unnecessary regulatory burdens that do not serve to improve actual aircraft safety," but that instead represented "process simply for the sake of process."[42] Besides, as another Republican congressman argued, no airline manufacturer would want to build unsafe planes—doing so would damage its reputation.[43] The market would sort everything out.

Except it didn't. Today we know that the company was aware of the problems with the MCAS system *before* the crashes took place.[44] When its cover-up came to light, Boeing was charged with a criminal conspiracy to defraud the United States. The company paid a $2.5 billion fine, of which just $500 million went to the families of those who had died in the crashes.[45] Boeing's new CEO, Dennis Muilenburg, walked away with a $62 million severance package.[46]

But this isn't just another story about the ruinous excesses of an unregulated market. Boeing's rise and fall was aided by the US state, which threw billions at the company in a bid to keep it afloat. A study from 2015 found that Boeing was one of the greatest beneficiaries of corporate welfare in the US, receiving $14 billion that year alone.[47]

In 2013, the state of Washington granted Boeing a $8.7 billion tax break—then the largest corporate tax break offered by any state to any corporation in history.[48] The justification for this giveaway was that it would protect and grow the airline industry in Washington. Within a few years, Boeing had laid off more than twelve thousand workers— more than 15 percent of its workforce in the state.[49]

In fact, the links between Boeing and the American state go even deeper. Donald Trump made Patrick Shanahan, who worked for Boeing for thirty-one years and supervised the development of the disastrous 787 Dreamliner, his acting defense secretary.[50] He adapted to his new role very quickly, making unannounced trips to Afghanistan and the US-Mexico border within a few weeks of his appointment. Weeks later he was placed under investigation over allegations he "improperly advocated on behalf of his former employer, Boeing Co."[51] While he was ultimately cleared of any wrongdoing, it was alleged that the acting defense secretary had pushed for Boeing to win lucrative military contracts at the expense of its competitors, as well as encouraging the government to increase its purchases of Boeing-manufactured aircraft.

The relationship between Boeing and the US state did not, of course, run entirely in one direction. Boeing returned the favor, naming Trump's former UN ambassador Nikki Haley as a board member shortly after Shanahan's appointment.[52] Trump even made a speech bragging about his corporate tax cuts while visiting a Boeing plant in St. Louis and reportedly "put pressure on U.S. allies to buy products from Boeing."[53] Between 2014 and 2018, Boeing made "$104 billion from unclassified defense contracts."[54]

These links are not peculiar to the Trump administration. Back in the 1990s, the Department of Defense facilitated a merger between Boeing and McDonnell Douglas, whose former CEO Stonecipher bore so much of the blame for the 737 MAX disasters.[55] The state needed McDonnell Douglas to survive, as it provided critical components to the US Air Force.

The firm was utterly "dysfunctional," the merger a disaster, and Boeing's workers resisted it at every step—including by striking for forty days. But the merger went ahead anyway, and McDonnell's corporate culture—based on cost-cutting, outsourcing, and corner-cutting—

became deeply embedded in the company.[56] There is a strong argument to be made that it was this cultural transition that created the environment within which the 737 MAX disasters took place—and it was a transition engineered by the US federal state.[57]

In the wake of the 737 MAX disasters and in the context of a global pandemic that severely damaged the airline industry, Boeing might have come close to collapse in 2020. But this outcome was, once again, forestalled by the American state. The CARES Act included $17 billion in loans "for businesses deemed critical to maintaining national security," of which Boeing was one. According to the *Washington Post*, this national security clause was "crafted largely for the company's benefit" and came on top of nearly $58 billion in loans provided to the airline industry—a figure strikingly close to the $60 billion demanded by Boeing executives for the industry in March 2020.[58]

But there was a catch. The Trump administration demanded that the company hand over some equity in exchange for the loans—a move that David Calhoun, Boeing's new CEO, deemed utterly unacceptable. They'd also have to limit layoffs and share buybacks, favorite tactics of Boeing's top team.

The company managed to find a way around this problem by going to the Federal Reserve for a backdoor bailout.[59] As bond markets started to seize up in March, the Fed stepped in to announce that it would purchase up to $20 billion in corporate debt—effectively agreeing to guarantee the borrowing of some of the most powerful companies in the world. Boeing realized it could issue new debt and investors, confident in the knowledge that the company was being propped up by the most powerful state in the world, would lap it up. Ultimately, Boeing ended up issuing $25 billion in new bonds, making its bond sale the largest of 2020 and the sixth largest on record at the time.[60]

The now-useless $17 billion slush fund created for Boeing and other businesses by the Treasury was hastily distributed to a wide assortment of other questionable companies, bringing them into the orbit of the US's already sizable military-industrial complex.[61] These included a company hoping to develop facial recognition software to track immigrants; a firm that relies on minimum-wage prison labor to make products for the military; and an "experimental spaceflight technology firm" already backed by wealthy venture capitalists.[62] How were these decisions made? By a private company, of course. The Treasury hired consultants to evaluate the applications that were submitted to the fund, paying the firm $650,000 for doing so.[63]

The growth of megafirms like Boeing, a company with deep links to the most powerful state in the world, makes it much harder to argue that capitalism is synonymous with free markets. The US is, after all, the world's foremost capitalist economy, and yet it could hardly be described as a free-market paradise. The pressures of competition are often very far from the minds of the executives running the country's largest corporations. Like those at Boeing, they're more concerned with boosting their share prices, lobbying politicians, and covering up the latest corporate scandal.

Boeing does not operate in the absence of competition: its rivalry with Airbus, which also receives massive state aid from the European Union, is often quite brutal. But the firms don't exist in a competitive market in which they need to compete on price. Instead, they operate in a duop-olistic market sponsored by states that have a vested interest in "their" manufacturer's market dominance. Rather than competing on price, the firms compete to keep their costs down (with the effect of making shoddy planes) and over relationships (with the effect of becoming embroiled in corruption scandals). Making backroom deals with airline carriers—like Boeing's agreement with Southwest—and putting pressure on suppliers also helps. Even when the market (or a curious journalist) does eventually catch up to a firm like Boeing, it can rely on its close relationships with the state for protection.

Just like the global aerospace market, many of the largest and most important markets that exist within capitalist societies are far from free: they are dominated by a few massive corporations with extremely cozy relationships to the state. States, meanwhile, are not autonomous entities floating on top of society and intervening in markets when doing so would maximize efficiency. The operation of state power is shaped by its rela-tionships with actors like corporations and financial institutions. Powerful businesses and financial institutions can act within the state to protect and promote their own interests. But the same power is not available to every-one else. This isn't a perversion of capitalism. This is capitalism.

In this chapter, we're going to look at how capitalism really works. Most people think that it means something along the lines of "free markets." This misconception benefits the powerful because free markets sound like a good—or at least a fairly benign—thing. How could one object to free markets without objecting to freedom itself?

In fact, capitalism isn't *defined* by free markets. It's defined by the domination of society by capital. People tend to assume that capital means money or resources, and this is how the term is often used in day-to-day life. But *capital* actually signifies a social relationship, as well as the stuff that defines that relationship. Capitalist societies are divided between a class of people who own all the stuff (capitalists) and those who are forced to work for a living (workers). And the profits of the capitalist come at the expense of workers. A capitalist society is one organized around the interests of bosses—not a free-market utopia.

Capitalism Isn't What You Think It Is

If you asked the average person what they think capitalism is, they'd probably say something about free markets and competition. In capitalist societies, we're told stories about heroic entrepreneurs who come up with brilliant new ideas that they develop into viable businesses, fending off fierce competition from incumbents to bring us fantastic new goods and services and often making substantial profits in the process. This view isn't far from the one held by mainstream economists, who see capitalist economies as those in which firms—led by entrepreneurs—compete to produce goods and services at the lowest cost, before selling those to consumers for a price, which reflects the market forces of supply and demand, in pursuit of profit.

Free markets and competition are supposed to be the features of capitalism that make it unique. But while markets, prices, and competition have all become more prominent features of the world economy since the advent of capitalism, they all predate it. Markets have existed for as long as people have traded goods and services with one another, and money is a political construct that dates back thousands of years. Competition is something that human beings and the organizations they create have engaged in for most of human history.

The reason we're told that capitalism is defined by free markets and competition is that those things sound good—or at least fairly innocuous. How could anyone object to a free market? Would doing so not effectively be objecting to freedom itself? And competition is clearly so important to humanity that denying its necessity would seem completely irrational.

Free markets and competition form part of the foundations of capitalism, but they do not define it. The thing that defines capitalism is capital.

So what, exactly, is capital?

Most people think of capital as a fixed thing—a stock of money or machinery. Everyone knows what it means when they read "your capital may be at risk" in the fine print on an advertisement for a new investment product—it means you might lose some money. Economists have a slightly more complicated view of capital, sometimes using it to refer to money, sometimes to the assets owned by a company, and sometimes to the equity of a bank. Some have gone so far as to argue that mainstream economics has no coherent view of what capital is at all.[64]

But the "capital" in *capitalism* has a meaning distinct from the way the word is used in daily life and in mainstream economics.

The "capital" in *capitalism* refers to a relationship that exists between different groups, as well as the physical stuff that defines that relationship. To understand what this means, compare the word *capitalism* to the word *feudalism*—the name for the social system that preceded capitalism across much of the world. The defining feature of feudalism was the relationship between peasants and aristocrats, whereby the latter owned all the land, and the former worked it in exchange for the stuff they needed to survive. Peasants had no real rights and politics was dominated by landowners. Land was the most valued asset within this social system, and the term *feudalism* refers both to the importance of land itself and to the dominance of landowners within feudal societies.

Under capitalism, a society's wealth is expressed not as land wealth but as "an immense collection of commodities."[65] The term *capital* refers to all the resources required to produce those commodities (what Marx called the means of production), and the term *capitalists* refers to the people who own all those resources. Workers are those who are forced to sell their labor power to capitalists for a living precisely because they don't own any of these resources. The wage these workers are paid is lower than the value of the commodities they produce over the course of the working day—this is the source of the capitalist's profit, and the worker's exploitation.

Capitalism is, at its core, defined by this divide: the divide between the people who own all the tools required to produce commodities and those who are forced to sell their labor power to the capitalists to buy those commodities.[66] The profit of the capitalist comes through the exploitation of the worker—the interests of the two are diametrically opposed.

Similar to *feudalism*, the term *capitalism* signifies both the importance of commodities and the dominance of the capitalist class. This is what it means to say that capital is a "social relationship."[67] The term's meaning refers not just to the means of production but also to the relationships that underpin how those resources are produced and used, much as feudalism refers not just to the importance of land in general but to the way it was controlled by an aristocratic class.

The people and institutions who control all the things we need to produce commodities, and the money gained from selling them, are the ones in charge. That's what makes capitalism capitalism, not the centrality of the market mechanism, but the domination of society by capital.

A corporation with significant market power can make decisions that have far-reaching implications for the lives of its workers, the choices of consumers, and even factors like the direction and rate of innovation, or the health of the planet. And all these decisions are made with little or no democratic accountability.

The control that bosses exert over workers is a form of political power that is often the subject of intense struggle. Bosses have authority over workers—sometimes significant authority—and the only threat a worker can wield in response is to withdraw their labor, a threat that in much of the world is illegal or tightly regulated.[68] Large corporations are also able to exert substantial amounts of power within the state. They can lobby within the state for the adoption of certain policies, donate to particular political parties to shape the outcomes of elections, and even develop and promulgate their own systems of private law and regulation.[69]

What's more, as Thorstein Veblen observed, competition itself encourages "alliance" and "conspiracy" among individual capitalists.[70] It is the very pressure of competition that encourages those subject to it to form alliances to strengthen their own position relative to other competitors. These alliance blocs are, in turn, better able to defeat their competitors and dominate the markets in which they operate. Ultimately, they are able to influence the very rules of the competitive game they are supposed to be playing.

Rather than understanding capitalism as defined by a free-market exchange between private actors interspersed with periods of state planning, we must understand capitalism as a whole system—one in which powerful firms, financial institutions, states, and empires work together to determine who gets what in the global economy. When viewed in these terms it becomes much easier to see that capitalism is a system of pervasive centralized planning.

So, what exactly is planning?

Planning involves the intentional design of a system—anyone can have a plan, as long as they have an image of the world and an intention about how they would like to reorganize it. But what makes planning manifest is the exercise of power.

Much as human beings have always had a tendency to "truck and barter," as Adam Smith put it, they have also always had a tendency to attempt to plan the production and allocation of resources. As Leigh Phillips and Michal Rozworski observe, "Planning has accompanied human societies as long as they have existed."[71] They cite the example of ancient Mesopotamia, in which "widespread permanent record keeping" facilitated a degree of centralized planning by the nascent state.[72] Markets and planning have always gone hand in hand.

But capitalist planning is different because of the many—often invisible—ways in which the power to plan is exercised. The power of capital is not simply expressed through brute force (although it quite often does take this form); it is also a kind of economic power.[73] The class division of society means that some people are forced to look for work under pain of starvation. The people who make decisions about employment therefore have a huge amount of power over everyone else. This is not a power that is exercised by any one individual—after all, workers are free to look for another job if they don't like their boss. It is a power that operates through the very structure of society itself: some people have to work for a living on pain of destitution while others do not.

But the economic power of capital is not simply a power wielded by bosses over workers. Large corporations, which as we will see emerge inevitably over the course of capitalist development, are able to shape the economic conditions in which all other actors participate. Those firms that are able to dominate an entire industry can set wages, prices, and the nature of technological change without any accountability to society as a whole. Today, we see that the economic power of capital is also ecological. Large firms, which are responsible for 71 percent of global carbon emissions, have the power to shape the future of life on earth.[74]

Capital can also work within the state to ensure that the state's violent and bureaucratic resources are deployed in its interests. When benefits claimants are forced to demonstrate they are actively searching for work in order to receive state support, it becomes easier for capitalists to exert their economic power over workers. When states turn a blind eye to anticompetitive practices, they facilitate monopolization. When central banks engineer bailouts or pump cash into financial markets, they protect certain powerful firms at the expense of others. On top of this, the state is also capable of wielding violent power on behalf of capital through the police and military. This power has historically been used very frequently against unionists and protestors—from Margaret Thatcher's violent repression of striking miners to the jailing of climate protestors today.

And as we will see, ideological power serves to reinforce the violent and economic forms of power deployed within capitalist societies. The wealthiest and most powerful are best able to influence the ideas we use to make sense of the world by shaping the ideas found within schools, universities, the media, and other sites of cultural production. They are even able to shape the way we understand ourselves, our obligations to one another, and our relationship to the state.

Mainstream economists don't tend to recognize these forms of domination that obtain within capitalist societies. After all, free-market economies aren't *supposed* to be defined by big inequalities of power. Corporations are supposed to be constrained by the market mechanism—unless these corporations are as efficient as possible, they'll be outcompeted by newer, leaner firms. Managers don't really have any power to set the wages and conditions of employment of their workers—these things are decided by the market. The abstract, impersonal forces of supply and demand are supposed to determine what happens in a free-market economy—not the decisions of any one individual.

But under capitalism, there exist many actors powerful enough to override the diktats of the market.[75] The world economy is dominated by a few massive monopolies over which the market exerts little control, yet these companies will use the threat of the market for labor to discipline their workers into submission, telling them that if they fail to meet the companies' expectations they will simply be replaced. They may also seek to crush their competitors or buy them up before they have the chance to pose a threat. The "free market" exerts brutal competitive pressure over some—those with the least power—while being controlled and manipulated for private gain by those at the top. As Marxist theorist Frederic Jameson memorably put it, "The market is thus Leviathan in sheep's clothing: its function is not to encourage and perpetuate freedom . . . but rather to repress it."[76]

But the power of capital is never all-encompassing. Capitalist societies, and the world economy of which they are a part, are immensely complex systems that can never be fully controlled by any one actor or group of actors. But some individuals and institutions are better able to determine who gets what than others. This observation holds even in the most competitive capitalist economies, albeit to a lesser extent. Capitalism is, then, a hybrid system balanced between competitive pressure and centralized control—between competition and planning.

Consider the example of Boeing above. This is a colossal firm that operates in a highly concentrated, some might say oligopolistic, market. The prices and practices we find in the aerospace market are more the result of active *decisions*—plans—made by Boeing's executives than they are the impersonal forces of the free market. Boeing's agreements with Southwest and other airlines, alongside its close relationships with other massive corporations and financial institutions, are more central to its success than the prices it charges. It is precisely the pressure of competition that encourages large firms like Boeing to attempt to bend the rules to its advantage.[77] Boeing's executives can afford to ignore the short-term pushes and pulls of the market precisely because their firm is so large and well connected—the ability to *ignore* market signals is precisely what market power is.

Boeing does still operate in a market of sorts. Indeed, its ferocious drive to beat its rival Airbus is part of what explains the cost-cutting—and corner-cutting—that characterized the development of the 737 MAX. But even when market forces come knocking—say, in the form of a collapsing share price—the firm can rely on its political relationships to save it from ruin. As we have seen, the United States is highly invested in ensuring the survival of firms like Boeing, almost regardless of the firm's competitiveness. In the unlikely scenario that all the firm's closest allies in the corporate and financial world finally abandoned it, the state would still step in to pick up the pieces.

The freedom of the free market was never much of a freedom at all—but today's megafirms are barely constrained by the pressures of market competition. While markets remain central to the operation of capitalism, and the pressure of competition is frequently brought to bear on those least able to resist, these markets are very far from free—they are, in fact, "distinctly 'unfree.'"[78] In place of the freedom promised through free markets, we find a world dominated by a few massive corporations, financial institutions, states, and empires. We find a world characterized by pervasive central planning.

The question we should ask ourselves, then, is not whether planning is possible in a capitalist economy. Instead, we should ask where planning is taking place, how it is being executed, and whose interests it is serving. We'll turn to these questions in the next chapter.

2

The United States of Fordlândia

enry Ford is perhaps one of the most famous American businessmen of all time. Not only did he found one of the world's largest auto manufacturers; he also gave his name to an entire model of
production—Fordism, the system of production that dominated in wealthy
economies throughout much of the early- to mid-twentieth century.[1]

Fordist production methods were based on the introduction of assembly line technology, in which the production process was broken
down into hundreds of discrete tasks, each performed by a different
worker. The work was incredibly dull and repetitive, and significant discipline and speed were required to ensure the highest possible productivity. But increases in productivity also facilitated increases in wages,
allowing working people to purchase all sorts of consumer goods that
had previously been the preserve of the wealthy.

Ford is often seen as a paradigmatic example of the American
dream. He was born on a farm into a family of immigrants only to become one of the richest men in the world. But Ford had a dark side. He
held extremely rigid views on what constituted ethical and upstanding
behavior—views to which he insisted his workers adhere—and he was
well known for his virulent anti-Semitism.

He paid for the printing and distribution of 500,000 copies of *The
Protocols of the Elders of Zion*, an apocryphal text purporting to show
Jewish plans for world domination.[2] He's mentioned in positive terms in
Adolf Hitler's autobiographical manifesto *Mein Kampf*, and in 1938, Ford
was awarded the Grand Cross of the German Eagle, the highest medal
the Third Reich could give to a foreigner.[3] Like most people sympathetic

to fascism, he was also bitterly opposed to the labor movement. Ford employed a former navy boxer and his team of wrestlers and gang members were known for beating unionists with clubs to prevent them from organizing.[4]

Antonio Gramsci, the Italian Marxist who coined the term *Fordism*, faced a childhood far harder than that of Ford.[5] Gramsci was born in 1891 with severe problems with his spine—initially thought to have been caused by a childhood accident but now recognized as a form of tuberculosis.[6] His back problems stunted his growth—he stood at less than five feet—and he suffered from acute health issues for the rest of his life.[7] His family was perpetually on the run from the police and his father was ultimately imprisoned when Gramsci was still young, plunging the family into poverty.[8]

Unlike Ford, Gramsci's experiences of poverty in early life made him into a socialist. And unlike Ford, who was sympathetic to fascism, Gramsci was the sworn enemy of fascists everywhere. He was arrested by Mussolini's regime and sentenced to five years' confinement on a remote Italian island. The regime later amended the sentence to twenty years; at his trial, prosecutors stated plainly that their aim was to "stop this brain from functioning."[9] Gramsci spent the next eleven years in prison, suffering from frequent extreme pain and constant discomfort. He died at age forty-six, having spent much of his early life struggling with crippling illness and poverty, and the last decade rotting in a prison cell.

But Mussolini's fascist regime did not succeed in preventing Gramsci's brilliant mind from functioning. While he was in prison, Gramsci wrote his *Prison Notebooks*, in which he provides an incredibly lucid and prescient analysis of what came to be known as Fordism.

Gramsci saw that assembly line technologies of the kind pioneered by Ford required the availability of an army of hardworking, semiskilled, pliant workers. The breaking down of the production process into a large number of tiny, discrete tasks meant that if one part of the "human machine" was missing, the entire production process would grind to a halt.[10] It was up to Ford—and his allies within the US state—to mold a new kind of worker who would fit easily into this modern production process; a worker who would submit willingly to their own exploitation.

The issue for Ford was that most of his workers found their jobs mind-numbingly dull, repetitive, and exhausting. As a result, the rates of absenteeism and turnover in his factories were strikingly high: turnover is estimated to have reached around 370 percent in the years before World War I.[11] The unions organizing Ford's workers attempted to translate this discontent into a movement demanding higher wages and better conditions. Ford responded with both carrot and stick. On the one hand, he recruited "the world's largest private army, and established the most extensive and efficient espionage system in American industry."[12] On the other hand, he introduced the Five-Dollar Day.

In exchange for this increase in pay, union organizing was out and strict controls on worker behavior were in. The Five-Dollar Day received a huge amount of publicity, but it was really composed of a basic salary of $2.50 plus another $2.50 per day in "profits" that the worker would receive if he obeyed Ford's rigid set of rules—both in the workplace and at home.[13] Ford workers were expected to pass a set of tests ensuring their behavior was in line with company policy: workers were told to abstain from alcohol, and Ford set up churches and education programs to encourage his workers to conform to his standards of morality.[14] Immigrant workers had to attend classes to become "Americanized" and men did not receive the bonus if their wives worked outside the home.[15]

Productivity increased dramatically and absenteeism and turnover declined proportionately.[16] The Ford Motor Company was not simply planning the amount of output it would be producing and the investment it would be undertaking, it was planning the labor process from beginning to end, including the lives of its workers. By the 1930s, Ford was essentially a "privately owned, planned bureaucracy, not unlike the Soviet Union."[17]

As Barry Lynn observes in his book *Cornered*, Ford was not alone. Giant auto companies increasingly served as "America's main economic planners." They coordinated activities including "the development and introduction of new technologies, the design and construction of the necessary production systems . . . the education of workers and consumers, and the gathering and structure of the capital necessary to power all these tasks."[18]

But the auto companies could never have become such successful planners on their own. For one thing, the seamless production process upon which Fordism relied required a level of macroeconomic certainty that had been elusive in the era of prewar capitalism. Gramsci realized that the success of Fordism not only required the creation of a certain kind of worker, it also required the creation of a certain kind of state: one that strove to create a society that aligned with corporate interests. Fordism required the construction of what Herbert Hoover, former secretary of commerce, called an "associative state," which took charge of "reconciling the vast complex of business interests through a multitude of public-private conferences."[19]

In 1928, Ford got his chance to build his own version of the Fordist state. He sought to realize his dream of creating a pure, Christian kingdom in his own image by building Fordlândia, a factory town in the depths of the Amazon rainforest.[20] The purpose of Fordlândia was to provide Ford with a secure source of rubber—a commodity then controlled by the British. Ford managed to negotiate a deal with the Brazilian government: in return for 9 percent of the profits generated by the site, the company would be granted control over 2.5 million acres of land in the Boa Vista area of Brazil.[21] Naturally, he also sought—and received—approval from the US state. The deal was a striking example of what academics would later refer to as "corporate sovereignty"; much like the British East India Company, the Ford Motor Company was being permitted to forge its own empire under the watchful eye of the state.[22]

Having been granted sovereignty over the area, Ford could treat it as "terra incognita," building the town and its laws on a blank canvas. He believed that workers at Fordlândia could be controlled more cheaply and easily than his entitled, unionized employees in the US. American managers—many of whom fell ill on the perilous journey to the rainforest—were brought in to manage local Brazilian workers.[23] While the Brazilians lived in basic local accommodations, the "American village" was furnished with American-style houses, a library, a swimming pool, a hotel, and even a golf course, at considerable extra expense.[24] Brazilian workers were closely monitored and forced to wear ID badges around the town.[25] Bans on alcohol, women, tobacco, and even soccer were stringently enforced by the town's American managerial class.[26]

Unsurprisingly, workers found a way to get around Ford's puritanical directives, establishing an "Island of Innocence" a few miles up the Tapajós River, complete with "bars, nightclubs and brothels."[27] Like their US counterparts, some refused to show up for work, and in December 1930, workers revolted in the cafeteria and ultimately ransacked the city, including much of the equipment needed to harvest rubber.[28] To make matters worse, the US managers had no understanding of how to plant and harvest rubber in a sustainable way, and many of the plants quickly succumbed to blight before any could be harvested.[29]

By the outbreak of the Second World War, Fordlândia was mired in failure. By that point, the US company DuPont—which we will meet later in this book—had discovered a formula for synthetic rubber, and Henry Ford II was forced to sell Fordlândia back to the Brazilian government at a loss of $20 million, equivalent to $325 million today.[30] Henry Ford never even visited his jungle utopia.

The failure of Fordlândia may have been a personal disappointment for Ford, but it didn't dent the Ford Motor Company's growth in subsequent years, growth that rested upon the company's close links with the US state. By the Second World War, Ford had become one of the largest and most powerful corporations in the world—and an integral part of the US military-industrial complex. By 1944, Ford was making 50 percent of all B-24 planes produced in the US, and by 1945, 70 percent, many of which were constructed at a new plant built by the company in Willow Run, Michigan.[31] When the factory was constructed in 1941 it was thought to be the largest war factory in the world; and the US government had contributed $200 million to its construction.[32]

Ford was also, of course, helping the other side. The company made "huge revenues" by manufacturing armaments for Hitler's Germany, even constructing a new plant "of a strictly military nature" in a safe zone near Berlin.[33] By 1939, Ford was one of the largest suppliers of vehicles to the German army. By 1941, Ford's German subsidiary had stopped producing commercial vehicles altogether, focusing instead on feeding the German war machine. In fact, "[o]f the 350,000 trucks used by the motorized German Army as of 1942, roughly one-third were Ford-made."[34]

Eventually, the Nazis took the German subsidiary into trusteeship.[35] The Ford employee who had been running the plant until that point—Robert Schmidt—was such an ardent supporter of the Nazis that he was kept on even after the change. Schmidt, who had been repeatedly praised by Ford's senior management, went on to supervise the introduction of forced labor into the plant to maintain wartime production. Workers were forced to work twelve-hour days with only a fifteen-minute break, fed on a diet of two hundred grams of bread for breakfast and a dinner of spinach and potato soup. Astonishingly, Schmidt was rehired by Ford of Germany after the war. He remained with the company until his death in 1962. Three years later, the company received over $1 million in compensation from the US government as a result of damage to its factories caused by Allied bombings.

Gramsci saw that the close relationships that were developing between the world's most powerful corporations and its most powerful states would pave the way to "the planned economy."[36] Gone were the days of isolated capitalist enterprises ruthlessly competing with one another for a scrap of market share—to the extent that this ideal had ever existed. Instead, Fordism involved the imposition of some centralized control over the anarchy of the free market. This coordination came in the form of both state and corporate control over society—from using public spending to combat boom and bust to the rigid behavioral guidelines to which Ford subjected his workers.

Gramsci was astute enough to recognize that the trends he was observing were not new.[37] Throughout the history of capitalism, one thing had remained constant: states, firms, and financial institutions all worked together to plan who got what. The nature of this planning process has, however, changed over time.

We're used to thinking of the postwar period as a time of extensive planning, where in many parts of the world the excesses of the market mechanism were tamed by the social democratic state. The neoliberal revolution is thought to have ended this era of planning and inaugurated a new era of free markets and small states.[38] But this narrative is false. What changed between the postwar period and the neoliberal period wasn't the presence or absence of planning. What changed was who was doing the planning and whose interests they were serving.

The problem with the postwar social democratic settlement was that it gave workers a seat at the table—however limited—which undermined the authority of capital over labor. What's more, Keynesian policies limited the threat of unemployment that disciplined workers into accepting low wages and refraining from strike action.[39] In other words, social democracy undermined the "governability" of society.[40] The shift toward neoliberalism fixed this problem by excluding workers from both corporate and state planning processes and further concentrating power in the hands of capital.

The planning problem for the neoliberals was, however, clearly distinct from that of the Keynesian planners of the postwar period. Rather than managing the relationship between workers and bosses to ensure industrial peace, the role of the state came to center more on supporting capital's relentless pursuit of profit and clearing up after the crises caused by this greed. At a more microeconomic level, state policy also came to be geared toward "nudging" individuals into adopting the "right" kinds of behaviors—the kinds that would be expected from rational, self-interested market participants—as well as disciplining those who rebelled.

As we'll see in this chapter, these continuities and shifts were clearly visible within the Ford Motor Company. In the prewar period of "laissez-faire" capitalism, Ford was able to exercise its corporate sovereignty largely unrestrained by competition or organized labor and supported by the state—at home and abroad. During the war, the line between Ford and the states in which it operated—particularly the US and Germany—became even blurrier, as the company was absorbed into the Allied and Axis military-industrial complexes, guaranteeing significant profits.

But, as I'll show in the next section, after the war Ford was forced to confront a much more powerful labor movement and a state that encouraged the company to cooperate with labor unions. The leadership of Ford executives was perennially frustrated by the limitations this placed on the company's formerly much less constrained sovereignty.

This period ended with the neoliberal revolution, when domestic and international shifts led to the defeat of formerly powerful labor unions. Within Ford, thousands of workers were laid off and, as international competitive pressure mounted, the company's profitability came to hinge on lending and financial engineering rather than production itself. Ultimately, Ford was bailed out by the US federal state when its irresponsible lending left it under a mountain of debt.

The neoliberals claimed that their policies were designed to protect and promote human freedom by ending the centralized planning of the postwar years. In fact, as the history of the Ford Motor Company shows, the neoliberal revolution did not end capitalist central planning—it simply changed who was in control of the process and whose interests it served. Rather than seeking to mediate between bosses and workers, the neoliberal state simply seeks to "save capitalism from its self-destructive tendencies, but without ever affecting the fundamental economic relationships that determine them."[41]

The Ungovernable Society

Organized labor emerged from the Second World War stronger than it had been in decades. Labor struggles that took place over the 1920s and '30s had led to the New Deal reforms, which established the eight-hour workday, the weekend, and the minimum wage with overtime pay. And the imperatives of wartime production had strengthened labor's position.

Workers at Ford were no exception. During the war, the company had recognized the UAW-CIO, and as soon as the war was over, workers wasted no time in organizing for a wage increase, which Henry Ford II was forced to grant.[42] By 1949, Ford's workers were so well organized that unionists negotiated a deal with Ford to provide workers with pensions, social insurance, and other benefits with no loss of pay—something Henry Ford had declared impossible just a few years earlier.[43] The contrast between the settlements of the postwar years and those of the prewar years was striking. As one history of the company notes:

"On the one hand, we can recall the loose, helpless agglomeration of Ford workers who learned on January 5, 1914, not from any leaders of their own, and not through any channels of negotiation, but from the newspapers that the company would thereafter pay a minimum of $5 per day . . . On the other hand, we can picture the firmly organized UAW-CIO union, a disciplined army, which forty-one years later negotiated with the Ford managers, as equal speaking to equal, in one of the most memorable agreements in the history of American labor."[44]

Workers were not only organizing for higher wages. In 1949, the UAW had organized a twenty-five-day strike at Ford over the speedup of operations, arguing that workers were not being compensated in line with increased productivity.[45] Unionists were also concerned about the automation of the production process, which could result in job losses and constrain workers' bargaining power.[46] But decisions over the pace and scale of investment were the jealously guarded prerogatives of management.

Workers weren't getting much support from state officials either, who were concerned to protect their close relationships with big companies like Ford. Robert McNamara was a former Ford chief executive and the first president of the company from outside the Ford family.[47] McNamara is remembered as a specialist in "management science": he sought to collect data on the organization and use it to build models that could show managers how to improve efficiency.[48] The executive had joined Ford after serving in World War II and was so successful at trimming the fat at the bloated company that he rebranded as the "whiz kid."[49] McNamara went on to serve as secretary of defense in both the Kennedy and Johnson administrations. (We'll come back to his career in government in chapter 7.)

Given the close links between Ford and the US government, the latter sought to support Ford in bringing industrial disputes to a swift conclusion. It was for this reason that President Kennedy created The President's Committee on Labor-Management Policy, otherwise known as the Tripartite Committee, a formal space within which workers, bosses, and other stakeholders could come together to litigate their disagreements, as well as identify shared goals.[50] The Tripartite Committee was one of the few examples of overt corporatist planning—planning based on formal cooperation between businesses and the state—ever to have been attempted in the US, and Kennedy was quick to give Henry Ford II a seat at the table.[51] The administration hoped that bringing workers and bosses together would help the US retain its international competitiveness with the consent of organized labor.

But this consent was not always easy to secure. At the time, auto workers were gripped by an antiauthoritarian spirit that saw them rebel against their "gold-plated sweatshops."[52] Grégoire Chamayou cites workers at General Motors who saw factory life as a "jail cell," in which they were forced to undertake ordinary acts of "indiscipline" merely to assert their freedom in the context of ever-greater managerial control. Worker representatives, including several from the UAW, were aware that they had significant power over the production process, and they were unwilling to concede to the demands of capital.

Some of the most significant disputes on the committee centered on the question of automation.[53] Workers sought the right to bargain with management over the pace and scale of automation, while management sought to retain the exclusive right to invest in new technologies as and when they saw fit. Ford argued that neither workers nor the state should be meddling in management decisions over when and how to invest in new technologies as this was "anathema to free market principles."[54]

Workers' attempts to influence the governance of corporations were a step too far for the bosses, who took their disputes outside the Tripartite Committee. Bosses—led by the implacable Henry Ford II—began to castigate union leaders for abusing their "monopoly power" over the labor market, appropriating the progressive anti-monopoly language of the New Deal and turning it against the unions.[55] Negotiations ultimately broke down and the Tripartite Committee became nothing more than a talking shop.

The failure of negotiations within the Tripartite Committee marked a shift in power away from organized labor. From the 1970s on, an increasing share of the US auto market was captured by imports, and US car manufacturers began to feel the pinch.[56] Management argued that the competitiveness problem resulted from an overly militant labor movement, which was pushing labor costs to unsustainable levels, and unionists often acceded to this interpretation of events. With the bosses pushing aggressively for greater automation and the US state shrinking from its commitments to maintain full employment, wage growth stalled and the workforce dwindled. Plants were closed and layoffs stepped up, "and the contracts negotiated in the 1980s reflected this power decline."[57] Between 1979 and 1980, the number of Ford hourly paid workers dropped by nearly fifty thousand.[58]

While wage growth and the workforce dwindled, Ford became a cash cow for shareholders, who financialized the firm beyond recognition. Over the course of the 1990s, the company increased its dividend payout by nearly 40 percent.[59] It also engaged in extensive M&A activity, purchasing Volvo and Land Rover to increase its market power. Despite all this lavish spending, the company was still sitting on a mountain of cash. By 2000, the firm's $24 billion cash pile was the largest of any firm in the world.[60]

Part of the reason Ford was able to remain profitable throughout the late twentieth century was that it effectively transformed itself from an auto manufacturer into an auto manufacturer–cum–financial institution. The Ford Motor Credit Company (FMCC), which provides cheap loans to Ford customers seeking to purchase new cars, had been founded in 1959 and began issuing credit in 1989. While the manufacturing arm of the firm lost "billions of dollars" from 2001, Ford financial had "excellent returns."[61] By 2015, Ford's total workforce had declined to 199,000—down from over 350,000 in 2001—and the FMCC was ten times more profitable than Ford Motor.[62] As one author put it, "Had it not been for the inflow of these funds through financial activities, the company would probably have gone bankrupt."[63]

But providing services that would ordinarily be reserved for a financial institution required Ford to take on a lot of debt, and in 2001 Ford's credit rating was downgraded as a result of its unhealthy balance sheet. By the time the financial crisis hit, Ford was weighed down by a mountain of debt.

Naturally, the US state stepped in to bail the firm out. Ford's rivals, Chrysler and General Motors, were the greatest recipients of government money during the bailouts that followed the crisis of 2008—together they received 20 percent of the funds the government dished out through the Troubled Asset Relief Program (TARP), worth around $80 billion.[64] Ford is usually credited with having refused a loan and repairing its balance sheet on its own, but, just like Boeing during the pandemic, the company received government money through the back door.

In the same year that GM and Chrysler were being raked over the coals for accepting billions in public money, Ford managed to secure $6 billion from the Department of Energy as part of a program designed to improve the fuel efficiency of US vehicles—a loan it took the company more than a decade to repay.[65] Naturally, the firm continued to focus on distributing profits to shareholders. Between 2012 to 2020, Ford paid "100% of net profit to shareholders."[66]

Ford's CEO at the time, Alan Mulally, argued during the midst of the financial crisis that the auto company bailouts had been necessary because the automotive industry was "uniquely interdependent."[67] Most companies, he argued, used the same suppliers, and if one of them went bankrupt, the suppliers would collapse too, creating problems for their competitors. The massive bailouts of other auto companies had, in other words, helped to protect Ford from collapse. And Mulally had inadvertently highlighted a key point about his industry. As one author put it, "Just as the many heads of the Hydra relied on one body, the automakers increasingly rely on a single common body of companies that supply the same components to all of them."[68]

The transformation of Ford from one of the US's largest employers into an oligopolistic financial institution that acted as a piggy bank for wealthy shareholders, whose greed ultimately brought the firm to the brink of bankruptcy, only to be bailed out by the US state, provides a pretty accurate indication of what the "free market" shift of the 1980s was all about. Rather than constraining the power of the state, the neoliberal turn was associated with a redistribution of power and wealth away from workers and toward owners and senior managers.[69] The neoliberal revolution was about restoring the authority of capital over labor.

The corporatism of the postwar years—cooperation between workers and bosses, mediated by the state—came to such an abrupt end because allowing workers a stake in the planning process threatened the true defining feature of capitalism: not the allocation of resources through the "free market," but governance by capital. Allowing workers a seat at the table through the labor movement had not placated them—far from it. As workers became more involved in the governance of both the firm and the state, they had started to believe they might be able to control these institutions without the help of owners, managers, and politicians.

Instead of meekly accepting the demands of bosses, organized workers had begun to make demands of their own, even attempting to undermine the managers' prerogative to determine the nature and direction of investment in labor-saving technologies. Workers, within and outside the labor movement, came to understand the stakes of the decisions that were being made within the state and realized the power they had to influence—and often disrupt—these decision-making processes to their advantage.

As a result, over the course of the mid-twentieth century, many rich countries became—as Grégoire Chamayou puts it—"ungovernable."[70] Bosses couldn't cede management of the production process to workers, because it would have undermined the distinction upon which the entire capitalist mode of production is based: the distinction between capital and labor. If workers were capable of planning the production process as successfully as managers, then why did they need to be managed at all? Why did they need to be paid a wage in exchange for their labor? Why didn't workers simply own and manage the firms in which they worked?

This crisis of governability within the firm was taking place within the context of a wider crisis of capitalist legitimacy.[71] It was not simply the authority of the boss over the worker that was being challenged, but the very "free enterprise system" itself.[72] Those in positions of power were faced with a crisis of management on two fronts—on the one hand, the "vertical" challenge of governing those beneath them in organizational hierarchies, and on the other hand, the "horizontal" challenge of responding to a social and political environment that was increasingly hostile.[73]

To make society "governable" again, the neoliberals had to unleash the power of capital, while creating a pliable class of consumer-subjects out of an organized class of worker-organizers.[74] In the words of Leo Panitch and Sam Gindin, "Neoliberalism was essentially a political response to the democratic gains that had been previously achieved by working classes."[75] Despite all their talk of shrinking the state, it was through the—often extraordinarily violent—exercise of state power that this project was achieved.

In the 1980s, restrictions on the lending and movement of money were removed, financial markets deregulated, tax rates cut, and industries privatized.[76] The religion of shareholder value was institutionalized, and firms did anything they could—either of their own will or under duress from "activist investors"—to cut costs and boost returns.[77] Unions were crushed, and atomized entrepreneurs and consumers of state services were created in place of workers and citizens.[78] When politicians like Thatcher and Reagan finally claimed victory over labor movements, governability was restored; the bosses once again had the sole power to plan.

The Neoliberal Lie

One thing that neoliberalism decisively did not give us was a smaller or weaker state.[79] State spending has continued to grow throughout the neoliberal era—as much due to lobbying for corporate welfare and crisis bailouts as to demands for higher spending on public services. In the US, state spending as a percentage of GDP is far higher today than it was during the 1970s, and much of the increase took place during the heyday of neoliberalism. In the UK, successive neoliberal governments managed to cut public spending, only to see it soar to its highest peace-time levels as they rushed to bail out the banks whose recklessness had been fueled by neoliberal macroeconomic policies. The observation that "the state grows because it grows"—first made in the 1970s—was not arrested under neoliberalism.[80]

And it wasn't just spending. As we'll see in chapter 5, the creation of "independent" central banks led to the capture of monetary policy by vested interests in the finance sector, which have secured billions in free handouts from these institutioins since the 1980s.[81] Regulation has also multiplied as financial interests have worked within the state to create new avenues for profit-making.[82] The financial crisis of 2008, for exam-ple, was not a crisis of deregulation—it was a crisis of regulatory cap-ture.[83] This kind of "regulation in denial" actually encouraged financial institutions to develop the kinds of products and take the kinds of risks that led to the crisis.[84]

The state has always played an active role in capitalist economies: it has never been "inattentive or quiescent."[85] But the exercise of this power has not remained constant across time and space. New policy paradigms, accompanied by new ideologies and new tools of governance, have emerged in different states at different historical periods. These changes are not the result of "pure" ideological shifts. Instead, they emerge from the struggles that take place between different groups on a constantly shifting terrain.[86]

What changed under neoliberalism wasn't the size or power of the state, it was who benefited from state intervention. Rather than investing in jobs creating infrastructure investment programs, or public services designed to support working people, neoliberal states instead handed out unfathomable amounts of cash to big businesses and wealthy indi-viduals while claiming to promote "free markets."[87]

Privatization, for example, was supposed to create efficient, profit-maximizing private corporations out of inefficient public behemoths run by unaccountable bureaucrats.[88] Instead, it simply transferred gov-ernance of vital national infrastructure from the public sector to an oligopoly of quasi-public corporations, whose profits were effectively guaranteed by the state. And these sales were undertaken via small investors who were able to buy up public assets on the cheap and sell them for a profit.[89]

In fact, the priorities of the neoliberal state are increasingly indistinguishable from those of the modern corporation.[90] States are judged according to economic metrics, and public bureaucrats learn to adopt a corporate register to describe their aims. Leading theorist of neoliberalism Wendy Brown quotes Donald Trump's son-in-law Jared Kushner, who argued that "the government should be run like a great American company."[91] As Brown highlights eloquently, one of the defining features of neoliberalism is the shrinking of the political sphere, and the replacement of the language and values of politics with those of economics. The result is the radical attenuation of the "exercise of freedom in the social and political spheres."[92]

At the same time, human beings become "human capital," responsible for maximizing their own particular interests through "hustling" and "entrepreneurialism."[93] We are no longer citizens, engaged in conflict and debate as part of a political sphere. Instead, we become passive "consumers," changing our votes based on a disinterested calculation as to which party is likely to provide us with the best and most efficient services. We are no longer collective owners of public assets, we are "mini-capitalists" charged with managing our own portfolios of assets and liabilities.[94]

Meanwhile, the rules of the economic game are seen as natural forces governing our lives, over which we as consumers have little control.[95] These economic rules are no longer subject to political contestation, yet they consistently seem to favor some over others. Less powerful individual consumers—much like smaller, less powerful firms—are destined to be buffeted by the ineluctable forces of market competition, while powerful individuals—much like large, powerful firms—are able to shape those very forces to their own advantage.

Outside the economic realm, the violent and coercive power of the neoliberal state is, if anything, greater than that of the social democratic state.[96] This violence is exercised *for* capital, not against it—which is why so few white-collar crimes are ever prosecuted. In fact, criminologists have argued that we live in a world of "state-routinized crime" in which governments permit—or actively facilitate—criminality on the part of large corporations.[97]

Meanwhile, the violence of the state is directed powerfully against those least able to resist. The dramatic expansion in the US prison population, through the prison-industrial complex that sees private corporations profit from state violence, is an excellent example of this trend—as is the astonishing force used by Margaret Thatcher to destroy the UK labor movement.[98] But the violence of the neoliberal state is most clearly on display in the Global South. In Chile, for example, tens of thousands of innocent people were murdered or disappeared by Pinochet's neoliberal regime, supported by neoliberal acolytes like Milton Friedman, all in the name of destroying socialism and building "free markets."

The neoliberals ultimately succeeded in "generating an antidemocratic culture from below, while building and legitimating antidemocratic forms of state power from above."[99] The end result has been the emergence of a kind of "crony capitalism" that Brown claims the original neoliberals would have abhorred. Hayek himself wrote in *The Road to Serfdom* that he would "prefer to have to put up with some such inefficiency than have organized monopoly control my ways of life."[100] And yet the movement that he spawned has birthed some of the largest and most powerful monopolies in human history.

Early neoliberal thinkers like Hayek would likely have argued that the expansion of domination and the curtailment of free-market processes seen under neoliberalism have happened only because their plans for a leaner state and freer markets have been subverted by vested interests, like unions and bureaucrats.

But this response defies reality. In most advanced economies, the labor movement was utterly defeated throughout the 1980s thanks to legislation introduced by neoliberal governments in order to destroy working people's capacity to resist the power of capital.[101] And it was state bureaucrats who were some of the most enthusiastic implementers of neoliberal policies. Not content to enforce these policies on the rest of society, they even set about enforcing them on themselves.

In the UK, the neoliberal shift toward "new public management" was all about bringing market efficiencies into the public sector by assessing the performance of civil servants according to rigid targets.[102] This approach appeared to contradict Hayek's perspective on markets and planning—after all, market outcomes are supposed to be unknowable and unplannable. But actually existing neoliberalism is based on a fusion between Hayek's free-market thinking and a longer managerialist tradition focused on developing ever more efficient methods through which to control workers.[103] As Hayek might have predicted, without any real marketplace to speak of, these reforms simply ended up increasing bureaucracy and leading to a dramatic expansion in middle management across the sector.

This bureaucratization isn't just a feature of the neoliberal shift; it's been associated with "free market" reforms since the dawn of capitalism. As David Graeber forcefully argues in *The Utopia of Rules*: "English liberalism, for instance, did not lead to a reduction of state bureaucracy, but the exact opposite: an endlessly ballooning array of legal clerks, registrars, inspectors, notaries, and police officials who made the liberal dream of a world of free contract between autonomous individuals possible. It turned out that maintaining a free-market economy required a thousand times more paperwork than a Louis XIV–style absolutist monarchy."[104]

Neoliberalism has become a monstrous regime of "managerial governance" premised upon ever greater levels of surveillance and control.[105] But this is a contradiction only if we take the neoliberals at their word when they said they wanted to build a "free-market economy." The idea behind new public management wasn't to curtail the power of the state, or even to subject state institutions to the power of the "free market." The idea was to replace democratic government with technocratic governance—to replace government by the people with rule by technocratic elites.[106]

Neoliberal "dreams of an apolitical state" are often couched in the language of freedom, in which neutral and objective policymakers can create laws that protect the private sphere from government interference.[107] These reforms were supposed to prevent "vested interests" from exercising undue influence over the policymaking process. If policies could be assessed with reference to the "science" of economics, there would be no need for contestation or deliberation among different groups. Policies could be developed without any "politics" at all.[108]

And yet, these claims to legal neutrality are always and everywhere undermined by the actual practice of neoliberal policymaking, in which policymakers are expected regularly to receive feedback from "key stakeholders."[109] These stakeholders are those with the most knowledge of the policy area under discussion, which generally means they are the very people the policy is most likely to affect. "Vested interests" return to the policymaking process in the guise of "technical experts."

Neoliberalism was never about "shrinking" the state, it was about "seizing and then retasking" it.[110] Many of the founders of neoliberalism would have admitted as much. As Philip Mirowski points out, the maxim of the neoliberals could be summed up as "[o]nly a strong state can preserve and enhance a free-market economy." Only a strong, "laser focused" state could hope to insulate itself from the demands of "the masses."[111]

In other words, state power hasn't expanded because the neoliberal dream was subverted; it has expanded precisely because the neoliberals took control. The foundations of this new world order were built on a lie—or what Hayek referred to as a "double truth." The elite would have to be trained in the art of repressing democracy and building a strong and powerful state, while the masses would be fed lines about "rolling back the nanny state" and "freedom to choose."[112] For some, such as Hayek himself, this "double truth" was a necessary evil that resulted from the difficult interaction between elegant neoliberal theory and the real, messy world of capitalist political economy.[113] For others, the neoliberal project, while framed as a project that aimed to deliver freedom, was always nothing more than a naked assertion of the power of capital.[114]

The lie at the heart of neoliberalism, despite having been debunked decades ago, retains huge sway over our politics. The idea that markets are "clean" and efficient is, as Wolfgang Streeck puts it, "propagated with remarkable success particularly by the economics profession, despite what is known about cartels, price agreement, 'bank rescues' etc."[115]

Neoliberal politicians will still claim they seek to shrink the state and create space for a free market, yet upon entering office they proceed to distribute public cash to private corporations, promulgate regulation that enriches vested interests, and violently repress all those who stand in their way. Perversely, the popular anger caused by the use of state power to support the interests of capital then serves to strengthen the very same politicians who claim to support "free markets."

This lie is sustained by a confusion about the nature of capitalism itself. Most people believe capitalism is defined by free markets and its opposite, socialism, by state planning. In fact, capitalism is a hybrid system based on a dialectic between markets and planning. Massive state intervention in the economy is not antithetical to capitalism—as we have seen, it is not even antithetical to neoliberalism. But the belief that it is serves the interests of the powerful. Dividing the world into capitalist markets and socialist states prevents us from understanding the nature of the system under which we live: a system defined by rule by capital.

As we have seen, the nature of capital's rule has changed over time. The competitiveness of markets shapes the extent of corporate power and executives' ability to plan. The nature and extent of cooperation between corporate and state actors shapes the kinds of policies we get. And the state of the perennial conflict between capital and labor determines whose interests dominate the planning process. But one thing that has remained the same is the fact of centralized planning under capitalism—whether undertaken by corporations, financial institutions, states, or empires.

When J. K. Galbraith observed the emergence of the "new industrial capitalism" after the Second World War, he was pointing both to an increase in planning and centralization on the one hand, and to the growing role of workers within the planning process on the other.[116] One result of this shift was a decrease in the frequency and ferocity of capitalist crises. In the 1980s, Scott Lash and John Urry claimed that neoliberalism meant the "end of organized capitalism," arguing that this era of stability had come to an end.[117] But while crises certainly did become more frequent with the advent of neoliberalism, this was not because planning had become less prevalent—it was because capitalists had figured out how to privatize the gains from economic booms, while socializing the losses from the busts.[118]

Neoliberals discouraged policymakers from attempting to attenuate the ups and downs of the business cycle, and instead argued that their efforts should be focused on cleaning up after the crash.[119] The idea was that the economic cycle should be allowed to run its course, rather than face interference from unaccountable state bureaucrats. In reality, this new approach to crisis management simply meant that powerful capitalists were able to reap all the benefits of booming financial markets, while being protected during the bust.[120] Workers were the ones forced to bear the consequences in the form of unemployment, lower wages, and cuts to public services and social security.[121]

Naomi Klein's account of disaster capitalism in *The Shock Doctrine* shows exactly how the most powerful firms and states often work together during moments of crisis to manage events in their interests.[122] Nobody *planned* the financial crisis. But the *response* to that crisis was determined by a tight-knit network of financiers and politicians deciding among themselves who would be saved and who would be sacrificed. Unsurprisingly, most of the big banks that caused the crisis survived in one form or another, as did all the states, while working people around the world paid the price for the reckless greed of big finance. Before long, many of these banks were back to making record profits.

The fusion of political and economic power that we see during these moments of crisis is integral to the way capitalist societies function, not an aberration resulting from conspiratorial networks or clandestine societies. Conspiracy theories—from the Illuminati to the Great Reset—tend to be based on a similar view of the world as that propounded by right-wing libertarians. These people believe that capitalism works, but that it is being corrupted by evil elites (and these elites are often overtly or covertly racialized as in the case of anti-Semitic conspiracy theories).

But capitalists aren't evil monsters, they're just people acting according to their own interests (though many of the characters mentioned in this book do have some fascinating foibles). The problem is that those interests are diametrically opposed to those of the majority. Even if we replaced every single politician, financier, and executive with a completely different person, the system would still function more or less as it does today.

The financial crisis couldn't have been avoided if Lehman Brothers had been Lehman Brothers and Sisters, as Arianna Huffington once put it. Capitalism is a class-based system that contains an inherent tendency toward instability and crisis. The only way to solve this problem is to dissolve the distinction between capital and labor upon which the system is based. The only way out runs through the democratization of our entire economy.

In the next chapter, we'll look at precisely how these crisis tendencies have manifested themselves over recent decades. We'll see how "disaster capitalism" works, and why, after every crisis, power seems to become more concentrated in the hands of the people who caused it.

3

Disaster Capitalism

In the early stages of the pandemic, the US state introduced an enormous stimulus package designed to prop up American capitalism. Eight hundred billion dollars in public money was distributed to millions of businesses through the Paycheck Protection Program (PPP), and more than 90 percent of the outstanding debt was forgiven by the government.[1] Workers received just $1 out of every $4 distributed through the program, with the other $3 going to business owners.[2]

The Small Business Association (SBA) refused to reveal which businesses had received this cash until a lawsuit was brought against it by a group of media organizations. The files revealed that the PPP loans had been a complete debacle. Barack Obama's inspector general, who oversaw the bailouts from the financial crisis, said that the program proved that "no lessons ha[d] been learned" from the crisis of 2008.[3] He told *Time* magazine that the PPP would "tilt towards the biggest and most established companies . . . because that's what always happens."

One of the largest companies to access support through the PPP was Shake Shack, which received a $10 million loan through the program.[4] At the time it received the loan, it had 7,603 employees—1,000 of which were later laid off.[5] Ruth's Hospitality Group, which runs restaurant chains throughout the US, received $20 million through two loans.[6] Companies like Ruth's and Shake Shack are consumer-facing enterprises that, when their participation in the PPP was revealed, caved to public pressure and returned their loans to the SBA.

But nearly 80 percent of the public companies that received PPP loans have not returned them, meaning that at least $1.5 billion in public loans ended up in the hands of big corporations.[7] After a House subcommittee wrote to five large companies asking them to return their loans, only one did.[8]

Many of these companies saw their share prices soar as the Federal Reserve intervened to prop up financial markets and the US economy returned to growth. ProPublica cites the case of Lazydays Holdings, a publicly traded company that sells recreational vehicles (RVs) and received a $9 million loan from the government, despite having $31 million in cash on hand at the end of 2019.[9] The value of the company's shares rose 500 percent over the course of the pandemic as consumers moved to holidaying at home, which raises the question as to why the company needed a loan in the first place.

And if that wasn't bad enough, twelve publicly traded companies that received large PPP loans recently used tax havens to cut their tax bills.[10] Of these, seven had paid no tax at all in the US in 2019. ZAGG Inc., a Nasdaq-listed company that makes phone accessories and which has a subsidiary in the Cayman Islands, received a PPP loan worth nearly $10 million.[11] The company paid no corporate tax in the US in 2019. The government knew about ZAGG's questionable tax practices because it had been hit with a penalty under the Global Intangible Low-Tax Income (GILTI) legislation. In fact, the previous year the company received a $3.3 million tax *refund*, on top of tax credits worth at least $7 million.

Several members of Congress benefited from the scheme as their family businesses were able to apply for loans. Republican Roger Williams of Texas owns a chain of auto dealerships that received relief through the PPP.[12] This was not the first time Williams had run into ethical controversies over his business affairs. In 2016, he was investigated by the House Ethics Committee for inserting a provision into a bill that would benefit dealerships like his. The committee found that Williams had violated ethics rules as his personal financial interests appeared to have "influenced his performance of official duties."[13]

The husband of Democrat Susie Lee of Nevada runs a chain of casinos that also received a loan through the program.[14] Lee had lobbied to ensure that the gaming industry could receive support through the PPP. The husband of House Speaker Nancy Pelosi has a stake in a hotel that received a loan, as did the shipping business started by the family of

Elaine Chao, the US transportation secretary and wife of former Senate majority leader Mitch McConnell. Three other Republican congressmen who own car dealerships and fast-food franchises also received loans, as did two law firms with links to Democrats.[15] Even the Trump family was found to have benefited from the program.

Lobbyists, political consultants, and firms linked to political donors also received money through the bailouts. OpenSecrets found that political donors whose businesses received PPP support made donations of at least $52 million during the 2020 election.[16] Later research from the Project on Government Oversight and the Anti-Corruption Data Collective found that 113 companies, which collectively received up to $300 million in PPP loans, went on to make donations of at least $25,000 each. The donations made by these companies totaled nearly $12 million.[17]

Geoffrey H. Palmer is a major Republican donor and real estate developer who has been described as the "most controversial" real estate tycoon in LA.[18] Palmer sued the city of LA after it rejected one of his development proposals for failing to meet affordable housing standards— and he has been a vocal campaigner against affordable housing standards ever since. The city later sued him for negligence after a fire at one of his buildings damaged an adjacent government building. Palmer, who is worth around $3 billion, even appears in the Panama Papers.[19] He received a PPP loan of up to $1 million before donating $2 million to a Trump-supporting super PAC.[20]

Film tycoon Joseph E. Roth received a PPP loan of up to $350,000 before donating $250,000 to a super PAC seeking to remove Senate majority leader Mitch McConnell, making him the largest single contributor to the super PAC.[21] A set of oil pipeline construction companies located in the same building each received PPP loans of between $5 and $11 million; one of the companies went on to donate $250,000 to a super PAC dedicated to Trump's reelection.[22]

In some particularly egregious cases, politicians seeking reelection received donations from companies that had received PPP loans, which were wholly or partly owned by themselves or members of their family. Marjorie Taylor Greene is a far-right congresswoman who has promoted white supremacist, anti-Semitic, and QAnon conspiracy theories and who compared the safety measures introduced during the pandemic to

the treatment of Jews during the Holocaust.[23] Taylor Greene even called for the assassination of high-level Democratic politicians before entering Congress.[24]

As a congresswoman, she has been reprimanded for promoting COVID-19 conspiracy theories and praising Vladimir Putin after his invasion of Ukraine.[25] The House later voted to remove her from all committee roles. Greene owns a construction company with her husband, which received a PPP loan of up to $350,000.[26] The company, Taylor Commercial, later donated $700,000 to Greene's election campaign.

In at least one case, a recipient of a PPP loan who went on to make political donations—Martin Kao—has been charged with fraud.[27] Kao, a former private defense contractor, exploited his political relationships to obtain PPP funds by citing correspondence with members of Congress when applying for a loan for his company, Navatek LLC. Kao insisted that the bank had to offer him a loan, referencing emails he had exchanged with a prominent senator involved in drafting the PPP legislation. He claimed that the senator had "confirmed directly that the [bank] is obligated to fund" his company and wrote—underlined and in caps—that this senator had "helped write the rules" on the PPP.

He received the maximum possible loan for his company from the bank, before securing another $2.8 million loan from another bank. Kao's company went on to make political contributions to various re-election campaigns—a continuation of a pre-COVID trend. One of the senators to whom Kao had donated spoke out in favor of an $8 million Pentagon contract that was awarded to Navatek, including a quote from Kao in her press release. Leaked emails show how Kao reacted to his staff's "personal fears" about COVID-19—he stated in an email to employees that he had "three words" for them: "I . . . Don't . . . Care."

Meanwhile, millions of people lost their jobs or were pushed out of their homes by companies that had received support from the US state. The US has seen a significant growth in corporate landlords: corporations like asset manager Blackstone that buy up swathes of real estate before renting homes out and hiking up rents.[28] Many of these companies used the pandemic to undertake mass evictions of vulnerable tenants, despite the imposition of a federal evictions moratorium. The Select Subcommittee on the Coronavirus Crisis found that four corporate landlords had filed at least fifteen

thousand evictions in the midst of the lockdown—often using intimidation and illegal tactics to force tenants out.[29]

The committee found that one corporate landlord—the Siegel Group—distributed copies of a court order wrongly suggesting that the evictions moratorium was not being enforced by the courts. A senior executive at the firm sent emails to his colleagues encouraging them to use this strategy to "bluff people out" of their properties.[30] Another Siegel executive suggested that one of his employees call child protective services on a family as a way to expedite their eviction.

Siegel received "millions of dollars" in emergency assistance distributed by the US government, which was intended to support tenants at risk of eviction during the pandemic. This is only one example of the extraordinary upward redistribution that took place throughout the pandemic. Governments and central banks distributed billions of dollars to multinational corporations and financial institutions while millions of people were pushed into poverty.

And it wasn't just the US.[31] Research from *VICE* in the UK found dozens of large companies that had accessed government support through the Bank of England's Covid Corporate Financing Facility (CCCF) went on to lay off workers and pay out dividends to shareholders. All in all, journalist Ben Smoke found that twenty-one of the companies that accessed the CCCF paid out £11.5 billion to shareholders during the first half of 2020. Twenty-six companies that accessed the fund had announced plans to lay off nearly forty-three thousand UK workers. Many of them, like the US IT company DXC, paid out large dividends *and* announced mass layoffs. The company paid £41 million in shareholder dividends before announcing that it would be cutting forty-five hundred jobs worldwide.

Bayer, the agrochemicals company, drew £600 million from the CCCF after paying a £2.75 billion shareholder dividend a few months earlier.[32] The German chemical company BASF was the largest beneficiary from the fund, drawing £1 billion, before proceeding to distribute billions to shareholders. BASF and Bayer have been fined in US courts for the "irreparable damage" caused by their products. The US oil company Schlumberger, based out of the tax haven of Curaçao, drew £415 million from the CCCF in June 2020 before announcing the next month it would be cutting twenty-one thousand jobs around the world. A day earlier, the company had voted to pay out £135 million in dividends. The firm had previously been fined $233 million for sanctions violations—at the time the largest such fine ever paid.

G4S, the global security and outsourcing company, drew £300 million from the CCCF before being hit with a £44 million fine for fraud for "dishonestly misleading" the government.[33] The CCCF has even been used by arms manufacturers like Chemring Group, which drew £50 million from the facility before paying out nearly £7 million in shareholder dividends. Chemring is one of the major suppliers of weapons to Saudi Arabia, which has been accused of war crimes during its military intervention in Yemen.

In France, all forty companies listed on the country's largest stock exchange, the CAC 40, benefited from public support—whether in the form of furlough money, loans, tax deferrals, subsidies, or access to the ECB's bond-buying program.[34] The government did introduce some "watered down" requirements to ensure that companies receiving public funds limited the amount they were paying out in dividends, but "the call for restraint was only moderately heeded." According to the Multinationals Observatory, only a third of CAC 40 companies canceled or suspended shareholder dividends.[35]

Total, the French energy giant, received indirect support from the state and increased its dividends payout, distributing nearly €7 billion to shareholders. The French companies Vivendi, Danone, and Sanofi all increased their payouts too, with the latter distributing nearly €4 billion to shareholders. Danone proceeded to cut two thousand jobs. All in all, France's top companies—all of which benefited from some form of government support—paid out a total of €34 billion to shareholders while cutting nearly sixty thousand jobs around the world. As the authors of one report point out, in France "public assistance to the private sector now exceeds the amount paid out in social welfare."[36]

In Australia, $12.5 billion in government money was distributed to companies that were later found to have been "largely unaffected" by the pandemic.[37] Many of these companies had actually increased their profits from prepandemic levels. In Canada, fifty-three public companies received more than $10 million (CD) through the emergency wage subsidy program. Thirty of them went on to distribute nearly $2 billion to shareholders, while seven also bought back their own shares.[38] In Germany, Volkswagen—which has been forced to pay out more than €30 billion in fines and settlements to authorities in dozens of countries due to the diesel emissions scandal—benefited from the country's furlough scheme before paying out billions in dividends to shareholders over the course of 2020 and 2021.[39]

All over the world, the story is the same: governments distributed vast sums of public money to large companies that then went on to lay off workers and pay out dividends to shareholders. This money came straight out of the pockets of people who need it for necessities like rent and monthly bills. Throughout the pandemic, powerful corporations, financial institutions, states, and international organizations worked together to protect their interests and ensure the stability of the status quo—as they do during every crisis.

Crises themselves may not be planned—capitalist economies experience frequent crises precisely because the actions of different market participants cannot always be coordinated. In a truly free-market system, such crises would be important for the health of the economy. Less productive businesses would fail and overleveraged financial institutions would go under. This is the nature of the ruthless anarchy of the market, which, in a crisis, should devastate rich and poor alike. In the minds of many economists, it is precisely this lack of discrimination that is what makes the market system just.

But within actually existing capitalism—a hybrid of markets and central planning—the largest and most powerful institutions in the public and private sectors can work together to save their own skin. Rather than bearing the consequences of the crises they have created, these actors shift the costs of their greed to those with the least power—working people, particularly those in the poorest parts of the world.

Capitalist crises often take the form of collective action problems: situations in which everyone would be better off if they cooperated to solve a problem but are nevertheless unable to do so. The issue is that in a crisis situation capitalists cannot trust one another to stand by their word. If they all agree to follow a particular plan—let's say, holding on to an asset rather than selling it—there will always be an incentive for one actor to abandon the plan, and the knowledge that this is the case often prevents such cooperation from taking place to begin with. Individual capitalists cannot see the wood for the trees—especially when engulfed in a serious crisis. It is during these moments that the state has to step in to act on behalf of the capitalist class as a whole.[40]

Governments can *force* capitalists to work together, backed by the coercive power of the state. In doing so, they can override the competing interests of individual capitalists and act on behalf of capital in general. Every recent crisis—from the financial crisis to the pandemic, to the cost-of-living crisis—has involved a key role for the state in solving capital's collective action problems. And even though capitalists have often wailed about the pain inflicted on them at the time, they have always come out on top.

AIG: American Insurance Grifters

The American investment banks were making more money than God before 2008, and the humble insurer American International Group (AIG) wanted to get in on the action.[41] The company started to issue insurance to big investment banks against the risk that the housing market would turn—if house prices fell, the company would pay out. AIG's executives believed this would be a one-way bet, so the company never bothered to insure itself against the risk that it might one day have to pay out on the insurance contracts it had sold. This was a great way to make a lot of money very quickly for as long as the mortgage market was stable—but as soon as things turned sour, AIG found itself on the hook to the big investment banks for eye-watering sums of money.

Within a few months of the collapse of Lehman Brothers, the firm's credit rating had been downgraded and it found itself on the brink of bankruptcy. AIG owed billions in insurance payments to some of the largest investment banks in the world, including Goldman Sachs, to whom the insurer owed at least $20 billion.[42]

AIG's liabilities to Goldman were particularly significant because the bank had been selling its clients dodgy mortgage-backed securities before taking out insurance against the risk that the value of these securities would fall. Goldman Sachs had effectively made a massive bet against the US mortgage market with its clients as counterparties. Its actions were, as one journalist put it, "tantamount to building a house, planting a bomb in it, selling it to an unsuspecting buyer, and buying $20bn worth of life insurance on the homeowner—who you know is going to die!"[43]

This fund was the basis of Goldman's claim against AIG—if Goldman wanted to collect the insurance on its shoddy fund, it needed the insurance giant to pay out. So, Wall Street lobbyists set about convincing the government to bail the firm out, arguing that it was the only way to protect AIG's other policyholders. But this argument was patently untrue. If AIG had gone down, the law stated that other policyholders would be protected.[44] AIG wasn't bailed out to protect ordinary policyholders; it was bailed out to save Goldman Sachs.

The Fed gave AIG a loan worth $85 billion in exchange for 80 percent of the company's equity, making it one of the largest bailouts in US history.[45] The former chairman and CEO of Goldman, Henry Paulson, was central to the decision to grant the bailout. In fact, during the crisis, "Goldman Sachs had at least four dozen former employees, lobbyists or advisers operating in the highest reaches of power both in Washington and around the world." One regulator captured "40 hours of audio recording . . . showing other Fed employees acting inappropriately by purposely not reporting on bad practices that they witnessed, in order to protect the bank."[46,47]

As the scale of the firm's losses mounted, the government had to channel even more money into the company, bringing the total injected into AIG up to $182 billion.[48] A condition of the bailout was that AIG agreed to honor all its insurance contracts, including those it had made with Goldman.[49] The bank walked away with nearly $13 billion of this public money, some of which ended up with the company's clients, but at least $2.9 billion was kept within the firm.[50]

Société Générale and Deutsche Bank each got $12 billion from the AIG slush fund.[51] But $11 billion of the cash that had gone to Société Générale went straight to Goldman under the conditions of a deal that had been made between the two banks. The money Goldman gained from the AIG bailout came on top of the $10 billion in cash the government provided the firm through the Troubled Asset Relief Program (TARP). A year later, the firm paid a record $11.4 billion in employee bonuses. AIG, meanwhile, paid out $168 million in "retention awards"—a figure that reached as high as $1.2 billion over subsequent years.[52] One of AIG's largest investors later brought a lawsuit claiming that the Treasury had "looted AIG to save Goldman and other firms from their own insolvency."[53]

During the financial crisis, the Treasury and the Fed sought to introduce a form of planning without the appearance of planning—they wanted to provide a public guarantee to the risky transactions that had been undertaken by the big banks, while claiming to be protecting the public. To achieve this end, the US state nationalized a massive insurer—at the cost of billions—and used it as "an enormous taxpayer-funded piggy bank from which the government could funnel billions to a throng of teetering banks."[54]

Despite the clear role played by the state in exacerbating the crisis and shifting the costs to working people, the financial crisis is often considered a classic lesson in the anarchic and unplanned nature of modern capitalism. In a complex and highly interdependent world, even something as safe as mortgage lending can ultimately lead to a "black swan" disaster that strikes everyone by surprise.[55]

In fact, the US state had helped to inflate the bubble that burst so violently in 2008. Without the implicit insurance provided by the central bank, the investment banks never would have taken the kinds of risks they took. Without decades of low interest rates and the removal of restrictions on lending, they wouldn't have been able to expand their mortgage lending so dramatically. Without the state-owned enterprises Fannie Mae and Freddie Mac, which drove the securitization boom, the big investment banks may never have entered the mortgage securitization game in the first place.[56]

The US government also created a system of oversight in which two government-sanctioned ratings agencies controlled 80 percent of the bond ratings market.[57] Cozy relationships between ratings agencies and bond issuers created significant conflicts of interests. In the lead-up to the crisis the ratings agencies "hid subprime junk within AAA-rated bonds," allowing hidden risks to build up unabated.[58] Regulators then referred to the ratings provided by these agencies when assessing risk within the financial system. Meanwhile, the agencies continue to rake in record profits. Moody's averaged a 77 percent return on invested capital, and S&P 84 percent, from 2016 to 2019, compared to just 24 percent for archmonopolist Google.[59]

But this wasn't just an American financial crisis, it was a global financial crisis—and its origins lay in the globalization of finance that had taken place over preceding decades. International financial markets expanded dramatically over the course of the second half of the twentieth century, with global cross-border capital flows rising to more than 150 percent global GDP by the time the financial crisis hit.[60]

Globalization is generally thought of as a "natural" phenomenon that takes place due to economic growth and technological change—and financial globalization was viewed no differently.[61] By the early 2000s, politicians in rich countries could often be found lamenting that it would simply not be possible for them to raise taxes, properly regulate multinational corporations, or control cross-border financial flows, because financial globalization had forced all countries to adopt the same neoliberal policies. But rich countries were not as powerless in this process as many politicians suggested.

As Eric Helleiner demonstrated as early as 1994, the financial globalization that took off in the 1970s and '80s had been set in train by states, particularly those of the US and the UK.[62] Governments and central bankers in these nations, under immense lobbying pressure, had decided as early as the 1950s that the constraints imposed on international financial flows created after the Second World War were restricting the potential growth of their powerful finance sectors. As a result, they implemented measures at both the national and international level to promote financial globalization.[63] These measures were generally described as deregulatory policies, but it is better to think of the process of financial liberalization as a "'reregulation' that required greater state intervention and cooperation."[64]

These policymakers did not, of course, intend to cause the financial crisis of 2008. But they could have seen it coming. The Asian financial crisis of the 1990s had demonstrated very clearly the dangers of allowing "hot money" to flow rapidly across borders without safeguards.[65] Joseph Stiglitz had pointed out that "capital account liberalization was the single most important factor leading to the [Asian] crisis."[66] And in its wake, there was a renewed attempt to place limits on financial globalization in some quarters.

But these attempts were stymied by an alliance of international financial institutions, politicians in the rich world, and bureaucrats within the international financial organizations. The response to the Asian financial crisis was simply to blame poor countries for economic mismanagement and shore up the neoliberal orthodoxy that had led to the crash in the first place.[67] As long as it was enriching and empowering Western financial institutions, the state was not going to stand in the way of financial globalization.

The financial crisis was driven as much by crooked coordination between powerful actors as it was by unrestrained "free market" capitalism. And when the crisis did hit, once again the state stepped in to shield powerful vested interests from the consequences of their own greed.

After the US savings and loan crisis in the 1980s, thousands of bankers were sent to jail on fraud and other charges. After the financial crisis of 2008, only one US banker was sent to prison—Kareem Serageldin, a banker at Credit Suisse who was convicted of fraud. Serageldin, who was born in Egypt and had a modest upbringing in Michigan, was earning nearly $7 million a year when he was arrested. Yet, according to the *New York Times*, he lived a "fairly modest" life.[68] Like many of his fellow investment bankers, he worked hard—but instead of partying on his nights off, he preferred reading economics books, earning him the title of "investment banking monk."[69]

The banker was convicted of lying about the value of Credit Suisse's mortgage-backed securities, a common practice among investment banks in what the judge described as the "evil environment" in finance that preceded the financial crisis.[70] Yet Serageldin was the only banker to go to jail, despite exhibiting more contrition in the wake of his sentence than many other arguably more blameworthy senior executives who were hit with large fines.

Executives at JPMorgan, for example, were found to have "knowingly packaged shoddy mortgages into securities that did not meet its credit standards and then sold them off to investors."[71] They then went on to fire the whistleblower who figured out what they had been doing. The bank ended up settling with various government agencies for $13 billion in a deal that kept many of its wrongdoings secret.[72]

Meanwhile, in the US, ten million people lost their homes[73]—many as part of illegal foreclosures that are still being litigated to this day. One Californian profiled by the *Los Angeles Times* had owned her home for a decade when her husband was forced to take a pay cut. The couple lost their home when the crisis hit, as well as $300,000 in pension savings, and a decade later were "still living paycheck to paycheck" in rented accommodations.[74]

Marx argued long ago that the state was nothing but "a committee for managing the common affairs of the whole bourgeoisie."[75] As we will see in chapter 6, the picture is usually a little more complicated than this, but crises are moments when it comes closest to being true. Most of the time, the powerful do not need to be collected in a single room to coordinate and plan. Institutions emerge within capitalist societies that can be relied upon to maintain the stability of the system and protect the powerful.

But during moments of crisis, these institutions are too slow and unwieldy to function effectively. Senior politicians will often literally bring representatives of the private sector together in a room to develop a solution to an evolving crisis—as US policymakers did during the financial crisis of 2008. In fact, research has shown that "individual banking executives with connections to the US Treasury made unusually large gains during and after the 2008 Troubled Asset Relief Program."[76] In other words, the policy choices made by governments after the financial crisis "ended up pushing power and wealth upward."[77]

Some see this as more evidence for racialized conspiracy theories. As one columnist for the *Jewish Chronicle* noted in 2009, *Rolling Stone's* description of Goldman Sachs as a "vampire squid" was "not without its problems for a bank with distinctly Jewish origins."[78] But the *Chronicle* went on to note that "the *Rolling Stone* writer does have a point." The point is not that a secret cabal of bankers runs the world; it is that the largest and most powerful institutions are protected from the consequences of their actions in a way ordinary people are not. Even the former chief executive of the International Monetary Fund wrote about a "quiet coup" that had been staged by a "financial oligarchy."[79]

This is not a bug, but a feature of capitalist economies. Capitalism is a system defined by a tension—a dialectic—between markets and planning, in which some actors are better able to exert control over the system than others, but in which no one economic actor—let alone individual—can control the dynamics of production and exchange entirely. Capitalism is a system that teeters on the knife edge between competition and coordination—this tension is what explains both its adaptability and its rigid inequalities.

Making a Killing for McKinsey

Before the pandemic, you may not have heard of the world's most influential management consulting firm. Unlike Boeing or Amazon, it's not an organization with which you're likely to have had any contact in your daily life. And unlike most of our major banks, it's historically been quite good at keeping its name out of the headlines.

This all changed during the pandemic, when the UK government granted McKinsey a contract worth more than half a million pounds to determine the "vision, purpose and narrative" of its Test and Trace program.[80] Emergency procurement rules meant that the tendering process for Test and Trace didn't even have to look competitive. McKinsey was given the contract without hesitation. The awarding of the contract was unsurprising given that Dido Harding, the Tory peer chosen to head the program, is a former McKinsey consultant.[81] If that wasn't enough, she is also married to a Conservative MP and studied at Oxford alongside former prime minister David Cameron.[82] Harding was later forced to defend the decision to spend upward of £1,000 a day on consultants during a national emergency in front of the Public Accounts Committee.[83]

Despite the scandal that surrounded the process, £563,000 for six weeks of work is pretty cheap for McKinsey, which is used to charging governments millions for its services. The company's executives were likely more interested in the clause stating that the firm could access valuable personal data—including "names, addresses, biometric data and medical data"—for up to seven years after the contract was signed if given the go-ahead from the Department of Health and Social Care.[84]

McKinsey doesn't exactly have a clean record when it comes to data protection. When the Saudi Arabian government hired the firm to assess public reaction to the kingdom's austerity measures in 2015, McKinsey wrote a report citing three Twitter users who were responsible for driving most of the negative reaction, before handing this information over to the authorities.[85] One of the three users identified by McKinsey was later arrested.

In fact, the history of the company is littered with scandals. After the 2008 financial crisis—which McKinsey had helped cause by encouraging its banking clients to load up on debt and enter the securitization game[86]—a former McKinsey executive was convicted for insider trading. Rajat Gupta, who sat on the board of Goldman Sachs, had used his McKinsey links to pass on inside information to friends that gave them an edge in financial markets.

Not long after, it was revealed that McKinsey had its own secretive internal investment arm, MIO Partners, which invested on behalf of a select group of senior employees and partners.[87] McKinsey had failed to disclose the fact that MIO was a creditor to Alpha Natural Resources while the firm acted as Alpha's bankruptcy adviser. The director of its bankruptcy division even sat on the board of MIO, along with many other former or current McKinsey partners.

In other words, McKinsey the advisory firm was helping to determine the compensation that would be provided to McKinsey the investment firm when a company to which the latter was a creditor collapsed. This created an incentive for McKinsey advisory to encourage the firm to place MIO Partners at the front of the line when it came to distributing the bankrupt firm's remaining resources. In 2019, McKinsey paid a $15 million fine in a settlement with the US Department of Justice—one of the largest ever levied in such a case, though significantly less than the profit McKinsey is reported to have made from the services it provided to Alpha Natural Resources.[88]

Valeant—once described as Big Pharma's Enron (another scandal in which McKinsey had a hand)—is a company now famous for buying up pharmaceutical companies in order to hike up the prices of lifesaving drugs. McKinsey, a prominent adviser to Valeant, actively encouraged this strategy. The fact that McKinsey was encouraging this extraordinarily unethical behavior would be scandalous enough, were it not for the fact that MIO was also investing in Valeant via several hedge funds at the same time, and several former McKinsey consultants sat on the company's management team.[89] In 2021, MIO settled a case with the SEC for $18 million over its failure to put in place proper safeguards to prevent information gleaned from McKinsey's advisory work from being used in the investment decisions made by MIO.[90]

But perhaps the greatest scandal to hit McKinsey in recent years has involved its role in the opioid epidemic in the US.[91] McKinsey advised Purdue Pharma on how it could "turbocharge" sales of the highly addictive drug OxyContin—as well as how the company might push back against regulators attempting to limit the use of the drug, and even how it might "counter the emotional messages from mothers with teenagers that overdosed."[92]

Before filing for bankruptcy in 2020, Purdue was given one of the largest fines ever levied against a pharmaceutical company after it was found to have "knowingly and intentionally conspired and agreed with others to aid and abet" medical professionals prescribing its opioids inappropriately.[93] Several McKinsey partners had worked for both the pharmaceutical companies and the government agencies that were supposed to be regulating those companies.

Yet the US government, which had intimate knowledge of McKinsey's failings, still hired the company to assist with its bungled pandemic response. Just as in the UK, emergency procurement rules were used to hire McKinsey quickly and without scrutiny. A former McKinsey executive working in the Department of Veterans Affairs (VA) received an email from a current McKinsey staffer offering emergency advice on pandemic support for the nine million veterans supported by the government.[94] The next day, the department signed a $12 million contract with McKinsey. Within ten days, two other government departments had jumped on board, bringing the total value of McKinsey's emergency government pandemic contracts to $22.5 million. Within weeks, "McKinsey had extracted a total of $40.6 million in no-bid contracts."[95]

And its involvement didn't stop there. McKinsey consultants supported the Federal Emergency Management Agency (FEMA) and the Department of Health and Human Services (DHHS) to obtain medical supplies and PPE, and the Food and Drug Administration (FDA) hired the firm for data analytics.[96] Confident in the firm's capabilities due to its megacontracts with the federal government, states—from California, to Massachusetts, to Tennessee—hired McKinsey to support their pandemic responses, as did several cities—from Los Angeles to Chicago and New Orleans.

In many cases, McKinsey's involvement either failed to help or actively impeded the response to COVID-19. In its work with the VA, McKinsey took precious weeks to compile the data required to launch the program, causing confusion and delaying the rollout. According to ProPublica, "The FEMA/HHS task force has faced harsh criticism for a slow and dysfunctional effort to procure supplies."[97] In Florida, ProPublica journalists found that McKinsey's support amounted to "compiling data . . . and putting it in pretty fonts."[98]

Yet McKinsey has profited handsomely from its involvement with the US state during the pandemic, to the tune of an estimated $100 million, as well as gaining access to precious data from the work. This data is particularly valuable as it can be sold to other parts of government that, in the absence of a centralized public database, have to rely on McKinsey for insights.[99] When governments hire firms like McKinsey to handle our personal data during a crisis, often riding roughshod over legislation designed to protect our privacy in the process, they are compromising civil rights that will be very difficult to restore once the crisis is over.

The pandemic is another in a long history of crises that have been used to plunge countries into "states of emergency" that augment the power of the state and capital. States of emergency often involve the suspension of legislation designed to protect individual and collective rights in the name of swift and effective crisis management.[100] In 1978, thirty countries existed under a state of emergency of some kind; by 1986, this had risen to seventy.[101] By the turn of the century, nearly every country in the world had created some legal mechanism to bring about a state of emergency. In the US, even before the pandemic hit, there were thirty-two active "national emergencies," the oldest of which dated back to the 1980s.[102] Today, there are forty-two.[103]

COVID-19 has provided the perfect justification for the use—and abuse—of these wide-ranging powers, allowing powerful actors to profit from a disease that has caused the deaths of millions. In 2020, 124 countries declared states of emergency in response to the pandemic.[104] In Moscow, quarantine rules were enforced through surveillance set up through the city's vast network of facial recognition cameras.[105] In Bahrain, the mandatory BeAware app transmits information on people's location directly to authorities—and similar measures have been used in Norway and Kuwait.[106] France implemented a decree allowing the government to monitor mask wearing on public transport using CCTV.[107] In Israel, the government's pandemic response made use of the dystopian-sounding database known as "the Tool," which sweeps up data from cell phones about "the location of the device, the cell and antenna zone to which it is connected, every voice call and text message sent or received by the cellular device, and internet browsing history."[108]

The Chinese state also developed its own app—the health code—

in partnership with the tech giants Tencent and Alibaba. The app uses "opaque algorithms to assess a user's risk of contagion and restrict their movements."[109] Users input sensitive personal data and are then assigned a red, yellow, or green QR code, which indicates the person's contagion risk and must be scanned to access venues. In some states, such as Hangzhou, the app is linked to a person's social security and medical records. Many states are now attempting to make the app a permanent fixture in China, including through proposals to expand it to include a "personal health index" that assigns the user a score based on their sleep, exercise, and eating habits.[110]

It would be easy to frame these developments as examples of states overstepping the line between public and private power. Many libertarians argue that the pandemic has shown that state spending needs to be pared back to create more space for the democratic interactions that take place within "the market." But, as we have seen throughout this chapter, states rarely work alone. Whether the British and American governments working with McKinsey or the Chinese government working with its big-tech giants, states almost always rely on some support from the private sector during moments of crisis.

In turn, through their cooperation with states, businesses have gained power over our lives that would be the envy of some of the most authoritarian governments in history. Cutting public services doesn't create more space for free markets, it simply encourages states to rely more on unaccountable organizations like McKinsey to do their dirty work for them.[111] These consultancies then gain immense influence over the exercise of state power—from the high-level advice they provide to lawmakers, to the pedestrian support they provide to the civil servants implementing these policies.[112]

The close links between the public and private sectors seen during the pandemic demonstrate the futility of attempting to draw a stark line between state and corporate power in capitalist societies, especially during crises. Throughout the pandemic, states and firms worked together to augment their power and wealth—and as they did so it became harder to see where the private sector ended and the state began. The costs of this corruption have been felt by working people, who are now being told there is no money left in public coffers to deal with a cost-of-living crisis that is seeing millions pushed into poverty.

Yet mainstream commentators lost no time in claiming that the increase in state spending seen over the course of the pandemic could be equated with "socialism." *Forbes* ran a piece on the rise of "Coronavirus Socialism."[113] More equivocally, a columnist for *The Hill* asked in March 2020, "Will coronavirus launch the second wave of socialism?"[114] *Scientific American* echoed the question with an article headlined "Will COVID-19 Make Us More Socialist?"[115] "The Free Market Is Dead," declared *Time* in April 2021; the only question that remains is "What Will Replace It?"[116]

Marxists have always insisted that higher levels of state spending cannot be equated with socialism. In *The State and Revolution*, Lenin critiques "the erroneous bourgeois reformist assertion that monopoly capitalism or state-monopoly capitalism is no longer capitalism, but can now be called 'state socialism.'"[117] The Irish political leader James Connolly wrote in 1899 that "state ownership and control is not necessarily Socialism—if it were, then the Army, the Navy, the Police, the Judges, the Gaolers, the Informers, and the Hangmen, would all be Socialist functionaries, as they are State officials."[118] As we have seen, the kinds of responses introduced in response to the pandemic have reflected the balance of class power within the society in question: more often than not, this has looked like socialism for the rich and ruthless individualism for everyone else.

The impact of the pandemic on corporate power and inequality is a good indication of whose interests were really served by the bailouts of 2020. The support provided by the state to big business has led to a bonanza in corporate profiteering. After Trump's $2.3 trillion corporate tax cut in 2017, US companies set a record for share buybacks, with companies in the S&P 500 purchasing $806 billion worth of their own shares. But 2021 beat even 2018's record, with S&P 500 companies spending $882 billion on share buybacks, up from $520 billion in 2020.[119] Corporate executives benefited substantially from the buybacks, making "eye-popping" amounts of money by selling their shares to benefit from inflated share prices.[120]

Many companies that didn't spend all their money on buybacks spent it on merging with or acquiring their competitors to shore up their market power. In the first six months of 2021, global M&A activity hit a record high, with most deals taking place among a few massive corporations. Two months later, total M&A activity for 2021 surpassed the value of all deals that had taken place in 2020, hitting $3.6 trillion and breaking the previous eight-month record, set in 2007. One of the greatest beneficiaries of all this M&A activity was none other than Goldman Sachs, which earned record profits in 2021. By the end of 2021, global M&A volumes had reached $5.8 trillion, up 64 percent on the previous year—and the first time in history that volumes had exceeded $5 trillion.[121]

Meanwhile, according to the International Labour Organization (ILO), 114 million people lost their jobs in 2020. In total, the ILO estimates that globally workers lost at least $3.7 trillion in earnings over the course of the pandemic.[122] Around the world, up to 124 million more people were living in extreme poverty in 2020 than had been expected based on pre-COVID projections, reversing decades of progress on poverty reduction.[123] At the end of 2020 the US saw the sharpest increase in the poverty rate since the 1960s.[124] Eight million Americans were living in poverty by the end of 2020, or 11.8 percent of the population.[125] In the UK, research from the Trades Union Congress showed that 50 percent of low-paid workers suffered a loss of income during the pandemic, next to 29 percent of high earners, and 30 percent of low-paid workers had to increase their borrowing as a result.[126]

Wealth inequality in the US also reached record highs. The net wealth of the top 1 percent is twenty-six times their liabilities, while the bottom 20 percent have wealth worth five times their liabilities.[127] By 2021, the wealthiest 10 percent of Americans owned a record 89 percent of all stocks;[128] and the wealth of US billionaires increased by 70 percent over the course of the pandemic.[129] By the end of 2020, just fifty people had the same wealth as the bottom 50 percent of all Americans, having increased their wealth by $339 billion over the course of the year.[130]

In the UK, the number of billionaires reached a record high during the pandemic, and twenty-four more people became billionaires over the course of 2021.[131] One think tank found that rising asset prices had "turbocharged" the gap between rich and poor, with the wealthiest 10 percent capturing five hundred times the gains of the poorest 10 percent.[132]

Even in Europe, billionaire wealth increased by $1 trillion over the course of the pandemic, hitting $3 trillion by 2021, with eighty new billionaires being added to the list.[133] By the end of 2021, 1.1 percent of the world's population held nearly 46 percent of the world's wealth.[134]

The increase in government spending seen over the course of the pandemic was not, as some columnists claimed, evidence of a shift toward socialism. Instead, governments and big business worked together to expand control over society and augment profits at the expense of workers. The capitalist state doing more does not, as Lenin and James Connolly realized more than a century ago, mean socialism. More often than not, it just means a rescue package for the capitalist class.

The Cost-of-Greed Crisis

In 1859, the Suez Canal Company commenced construction on the eponymous canal. The canal would take a decade to construct, costing $100 million[135]—roughly $2.3 billion in today's money—and thousands of lives. Prior to the opening of the canal, ships had to sail all the way around the Cape of Good Hope to travel by sea between Europe and America on the one hand, and India and the Middle East on the other. The opening of the Suez Canal reduced the journey from London to the Arabian Sea by one month.

In 1956, General Gamal Nasser, the second president of Egypt, nationalized the Suez Canal, sending shock waves throughout Britain and France. While Nasser pledged that trade through the canal would continue as normal, the two former empires were not content to allow their capitalists to be expropriated by a foreign government. So they allied with Israel to invade Egypt with the express purpose of taking it back, winning decisively against the Egyptians.

But the world's newest imperial power was not satisfied with this outcome. The US was keen to remind both France and the UK that they were no longer empires and threatened economic retribution against the British government if it did not back down. In an event still remembered as a national humiliation, the British complied, and the concession to run the canal was granted to the Egyptian state-owned Suez Canal Authority.

In the wake of the Suez Crisis, tensions mounted between Egypt and Israel. During the Yom Kippur War, Egyptian forces crossed the canal into the Sinai Peninsula—then occupied by Israel. The Israeli army launched a counterattack, with the aid of the United States, which sought both to support its ally and ensure the ongoing operation of the Suez. In response to US-sponsored aggression, the OPEC-producing countries hiked oil prices and imposed an embargo on the US, leading to the first oil price spike, which sent inflation soaring all around the world.

Neoliberal politicians attempted to present the inflationary shock seen in the 1970s as a natural result of attempts to disrupt the operation of the "free market." They contended that the crisis had resulted from workers demanding wage increases over and above what they deserved, not the US meddling in other countries' affairs.

The neoliberals claimed that unionists were acting like monopolists in the labor market, banding together to hike the price of their labor, to the detriment of everyone else—and that this was what was really causing inflation. The success of these arguments saw the election of a series of neoliberal governments—from Thatcher in the UK to Reagan in the US. Once elected, these administrations battered their domestic labor movements, while hiking interest rates to engineer a recession and show workers who was really in control.[136]

Sixty-five years after the first Suez crisis, on March 23, 2021, the Taiwanese ship *Ever Given* became stuck in the Suez Canal after it was blown off course by strong winds. The 1,300-foot container ship—roughly the height of the Empire State Building—remained lodged in the canal for six days, blocking all other vessels from passing through. In the time it took to dislodge the *Ever Given*, 369 ships became stuck in a line in the Suez in both directions, forcing others to take the far longer journey around the Cape of Good Hope. All in all, the crisis is thought to have prevented up to $10 billion in trade each day.[137]

The second Suez crisis was part of a crisis in logistics that increased prices across the global economy throughout 2022. Higher shipping rates drive up the cost of anything that has to be transported by sea—that's roughly 90 percent of the world's goods—and those costs were passed on to consumers.[138] But the effects weren't felt until those goods found themselves on the shelves months after they'd been shipped, so much of the inflation experienced at the start of 2022 was in part the result of shipping disruptions during 2020.

Yet the shipping companies profited handsomely from this chaos. In 2021, ten companies—all based either in Asia or Europe—controlled 85 percent of global shipping capacity.[139] And these firms all collude with each other in plain sight of regulators. The largest ones made operating profits of $110 billion in 2021 alone—more than the operating profits from the previous ten years combined.[140] And 2022 was even more lucrative, with profits hitting record levels of $208 billion.[141]

Meanwhile, the workers employed by these companies are paid poverty wages and denied basic rights.[142] The ships sail under "flags of convenience," which allow them to register in jurisdictions with weak labor laws and low taxes to avoid obligations to their workers and society. During the pandemic, conditions became even worse when workers were trapped on board ships that had been unable to dock for as long as fourteen months—far in excess of what is allowed under international maritime law.[143]

There is a direct line running from the Suez Crisis to the inflationary shock of the 1970s to the neoliberal shift of the 1980s. And, oddly enough, a similar line can be drawn from the Suez crisis that shook the world in the midst of COVID-19 to the inflationary shock of 2022 to the economic turmoil of 2023. Far from being natural results of either unrestrained free markets or greedy unionized workers, both crises resulted from political choices made by states and corporations in response to shifts in power and wealth then underway in the world economy. Naturally, these choices tended to consolidate the status quo and benefit the powerful.

The significant uptick in inflation seen around the world in the wake of the pandemic has been presented by many as a "natural" result of the decision to lock down and then reopen the global economy. Governments upset the operation of the price mechanism, and now they are paying the price.

But the inflationary crisis we're seeing today is not natural; it is political. Some economic actors—those with the most power—have made huge amounts of money from the crisis, while others have been plunged into poverty. The relentless pursuit of profit among a few powerful actors in the global economy is creating the inflationary pressure that everyone else is being forced to pay for. The cabal of shipping companies that has enclosed the infrastructure responsible for transporting 90 percent of goods used the pandemic to increase prices far beyond their costs, making huge profits in the process. In fact, the trade crisis might not have been so significant had those same companies not spent the previous few decades building ships so large that they take days to load and unload, can enter only certain ports, and occasionally get stuck in the Suez Canal.

And the shipping companies weren't the only ones benefiting from the chaos. Energy prices around the world shot up after the pandemic thanks to the sudden increase in demand that followed the reopening of many economies, the war in Ukraine, and decades of failure to invest in renewables. Economists and their friends in the energy sector claimed that these price increases were a natural and unavoidable result of rising costs. Yet somehow the fossil-fuel companies managed to make record profits while people around the world struggled to pay their heating bills.

In 2021, ExxonMobil announced its highest annual profits since 2014, more than making up for the losses it suffered in 2020.[144] The company could have used this boost to accelerate the transition to renewables. Instead, it used the cash to launch a $10 billion share buyback program, handing its shareholders billions in capital gains.[145] Shell reported its highest-ever profits of nearly $40 billion for 2022—more than double what it made the previous year.[146] BP more than doubled its profits between 2021 and 2022, surpassing its previous record of $26.3 billion. BP also dished most of this money out to shareholders, increasing its dividend payment by 10 percent, while backtracking on pledges to reduce its greenhouse gas emissions.[147] Between them, Shell, BP, ExxonMobil, and Chevron made around $70 billion worth of profit during the first three months of 2022.[148]

Even as massive corporations have profited from the chaos caused by the pandemic and the energy crisis, rising prices have been blamed on workers—just as they were in the 1970s. Some economists alleged that the inflation seen in 2022 was the result of a wage-price spiral, in which workers demand higher wages to compensate for rising prices, which in turn drives up inflation. In the UK, the governor of the Bank of England, Andrew Bailey, pleaded with workers not to demand a wage increase in line with inflation.[149] Bailey neglected to mention that he earns half a million pounds a year.

But the wage-price spiral argument was utterly without foundation. In fact, 2022 was the worst year for real wage growth in the UK since 1977.[150] The inflationary crisis is not being driven by a wage-price spiral. If anything, it is being driven by a profit-price spiral, in which large corporations use their market power to raise prices far more than the increase in their costs, using inflation as an excuse.[151] This idea—termed *sellers' inflation*—was proposed by economist Isabella Weber in December 2021. At the time, her arguments were dismissed as "stupid" by some of the leading lights of the economics profession. But now even those who once mocked her have been forced to accept many of the insights of her research.[152] Ballooning profits are responsible for embedding inflation—not rising wages.

Yet central bankers have once again decided that the only response to rising prices is to hike interest rates, in the hope that the resulting fall in investment will cause an increase in unemployment. While they claim to hope to engineer a "soft landing" in which rates are raised without causing a downturn, policymakers know their actions could tip many economies into recession in 2024. What's more, unexpected increases in interest rates can cause immense instability in financial markets—rising rates were part of what brought down Silicon Valley Bank in 2023. Though the bank's megawealthy clients were, of course, swiftly bailed out by the US state.

Central bankers know that *they* are not going to be the ones bearing the costs of this crisis. Millions of working people will lose their jobs due to rising interest rates. Millions more will find themselves pushed into poverty as the cost of servicing their debt increases at the same time as their heating bills go through the roof. Meanwhile, poor countries all over the world will be pushed into debt distress—just as they were in the 1980s—as investment flees the poor world to take advantage of higher returns in the rich world. As interest payments on government debt increase, there will be less public money available for poverty reduction, health care, and education.

The cost-of-living crisis is being driven by a toxic melding of public and private power. Powerful corporations are taking advantage of shortages to raise prices, before handing the windfall to shareholders and executives.[153] States largely refuse to tax these windfall profits, preferring instead to rely on central banks to raise interest rates to curb inflation, increasing the cost of debt servicing for everyone else. Commodities traders have made a killing from gambling on the prices of the basic goods people rely on to survive after their trade was deregulated by government.[154] Meanwhile, politicians, central bankers, and powerful business leaders can be found arguing that they couldn't possibly consider increasing wages for fear of increasing workers' power.

No economic crisis is a truly natural event, like an earthquake or a thunderstorm. Economic crises are caused by the dynamics of modern capitalism, and they are resolved in favor of the most powerful. This is as true of the inflationary crisis we're seeing today as it was of the one in the 1970s. Even as the world economy stares down the barrel of a gun, there are powerful vested interests making money from the chaos.

But the energy crisis that consumed the world in 2022 is only a taste of things to come if we do not make radical changes to the structure of our economy. Climate breakdown is the single greatest challenge that any capitalist society has ever faced. While capital is quite happy to profit from the crisis over the short term, over the long term everyone knows that a warming planet threatens the very foundations of capitalism itself.

Out of the Frying Pan and into the Fire

In July 2021, the *Financial Times* ran an opinion piece entitled "For Sustainable Finance to Work, We Will Need Central Planning."[155] A few months later, the *Economist* followed with an editorial arguing that when it comes to climate breakdown, the market might not always deliver the goods. Sometimes "a more centrally planned approach will be necessary."[156] Some have taken this as an admission from some of the oldest and most respected free-market journals that capitalism cannot deal with the all-encompassing crisis of climate breakdown.

But, as we have seen, more state planning does not equal socialism. The *Economist* and the *Financial Times* have, for decades, acted as the journals through which the ruling class debates, discusses, and coordinates its approach to the management of capitalist societies.[157] Turkeys don't vote for Thanksgiving; and the leading papers of the capitalist ruling class are not calling for the abolition of capitalism. Their pleas for central planning are not an admission that capitalism is failing; they merely recognize that all capitalist societies require some level of central planning to function.

As we have seen, many of the challenges faced by businesses in a capitalist economy take the form of collective action problems. When a crisis like climate breakdown threatens capitalism's very foundations, private businesses must coordinate to respond. In more competitive economies, such coordination is difficult. If every business leader agreed to decarbonize, a few less responsible companies could edge ahead of their competitors by continuing to use fossil fuels.

It's up to capitalist states to solve these problems by forcing capitalists to cooperate. Whether the state is levying taxes to reduce inequality, investing in infrastructure, or employing workers during a recession, state institutions act as an organizing and coordinating force in nominally free-market economies. Climate breakdown is the next in a long line of collective action problems faced by global capital. It is, however, by far the greatest challenge in its history.

The science is now completely indisputable. According to the Intergovernmental Panel on Climate Change's most recent report, released in 2021, in 2019, atmospheric concentrations of carbon dioxide were higher than at any time in the last two million years. The last decade saw Arctic Sea ice at its lowest level since 1850. Global mean sea levels have risen faster since 1900 than at any other time over the last three thousand years. Not only is the planet getting warmer, but the rate of change is accelerating. Global surface temperatures increased faster since 1970 than in any other fifty-year period over at least the last two thousand years.

The year 2020 was tied with 2016 as the warmest on record, followed by 2019, 2015, and 2017.[158] The year 2021 comes in as the fifth-warmest on record, and it is "virtually certain" that 2023 will rank among the ten warmest years on record.[159] In July 2023, as I was finalizing this book, the world experienced its hottest month on record. Global average sea temperatures have also hit new records, reaching 69.8 degrees Fahrenheit in March 2023.[160] Extreme weather events have become far more common, with astonishing heat waves hitting the Middle East, India, and Pakistan, lifting temperatures to nearly 122 degrees Fahrenheit. Forest fires in Canada covered much of the country, plus the East Coast of the US, in smoke for several days in spring 2023, releasing billions more tons of carbon dioxide into the atmosphere.

When world leaders met in Paris in 2015, they agreed to take action to keep the rise in global temperatures to well below 2 degrees Celsius above preindustrial levels, and preferably to limit the increase to 1.5 degrees above those levels. A recent report by the Intergovernmental Panel on Climate Change (IPCC) confirmed that in almost any imaginable scenario, we will fail to keep to the 1.5-degree target, finding that "the scale of recent changes experienced across the climate system and much of its present state are unprecedented over thousands of years." Many of the changes, the IPCC's scientists said, are already irreversible. At the start of June 2023, average global surface air temperatures were more than 1.5 degrees above preindustrial levels for several days.[161]

And it's not just that the world is warming; human activity is fundamentally altering global ecology in a host of other ways. We are currently living through the sixth mass-extinction event in the earth's history, driven by everything from climatic changes to the overuse of chemical pesticides.[162] We have disrupted the nitrogen cycle through the overuse of chemical fertilizers that have compromised the quality of our drinking water and the air we breathe, as well as accelerating climate breakdown and biodiversity loss.[163] The overuse of antibiotics has led to the emergence of resistant strains of many potentially deadly bacteria, and the overuse of pesticides has resulted in pollinator decline that is putting at least $600 million in global crops at risk every year.[164] Meanwhile, up to 40 percent of the earth's land is now degraded, potentially compromising our ability to grow the foods we need to feed ourselves.[165]

Marx realized more than a century ago that the wealth provided by nature was treated by capital as a "free gift"—a store of wealth that could be drawn on, apparently indefinitely.[166] The pandemic was a wake-up call for those who have grown used to exploiting the natural world without consequence. As the author and activist Mike Davis perspicaciously warned in 2005, zoonotic diseases have become far more common in the era of industrialized agriculture, and they spread more quickly due to globalization.[167]

Capital is now waking up to the fact that nature's free gifts are close to running out—not simply the resources that we have extracted from the earth for generations, but the very environment we rely on to survive. Today's captains of industry know that they can do very little to solve the challenges associated with climate breakdown on their own; they need the state to force a solution on the private sector and hold companies to their decarbonization goals.

So-called market-based approaches to tackling climate breakdown have already been trialed extensively over the course of the last forty years, primarily in the form of emissions-trading schemes that rely on carbon pricing. Few of these schemes have been successful. The European Union's Emissions Trading System, for example, was deeply flawed from the outset as fossil-fuel lobbyists forced the adoption of a lower carbon price than initially intended.[168] In fact, fossil-fuel lobbyists spent more than €250 million pushing the EU to adopt policies favorable to the sector between 2010 and 2019.[169] The result of the scheme was that many polluting companies actually ended up *making* money from the ETS, and it roundly failed to reduce carbon emissions.

The idea of a centrally planned response to climate breakdown is now being promoted as the progressive alternative to market-based solutions, after years of failure have brought us to the point of climate chaos.

In 2020, both the United States and the European Union, which together have done the most to embed the neoliberal consensus at the level of the world economy, pushed through "green" stimulus packages designed to promote recovery from the pandemic and meet the challenges of climate breakdown. Meanwhile, Larry Fink—the CEO of BlackRock, whom we will meet in chapter 5—was writing to the heads of the companies in which he invests (i.e., pretty much every large company in the rich world) to tell them that BlackRock would be paying close attention to their approaches to decarbonization.

Yet this veneer of consensus obscures deeper divisions about precisely how the world should adapt to climate breakdown. BlackRock has consistently voted against activist investors pushing for sustainability, and one activist accused the company of "undermining the objectives of a climate coalition it just joined."[170] Both President Biden and EU leaders adopted the language of the Green New Deal to describe their stimulus packages, yet both fell far short of the kinds of measures that would be necessary even to make a dent in global emissions.

Just as responses to the pandemic reinforced preexisting inequities, the planned response to climate breakdown is unlikely to issue any fundamental challenge to the power of capital. The *Economist* and the *Financial Times* may write of the dramatic transformation that is likely to come as the world shifts away from fossil fuels, but their prescriptions fall short of the deep transformation of global capitalism required to decarbonize.

Calls for environmental sustainability from within the halls of power obscure the fact that the same small group of people and institutions that gave us climate breakdown, and who have profited handsomely from it, are now expected to develop a solution to the problem. Naturally, they will seek to protect and promote their own interests—not those of the majority. The planning we have seen in response to the pandemic and climate breakdown has differed little from the central planning seen in response to the financial crisis: once again, capital faces a collective action problem, and once again the capitalist state rides to the rescue.

In fact, as Joel Wainwright and Geoff Mann argue in their book *Climate Leviathan*, climate breakdown may end up being used by powerful actors within the state to augment their control over citizens.[171] In place of the liberal and neoliberal view of the limited state, a Hobbesian justification for state power[172] may reemerge, in which a government's legitimacy hinges on whether it is able to protect its citizens from rising global temperatures. Authoritarian legislation may come to be seen as a necessity, and democracy itself might come under threat. This authoritarian shift is already evident in many countries, like the UK, where the government has sought to criminalize climate activists with some notable successes.

As was the case with the response to the financial crisis, those without access to the corridors of power will remain unheard. States in the Global South are already being forced to deal with the impact of climate breakdown without access to the technology, resources, and financing required to mitigate the effect of rising temperatures—let alone decarbonize.

The prime minister of Barbados, Mia Mottley, took to the stage at COP26 to implore world leaders to "try harder" to avoid the kinds of temperature rises that would leave low-lying and island nations like hers literally underwater.[173] She told delegates including President Joe Biden and Prime Minister Boris Johnson that their "failure to provide enough critical funding to small island nations is measured in lives and livelihoods in our communities." These failures were, she told delegates, "immoral and . . . unjust." Yet the agreement that was hammered out at COP26 fell far short of the action that would be required to meet Mottley's call to arms.

Democracy and decarbonization are often seen as enemies. Democratic processes are slow, and time is running out. But unless we are able to democratize our society, political and economic decision-making processes will continue to be dominated by those who have helped to cause climate breakdown up to now.[174]

We cannot rely on the hope that the powerful will suddenly realize the need to tackle climate breakdown and take appropriate action. Even if they do realize in time, they will seek to protect their interests at the expense of the general interest. It is not hard to envisage a world in which wealthy nations respond to climate breakdown by building walls to keep at bay those displaced by rising temperatures.

Much like the separation between states and markets, the separation between man and nature is a liberal myth.[175] Humanity is a part of nature. The fight against climate breakdown is not a fight to save "the planet"— the planet will continue to exist long after it is rendered uninhabitable for humans. The fight against climate breakdown is a fight to protect human life on earth. And that fight cannot be won by sacrificing millions of lives or the freedoms that make life worth living. But if we continue to allow the response to climate breakdown to be shaped solely by the powerful, this is the kind of "solution" we will get.

More overt centralized planning undoubtedly will be introduced in response to climate breakdown, but this does not mean that the response to it will be progressive. The anarchy of capitalism creates crises that harm the poorest far more than the wealthy, but a central plan drawn up by the wealthy and powerful is no solution.

To understand how to fight back against the central planning practiced by the powerful, we need to know how it works. In the next part of this book, we'll look at how firms, financial institutions, states, and empires are able to plan the production and allocation of resources in nominally free-market societies. And in the final part, we'll look at how we can democratize political and economic life to the benefit of all.

PART II

THE PLANNERS

4

American-Made Sweatshops: How Big Business Plans

Jeff Bezos could be described as the Henry Ford of our era. Just as Ford rose from humble beginnings to become one of the world's richest men, Bezos was born into difficult circumstances—his seventeen-year-old mother was forced to study at night school while bringing up the young Jeff[1]—before briefly becoming the world's richest man. Just like Ford, Bezos was a serious child with a penchant for tinkering and experimenting with common household items. And just like Ford, Bezos has never warmed to the labor unions formed by his employees. Apparently, the feeling is mutual. In 2014, Jeff Bezos was named the world's worst boss by the International Trade Union Confederation.[2]

Ford, as the owner of the only company from which US consumers could buy a car in the early 1900s, was one of America's first and most successful monopolists. And Bezos clearly believes he can follow in Ford's footsteps. As of 2022, Amazon dominated US ecommerce, with conservative estimates placing its market share at nearly 40 percent.[3] Other estimates from 2021 placed the company's market share in ecommerce as high as 60 percent.[4] Within this market-dominating position, the company accounts for more than half of all computer and consumer electronics ecommerce sales and 80 percent of books, music, and video sales.[5] Its share of US advertising revenue has also been climbing—its share of ad spending is expected to reach 12.4 percent in 2023, up from 11.7 percent in 2022. Amazon Web Services (AWS), which offers cloud computing services, is by far the most profitable part of the company, accounting for nearly 75 percent of the company's total operating profit and 32 percent of the *global* cloud infrastructure market.[6]

All of this is not enough for some economists to classify Amazon as a monopoly. Economists tend to assess market power by looking at the markups a company charges—that is, how much more expensive its products are than would be expected in a competitive market. But, in this regard at least, Amazon often behaves like the opposite of a monopoly. Rather than cornering one market and using its power to hike prices, Amazon seeks constant expansion, using its market power to *cut* prices and operate at a loss to expand its customer base.[7]

The cornerstone of this strategy is Amazon Prime; once they've signed up for Prime, customers are more likely to buy everything they need on Amazon, allowing it to capture an even greater share of the ecommerce market. The service also allows the company to direct customers to its own products, a practice for which Amazon has frequently been hauled in front of competition authorities. But given the company's size and scope, it's hard to accurately determine the benchmark according to which Amazon's market power should be assessed. It's a giant conglomerate with sales in multiple markets, but it is also a market itself.

Amazon is clearly not a small price-taking firm automatically translating inputs into outputs, as firms are depicted within microeconomics. But neither can it be understood as a traditional monopoly: its strategy isn't to enclose a single market, erect barriers to entry, and raise prices—it's to dominate the market for everything. In fact, the company was not even profitable for much of its history. Amazon survived *despite* market forces, not because of them. Even today, its structure looks highly irrational: certain areas, like Amazon Web Services, are highly profitable, while services like Prime have made large losses. The market is telling Amazon one thing, but it seems to be doing another.

Market power is precisely the power to *avoid* the pressures imposed by the market: it is the power to control the market, rather than be controlled by it. As one author puts it, "Market power is the ability to act independently and without serious repercussions."[8] In this sense, market power is a form of political power—not dissimilar to the power wielded by a state. Amazon, like all powerful firms, is a political institution as much as a simple firm. Its aim is not to maximize short-term profits—its central aim is to maintain and expand its power. Arguably, Bezos's aim was to create the most powerful company in the world, and to become one of the world's most powerful men in the process.

As is always the case in capitalist enterprises, the success of the CEO has come at the expense of his workers. Amazon workers have accused the company of treating them like "robots"; one described the experience as like working in an "existential shithole," another as an "American-made sweatshop."[9] The US Occupational Safety and Health Administration (OSHA) found that Amazon workers were being injured at nearly twice the rate as workers for the company's competitors, and in one case five times higher.[10]

In 2019, one forty-eight-year-old worker had a heart attack and was left lying on the floor for twenty minutes before internal safety responders reached him.[11] Everyone was instructed immediately to return to work. History repeated itself in 2022, when employees in Colorado claimed they had been forced to "literally walk over a dead body" after an employee suffered a fatal heart attack.[12] Throughout 2022, five Amazon workers died across the US.[13] The year before, six people died at a single warehouse in Bessemer, Alabama, where workers have been trying to unionize.[14]

Bezos can often be found bragging about the high wages Amazon workers and delivery drivers are paid.[15] Not only do these wages fail to compensate for the horrendous conditions faced by Amazon workers, they also aren't offered to everyone. Amazon also relies on a range of so-called delivery service partners, through which workers are subcontracted to deliver parcels.[16] These subcontractors often pay much lower wages than Amazon itself and have been accused of breaking labor laws by underpaying workers.[17] Amazon's private infrastructure even extends into the skies. Its "Amazon Air" subcontractor, Atlas Air, pays pilots from 30 to 60 percent less than the industry standard. In 2019, one Atlas Air flight carrying Amazon packages crashed, killing three crew members.[18]

And it's not just the US. In the UK, an investigation by the *Mirror* found that workers are treated like "slaves" and "robots."[19] They have to process a package every nine seconds between when they start work at 7:30 a.m. until they leave at 6 p.m. Fifty-five percent of Amazon workers have been criticized for taking sick days, with female workers penalized for taking time off while pregnant. Ambulances have been called to Amazon warehouses over six hundred times—including 115 ambulance calls to one Amazon warehouse in the Midlands alone.

So why aren't Amazon workers organizing to resist their exploitation? They are—but Amazon is trying to stop them. In the US, Amazon was accused of "aggressive" anti-union tactics after the release of a leaked training video that included "warning signs" of union activity for managers to look out for, including "use of words like 'living wage' and 'steward'" and "increased negativity in the workplace."[20] A New York judge has ordered the company to "cease and desist" its anti-union practices, which included surveilling workers and firing those who engage in union activity.[21]

Amazon's new CEO, Andrew Jassy, has told workers outright that they will be "less empowered" if they join a union. In response, the National Labor Relations Board (NLRB) accused Jassy of illegal coercion and intimidation.[22] One fifty-year-old Amazon worker, who had been warned he would be fired due to his union activity, was later forced to take time off to undergo knee surgery.[23] While he was still in the hospital, he was informed he had used up all his medical leave and would be dismissed.

In the UK, the union Unite has accused Amazon of using union-busting tactics based on information from whistleblowers.[24] In Australia, the police were called to forcibly remove two union officials from an Amazon warehouse in Sydney while they were investigating a worker complaint.[25] In Canada, workers trying to organize during the pandemic said they faced a targeted anti-union campaign.[26] One of the workers claimed that he and fourteen of his colleagues were fired in retaliation for their efforts.

In Europe, where laws protecting workers are often stronger, it's been harder for the company to clamp down on unions. In Germany, workers in one factory launched a two-day strike for better wages and conditions.[27] In Spain, workers have launched an indefinite strike over the closure of a factory.[28] In Poland, workers across the country's many Amazon warehouses have been organizing for years, including organizing in solidarity with German workers when they announced strike action.[29] In Italy, workers went on strike demanding Amazon improve working conditions at its warehouses during the pandemic.[30] On Black Friday 2022, Amazon workers across thirty countries went on strike in a coordinated campaign over wages, conditions, and decarbonization.[31]

Amazon's business model depends on hyperexploitation of its workforce—particularly those in its distribution centers and logistics. But the company's success also depends on its ability to avoid taxes and ravage the natural environment. For two years in a row now, Amazon's main UK division has paid no corporation tax.[32] In the US, the company managed to avoid more than $5 billion in corporate federal income taxes in 2021, paying just 6 percent of its total profits in taxes.[33] In 2020, Amazon made €44 billion in revenue in Europe and paid no corporation tax by shifting its profits to Luxembourg, where the firm reported an overall loss that allowed it to claim tax *credits* that can be offset against any future profits declared in the tax haven.[34]

While brutally exploiting its workers and avoiding taxes, Amazon is also accelerating climate breakdown. According to its own estimates, the company released 71.54 million metric tons of carbon dioxide equivalent in 2021, up 18 percent over the previous year.[35] If Amazon were a country, its total emissions would be roughly equivalent to that of Kenya, a country of fifty-three million people.[36] Yet Amazon has also been accused of "drastically underestimating" its carbon footprint, allowing it to portray itself as a "green" company.[37] AWS, while supposedly a "clean" digital part of the company, has significant energy needs and mostly uses nonrenewable energy sources. And a shocking investigation into the company recently revealed that it is destroying millions of items of unsold stock—from unused TVs to smartphones—every year.[38]

Amazon's power is so great that it is able to influence the political systems of the countries in which it operates. In 2017 in Seattle, where the firm is based, Amazon donated $345,000 to the mayoral campaign of Jenny Durkan, whose opponent, Cary Moon, had previously spoken out against the firm's power.[39] Amazon's candidate, meanwhile, was discussing the need to develop "partnerships" with businesses like Amazon as part of a neoliberal "smart city" agenda that seeks to integrate big tech into the veins and arteries of the city. This is all part of Amazon's strategy to "[pit] cities against one another and [pluck] tax subsidies for facilities it already needs to build, reeling in at least £2.7 billion as of August 2019."[40]

Amazon also donated $1 million to the Seattle Metro Chamber of Commerce's pro-business political action committee, which spent nearly half a million trying to oust city councilmember Kshama Sawant, a member of the Socialist Alternative party and vocal critic of the company.[41] Sawant made her name by introducing a tax on big business she dubbed the "Amazon tax" and protesting the company's impact on living costs in the city.[42]

As if all that wasn't enough, Bezos has sought to extend his grip over the media too. In 2013, Bezos bought the *Washington Post*, appointed a new CEO, and changed the paper's business model. When asked in an interview why he purchased the paper, Bezos didn't say anything about profits. Instead, he said: "It is the newspaper in the capital city of the most important country in the world . . . [it] has an incredibly important role to play in this democracy."[43] In 2021, he used the *WaPo*'s homepage to launch a giant advertising campaign for Amazon. Critics have said he's using the paper as his "personal megaphone to push back against criticism over wages and working conditions."[44] And if that wasn't enough, Amazon has also been accused of bullying, manipulating, and lying to journalists from other outlets when they portray the company in a negative light.[45]

In his book *The Everything Store*, Brad Stone mentions that a key part of Bezos's business philosophy rests on the idea of positive feedback loops: your business grows, its costs fall, and it can invest in more growth.[46] Bezos's self-reinforcing cycle can be viewed as a formulation of the simple economies-of-scale argument that can be found in any economics textbook. But it could also be viewed as a depiction of the reinforcing cycle between economic and political power. As Amazon grows its customer base, it generates economies of scale that allow it to offer lower prices. If Bezos's aim was merely to maximize profits, he would start to raise prices in certain areas to exploit that market power.

Instead, his aim is to generate sovereignty for his firm—to give it the financial, regulatory, and competitive space to do whatever he wants it to do: to plan, without pressure from the market. So, rather than raising prices, Amazon uses its growth to cut prices, expand market share, and gain political power. As one of the only large employers in many places, the company can impose horrendous conditions and still access plenty of workers. As a powerful political actor, Bezos can use personal donations as well as his company's economic clout to pressure legislators into adopting his preferred policies. And as a powerful voice in the media, he is able to shape the views of policymakers and the public. The company has even built its own system of "private law" to govern its marketplace—one that prevents third-party sellers from taking any legal action against the company. It's been described as the "largest employment-based arbitration agreement in America."[47]

Amazon isn't alone. This kind of corporate planning is the norm among the world's largest enterprises. But because it is a form of planning that exists at the intersection between economics and politics, it is invisible to many academic economists.

Centralized planning isn't supposed to take place within free markets—it's supposed to be something that only states can do. Yet the world's biggest firms aren't just capable of planning production, often relatively insulated from market forces. They're also capable of influencing everything from the candidates we're faced with at election time to the stories we see in our media. Modern capitalist societies are characterized by "a hierarchy of power in which a few immense trading companies—in control of and to some degree in cahoots with a few dominant supply conglomerates—govern almost all the industrial activities upon which we depend, and they back their efforts with what amounts to police power."[48]

So how does this planning work in practice? And how can we resist this planning in our workplaces? We'll turn to these questions over the course of this chapter.

Black Box Businesses

Ronald Coase was a Nobel Prize–winning economist best remembered for providing an explanation as to why businesses were necessary under capitalism. This might seem like a rather trivial matter for which to award a Nobel Prize—after all, most of us consider business the lifeblood of capitalist economies. Even the word *capitalism* is likely to conjure up images of famous brands like McDonald's and Coca-Cola.

But for early economists, it was a challenge to explain why businesses should need to exist at all. Firms—which is how economists tend to refer to what we might call businesses—are quite rigid institutions that get in the way of the operation of the free market.[49] After all, bosses don't go out into the market every day to purchase the inputs they need for production—they lock in long-term contracts with suppliers and workers that mean these inputs become "trapped" within the firm for long periods of time.[50]

For this reason, it can be difficult for resources to move from one firm to another: a certain amount of money, a certain amount of stuff, and a certain number of people are locked into individual firms, at least over the short to medium term. All the buildings, machinery, and labor that are owned by a firm cannot be used by another firm—even a more competitive firm—unless that first firm goes under. Firms are like "lumps of butter coagulating in a pail of buttermilk."[51]

The question that economists had to answer was, if we really do live in a free-market system, then why does the firm exist at all? In this section, we're going to take a closer look at this question, and what it can tell us about the way corporate power is conceptualized in mainstream economic theory. We'll look at why the corporate world doesn't work the way it is presented in an economics textbook. In the real world, corporate owners and managers have power—power that derives from their control over their workers, their ownership of the physical resources used in the production process, and their close relationships with states. Corporations are a form of despotic private government.[52]

For a long time, economists didn't pay much attention to the problems of the firm. They were more focused on providing a panoramic view of the capitalist economy, and so they left the thorny question of the capitalist enterprise to one side. In most macroeconomic models, businesses are treated as "black boxes": resources go into the box before being transformed through the firm's mysterious internal processes and emerging on the other side for sale in the market.[53]

One early economist who was interested in opening the black box was Karl Marx. Marx realized that understanding capitalism required us to leave the realm of exchange and enter the "hidden abode of production."[54] He believed that one could not understand capitalism without studying what went on inside the capitalist firm. Studying businesses allowed Marx to show that the defining feature of capitalist production was not the free market, but the social division of labor—the class division between those who own the tools we need to produce commodities (capitalists) and those forced to sell their labor power for a living (workers). Marx realized that capitalism could only function through the exploitation of workers by bosses.

But this explanation wasn't particularly compelling to mainstream economists who wanted to show that capitalism worked for everyone—including workers. To do so, they came up with a theory of the capitalist firm that disguised the political power of modern corporations. As Isabelle Ferreras puts it, "The economic theory of the firm, while claiming scientific neutrality, has in fact upheld and validated a very narrow approach to the firm"—one that uses the obscure language of economics to conceal power and politics.[55]

Coase was one of the first mainstream theorists to provide a convincing mainstream explanation for the existence of the capitalist firm. Here was an economist born in 1910 into a working-class family—both his parents were telegraphists for the Post Office[56]—who had initially considered himself a socialist.[57] But while at university, he came to moderate his socialist principles with a belief in the "virtues of a competitive system."[58] Coase's socialist leanings (discarded later in life) were perhaps what allowed him to pay such close attention to the inner workings of the firm—and particularly the relationship between workers and bosses—whereas most other economists had glossed over this important subject.

Coase developed the "transactions cost" theory of the firm.[59] Without businesses, he argued, producers would have to write new contracts every time they wanted to buy something or employ a worker, and this would be expensive and time-consuming, especially when it came to employment contracts.

When you started your job, you probably weren't completely aware of what you'd be doing every day, even if you'd read every page of your employment contract. And your boss probably wasn't either. Your boss might even occasionally ask you to do things that are outside the scope of your employment contract, and most of the time, you probably agree to do them.

Why do you do what your boss tells you to? Because he has authority over you that is implicit in the contract you've signed with the organization for which you work. If you have a standard employment contract, it likely gives your boss broad control over the activities you undertake while you're at work. In fact, this authority is precisely what formal employment boils down to: the common law control test defines the employer-employee relationship based on an assessment of "whether the employer has the right to control the actions of the employee within the scope of employment."[60]

If your boss didn't have this broad authority, you'd have to agree to a new contract every time your boss wanted you to undertake a new task. Economists refer to such a situation as the problem of "incomplete" contracts: a contract may be incomplete because it has been poorly written, but it may also be incomplete because of uncertainty—because it is impossible to know all the things I might need from my counterparty (the person with whom I'm agreeing on the contract) over the course of our relationship.

For Coase, firms solved this problem of incomplete contracts by binding people together over long periods of time in hierarchical relationships that allowed some people (bosses) to control the behavior of others (workers).[61] Within the firm, the authority of the boss substitutes for the contractual relationships that exist within the market. In other words, resources within the firm are allocated based on a form of economic planning: the bosses decide where and how the firm's limited resources will be used. They do so based on cues they receive from the market, but nonetheless, the basis of resource allocation within the firm is *authority* rather than prices.[62]

The rise of managerialism and "management science" were radical new tools that have allowed bosses to exercise this authority in ever more effective ways.[63] Managers have sought out new and ever more totalizing ways to control work processes (and, as we will see in chapter 6, the neoliberal state also adopted this managerial ethos in policymaking).[64] Today's corporate bosses hold "despotic power" over their workers.[65] The modern corporation is a legal form designed to formalize the power of the boss over the worker, while protecting the former from risk.[66]

The modern corporation is, in other words, a *political* entity. In fact, it is a form of "private government."[67] But it is a government based on the principle of centralized control and hierarchy rather than democracy.[68] This is not merely a Marxist interpretation. Coase's own theory of the firm seems to suggest that, rather than rule by the market, capitalism is a system based on rule by bosses.[69]

Marx was highlighting the unequal relationships that exist within the corporation as part of a critique of capitalism, while Coase was seeking to defend and explain it. The economics profession accepted Coase's theory, but to avoid sounding like Marxists, they needed to show that, even though bosses seemed to have a lot of power over their workers, this power is limited by the operation of the market. They needed to show that bosses couldn't abuse the power they had over workers because they were constrained by the market mechanism.

This is where Joseph Schumpeter came in. Born in 1883, Schumpeter was an Austrian economist who is now remembered as one of the giants of classical political economy. He was also an ardent anti-communist and anti-Keynesian, who believed that social democracy had encouraged a lazy corporatism that would ultimately undermine the entrepreneurial spirit that allows capitalism to survive. But unlike most critics of Marxism, Schumpeter had read Marx carefully. As such, he had a far more acute understanding of the "laws of motion" of the capitalist system than many of his contemporaries.

Like Marx and Coase, Schumpeter believed that bosses exercised authority over workers and profited from their labor—but he did not see this as inherently unfair. He thought the bosses—or, in Schumpeter's more romantic language "entrepreneurs"—deserved to be in charge because they were smarter and more dynamic than workers.[70] The reward for this superiority is profit, and not just the normal profits of the kind found in mainstream economics.

Schumpeter believed that the incentive for entrepreneurialism under capitalism was market power—or temporary monopoly power. A firm that developed a powerful production technique should be able to charge higher prices than its competitors for a while to make sure the entrepreneur was fairly compensated for the investment undertaken in developing the innovation. If that meant that the most innovative firms sometimes became monopolies, so be it. Entrepreneurs needed to be rewarded for their brilliance, or they wouldn't innovate and capitalism would stagnate. In place of Adam Smith's invisible hand regulating supply and demand through the price mechanism, we find the grasping fist of the entrepreneur, pulling everyone else forward by their bootstraps.

But Schumpeter did believe that the rewards of monopoly power would—or, more accurately, should—always be temporary. If a firm did not continue to innovate once it had reached a market-dominating position, then it would eventually be outcompeted by other firms. Crisis was particularly important in Schumpeter's model, as economic crises were times when these older, more inefficient firms would collapse to pave the way for newer, more competitive ones.

"Creative destruction," Schumpeter argued, limits the power of the boss over the worker—and indeed, the power of the corporation over society. In his model, if a corporation didn't play the free-market game in exactly the right way, over the long run it would die. If it charged too much for its products, it would lose market share to its competitors. If it didn't pay its workers enough, or treated them poorly, it would suffer from a loss of labor power. If it didn't innovate to beat its competitors, it would be outcompeted. Bosses might be able to exercise authority over workers, but the free market exercised authority over them. This kind of planning—planning dictated entirely by the market—isn't really planning at all.

There's one issue with the Schumpetarian framework: creative destruction doesn't really happen very much anymore—at least not for the largest and most powerful firms. In actually existing capitalist societies, powerful firms do not die nearly as often as we might expect—even when, as with Boeing or Ford, they make big mistakes. Just think about all the brands that dominate our shelves—many of them have existed in one form or another for decades, some for a century or more. And this observation is borne out by the evidence: the average age of a public company in the US was eighteen years in 2019, up from twelve years in 1996.[71]

The problem with the idea of temporary monopoly is that even allegedly temporary monopolists have the power to "lock in" their past successes. When a firm makes excess profits, it can use these profits to erect barriers to entry for other companies, or simply buy up its competitors, making it better able to dominate the markets in which it operates.[72] Large incumbents do not, as Schumpeter argued, have to continue to innovate to remain on top—in fact, the evidence shows that competition is far more likely to spur innovation than monopoly power.[73] Monopolistic firms are much more likely to buy up or eliminate their rivals, "[embed] their own technology in the industry" and "[control] the dissemination of ideas" than they are to genuinely innovate.[74]

In Schumpeter's model, crises are supposed to clear out uncompetitive monopolists, but monopolists are actually better able to survive crises than smaller firms. They generally have higher margins, so they can withstand long periods of low profits. They have closer relationships with financial institutions, so they can often borrow money more cheaply and easily during tough times. They're also able to use their market power to exploit suppliers and workers to push down their costs. And as we have seen in the cases of Boeing, Ford, and Amazon, even if they do find themselves vulnerable during a crisis, powerful firms are able to exploit their close relationships with states to secure bailouts.

For all these reasons, market power doesn't tend to dissipate as capitalism develops—it tends to strengthen. In fact, there is now strong evidence that market power is increasing across the board in the rich world. In *The Great Reversal*, economist Thomas Philippon shows how the US economy has become increasingly monopolistic in recent years, with negative effects for consumers.[75] Powerful corporations have been able to lock in their success—whether because of economies of scale, by crushing or buying their competitors, or by lobbying politicians to restrict competition. As a result, consumers are faced with higher prices, which means higher corporate profits. But these profits aren't being channeled into new productive investment; they're being distributed to shareholders and executives, driving down productivity and driving up inequality.

Philippon's argument is that prices are higher in the US than Europe thanks to the more stringent competition law enforced in the latter. It is true that the EU often takes a more active approach to the enforcement of competition law than does the US, but this isn't saying much. Between 1990 and 2019, the European Commission rendered over 7,000 merger decisions and blocked only 30.[76] As a result, many European markets are also characterized by a high degree of monopoly power.[77]

Jan Eeckhout shows that markups have increased across both the US and Europe, and these higher prices are a significant factor in driving higher profits.[78] This, in turn, has affected wages by reducing aggregate demand: monopolistic firms are charging higher prices, meaning they are selling less, employing fewer workers, and investing less in new technologies. These practices have had a long-term impact on growth and productivity across Europe and the US.

In fact, levels of concentration are likely higher than either Philippon or Eeckhout suggest. Both attempt to measure monopoly power using variations of the neoclassical definition of monopoly, which centers on whether firms are charging higher prices than what would be expected in a competitive market. But, as Michelle Meagher argues in her excellent book *Competition Is Killing Us*, this definition is too technocratic to act as a real brake on corporate power—it fails to consider questions of power, democracy, and social justice, and instead focuses on "narrow [assessments] of economic welfare."[79] As we have seen with the example of Amazon, large firms often do not use their market power simply to raise prices, instead focusing on how to deepen and expand their power over every area of society.

The evidence suggests that Schumpeter's temporary monopolies are becoming increasingly permanent. So, not only are relationships within the firm based on authority rather than market exchange, but the authority of the boss is also relatively unconstrained by the discipline of the market. Bosses are increasingly able to act as powerful planners within their domain. And in doing so they are able to exercise significant power over society as a whole.

In their book *The People's Republic of Walmart*, Leigh Phillips and Michal Rozworski show the many complex ways in which the US retail giant Walmart plans its operations.[80] Within the corporation, "there is no internal market," because "everything is planned."[81] The pair argue that Walmart provides a fascinating example of how new technologies are facilitating centralized planning on a large scale within nominally free-market societies. But this power is monopolized by capitalists and deployed for the sole purpose of maximizing their own wealth and power.

Capitalist economies are supposed to be efficient; any other system, the argument goes, would waste precious scarce resources. So even if capitalist economies produce some "negative externalities"—like inequality, climate change, and corruption—these economies are so much more efficient that it is more rational to correct these problems after they emerge than it would be to prevent them from emerging in the first place.

But when an economy is dominated by large corporations over which the discipline of the market has little sway, efficiency goes out the window. If a firm is able to operate in the absence of competition, or in a limited form of it, then it can break many of the fundamental rules of free-market economics. It can charge higher prices, it can pay its workers less than in an imagined free-market scenario, and it can drive down costs throughout the supply chain. Once it has reached a certain size, other businesses will find it harder to enter the market, making it easier for this one big company to grow even larger over time.

When a few colossal firms begin to dominate the whole economy, suddenly the average consumer is paying more than they should for their groceries, even as the average worker is being paid less than they should be for the work they do. Without real competition, consumers can't shift their shopping habits and workers can't find another job, let alone try to bargain for higher wages. Resources are being wasted: too much money is being sucked up to the top of the economy, while those doing all the work find themselves on the sharp end of this shift.

And these observations are borne out by reams of economic evidence. As Jonathan Tepper and Denise Hearn systematically document, successive economic studies have shown that monopoly power leads to a "toxic cocktail of higher prices, less economic dynamism, fewer startups, lower productivity, lower wages, greater economic inequality and damage to smaller communities." David Dayen quotes one of his interviewees, talking about the grossly concentrated agricultural "industry" in the US, as saying: "The system now is no better than the collective communist farms of the USSR."

Even were it not for the gross inefficiencies created by massive capitalist firms, their dominance over so many areas of our lives undermines the very freedom that neoliberals allegedly sought to protect. Workers are subject to the "despotic" control of the boss at work.[82] Consumers have the false choice of opting for different brands of the same products, all owned by one or two corporations.[83] And citizens are forced to watch as these same corporations co-opt governments that are supposed to be accountable to the people.[84] As we have seen, Hayek himself wrote that he would "prefer to have to put up with some such inefficiency than have organized monopoly control my ways of life."

....

We've now seen how the operation of actually existing capitalist enterprises is a little more complicated than the picture shown in an economics textbook. Corporations have power—over their workers, over markets, and over society in general—and those leading these organizations use this power in the relentless pursuit of personal gain.

These observations would come as no surprise to Marxist theorists, who saw decades ago that capitalism would lead to a concentration of wealth and power in a few hands. In the next section, I'll outline some theories that seek to explain why we've seen such an increase in corporate power over the history of capitalism—and the costs this centralization has imposed on everyone else.

Chemical Imbalances

In 2016, the pharmaceutical company Bayer agreed to buy the agrochemical company Monsanto in a megamerger that was approved by both European and American competition authorities. A year later, DuPont, another big player in agrochemicals, bought its rival Dow Chemical. A few months after that, the Chinese state-owned company ChemChina purchased the agrochemical company Syngenta.

Within a few years of the Bayer merger, three companies controlled nearly 70 percent of the world's agrochemical industry and 60 percent of the world's commercial seeds, protected by strict intellectual property rules.[85] Agrochemicals and seed production may sound like obscure industries to your average consumer, but these three corporate behemoths produce materials and control processes that form the foundations of the global food system. In other words, they control the systems that provide for the maintenance of human life on earth: most of the readers of this book will have ingested a product touched by one of these three companies in the last twenty-four hours.

And yet, readers may well recognize the names of some of the companies in the previous paragraphs as firms responsible for ending human life, rather than sustaining it. Union Carbide India Limited, purchased by Dow Chemical in 2001, was responsible for the infamous Bhopal gas tragedy in India, which has been described as one of the world's worst industrial disasters.[86] Monsanto is well known for producing Roundup, which contains glyphosate, a chemical that the World Health Organization warned is linked to cancer.[87] After acquiring the company, Bayer was forced to pay out at least $10 billion to settle claims brought against

Monsanto by tens of thousands of people who said the product had made them sick.[88]

In 2007, a group of gunmen shot at protestors occupying a site in Brazil where Syngenta was illegally planting GMO crops, killing at least two people.[89] Syngenta was later convicted of murder and ordered to pay compensation.[90] DuPont was the subject of *Dark Waters*, a film produced by and starring Mark Ruffalo, which tells the story of the toxic chemicals used in the production of Teflon. DuPont's scientists knew about the harmful effects of Teflon as early as the 1960s, but the company continued to dump the toxic waste left over from the production process into local waterways.[91] Today, we know that the chemical used to manufacture Teflon—C8—is linked to six human diseases. Ninety-nine percent of Americans have C8 in their bloodstreams.

Bayer, DuPont, and ChemChina now form a global triopoly in the market for agrochemicals and seeds, and have been accused of practices that harm consumers, the environment, and small-scale farmers. At the most benign level, rates of corporate concentration in these industries have been associated with a slowdown in innovation, the continuation of which is critical to ensure the growing global population is able to feed itself in the context of climate breakdown.[92]

More worryingly, they continue to make billions from selling products that are actively harmful to both humans and the environment. Pesticides sold by these companies and their competitors have been linked to a wide range of health problems as well as the serious environmental problem of pollinator decline.[93] The ability of subsistence farmers to access generic seeds has also been compromised by the mergers: companies like Monsanto have frequently threatened to sue farmers for using seeds that it claims as its intellectual property.[94]

And it's not just agrochemicals. Market concentration in industries like pharmaceuticals, food, and technology has increased since the 1980s, with far-reaching implications for consumers, workers, and the planet. Rising monopoly power has been linked to rising national and international inequality, a global race to the bottom on tax, declining innovation, falling wages, regulatory capture, and even the erosion of democracy.[95] Concern about these problems is not confined to progressives: ardent defenders of capitalism can frequently be found lamenting the problems created by corporate concentration.[96] But the solutions they offer—from more stringent antitrust law to better corporate governance—fail to cut to the heart of the issue. Monopolization is as central to capitalism as profit maximization: you can't have one without the other.

Marx's understanding of the capitalist firm allowed him to show that what he called centralization—the concentration of production into a smaller number of larger corporations—was an inherent part of the development of capitalism.[97] As production becomes more technologically advanced, the amount a business needs to invest to commence operations increases.[98] Building a factory from scratch requires more investment today than it did a hundred years ago because you need more technology to compete with incumbents. Smaller entrepreneurs are unable to compete with existing giants, so they enter industries with fewer large incumbents, leaving large firms in established sectors with less competition.

As we've seen, economists tend to assume that monopoly power is expressed in terms of higher prices—powerful firms that can dominate an entire industry will use their power to maximize their profits by hiking prices. And while there is evidence of high markups across a range of industries today, there's no evidence of a constant tendency toward higher prices over the course of the history of capitalism—if anything, the opposite is true.

Monopoly power does not, however, involve the total elimination of competition. As Marx observed in his discussions of concentration and centralization, competition in capitalist societies never disappears altogether.[99] Instead, a few large corporations concentrate ever more power among themselves, often colluding to maintain market prices while competing to push down their costs, including wages and taxes. These corporations push competitive pressures to "the people under [their] power."[100] They force workers, suppliers—and even small states—to compete simply in order to survive in a world populated by seemingly indestructible corporate behemoths.

For this reason, market power doesn't always lead to higher prices. Firms prefer not to get stuck in "mutually destructive price warfare" with their competitors.[101] Rather than trying to exercise power over consumers by price gouging, they try to use their power over workers—a power that workers have generally struggled to resist—to push down wages.[102]

Firms can reduce their wage bill by reducing take-home pay, or they can attempt to curtail other benefits and entitlements such as pension contributions, sick pay, and parental leave. This latter form of wage suppression is particularly common in the so-called gig economy, where many big-tech companies have pioneered a model of bogus self-employment in which workers are denied benefits and are often also required to pay for the tools needed to undertake their jobs. This kind of power—which economists refer to as "monopsony power"—has, by one estimate, reduced labor's share of national income in the US by 22 percent.[103]

Another way to cut costs is for firms to use their market power to gouge their suppliers. Powerful retail companies in the Global North, for example, use their market power to suppress the rates paid to garment manufacturers in the Global South—and this pressure is then felt by workers in the form of wage suppression, as garment producers seek to maximize their own squeezed profits.[104] These processes in turn put pressure on the garment manufacturers to consolidate, spreading monopoly power throughout the global economy at the expense of workers (though this can also create opportunities for worker organizing, as we'll see in chapter 9).[105]

Big businesses can also exploit their close relationships with states to reduce their tax burden. Corporations can lobby both to change headline rates of taxation and to create loopholes that benefit them, as well as benefiting from forms of tax arbitrage that allow them to report profits in low-tax jurisdictions—an activity that is permitted, and often actively facilitated, by many powerful states.[106] As we'll see in chapter 5, large corporations also work closely with financial institutions, both to facilitate these forms of tax avoidance, and to reduce their overall financing costs. And they can threaten states that do not legislate according to their interests with capital flight, as we'll see in chapter 7.

The pioneering political economists Paul Baran and Paul Sweezy are perhaps the best-known Marxist theorists of corporate power. Baran was born in 1909 in Russia, to Jewish Menshevik parents who left the country for Germany in 1917, where he stayed until the Nazis came to power.[107] In 1939, he was forced to flee to the US, where he continued his studies at Harvard while working several high-level government jobs. It was at Harvard that he met Paul Sweezy, who was to become his lifelong friend and collaborator.

Sweezy was born the year after Baran to a well-off family in New York and, unlike Baran, didn't become acquainted with Marxist ideas until his early twenties.[108, 109] The easygoing upper-class Sweezy took to the halls of Harvard far quicker than the grumpy, intellectual Baran, penning dozens of articles in which he sought to apply Marxist ideas to mainstream economic problems—work that is still used in mainstream economic theory today. He even took up a post at Harvard once occupied by one Joseph Schumpeter.

But despite—or perhaps because of—their different upbringings and temperaments, the two had a fruitful intellectual collaboration during their lifetimes. They worked to adapt Marx's theory of capital, which had been written in the age of "the railroad and the steamship," to the age of computers and airplanes.[110] Modern capitalism was, the pair wrote, a highly concentrated economic system dominated by powerful monopolies and oligopolies.

Mainstream economists might not be able to detect the existence of a monopoly because many market-dominating firms do not seek to restrict output and raise prices. Drawing on Marx's work on the subject, Baran and Sweezy realized that, more often than not, modern monopolies (or, really, oligopolies) collude to keep prices stable. This tacit collusion has been likened to the division of "turf" by rival mobsters, and it is pervasive within modern capitalist societies.[111] While the US Department of Justice convicted 128 companies of criminal price-fixing between 1996 and 2010, estimates suggest that this accounts for only 20 percent of collusion cases. As Marx observed, "capitalists are like hostile brothers"—they compete, while cooperating over the basic structures required to keep the system afloat.[112]

As we have seen, rather than competing on price, oligopolies will instead compete by keeping costs low, resulting in low wages, tax avoidance, and environmental destruction of the kind outlined in the examples in this chapter.[113] They also push competition into the realms of advertising, relationship building, branding, and other tools of what Baran and Sweezy call the "sales effort."[114] Indeed, some argue that the interaction between this fierce competition over sales and technological innovation has led us into a new era of capitalism—surveillance capitalism or technofeudalism—in which a firm's competitive edge depends upon its ability to predict its customers' needs by exploiting the data they produce when interacting with big-tech companies like Google and Facebook.[115]

Today, competition has given way to monopoly and oligopoly across the economy. In the US, 75 percent of industries have seen a fall in the number of competing firms, and a corresponding rise in market concentration, over the course of the 1990s and 2000s.[116] In Europe, 80 percent of industries experienced a similar increase over the same period.[117] And these firms are richer than ever before.[118] Whereas in 1995, the top one hundred companies accounted for 53 percent of all income among public firms, by 2014 this figure had reached 84 percent.[119] In fact, "the vast majority of the value of publicly listed companies comes from their market power."[120] As Warren Buffett has frequently opined, smart investors know that a firm with market power is going to be one that generates the strongest returns over the long run.[121]

What, you might ask, has happened to Schumpeter's powerful forces of creative destruction? Barriers to entry—whether regulatory barriers, the cost of investment, or anticompetitive behavior by the corporations themselves—allow monopolistic firms to retain their power by preventing new firms from entering the industry. In big tech, large incumbents police the so-called kill zone in their marketplaces by "hoovering up or squashing any potential competitors."[122] Google, Amazon, and Microsoft have, between them, "collectively bought over 436 companies and startups in the past 10 years and regulators have not challenged any of them."[123]

Even in sectors where competition is fiercer, big corporations are able to use their relationships with other economic and political actors to shore up their market power. First, large firms can put pressure on other businesses—particularly their suppliers—to maximize their own profits at the expense of smaller capitalists. This pressure can come through legitimate avenues—like buying in bulk—but it can also be exercised more nefariously. Small businesses often complain that when they are supplying a big company that company will take longer to pay them than a smaller customer—big businesses know that they can afford to take advantage of their suppliers because they dominate their industries.

Second, as we'll see in chapter 6, companies can put pressure on politicians to protect themselves from competition. As we saw in the introduction, the relationship between the corporation and the capitalist state has been far closer throughout history than liberal theory suggests. The state and the "free market" are not separate self-regulating spheres, and market power is not separate from political power. The state and the corporation are intimately connected, and powerful companies are uniquely able to influence political outcomes. As we saw with Amazon, Ford, and Boeing, states frequently step in to shield their most powerful businesses from domestic or international competition. And, as we'll see in chapter 7, powerful corporations can threaten those states that fail to bend to their will with capital flight.

Third, as I'll show in the next chapter, big companies often have close relationships with investors and financial institutions, which makes it easier for them to access the financing they need to thrive and grow. When a financial institution is deciding whether to give a loan to a small business with low margins, or a large, powerful, multinational corporation, it is generally going to consider the latter a safer bet. Either that means the small business is paying higher interest rates to access financing, or it means the small business doesn't get the loan at all. And all that cheap cash makes it easier for bigger businesses to beat the competition.

"All this means," Baran and Sweezy argue, "is that Schumpeter's perennial gale of creative destruction has subsided into an occasional mild breeze."[124] Without the constant competitive pressure that constrains their smaller peers, large corporations have a great deal more leeway to make active decisions about the future of their firm. And they also have the political and financial relationships necessary to enact their plans. The largest firms are able to work with other actors to determine—within limits—what happens in the rest of the economy. And this has created a lot of problems for modern capitalism.

For example, monopolistic firms tend to limit investment.[125] This results in lower growth and, crucially, lower levels of innovation over the long run. Unlike in Schumpeter's vision of temporary monopoly, longer-lasting monopolies don't need to innovate to retain their market power; rather, they can buy up smaller firms, or boost their share prices through accounting tricks. Today's tech giants are sitting on vast amounts of cash that could be invested in developing new technologies, but that instead either lies idle or is invested in financial markets.[126] Low levels of investment mean lower productivity over the long run, and some argue that the low rates of productivity seen in many advanced economies today can be ascribed to corporate practices in sectors like tech, where powerful monopolies are often more concerned with increasing their market share than undertaking any genuine innovation.[127]

Monopoly power is also associated with higher levels of inequality. This is driven by a number of factors—for example, the total amount of income accruing to workers tends to fall in sectors where market concentration is high because large, powerful firms are able to produce output with fewer workers. Monopolists (the dominant sellers) are also often monopsonists (the dominant buyers) in labor markets, and therefore have the power to reduce wages for the average worker and redistribute the returns to senior executives and shareholders.[128]

As Baran and Sweezy show, "free-market capitalism" is a misnomer. As capitalist societies develop, the free market becomes less significant in determining how resources are produced and allocated, while concentrated corporate power becomes far more significant. Marxist economist Michel Kaleki once wrote that "monopoly appears to be deeply rooted in the nature of the capitalist system: free competition . . . may be useful in the first stage of certain investigations, but as a description of the normal stage of capitalist economy it is merely a myth."[129] Corporations exercise power over the production and allocation of resources in a capitalist economy—and they do so to promote their own interests, rather than the general interest.

Rather than living in a world of perfect competition as described in an economics textbook, we live under the awesome power of what J. K. Galbraith called "the industrial system."[130] Giant firms within this system are not merely concerned with maximizing profits; instead, they are governed through a "technostructure," which prioritizes maintaining the organization's *power* just as much as increasing its profits. And they do so with the active support of the state, the collusion of other firms, and financing from huge financial institutions.

Galbraith saw these trends as paving the way toward a new form of socialized capitalism, in which production was consciously organized rather than shaped by the caprices of the market mechanism.

Galbraith observed that society may become more democratic and less chaotic as a result of the heightened cooperation both among capitalists themselves, and between capital and the state.

But, as we have seen, free-market capitalism has never been as unplanned as its advocates have suggested. Firms have always colluded with one another, and the state has always stepped in to support the interests of capital. This cooperation may have become more entrenched and formalized over time, but what Marx called the tendency toward centralization has always been a feature of capitalist societies.[131]

The tendency toward centralization never completely overcomes the role of competition—there will never emerge a total industrial state, or even world government, within a capitalist economy. Instead, competition and cooperation exist in constant tension. The only constant is that capital always comes out on top. And, contrary to Galbraith's somewhat benign vision of capitalist planning, Marx saw that this would lead to an increase in "the mass of misery, oppression, slavery, degradation, exploitation" as capitalist societies develop.

Some might respond to this gloomy picture by pointing out that big businesses also create a lot of good, steady jobs that have supported the emergence of a broad and deep middle class. The transition from manual labor to service work in the rich world—a transition that many economists claim any country can undertake if it introduces the right policies—has led to an increase in living standards. Not only do these jobs generally come with higher salaries, they're also safer and allow for more autonomy and freedom than the blue-collar jobs of the past.

There are a few issues with this argument. First, as we'll see in chapter 7, the expansion in service work in the rich world has been dependent upon an increase in horrendously exploitative, poorly paid, and dangerous manual labor in the poor world. But it's also worth pointing out that even in the rich world there's a sizable gap between the wages and job quality of those employed to manage other people's labor and those employed to do as they're told.

Over the course of the pandemic, demand for call center workers rose, but some were forced to work from home, potentially compromising bosses' ability to surveil their workers. Teleperformance, one of the largest call center operators in the world, responded by introducing rigid new home surveillance technologies that would allow bosses to "check whether [workers] are eating, looking at their phones or leaving their desks while working from home."[132]

In Colombia, Teleperformance workers raised concerns about conditions in the call centers during the pandemic, as they were not given adequate personal protective equipment and many were forced to share headsets.[133] The company responded by allowing workers to work from home if they accepted the installation of Teleperformance cameras on their laptops to monitor their activities *all day long.*

The US news network NBC reported that 95 percent of Teleperformance's thirty-nine thousand employees in Colombia received an alteration to their contracts requiring them to consent to at-home surveillance that would allow "monitoring by AI-powered cameras in workers' homes, voice analytics and storage of data collected from the worker's family members, including minors."[134] The addendum even required workers to consent to taking lie detector tests if requested. Workers were reportedly told they would lose their jobs if they did not sign the new contracts.

Office-based jobs like those provided by Teleperformance are supposed to be examples of the easy, low-stress labor characteristic of the modern service-based economy. Harry Braverman, a Marxist thinker inspired by Baran and Sweezy, thought otherwise. Braverman was born, like Baran, to working-class Jewish parents and was raised, like Sweezy, in New York. He studied at Brooklyn College for one year before being forced to drop out for financial reasons, and it was during that year that he became acquainted with Marxism.[135]

Unlike either Baran or Sweezy, Braverman had direct experience of blue-collar work under monopoly capitalism. He spent four years working as a coppersmith apprentice at the Brooklyn Navy Yard, before joining the army and then working as a steelworker in Ohio. He was an active member of various socialist groups during this time and was eventually fired from one of his jobs "at the instigation of the FBI."[136]

Over the course of the 1950s, Braverman began working on what would eventually become *Labor and Monopoly Capital*, his seminal study of work under monopoly capitalism. He argued that Taylorism—a theory of scientific management that laid out the most effective ways to transform the worker into an "appendage of the machine"—was alive and well in modern American capitalism, and that the workforce was, if anything, more alienated than ever.

Braverman observed that with the growth of megacorporations, workers had become tiny cogs in a giant machine.[137] The labor process has become so specialized that the worker no longer has any control over their own labor. Whereas previously a worker might have had some autonomy in deciding how to conduct a task, in a giant multinational corporation bosses decide how workers work for them.

But the capitalist doesn't supervise the labor process himself—he employs a manager to do it for him. Managers may be employees, but they are privileged employees who are paid more than the workers they supervise precisely because they are charged with wielding the managerial power of the capitalist.[138] Larger firms need more managers because the people who own these firms can't be expected to supervise their workers themselves. This is one of the causes of the expansion of the "professional managerial class" in recent years—not the presence of a greater number of productive white-collar jobs, but the creation of a sizable managerial class to control an alienated class of workers.

The divide between those who own and govern the production process on the one hand, and the exploited workers who actually produce things on the other, has even led to changes in the development of technology.[139] We can see this today in the increasingly draconian tools used to control the worker, termed the "New Taylorism"—whether Amazon's use of wristbands to monitor their warehouse staff, or the monitoring of employees' computer usage in office workplaces.

Huge resources have been directed toward designing and implementing these technologies aimed at controlling worker behavior, which has shaped the direction of technological development. Had those resources been used in everyone's interests, rather than in service of capital, the nature of the technological knowledge we possess today would be different. Imagine what the world might look like if all the resources that go into surveilling workers had been devoted to figuring out solutions to climate breakdown.

We live in a world in which individuals are being crushed under the immense weight of corporate power and planning. Neoliberals like Hayek claimed to want to protect human freedom from the overbearing power of the state, yet today, individual freedom is drastically restricted by a toxic fusion of state and corporate power. Those forced to sell their labor power for a living under capitalism are profoundly unfree. The corporations for which they work, on the other hand, have more freedom than ever. In fact, as we'll see next, many of them benefit from some of the hallmarks of sovereignty usually considered the prerogative of states.

Government 4 Sale

G4S is the largest security company in the world, with over eight hundred thousand employees in eighty-five countries.[140] It is a corporation that does a lot of things we would ordinarily think of as the preserve of states, including providing services such as prison management, immigration detention, and health and education services. But G4S isn't a democracy. It's a corporation, run based on the authority of unelected bosses and shareholders. This combination of power without accountability has proved controversial, and extremely profitable, for the company, which has been mired in scandal since its inception.

One notable scandal came with the London 2012 Olympics. G4S was paid $355 million to provide thousands of private security guards for the event, but a month before the opening ceremony the company told the UK government that it was more than thirty-five hundred guards short of what was required.[141] And many more failed to turn up because of a critical lack of communication from the company. The government announced it would be imposing penalties on the firm for breaching its contract. In the end, the army had to be called in to police the games.

Mismanaging such a high-profile event was a PR disaster for the company. But this was not the first, or the last, or worst, scandal to hit G4S in recent years. In 2010, the company was implicated in the killing of Jimmy Mubenga, an Angolan refugee and father of five. Mubenga was on a plane being forcibly returned to Angola in an outsourced deportation process managed by G4S in 2006 when three security guards restrained him, holding his head down while cuffing his hands behind his back. This is a technique known in the security world as "carpet karaoke" due to the well-known risks of asphyxiation.[142] In a chilling precursor to the murder of George Floyd in the US several years later, fellow passengers heard Mubenga cry out, "I can't breathe!" and "They're killing me!"[143]

Mubenga eventually lost consciousness and was pronounced dead at the scene by paramedics.[144]

The guards were arrested, before being released on bail. G4S was concerned that it could face charges of corporate manslaughter. But the Crown Prosecution Service (CPS) refused to bring charges against the company or its employees, citing "insufficient evidence."[145] The CPS later revised its decision, after a public inquest found that the guards were aware that their actions could have caused serious harm and acted in an unlawful manner. The guards were found not guilty.[146]

In the wake of the verdict, it was revealed that one of the guards had written a text message in which he used viscerally hateful language to describe the migrants the company was deporting: "Fuck off and go home you free-loading, benefit-grabbing, kid-producing, violent, non-English-speaking, cock suckers and take those hairy-faced, sandal-wearing, bomb-making, goat-fucking, smelly rag head bastards with you."[147]

This racist text, along with others, was not shown to the jury during the trial as the judge decided that the messages were "not relevant" to the case.[148] Nor was the jury told about the findings of the public inquest, including concerns raised by the coroner that the G4S staff may have racially abused the people in their custody. Later investigations revealed that the guards were being paid through an incentive structure that meant they stood to lose £170 if the plane did not depart on time.[149]

When it comes to the abuse of migrants, G4S has a record. Hundreds of complaints have been lodged by people being held in G4S detention centers throughout the UK over the course of the last several years. In 2017, the BBC program *Panorama* revealed footage of guards bullying and racially abusing those in their custody, including footage of one person being choked by a staff member.[150] Many of the complaints came from one center, Brook House, from which the company had made nearly £15 million in profit over five years.[151]

Five years earlier, the chief inspector of prisons had released a report into services provided by G4S for the UK Border Agency. The report found that many officers were using unacceptable levels of force with people being held in deportation centers, including one incident in which a pregnant woman was tipped out of her wheelchair while a guard held down her feet.[152] A year after that, G4S was accused of using torture techniques—including electroshock therapy and forced injections—at its network of prisons in South Africa.[153] In 2014, the company was accused of using migrants in its care as prison labor, paying them far under the minimum wage.[154] In 2016, a G4S employee, Omar Mateen, murdered forty-nine people in a homophobic attack at the Pulse nightclub in Florida—the second-deadliest mass shooting in US history.[155]

Firms like G4S are able to wield such extraordinary power because of their close relationships with states, which charge them with exercising public authority on their behalf. As we have seen, a state is often defined as an entity with a monopoly on the legitimate exercise of force: but companies like G4S blur this line. This privatization of authority is clearest when it comes to outsourcing, but it is true of all corporations, which are granted legal privileges that allow them to exercise significant power within our society.[156] Yet this power is exercised with little or no democratic accountability. G4S has repeatedly escaped prosecution for gross examples of wrongdoing that, if undertaken by individuals rather than firms hired by the state, would have resulted in long prison sentences.

The reason corporations are able to exercise this kind of power is that they are, in many ways, sovereign entities.[157] They often have the kind of unaccountable power over people, territory, and security that would usually be the preserve of states. And this phenomenon is not new—the fusion between state and corporate power lies at the origins of capitalism itself.

At the turn of the seventeenth century, Queen Elizabeth I granted a group of merchants a royal charter to explore the area of the world then known as the East Indies. Over the next few centuries, the East India Company (EIC) became the most powerful corporate entity on the planet. Conservative statesman Edmund Burke referred to the EIC as the "state in the disguise of a merchant."[158] An Indian lawyer later observed that the English monarch had granted to the EIC many of the characteristics of sovereignty that would ordinarily be reserved for a state.[159] The company could "dispose of and alienate land, draw rents and assess taxes . . . appoint and dismiss governors and make laws."[160]

Adam Smith saw this situation as a "strange absurdity."[161] States and markets were supposed to be separate entities; the latter governed by the clean, natural laws of economics—which Smith famously conceptualized using the metaphor of the invisible hand—the former governed by the mucky, conflictual realm of politics. And the East India Company has been seen as something of an aberration of the capitalist mode of production ever since. Yet as recently as 2017 Erik Prince, founder of private military company Blackwater and close ally of US president Donald Trump, was calling on the US government to create an "American South Asia Company," based on the "East India Company model," to govern Afghanistan.[162]

Seeing corporations like the East India Company and G4S as sovereign jars with mainstream political and economic theory. Both ideologies see states and markets—politics and economics—as fundamentally different spheres of activity. The state is seen as a political institution with a monopoly on the legitimate use of force, whose legitimacy derives from the consent of the governed. The corporation, meanwhile, is seen as a merely economic institution, which exists to facilitate production and exchange.

In fact, corporations are *political* entities.[163] They are "fictions created by states" to facilitate certain kinds of activity.[164] The capitalist corporation was developed as a legal concept to formalize certain relations of production, minimizing bosses' exposure to risk, while maximizing their ability to exploit and control their workers.[165] As one Marxist corporate law theorist puts it, the corporation was constructed as a "structure of irresponsibility," designed to ensure "corporate impunity."[166] The corporation has become "capital personified," its singular drive to amass ever more wealth and power at the expense of people and planet.[167]

The political power of the corporation cannot neatly be separated from its economic power. Corporations do not exist simply to facilitate production—they exist to facilitate a certain kind of production, one premised upon the domination of one class by another. When this power is centralized in a few hands, corporations are able to exercise sovereignty in a similar way to states. Take the example of the East India Company. The very existence of the EIC shows that corporations are born out of state power; that corporations have always had features of political sovereignty; and that the capitalist state has used corporations to project its power over people and spaces throughout its history.

The most obvious objection to the idea that corporations can have sovereignty, like states, is that they don't have armies or police or legal systems. States are the only entities within a particular territory that can *force* other actors to behave in certain ways—that's what makes them states. Only in territories where a functioning state doesn't exist—in war zones or refugee camps or similar liminal spaces—could a corporation hope to "govern" in the same way as a state.

The first objection to this view is that there are many parts of the world—in Iraq, for example, which we will study in chapter 5—where private corporations are able to exercise force, sometimes legitimately and sometimes with a monopoly, often by exercising this power on behalf of a state. Private armies, staffed by mercenaries, are common even in functioning states all over the world—though they generally work in cooperation with those states. And, as we have seen, the outsourcing giants are tasked with meting out punishment, and even death, on behalf of states like the UK.

But state power can't just be reduced to force. Michel Foucault—whom we will meet later—argued in 1977 that the maintenance of life has become more important to a state's legitimacy than the ability to threaten death and punishment.[168] We saw this logic demonstrated quite powerfully during the pandemic, when rankings indicating mortality from COVID-19 provided a metric according to which the competence and legitimacy of different states could be measured.[169]

This power over life—what Foucault called biopolitics—is underpinned by law, or the "rules of the game" that everyone is expected to follow.[170] One thing that makes a sovereign sovereign is its capacity to determine where these rules of the game apply, and where they do not. States can designate particular places within which, and people over which, the rule of law does not apply—for example, prisons or refugee camps.[171]

Corporations are one kind of organization that the state grants limited power to set its own rules of the game.[172] Most of the time you don't do what your boss tells you to based on a reference to your employment contract; you do as you're told because you recognize your boss's power as somehow legitimate. Equally, your company has certain responsibilities to look after your well-being while you're at work—and where it fails to do so, as in the case of Amazon, its legitimacy can be called into question.

Because the corporate form is a legal construct, corporations have a significant stake in influencing the legal architecture that regulates their existence—and their capacity to do so is far greater than that of individuals, NGOs, or labor organizations. Corporations both directly lobby governments to adopt certain policies and use their power to shape wider public debate (e.g., through funding think-tank research or speaking in the media).

In 2022, lobbying at the federal level in the US reached a staggering $4.1 billion.[173] Several health care and pharmaceutical companies rank among the top ten spenders, and Amazon alone spent more than $20 million lobbying the US government, with Meta following closely behind. The National Association of Realtors is, however, the top lobbyist in the US, spending $84 million in 2022. It is worth noting that the government drive to expand mortgage access and boost the property industry was a big part of what caused the financial crisis of 2008.

Lobbying behavior is concentrated among large and powerful firms—and it makes them larger and more powerful. Bayer and Monsanto are two of the top-spending lobbyists in the US, the former spending $10.5 million on lobbying in 2017 alone, next to $6.5 million for the latter.[174] One study showed that every dollar spent on lobbying yielded $220 worth of tax cuts.[175] A consulting firm put this theory to the test, creating an investment portfolio composed of the biggest lobbyists, betting that these firms' ability to shape the rules of the game would boost their returns.[176] Over a decade, the portfolio beat the S&P 500 average by more than five percentage points every year.

In the US, a fascinating example of corporate lobbying interfering with potentially more efficient processes can be found in the tax system. In most other wealthy nations, income taxes are calculated by the state and deducted directly from an employee's paycheck. But in the US, a group of powerful private firms has consistently lobbied to prevent such a system from being introduced, pressuring lawmakers to maintain a system in which individuals are forced to calculate and submit their own taxes, using software like TurboTax. The two largest sellers of tax accounting software—Intuit and H&R Block—spent over a combined $5 million trying to defeat bills that would either introduce a simpler, centralized system for the calculation of individual taxes, or which would have allowed the IRS to provide free software that individuals could use to file their own tax returns.[177] And they won, despite the fact that this system is deeply inefficient and resented by millions.

Corporations aren't only working within the state to change the law, the state often allows them to *break* the law with impunity. As Gregg Barak observes in his book *Unchecked Corporate Power,* capitalist societies are marked by an immense amount of "state-routinized crime."[178] Essentially, states permit—and sometimes actively facilitate—systematic lawbreaking by large corporations. In the words of anti-monopoly campaigner Michelle Meagher, "There is very little that big companies are not able to do, and we have relinquished the tools that were once designed to enclose them."[179]

Barak argues that the very nature of the corporate form in capitalist societies has been designed to ensure that the people who own and run corporations can "personally profit from their legal and productive activities without having to be fully liable for their illegal and harmful activities."[180] In the US, the ruling that corporations are legally people allows them to benefit from all the rights a human being enjoys with few of the responsibilities—there is, for example, no such thing as "corporate manslaughter" in US law.[181] And even when they are found to have broken the law, large corporations are able to deploy armies of expensive lawyers to bend the legal system to their will.

The reason for this imbalance in the legal treatment of individual and corporate crime is that, as we will see in chapter 6, corporate and state power are not as separate as we are taught to believe. Instead, the outcomes that take place within the state—and within the legal system— tend to reflect struggles between social classes that are influenced by the balance of power between those classes.[182] In a capitalist society, in which capital dominates labor, the state will more often than not seek to "repress the . . . property crimes of the street and to normalize the multinational crimes of the suite."[183] Under neoliberalism, which has shifted the balance of power further in favor of capital, "the brand of state regulation known as corporate crime has basically disappeared."[184]

In fact, it is precisely because of the law's relationship with capital— mediated by the state—that the law cannot be used successfully to prosecute corporate criminality.[185] The rare exceptions to this rule stand as proof to the underlying principle that, while legal rules "may curb some corporate behavior some of the time," they cannot challenge the unaccountable power of the corporation itself.[186] The unprecedented level of corporate power and corporate impunity in most rich economies requires corporations to be "held accountable"—yet the very fact of that corporate power and impunity means that this accountability will never be fully realized. Indeed, one scholar refers to this absence of accountability for corporate wrongdoings as "planned impunity."[187]

The main takeaway here is that corporations are political—as well as economic—entities. Within the corporation, relationships are shaped by the social division of labor: the fact that some own the things we need to produce commodities, while others are forced to sell their labor power as an input to production merely in order to survive. The corporation came into existence to formalize this unequal and exploitative relationship between worker and boss, while insulating owners from risk. The corporation is capital personified.

As corporations have become bigger, they have gained more power over both the markets in which they operate and the workforces they control. Complex corporate hierarchies have institutionalized the power imbalance between workers and bosses, mediated by a large class of professional managers. Ultimately, these corporations have become sovereign actors within our society—capable of delivering punishment, governing life, and making and breaking law in much the same way as states.

The effects for everyone else have been disastrous. If Hayek really cared about individual freedom and autonomy, he would have considered the sprawling, sovereign capitalist enterprise just as great an enemy as the capitalist state. But corporations can't plan on their own—they rely on the support of other powerful actors, like the state and big financial institutions. We'll explore these relationships in the following chapters.

5

Buying Time: How Big Banks Plan

Readers may be familiar with the sci-fi series *Doctor Who*—one of the longest-running television series in the world. The show is based around the adventures of a mythological "Time Lord"—the eponymous Dr. Who—who is able to travel through time and space in a spaceship—the TARDIS—that, to common earthlings, looks like a blue telephone box. The Time Lords, most of whom were destroyed in a lengthy war, were a race of technologically advanced beings that used their power over space-time to act as guardians of time itself—preventing less advanced species from warping or damaging the fabric of the universe.

Capitalism has its own time lords—financial institutions that shape how different economic actors experience time. By allocating investment across time and space, finance shapes which entities last and which don't. Many good companies collapse when they are unable to access cash, while many unviable companies that have close relationships to financial institutions are able to survive long beyond what might have otherwise been expected.

In determining which companies are able to survive and which ones fail, which innovations are developed and which fall by the wayside, and which states are able to borrow and which ones default, financial institutions are some of the most powerful planners in the capitalist system. According to one author, modern banks are the private equivalent of Gosplan—the central planning agency of the USSR—in that they determine which companies will receive the "judgement of the market," as Schumpeter put it.[1]

Adam Neumann, the founder and former CEO of WeWork, is someone intimately familiar with the ability of financial institutions to act as masters of time in capitalist economies. Once hailed as one of Silicon

Valley's most successful and ambitious "disruptors," Neumann's career became mired in controversy after it emerged that he had been cooking his company's books ahead of an attempted IPO in 2019.

Born in Israel in 1979, Neumann headed off to New York in 2001 to study at the Zicklin School of Business at Baruch College. Shortly before dropping out, he met his future wife, Rebekah Paltrow—cousin of the actress Gwyneth Paltrow—and some of his earliest business pitches included an idea for collapsible high-heeled shoes for women and baby clothes with built-in kneepads.[2] He managed to find funding for the latter and launched Egg Baby in 2006, which still exists.[3] Soon after, he developed the idea for WeWork: a company that would rent out unused office space to fast-growing startups.

The company forged close links with rapidly scaling tech startups that used WeWork for flexible office space, which allowed its founder to market the company as something like a technology company itself. In the wake of a financial crisis that had witnessed the collapse of many financial and real estate giants alongside the dramatic rise of "big tech," this perception allowed WeWork to attract large amounts of cash, facilitating its expansion to multiple American and eventually European cities. By 2016, WeWork was worth $10 billion and featured on *Fortune*'s list of "unicorns"—private companies worth more than $1 billion.[4]

Enter Masayoshi Son, infamous founder of the Japanese financial institution SoftBank, known for investing with his gut and making big wins as well as some massive losses. Son was raised in a poor family of Zainichi Koreans—early Korean migrants to Japan—who eventually made enough money to send Son to school by selling illegal sake.[5] At age sixteen, Son moved to the US to finish high school, after which he studied at Berkeley in California.[6] While at Berkeley, he developed a fascination with computing technology and started several successful small tech businesses.[7]

Son invested the money he made from these early businesses during the tech bubble through his new company, SoftBank. After purchasing a stake in Yahoo! in 1995, he made his name, and his fortune, as an early investor in Alibaba—the Chinese tech giant. He placed a $20 million bet on Alibaba in 1999 in exchange for a 30 percent stake in the company, the market capitalization of which had grown to more than $800 billion by 2020. This was to be Son's most successful investment. Since then, he has become famous for making a string of bad bets and holds the dubious honor of being the man who has lost the most money in history after losing $70 billion during the dot-com crash.[8]

One of those bets was made in 2017 when, taken in by the image of WeWork as a fast-growing start-up, Son invested $4.4 billion in the company, then valued at more than $20 billion.[9] Son's investment came after a tour of the company's headquarters that lasted twelve minutes.[10] Once Neumann had been granted Son's confidence, his ambitions—and his ego—grew to gigantic proportions. He sought to translate his "We" vision into many more areas of social life, changing the name of the company to the We Company, opening a WeLive apartment building, and floating ideas like "WeBank," "WeSleep," and even "WeFly."[11]

By this point, Neumann had reportedly taken to wandering around the office barefoot as well as organizing "debauched" summer camp parties for his employees, encouraging them to drink tequila at work and even buying a G6 private jet to hotbox with his colleagues.[12] The *Wall Street Journal* wrote that some of Neumann's modest aims for life included becoming the world's first trillionaire and building a WeWork on Mars.[13]

But when Neumann and Son sought to take the company public, things started to unravel. In the summer of 2019, after another cash injection from Son, WeWork was valued at $47 billion.[14] If the company had gone public at that valuation it would have been the second-largest IPO of 2019, after Uber. But going public meant giving investors, journalists, and regulators a look into the inner workings of Neumann's empire, and what they found wasn't pretty. The paperwork WeWork filed ahead of the IPO showed that Neumann was, according to *Forbes*, "burning through cash" and had "some of the worst corporate governance practices" the journalist had ever seen.[15]

The company was taking massive losses, and Neumann was getting personally rich on the back of the chaos. First, he had bought several of the buildings WeWork was leasing, meaning the company was paying him a significant personal rental income.[16] Second, Neumann had taken several personal loans from the company at very low interest rates.[17] Third, and most ridiculously, Neumann had personally trademarked the word *we* and sold it to the company in exchange for $5.9 billion in stock options.[18] At the time of the IPO, Neumann had personal lines of credit open with several banks that were underwriting the floatation, and the *Wall Street Journal* reported he planned to sell $700 million of his company stock before going public.[19]

Investors took one look under the hood of WeWork and balked. The company's valuation dropped from $47 billion to under $15 billion almost overnight, and it was forced to pull its IPO.[20] After pressure from investors, which Son had attempted to dispel until the last possible moment, Neumann was forced to step down as CEO, but he still managed to walk away with $1.6 billion.[21]

SoftBank effectively agreed to bail the company out of its financial difficulties and provide Neumann with a hefty windfall by purchasing a chunk of his shares before their value plunged even further. Astonishingly, he was also paid millions in "consulting" fees. Later, after Son was forced to apologize for the debacle to his own investors, SoftBank reneged on the deal with Neumann and in 2021 agreed to a settlement that left WeWork's former CEO with close to $450 million.[22]

As readers may have noticed from walking around city centers, WeWork still exists. After investors forced management to dramatically cut costs, lay off at least 20 percent of the workforce, sell the G6, and completely transform its corporate governance, the company managed to survive.[23] The COVID-19 pandemic hit its business model as freelancers moved to working from home, but the company benefited from the post-pandemic transition away from permanent office space toward more flexible, and fun, workspaces. In 2021, WeWork finally went public—this time via a special purpose acquisitions company (SPAC)—at a $9 billion valuation.[24] In the time between WeWork went public and the time of this writing in August 2023, it had lost 98 percent of its value.

The most significant factor explaining WeWork's ability to avoid complete collapse was the bailout from SoftBank, which ended up losing about 90 percent of its initial investment after write-downs.[25] There was a viable business at the core of WeWork, but in almost any other scenario the staggering corruption and mismanagement that took place under Neumann would have forced the company into insolvency, allowing a better-run competitor to buy up its assets. Masayoshi Son bought WeWork *time*, and this is what allowed it to restructure itself into a viable (and much smaller) corporation. Though doubts still remain as to the company's ability to survive much longer, even after all this external support.

As the twentieth-century renegade economist Hyman Minsky noted, companies face a "survival constraint," which makes access to cash one of the most important factors in determining which ones last.[26] Powerful financial institutions are not simply responding to wider economic conditions; they play a role in shaping those conditions by buying time for those they support. Yet they do so without the slightest democratic oversight. In our economy, the power wielded by the financial sector is directed toward securing the greatest wealth and power for those at the top—even if it means turning a blind eye to, or indeed actively supporting, large-scale fraud.

So how does all this planning work? Answering this question requires taking a look under the hood of modern finance. Financial institutions allocate investment in capitalist societies—that means they help to decide which companies, states, and individuals can thrive. Banks are one type of financial institution that have the special privilege—granted to them by the state—of being able to create money out of thin air.[27] It is this power over the allocation of investment that gives financial institutions the capacity to plan.

But they do not do this alone. Financial institutions could not exist in their modern form were it not for the support provided to them by capitalist states. Somewhat counterintuitively, this support comes primarily in the form of regulation—the constraints placed on banks are what allow them to maintain the confidence of their investors and depositors. Of course, states also frequently step in to bail out financial institutions when they fail to abide by the spirit—and sometimes the letter—of this regulation in pursuit of profits.

The relationship between banks and corporations is also extremely important to modern capitalism. Financial institutions lend to and invest in businesses, determining the pace at which certain businesses grow, as well as which ones survive. At the core of these processes are relationships. Big businesses and big banks—and the individuals who run them—tend to have very close relationships given their interdependence. And sometimes, as with Masayoshi Son and Adam Neumann, these close relationships allow poorly run firms to survive far longer than they should.

The planning power of modern finance is not, in other words, used in the public interest. Instead, it is used by a close network of corporate and financial executives to generate profit for themselves and their shareholders. As we will see, as the financial sector has become larger and more deeply enmeshed with the capitalist state, much of this profit has been earned through reckless short-termism, fraud, or outright corruption. As one author puts it, "The planning of our economic architecture has been transferred from democratic institutions into the hands of bankers and executives, both working in concert, knowing that they personally benefit from consolidation."[28]

Dr. Debt

In the wake of the financial crisis of 2008, Queen Elizabeth II asked a room full of economists at the London School of Economics why none of them had seen it coming.[29] They bristled at the Queen's question. Some argued that there had been a lack of communication between different sections of the financial system, others said it was a problem of insufficient regulation, others speculated that 2008 had simply been a "black swan" event of the kind that always would have been impossible to predict.

Yet some economists did see the crisis coming. In 2006, Dr. Nouriel Roubini told a room full of economists at the International Monetary Fund that the world economy was staring down the barrel of a gun.[30] A huge amount of risk was building in the global financial system, much of it linked to subprime mortgages in the US. As soon as some home-owners started to default on their loans, it could bring down some of the largest banks in the world. Dr. Roubini was disparagingly referred to as "Dr. Doom" by his colleagues for his perspicacious comments.

Steve Keen, an economist who specializes in the theories of Hyman Minsky, also predicted in 2005 that the buildup of private debt in the global financial system was paving the way for a "Minsky moment," in which credit markets tighten and fire sales of assets lead to an insolvency crisis.[31] That same year, an insider—Raghuram Rajan—told an audience of economists at the annual central bankers meeting in Jackson Hole, Wyoming, that financial "innovations" like collateralized debt obligations and credit default swaps were generating the possibility of a "catastrophic meltdown."[32]

What did these economists know that their colleagues didn't? Keen puts it down to the failure of mainstream economists to consider the dynamics of debt.[33] In this section, we'll look at precisely why debt is so central to modern capitalism, and how orthodox models of the economy underplay—or even overlook entirely—the dynamics of lending and borrowing. One thing missing from mainstream models is the insight that, through lending, banks have the capacity to create money out of thin air, and this privilege gives banks immense power to plan what goes on in our economy.

Open any economics textbook and you'll be introduced to the idea of loanable funds—the stock of savings within an economy.[34] Private savings are supposed to represent a fixed stock of money that can be used for investment: the object of finance is to determine how this money should be invested most efficiently. The interest rate (the "price" of money) is said to be determined by the supply and demand for these savings.

In this banking model, savers deposit their money in banks, which lend that money to investors in exchange for interest, a portion of which will then be paid to the saver. But the bank can't lend out all its money—it has to keep some money "in the bank."[35] This system is termed *fractional reserve banking*, and it gives banks the capacity to create money. If I deposit $100 in the bank and the bank lends another consumer $90 on the basis of my deposit, the total amount of money in the economy has increased from $100 to $190.

The idea behind this model—the so-called loanable funds model—is that banks provide households with a safe place to store their savings, and then lend these savings out in such a way as to minimize risk. Rather than lending all your money to a friend who wants to start a new business, you might instead deposit your money in a bank, which will then vet loan applications based on risk. In other words, banks simply mediate the relationship between savers and borrowers.[36] There's just one problem: the assumptions on which this model is based are wrong.

As the title of Bank of England working paper 761 makes abundantly clear, "Banks are not intermediaries of loanable funds."[37] In most modern economies, banks are able to create money *ex nihilo* (out of nothing) before first gaining access to deposits. A bank could lend out £100 without having £100, or even £10, in deposits "in the bank." So, when a big bank decides to lend $100,000 to one of its clients, it is increasing the amount of money in the economy commensurately, without drawing on any pre-existing stock of savings.

When you think about it, this ability to create money gives banks significant power. Access to credit is one of the key factors that determines which businesses survive, which individuals succeed, and which states are able to grow. What's more, the total amount of money in the economy has macroeconomic implications for variables like growth and inflation, both of which the government seeks to influence. Yet the state allows the big banks to play the role of moneymakers with little oversight, handing over all this power to the private sector.

So what, if any, limits *are* placed on banks' ability to create money in this way? Banks have to abide by regulations set by states and central banks—for example, most banks have to maintain a certain ratio between their assets (i.e., the loans they make) and their liabilities (i.e., their deposits)—but they can raise the funding to meet those requirements after they have made their loan.[38]

The main factor determining how much money is created by the banks is the *demand* for lending.[39] Banks don't need to worry about getting access to deposits to facilitate their lending. Instead, their primary concern is making sure they can make as many profitable loans as possible. The thing that limits this lending—aside from regulation—is how much people want to borrow. And how much people want to borrow is influenced by the state of the economy. And the state of the economy is, in turn, influenced by banks' lending decisions!

It's not hard to see how the wild ups and downs found in the modern economy can be attributed to this circular dynamic. Banks lend, boosting economic growth, making businesses want to borrow more, and allowing banks to lend even more. So, what causes the boom to grind to a halt?

The most important thing to note is that the main factor influencing the way this cycle plays out isn't just objective economic variables like interest rates or economic growth—it's a feeling: confidence.

When entrepreneurs or managers are making decisions about investment, they're essentially making predictions about what the future is going to look like.[40] They know for certain the costs they face today, but they have no idea what their returns are going to look like tomorrow—there could be a recession around the corner, which would make the factory they built far less profitable than they anticipated. This problem of uncertainty is exactly why Schumpeter thought successful entrepreneurs were so brilliant, and so important to capitalism.

Economists often try to avoid dealing with uncertainty, because it's a very tricky beast. When an outcome is uncertain, you can't simply weigh all the different options, assign them a number, and solve an equation to tell you which one to choose. Making investment decisions isn't like rolling dice; it's more like deciding whether to get married.[41] Whether you go ahead with the decision will be determined by how you feel today, because you can't possibly know what's going to happen tomorrow.

Financial institutions are supposed to manage this uncertainty on our behalf. They allocate investment to some uncertain ventures over others without any perfect information about the future. Mainstream theory teaches us that as long as banks and investors are responding correctly to the information provided to them by businesses and financial markets, then this shouldn't be a problem: investment will end up where it is supposed to end up. As long as banks direct investment toward the most profitable companies, they're doing their job.

But this theory avoids uncomfortable questions about uncertainty. What if not one but multiple efficient outcomes are possible? And what if our expectations about the future end up shaping that future itself? What if the banks' decisions about which companies to lend to actually influence which become the most profitable?

WeWork is one example of the power of people's expectations. Had financial institutions like SoftBank not stepped in to prop up WeWork based on a prediction the company would grow, it would likely have failed much faster than it did. Yet those expectations allowed the company to survive much longer than anyone expected. In such a context, the challenge is not only that the most efficient outcome is unknowable, but that there is no one "right" solution to the problem of where credit and investment should be allocated.[42] The power to determine the allocation of credit is the power to determine the future.[43]

The neoliberals were intimately aware of this power, and they sought to use it as an effective way to control and discipline citizens. Through the regime of "privatized Keynesianism," individual consumer debt substituted for public spending and investment.[44] Not only did this private debt-creation help to conceal the underlying stagnation of many economies in the rich world, ultimately leading to the financial crisis; it was also a powerful disciplining tool that could be exercised against workers.[45]

As we will see in chapter 6, privatized Keynesianism was part of a swathe of neoliberal reforms that sought to create particular kinds of subjects—ones who saw themselves as individual investors and entrepreneurs competing for their share of the economic pie, and not as part of a working class working together to resist their exploitation. To achieve this aim, neoliberal governments destroyed the labor movement before setting their sights on creating a class of "mini-capitalists" who viewed their lives as a balance sheet of debts and investments.[46]

On the one hand, pension privatization would create a class of "investor-capitalists" who saw their interests as identical with the finance sector as a whole.[47] On the other hand, the removal of controls on credit creation would create a class of indebted subjects, many of whom would live in constant terror of default and would therefore be much less likely to resist their own exploitation.[48] Meanwhile, large corporations and financial institutions were shielded from the consequences of their own recklessness by a state geared toward protecting the interests of the powerful.

The power to create and manage debt is an extraordinarily potent political tool. But this power has been enclosed by capitalists and politicians who use it to augment their control over everyone else. Imagine if, rather than being tightly controlled by a few massive financial institutions, all this power lay in the hands of the people. We could invest in infrastructure and technology that would make the world better, rather than directing investment toward those projects expected to generate the most wealth and power for those at the top.

We've seen that banks have the capacity to create money out of nothing. This privilege, granted by states, gives them immense power to shape the way our economy works. Banks help to determine which businesses, individuals, and even states succeed, with no real democratic accountability. In other words, they have the power to plan. But financial institutions don't plan on their own—their power is based on the relationships they have with nonfinancial corporations and with states.

Bernie's Bros

Banks and businesses are often seen as two very different kinds of capitalist institutions, the former representing the clean, efficient financial capitalism of the twenty-first century and the latter the dirty industrial capitalism of old. But the most powerful banks and the biggest businesses have a lot more in common than you might think, and they often work together—whether for good or ill. In fact, take a look behind every major corporate scandal of the last century, and you'll find one of the world's largest and most powerful financial institutions. The companies may be dead, but their banks live on.

Take Enron. Enron's bankruptcy in 2001 was then the largest in history after it emerged that the entire company was built on massive, institutionalized fraud. The company's top executives had developed a series of opaque accounting structures to disguise billions in debt. Enron no longer exists, but one of its biggest lenders—JPMorgan Chase—is the largest investment bank in the United States. JPMorgan was "deeply involved" in the company's finances, "simultaneously investing in the company, buying Enron stock for funds it managed and recommending the energy company's stock to investors."[49]

As a significant holder of the company's stock, the bank had a vested interest in ignoring any accounting incongruities. Analysts later found that the bank was recommending that investors purchase Enron's stock despite being aware of its hidden debts.[50] JPMorgan also helped Enron access billions in financing from investors, creating a convoluted financial structure designed to make the company appear less indebted, and more creditworthy, than it really was.[51] When their role in the scandal came to light, Enron's investors filed lawsuits against ten banks, including JPMorgan, which settled for $1 billion.[52]

One year after Enron's collapse, an audit revealed that senior executives at the telecom company WorldCom had used illegal accounting techniques to inflate the company's share price to the tune of $11 billion. The WorldCom scandal quickly overtook Enron as the largest accounting scandal in US history.

WorldCom was founded by Bernard Ebbers, born in 1941 to a traveling salesman father, who took the money he had made from running a chain of motels and used it to invest in the telecoms sector.[53] Ebbers, a former college basketball star, had been called the "Telecom Cowboy," given his habit of walking around in jeans and cowboy boots. He had never excelled at school and, when pressed at his trial, he admitted that "to this day, I don't know technology and I don't know finance or accounting."[54] His strategy for WorldCom was to expand the company aggressively through acquisitions. By the time the dotcom bubble burst, the company was saddled with $30 billion in debt.[55] Investors and regulators were left scrambling to figure out precisely how the company had managed to borrow so much.

In the investigations that followed WorldCom's bankruptcy, it emerged that Ebbers had had a remarkably close relationship with senior executives at Salomon Smith Barney, an investment bank later absorbed into Citigroup.[56] When the former attorney general found that the bank "gave extraordinary financial favors and assistance" to Ebbers to convince him to give them his business, Citigroup settled with WorldCom's shareholders for $2.65 billion.[57] JPMorgan, which had helped to underwrite $15.4 billion of WorldCom's bonds with Citigroup, paid out $2 billion.[58] Ebbers himself was convicted on fraud and conspiracy charges. He is remembered as the fifth-worst CEO in US history.[59]

Or, if those two examples aren't enough, let's take a look behind the scenes of Bernie Madoff's 2009 conviction for fraud. In 2009, Madoff, the former chair of the NASDAQ stock exchange, admitted that his wealth management company, Bernard L. Madoff Investment Securities LLC, was a giant Ponzi scheme, in which new investment was being used not to grow the business but to pay off previous investors.

Madoff had started the firm in 1960, with $5,000 he'd saved from working as a lifeguard and a sprinkler installer,[60] alongside a $50,000 loan from his father-in-law—the first, but not the last, person to be duped into supporting Madoff's schemes.[61] In 2009, he was sentenced to one hundred and fifty years in prison for operating the largest Ponzi scheme in US history. Madoff had defrauded investors to the tune of an estimated $64.8 billion.[62]

Madoff's bank was none other than JPMorgan, which, despite being aware of some incongruities in Madoff's financial arrangements, didn't make authorities aware of the potential fraud until the last possible moment. Prosecutors stated that the bank "knew, or should have known" that Madoff was perpetrating a massive fraud, but the bank claimed ignorance rather than any overt wrongdoing.[63] Madoff himself stated in an interview from prison that "JPMorgan knew" about the fraud.[64] The bank paid $2.6 billion in fines and penalties, including forfeiting $1.7 billion, at the time the largest forfeiture a bank had ever paid for money laundering violations.[65]

Why did all these huge, international banks fall for frauds perpetrated by a few individuals? Banking and finance are built on relationships. To invest money in an institution, a banker has to trust the executives running that institution. And to take the money, these executives have to believe that the investor is good for their promises. The relationships formed between the largest banks and the largest businesses are key to understanding modern capitalism—and the planning that takes place within it.

As we'll see in the next section, modern finance was the creation of the nation-state. But as capitalism developed, banks became intermediaries in the production process, providing various forms of financing, clearing balances between firms, and accepting deposits, while continuing to meet the financing needs of governments. Banks also became intimately involved with the development of capital markets, helping firms to float on stock markets and acting as midwives for the birth of modern corporations. The changing nature of the relationship between banks and firms is a process called financialization.[66]

One of the best-known Marxist theorists of financialization was Rudolf Hilferding, who saw that this process would transform financiers into powerful capitalist planners.[67] Hilferding, born into a Viennese Jewish family, became involved in the city's circles of socialist thinkers and agitators from an early age.[68] He studied alongside leading Marxist intellectuals, including Karl Kautsky, a friend of Friedrich Engels who edited some of Marx's writings before his death.[69] Today, Hilferding is most famous for his role as the minister of finance in Germany's short-lived Weimar Republic at a time when the German government had begun printing paper money to finance its foreign debts, leading to hyperinflation.

Hilferding followed Kautsky to Germany, where he became editor of the German social democratic newspaper *Vorwärts*.[70] It was during these early years in Germany that he worked on his magnum opus *Finance Capital*, published in 1910, before being elected to the Reichstag in 1924. As a prominent Jewish intellectual and social democratic politician, Hilferding was forced to flee Germany when the Nazi threat became apparent. He escaped to France but was unable to avoid the Vichy authorities and was turned over to the Gestapo in 1941.[71] Historians believed he was tortured before dying in a prison in Paris.

Hilferding was a social democrat, and a personal opponent of Lenin, but he remained a Marxist throughout his life—and indeed much of Lenin's work can be traced back to Hilferding's.[72] *Finance Capital* built on Marx's theories of centralization and financialization to show that financial institutions are important planners in the world economy—and that the construction and maintenance of *relationships* with actors in other sectors are central to the maintenance of their power.

The reason these relationships are so critical comes down to the nature of capitalist development. As capitalist economies mature, production comes to rely more on machinery, technology, and infrastructure, which makes starting a new business more costly. To invest in all the machinery and equipment they need to start a business under these conditions, new companies are forced to borrow to purchase the resources they need to compete with incumbents. The relationships between banks and businesses therefore deepen as time goes on, and banks become more interested in the conditions within the enterprises to which they are lending.[73]

Over time, Hilferding argued, the divide between the businessman and the banker would become narrower. Financial institutions would come to manage a business's relationship with investors, allowing executives to focus on the day-to-day operations of the firm.[74] At the same time, CEOs would be transformed from managers to owners—they would not just be paid a salary to manage the firm, they would be remunerated in stock options that turn them into "mini-capitalists." As banks and businesses became ever more closely entwined, markets would become less significant in determining how the economy works. Instead, the close relationships between these institutions on the one hand, and the capitalist state on the other, would allow for some centralized planning within the largest businesses and financial institutions. As one of Hilferding's contemporaries wrote in one Wall Street publication, "The elimination of competitive methods, [the] close welding together of the private banking with the government financial apparatus, the increase of control and coordination—all are elements of strength of the future financial capitalism."[75]

Hilferding, influenced by Kautsky, came to believe that the fusion of capitalist interests would result in the emergence of a "general cartel"—almost like one big capitalist megacorporation that would be able to plan everything that took place in the world economy. This prediction has not come true. While capitalist economies can be more or less competitive, competition will never cease to exist entirely. It's very important to remember that capitalism is a hybrid system in which planning and markets exist alongside each other—so Hilferding's "general cartel" is unlikely ever to come into existence.

Marx, of course, realized this. His theory of centralization did suggest that corporate power would grow over time, but never suggested that competition would disappear altogether. Marx was always sensitive to the tensions that exist within capitalism—tensions that help the system to grow, change, and adapt. The push and pull between coordination and competition—between the planning power of big institutions and the anarchy of the market—is central to the way modern capitalism functions. A small number of institutions have a lot of power to shape the way the system works, but they don't control it entirely.

We can see these tensions—what Marx would have referred to as a "dialectic"—very clearly in the finance sector. Financial institutions are in competition with one another, as well as providing finance to firms that are also competing for market share. But the relationships that financiers build with businesses and politicians, as well as the relationships they help to forge between these actors, ultimately undermine competitive markets and make the economy far more centralized.[76]

Take the series of agrochemical mergers described in the last chapter—none of these would have taken place without the support of large investment banks. When Bayer bought Monsanto in 2016, it did so with the support of Credit Suisse, Bank of America, and Rothschild, which split up to $80 million in fees between them.[77] Morgan Stanley and Ducera, which were advising Monsanto, stood to split up to $110 million from the deal.[78] Given that the deal was partly financed with debt, several banks—including Credit Suisse, Goldman Sachs, and

JPMorgan—stood collectively to gain between $150 and $200 million in fees from the bridge loan required to pull off the deal.[79] The merger was later dubbed one of the worst deals in history, as Bayer faced millions in lawsuits levied against Monsanto for its use of the carcinogenic chemical glyphosate in its herbicide Roundup.[80]

When Dow Chemical merged with DuPont, a large portion of the advisory fees went to Michael Klein. Klein is a former CEO of Citigroup who worked with then-CEO of Dow Andrew Liveris when Liveris served on Citigroup's board. Klein split fees of $80 to $100 million with Morgan Stanley, making it his biggest deal ever.[81] ChemChina was advised by HSBC and China CITIC Bank International, which split between $65 and $95 million in fees, while Syngenta was advised by the boutique investment bank Dyalco—set up by former Goldman Sachs investment banking cochairman Gordon Dyal—as well as JPMorgan, UBS, and Goldman Sachs, which all split between $59 and $71 million in fees.[82] Big mergers don't just mean more market power for the companies involved; they also mean more money for the big banks.

Banks play a sizable role in organizing the processes of capitalist production and exchange by helping to consolidate power in the hands of a few large corporate and financial institutions. Far from being rivals, big banks and businesses tend to work together to achieve their goals—and a lot of the time they are successful.

But—as Marx realized—the power of the finance sector is not unlimited. Not even the most powerful bank can control the ups and downs of the financial cycle. In fact, many times throughout the history of capitalism, the big banks' relentless pursuit of profit has brought the global economy to the brink of collapse. Conveniently, powerful states have always been there to bail them out.

The King's Coin

In the late seventeenth century, European sovereigns were engaged in near-constant struggle for control over territory and people. The Nine Years' War of 1688–97, sometimes referred to as the first global war, was one in a long series of wars fought between Europe's great imperial powers—in this case, the French were fighting against a coalition including the Holy Roman Empire,[83] the Dutch Republic (the Netherlands), Spain, and England. England's new monarch—William III—was feeling embattled after the Jacobite risings that followed the Glorious Revolution. He lacked the cash necessary to continue England's participation in the war, and there weren't too many bankers willingly offering to lend to him.

In the end, William's quandary laid the foundations for the emergence of modern central banking. William assembled a group of bankers to provide him with the loan he needed. In return, they would be allowed to form a limited company—the Governor and Company of the Bank of England—that would be entrusted with holding the government's balances. It also gained the exclusive privilege to issue banknotes on the sovereign's behalf. The lenders provided the king with the gold he needed to build his navy, and in return they were able to issue paper notes backed by the power of the king.

As David Graeber writes in his *Debt: The First 5,000 Years*: "This was a great deal for the bankers (they got to charge the king 8 percent annual interest for the original loan and simultaneously charge interest on the same money to the clients who borrowed it), but it only worked as long as the original loan remained outstanding. To this day, this loan has never been paid back. It cannot be. If it ever were, the entire monetary system of Great Britain would cease to exist."[84]

Or, in the words of Karl Marx: "The Bank of England began with lending its money to the Government . . . at the same time, it was empowered by Parliament to coin money out of the same capital, by lending it again to the public in the form of banknotes. . . . It was not long ere this credit money, made by the bank itself, became the coin in which the Bank of England made its loans to the State."[85]

All over the world, central banks were modeled on the Bank of England. Its power and wealth continued to grow over the course of the eighteenth and nineteenth centuries, and it eventually became the "bankers' bank"—settling payments between and providing credit for other financial institutions. Today, the world's most powerful central banks act as guardians of the entire financial system. And this role has become more important as the destructive power of finance has increased.

Ever since financial markets first came into existence, it has been possible to observe "manias, panics and crashes" that nearly bring down the whole system.[86] From the tulip bubble in the 1630s, to the sub-prime bubble before the 2008 financial crisis, to the recent cryptocurrency bubble, these tend to follow predictable patterns.[87] A new trend emerges, investors pile into a new asset, betting that it will revolutionize the world economy. The price of the asset rises, before reaching a peak and then falling. Most previous bubbles have followed almost the same graphical pattern. And yet, when they're happening, most investors fail to realize what's going on.

People are swept up in the excitement of the new, so they borrow to invest in their hunches, and this borrowing can create new money out of thin air. All this new money finds its way into assets like tulips or houses, encouraging producers to supply more and more of the thing in the hope of realizing spectacular profits. Markets become flooded with this new asset until everyone realizes that it's not going to be as revolutionary as they initially expected, and they all start to sell. But everyone can't sell at once without affecting the value of the thing they're trying to sell—as Keynes observed, "There is no such thing as liquidity of investment for the community as a whole."[88] The bubble bursts and lots of people find themselves with egg on their face and holes in their pockets.

At least, that's how it should work.

On the surface, the wild swings we see in financial markets disprove the idea that capitalist economies are shaped by conscious planning. After all, manias, panics, and crashes result from actors investing in financial markets *without* a central plan. Investors pile into a certain asset because they see everyone else doing it, but they can't determine what happens next.

As we saw in chapter 3, the tension—the dialectic—between planning and anarchy is key here. The emergence of crises may be outside the control of any one actor, or group of actors. But some are better able to shape how these crises play out than others. The close links between financial institutions and the state ensure that those who cause financial crises—financiers—rarely suffer the consequences of their greed. Instead, the costs of a financial crisis are borne by the people, while the profits are taken by the banks.

After the 1987 US stock market crash, the Federal Reserve slashed interest rates and made billions of dollars worth of "repurchase agreements" with US investment banks.[89] These "repos" were effectively short-term loans that allowed banks to buy up cheap assets after the crash—like a corporate landlord buying up cheap property in a declining area after a financial crisis. The most powerful and nimble investors made vast sums of money during the boom and were then insulated from the effects of the bust. It was smaller retail investors and overindebted homeowners who ended up paying the price.

The Fed's response to the crash was referred to as the "Greenspan put," after its then-chairman, Alan Greenspan.[90] A put option is a bit like an insurance policy—it's a one-way bet in which the buyer has the right, but no obligation, to sell a security back to the owner at a particular price. Greenspan, darling of the neoliberal economists and sometimes referred to as the "rock star" of the Fed, was effectively providing a state-backed insurance policy to the big banks, telling them that even if they took huge risks during the upswing of the financial cycle, the state would always be there to bail them out when things got hard.[91] This was merely the start in a long chain of "crisis responses" that laid the foundation for future crises.[92]

Investors quickly learned how to play the game Greenspan had set up for them. They knew that central banks would slash interest rates when a bubble burst, which disincentivized caution during the upswing of the financial cycle. By the time the 2008 financial crisis hit, a familiar pattern had emerged: central bankers would stand idly by while a bubble inflated, allowing asset prices to rise and the rich to become even richer, and when these speculative gains were wiped out—generally at the expense of workers and retail investors—they would take all necessary measures to get the boom going again.

But when Japan's housing boom had ended in a similar way in the 1990s, policymakers encountered a problem. The crash had been so dramatic that cutting interest rates wasn't enough to stimulate the economy. Even if the central bank made credit very cheap, people still didn't want to borrow.[93] So, the Bank of Japan came up with a new way to transfer money to the financial sector: quantitative easing (QE). And after the crisis of 2008, banks all over the world followed suit.

While it worked differently from country to country, the underlying logic of QE was the same: central banks would create new money and use it to purchase assets from the private sector. At first, central banks limited their purchases to long-term government bonds, but eventually they started to buy all sorts of assets—from corporate bonds to the mortgage-backed securities that helped cause the financial crisis in the first place.

Initially, the central banks contended that QE would raise growth rates by providing banks with more cash that could be lent to consumers and businesses. But this was never going to work in an economy in which everyone was trying to pay down existing debts. The supply of money was never the problem—the problem was that no one wanted to borrow. And no one wanted to borrow because the economy was in dire straits and they were already up to their eyeballs in debt.

But some economists saw that QE might help solve this problem of a lack of demand for lending in another way. Rather than encouraging lending directly, QE would boost growth by making the rich richer. Central banks would purchase assets, helping to prop up asset prices in the wake of a crash in which lots of people were trying to sell and not that many were trying to buy. In doing so, they would make the owners of those assets feel more confident about the future, encouraging them to borrow to undertake investment. This investment would create jobs and stimulate growth, helping to kick-start the upswing of the financial cycle.

But only one part of this theory came true—the part where the rich got richer. With central banks pumping new money into the financial system through purchases of safe assets like government bonds, investors have been pushed toward investing in riskier assets, and the obvious result of this has been rising asset prices.[94] Asset prices have risen faster than prices in the rest of the economy (including wages)—meaning the gap between the people who own all the stuff and everyone else has widened even further since 2008.[95] All this new money was supposed to "trickle down" to the rest of the economy through investment undertaken by the rich. Unsurprisingly, this effect has been slow to materialize.

In 1987, with the Greenspan put, the Fed's mask slipped. Greenspan showed that the US state was willing to pull out all the stops to protect Wall Street, even while doing very little to support workers and small businesses. With the 2008 financial crisis, the mask came off completely. Central banks were repurposed to meet the needs of large financial institutions and big businesses, even as millions lost their jobs and were evicted from their homes.

In the words of Frederic Durand, "The great mission of governments and monetary authorities faced with each financial upheaval since the 1980s . . . has been to guarantee [the] continuity of financial profits."[96] The financial crisis exposed the toxic synergies that exist between the most powerful central banks in the world and their friends in the financial sector. It has now become very clear that our public economic institutions don't work for us, they work for capital.

This shift has, however, created some problems for the legitimacy of central banks. As the political economist Benjamin Braun has argued, the problem with QE is that it shows that central banks aren't as "independent" as they claim to be.[97] The idea behind central bank independence is that there is a natural long-term rate of interest—the rate at which supply and demand for money are in equilibrium, prices are stable, and full employment is maintained—and the job of central bankers is to align the central bank rate with this "real" interest rate. They're not supposed to influence the long-term state of the economy; they're just supposed to align the state of the economy today with its long-term potential.

With the emergence of QE, the idea of the natural long-term rate of interest suddenly disappeared. Rather than attempting to influence short-term interest rates to bring them closer to their long-term "natural" rate, central banks have shown that they are actively trying to influence macroeconomic conditions.[98] Central bankers have abandoned the pretense of following the market and started instead to lead it. And to no one's surprise, they have led the market in a direction that benefits the already wealthy and powerful, while claiming to act in the general interest.

The political nature of central banking has become even clearer during the cost-of-living crisis. While interest rates were kept low after the financial crisis to protect asset prices, they're now being raised very quickly to keep down consumer prices. Why? Because rising consumer price inflation makes assets relatively less valuable. If, say, food prices are rising sharply but your house is worth the same as it was last year, you can buy less food with the equity you have in your house.

Consumer price inflation wasn't a problem after the financial crisis, because growth was so low, so central banks could afford to pump money into financial markets and artificially inflate asset prices. But as soon as consumer prices started to rise, they panicked and hiked interest rates, making borrowing more expensive for those with lots of debt. Given that borrowing was already more expensive for the poorest, and high prices were being driven by supply-side factors and corporate profiteering, this move has had a highly regressive impact.[99]

As Braun argues, the actions of central bankers in recent years have made it very clear that they're not neutral, technical experts with superior knowledge of the operation of the economy.[100] The idea of a long-term natural interest rate has been sacrificed on the altar of preserving the stability of the financial system.[101] Instead, central bankers have revealed that they are actively planning what happens in the economy, with no democratic accountability whatsoever.

And it's not just central banks. The entire regulatory apparatus that governs the modern financial system was built by and for powerful financial institutions themselves.

Modern finance would not be possible without the legal architecture that governs it—from deposit protection schemes to capital requirements to bankruptcy law. Because the law is so central to the operation of the financial system, financial institutions spend a great deal of time and money lobbying legislators and regulators to influence that system.

While society would clearly benefit from better and more restrictive financial regulation, the battle to shape this regulation is, by its nature, intensely uneven. Financial regulation is an incredibly complex area of law, and few outside parties have either the incentive or knowledge to challenge the coordinated lobbying power of the large financial organizations. Public campaigns like, for example, the campaign in Europe to introduce a financial transaction tax, are often defeated at the first hurdle—in this case thanks to a powerful and coordinated lobbying from the finance sector.[102]

In fact, financial regulation is so complex that financial institutions are often allowed to determine it for themselves. Financial institutions are part of a deep and extensive international system of *private law*.[103] On the surface, the idea of "private law" sounds like a contradiction in terms: laws are made and enforced by states. But just as corporations can have sovereignty, the power to make law is not confined to the state.

The way the law works is as much about codes and norms as it is about force. After all, most people don't follow the law merely out of a fear of getting caught; they follow the law because "it's the law." The "power, the violence, and the legitimacy of law" all stem from its designation as law[104]—a set of rules to govern human conduct to which all parties seem to have consented, merely by virtue of having entered into the "game" to begin with. In fact, obedience to the law doesn't even require coercion by one central authority—though the presence of such an entity undoubtedly helps. Rather, it is implicit in the very idea of "law" itself.[105]

So, the norms and rules promulgated by private institutions can, if they have enough legitimacy, function in a similar way to laws promulgated by states. As legal scholar Katharina Pistor argues, it is often the case that "capital [rules] not by force, but by law."[106]

One of the main ways private bodies can build their own private legal architecture is by exploiting the gaps in the formal legal system.[107] Like contracts, legal systems are always incomplete—legal codes can't account for every possible eventuality. This is precisely why we have a judiciary to interpret how abstract laws can be applied to specific cases. Lawyers are able to take advantage of the indeterminacy of law not just to defend their clients but also to shape the way the law is applied in general.[108]

Pistor uses the example of the trust, which was created in the Middle Ages to protect the property of knights going to fight in the Crusades, but which ultimately ended up being used as a mechanism to avoid tax. More recently, financiers in the City of London exploited gaps in international regulation to make the city a center for the offshore trading of dollars—so-called Eurodollars—which couldn't be regulated by the US state.[109] By the time the Bank of England started to pay attention to the unregulated dollars being traded in the city, the market was so big that regulators decided essentially to ignore it. Banks make the law just as much as the law makes the banks.

And, just like corporations, financial institutions are also often able to bend and break the law without sanction. As with corporations, states often turn a blind eye—or even actively support—the criminality of large financial institutions. In the wake of the financial crisis, for example, most states demurred from prosecuting those most involved.

As Nicholas Shaxson demonstrates in his book *Treasure Islands*, the state routinization of crime is very clear when it comes to international tax avoidance and evasion, facilitated by the finance sector.[110] It is not merely that tax havens like the Cayman Islands and Panama create laws that undermine financial transparency; these countries are protected from scrutiny by more powerful states whose financial systems also benefit from the availability of tax havens around the world—whether to support tax evasion or hide dirty money. Estimates suggest that $7.6 trillion of wealth is hidden in tax havens all over the world.[111] The international finance sector acts as a "circulation system for criminal money acquired through drug trafficking, terrorism, piracy, human trafficking, proliferation and tax evasion."[112]

When we look at the international financial system, we don't find a free-market paradise. Instead, we find incredibly powerful institutions in both the public and private sector shaping the conditions faced by everyone else. Financial institutions "[dress themselves] up in the liberal trappings of the market, yet [capture] the old sovereignty of the state all the better to squeeze the social body to feed [their] own profits."[113]

Yet all this power is held without any democratic accountability. Politicians, technocrats, and financiers work together to decide everything from the interest rates we pay on our loans to who gets what when a state files for bankruptcy. If everyone had a say in determining how these rules were made and enforced, rather than just a privileged few, we'd live in a very different world.

BlackRock's Black Ops

Most people have heard of Amazon. Its monopoly power, like that of other large consumer-facing corporations, is highly visible and is the subject of ongoing political debate. Jeff Bezos, once the world's richest man, has a net worth of $150 billion. Most people have not heard of BlackRock, and yet Larry Fink, the CEO of the asset manager whose personal fortune of $1 billion pales in comparison to that of Bezos, is in many ways more powerful than the former CEO of Amazon.

Fink has been called the "king of Wall Street"—a man who has built a "vast financial empire, the likes of which has never been seen before."[114] After flirting with a few different majors at college, Fink decided to try a career on Wall Street. He received multiple job offers—though he reports being "devastated" after being rejected for a role at Goldman Sachs. Nevertheless, he flew up the ranks at First Boston, becoming the youngest managing director in the firm's history, despite (or perhaps because of) acting like a self-confessed "jerk."[115]

Fink eventually left the firm after losing $100 million on a bad bet on interest rates in 1986.[116] It was at this point that he started BlackRock, which grew up in the offices of its future competitor Blackstone. BlackRock began its life as part of Blackstone Financial Management, before splitting with the firm in the early 1990s. Blackstone had initially stipulated that the firm's new name could include neither the words *black* nor *stone*, yet Fink managed to convince the top brass that naming the firm BlackRock—in homage to its origins—would benefit both parties. In a twist that continues to confuse the uninitiated, Blackstone agreed, and BlackRock was born.

After the dot-com bubble, when the firm's ill-timed 1999 IPO had gone sour, BlackRock began to grow very quickly indeed. As well as growing organically, Fink was able to achieve rapid growth through mergers and acquisitions financed by cheap debt. By 2006, after a merger with Merrill Lynch Investment Managers, BlackRock finally reached the threshold of $1 trillion assets under management.[117]

Today, Amazon is the fifth-largest company in the world by market capitalization, after Saudi Aramco and Alphabet (Google), with a market capitalization of $1.35 trillion. BlackRock, the world's largest asset manager, controls more than *$10 trillion* in assets. One of the Big Three asset managers—BlackRock, Vanguard, or State Street—is the largest shareholder in around 88 percent of S&P 500 companies.[118] BlackRock alone is the largest investor in thirty-eight such companies, and also has a 5.7 percent stake in Amazon. Together, the Big Three oversee $22 trillion in assets and hold about a fifth of all the shares in the S&P 500.[119]

Asset managers are financial institutions that manage other people's money.[120] If you have a pension, you'll hand your money over to a pension fund, and chances are that pension fund will hand some of your money over to one of the Big Three, which will decide how that money is invested. In this sense, BlackRock's money doesn't really belong to BlackRock; it belongs to us. Yet that money is being used to augment the power and wealth of those at the top at the expense of everyone else.

Asset management is supposed to be a very boring business. Most of

BlackRock's clients aren't looking to beat the market in the short term with clever trading strategies; they're looking for long-term returns and a safe place to put their cash. Historically, asset management was a relatively small sector, dominated by lots of midsized players guarding the savings of the very wealthy. But thanks to an aging world population, pension privatization, the erosion of the welfare state and growing wealth inequality—among other things—the stock of savings has ballooned.

BlackRock benefited from this trend and overtook its competitors by pioneering the use of low-cost passive investment strategies.[121] Rather than providing its clients with specialized advice, many of the products Black-Rock offers simply track indices like the S&P 500 or the FTSE 100. This automated process allows BlackRock to outsource its advisory work to an algorithm, which is far cheaper than employing staff to consult with and invest on behalf of clients directly. While many investors were initially skeptical about the value of passive investment strategies, these algorithms have proved highly successful at beating even the most talented fund managers.[122]

But there's a problem with passive investment funds. By pushing investment into a preselected group of corporations, without much regard for what those firms are doing, passive funds undermine the operation of the "market" for investment.

Investors are supposed to pay attention to decisions being made by senior managers and invest accordingly. Good managers are rewarded while bad ones are punished. This is the foundation of modern corporate governance. But BlackRock can't punish managers, because it can't sell its shares. The firm's stakes in companies like Walmart and Amazon are too large to off-load, and, in any case, BlackRock's market-tracking funds are always going to be heavily invested in the largest corporations. Almost regardless of how these firms perform, they can rely on the fact that BlackRock, Vanguard, and State Street aren't going to sell their shares.[123]

As *The Economist* pointed out, one of the main features of healthy financial markets is that "a cacophony of diverse actors come to different conclusions on the price of things, based on their own idiosyncratic analyses."[124] But rather than a cacophony of diverse voices, financial markets are increasingly starting to resemble a crowded room in which one or two people have a megaphone.

In fact, asset managers like BlackRock may be helping to drive concentration across the whole economy. Economists have found consistent evidence of anticompetitive effects of common ownership—the ownership of multiple firms within a sector by one shareholder.[125] Where a few powerful asset managers have a stake in most big firms, why would those investors want these firms to compete with each other? It's better for BlackRock when the corporations they own collude—and perhaps merge—with one another. High levels of common ownership lead to a situation "equivalent to an economy-wide monopoly."

But what if this shift is a positive thing? As the "universal owners" of most of the world's largest companies, the Big Three should be less interested in "the performance of each individual firm it owns" and more interested in "the performance of the economy as a whole."[126]

The argument that people like Fink could become the guardians of a new, responsible "stakeholder capitalism" is a familiar one, which has been promoted by organizations like the World Economic Forum—host of the annual Davos economic conference.[127] Advocates of this perspective tacitly acknowledge that corporations and financial institutions have the power to plan our lives, while pleading with them to do so in the general interest.[128]

In 2020, Larry Fink wrote a strongly worded letter to the CEOs of the world's largest companies stating that BlackRock would be using its power as a major shareholder to pressure these firms into becoming carbon neutral by 2050.[129] But beneath Fink's alleged commitment to decarbonization, BlackRock has voted with management against the majority of shareholder resolutions in favor of decarbonization. Academic research has shown that, most of the time, the Big Three "generally vote with management."[130] And BlackRock has now said it plans to vote against most climate motions put forward by activist shareholders as they are becoming too "prescriptive."[131]

Stakeholder capitalism is a kind of "autocritique" of capitalism by capitalists themselves. These critiques tend to emerge when capitalism is in crisis without a powerful movement to present an alternative.[132] The "responsible capitalists" of the world believe that if they can demonstrate a record of self-regulation, stakeholder engagement, and philanthropy, they can avoid the threats of regulation, redistribution, and unionization.

Governments around the world have bought this message hook, line, and sinker. The idea that firms like BlackRock represent the interests of "responsible" capitalists is what has allowed political parties and central banks to build such strong links with the firm. BlackRock has close relationships with governments and central bankers all over the world and has been described as a global "fourth branch of government."[133]

In the US, President Biden brought several former BlackRock executives into his cabinet.[134] The Federal Reserve has given the company responsibility for managing the corporate debt it bought through QE.[135] The Fed's interventions over the last few years have benefited BlackRock—for example, by providing bailouts for corporations in which the company has substantial stakes. And this isn't the first time BlackRock has benefited from a bailout. The firm was brought in to manage the assets of Bear Stearns and AIG when they were effectively nationalized during the financial crisis.[136]

The Bank of Canada hired BlackRock to advise on monetary policy during the pandemic, and Fink personally advised Justin Trudeau on the establishment of the Canada Infrastructure Bank, which critics refer to as "the privatization bank."[137] The European Union also hired Black-Rock to advise on environmental, social, and governance (ESG) regulation for European banks, before being accused of failing to consider the conflicts of interest entailed in such an arrangement.[138] So much for the separation of state and market.

In fact, as Brett Christophers shows in his book *Our Lives in Their Portfolios*, asset managers own much of the basic infrastructure that most of us use every day.[139] It's not simply the case that asset managers have extraordinary control over the financial system, massive firms like Black-Rock "own, and extract income from, things—schools, bridges, wind farms and homes—that are nothing less than foundational to our daily being." Their control over these assets is, of course, used to maximize their returns. And this requires them to "relentlessly squeeze" profits out of their holdings—whether that means hiking rents for vulnerable tenants or charging for the use of common infrastructure.

Rather than efficient financial markets that allocate investment based on the best available information, we have a few giant, unwieldy organizations that act as the "new permanent owners" of the world's largest corporations and the infrastructure upon which we all depend.[140] In fact, it is possible to observe the centralization of global capitalism empirically. The authors of one paper show that "three-quarters of the world's 205 largest firms by sales are linked to a single global company network of concentrated ownership ties."[141] The network they observe is hierarchical, with control centralized in the hands of a few US fund managers (one of which is BlackRock) "ringed by a more geographically diverse state capitalist periphery."

Alongside the Big Three institutional investors, developmental states like China, Singapore, and Norway emerge as some of the most significant holders of equities. The authors conceptualize the growing role of state ownership as a response to the volatility of world capitalism, which encourages governments to insulate their economies from market movements beyond their control. Free-market capitalism, the authors argue, paradoxically becomes increasingly statist as the drawbacks of marketization become clear—a trend that will be analyzed in the next chapter.

At the same time, as more and more money has flowed into these successful passive funds, the managers of those funds have come to compose a "de facto permanent governing board for a growing share of major global companies." The combination of rising state ownership and the centralization of asset ownership among the Big Three institutional investors leads the authors to question "whether global finance can still be characterized, fundamentally, as a marketplace."

In a truly free-market society, pervasive private power of the kind exposed in the last several chapters should not exist. All capitalist institutions should be—to a greater or lesser extent—subject to the overwhelming power of the market mechanism. Instead, we find a world in which private institutions are able to dominate and control markets, while also dominating and controlling workers and manipulating entire states. Capitalism means rule by capital—not free markets.

6

Capital's Cronies: How States Plan

In 2015, an investigation revealed that ExxonMobil has known about the causes of climate breakdown—and the dangers it poses—since at least the 1970s. A report produced by Exxon in 1968 stated that carbon dioxide levels in the atmosphere were clearly rising, causing potentially devastating effects, and that fossil fuels were the most likely culprit.[1] In 1982, Exxon's Environmental Affairs Programs manager sent management a paper describing the "potentially catastrophic events" of continuing to burn fossil fuels at the current rate.[2]

One year later, when its profits hit $5 billion, Exxon slashed the funding for its climate research team from nearly $1 million to $150,000 per year.[3] Then, in 1989, the company worked with several other fossil-fuel producers to fund the Global Climate Coalition, which created a briefing document for legislators stating that "the role of greenhouse gases in climate change is not well understood."[4] In 1996, the then CEO of Exxon, Lee Raymond, said in a speech that the scientific evidence surrounding the impact of human activities on the climate was "inconclusive."

Raymond is remembered by the *Wall Street Journal* as a "strikingly politically incorrect" character.[5] That's one way to put it. He issued a speech railing against the Kyoto Protocol to tackle global warming, received what was at the time the second-largest retirement package (nearly $400 million) from a US public company,[6] and, just for good measure, refused to amend the company's antidiscrimination policy to protect gay employees throughout his time at Exxon. Raymond eventually stepped down in 2006, but not before Exxon released an ad casting doubt on the impact of human activity on the climate at the turn of the millennium, when its profits hit $17.7 billion.

Since 1998, the company has spent nearly $290 million lobbying the US government, an average of $13 million a year, including nearly $30 million in 2008 alone.[7] These figures are only the direct lobbying expenditures listed in the company's annual reports; in 2015, a year when the company reportedly spent nearly $12 million on direct lobbying, a report from InfluenceMap found that its total expenditure was more like $27 million when staffing and advertising costs, direct political contributions, and support of sector associations were taken into account.[8] And between 1998 and 2014, the company spent around $30 million funding "shadow groups" that spread misinformation about climate breakdown.

The links between ExxonMobil and the Republican Party are lasting and deep. Exxon donated $100,000 to George W. Bush's inaugural fund and piled pressure on the administration in the following years to push back against the research of the IPCC.[9] In 2006, Lee Raymond was replaced by the equally politically incorrect Rex Tillerson as the chief executive of ExxonMobil. Tillerson is remembered for building close ties with authoritarian regimes like Saudi Arabia and Russia, including personal ties with Vladimir Putin—ties he took with him into the US state when he left Exxon in 2017 to become Donald Trump's secretary of state.[10]

While at Exxon, Tillerson cynically lobbied for the implementation of a carbon tax to tackle climate breakdown, which activists argued was a ploy to avoid harsher regulation of the industry.[11] As late as 2016, Tillerson stated that the world was going to continue to use fossil fuels, "whether they like it or not." When a lobbyist was confronted by an undercover reporter who asked him how much influence the company had had over the Trump administration, he laughed, saying, "It would be difficult to categorize" all the wins they'd had with Trump, which were "probably worth billions."[12] The Trump administration dished out between $10.4 billion and $15.2 billion in direct economic relief to Big Oil.[13]

But it's not just the Republicans benefiting from Exxon's largesse. In 2021, a senior ExxonMobil lobbyist told an undercover Greenpeace reporter that the company had been lobbying Democratic senators seen as amenable to the corporation to resist Biden's climate plans.[14] The lobbyist described the Biden administration's plans to cut carbon emissions as "insane" and stated outright that Exxon had "aggressively fought some of the science" through "shadow groups" to protect its bottom line. The lobbyist also admitted that the company had indeed been backing calls for a carbon tax, which would be levied on consumers rather than producers, on the basis that it knew such a tax "on all Americans" was "not going to happen."

The lobbyist told the reporter that Exxon was having weekly meetings with Democratic senator Joe Manchin—the most conservative Democrat in the Senate, who has worked with Republicans on a variety of issues[15]—with the aim of curbing the impact of any proposed legislation on the fossil-fuel giants. Manchin has made his name in the Senate by blocking almost all progressive legislation that has passed his desk, particularly on climate. Manchin's personal investments in fossil-fuel companies net him an income of nearly half a million dollars a year, three times his salary as a senator.[16]

The lobbyist also said that Exxon was targeting five other Democratic senators—Arizona senators Kyrsten Sinema and Mark Kelly, New Hampshire senator Maggie Hassan, Montana senator John Tester, and Delaware senator Chris Coons. Later analysis from the *Huffington Post* found that the six Democratic senators (including Manchin) had received a total of $333,000 in donations from "lobbyists, political action committees and lobbying firms affiliated with Exxon over the past decade."[17]

Unsurprisingly, the Biden administration's commitment to tackling climate change, which was arguably the issue that dominated his campaign, has ebbed significantly since the he took office. In September 2021, Biden announced that his administration would not only allow oil companies to continue with offshore drilling, but would expand it, allowing seventy-eight million acres in the Gulf of Mexico to be leased by fossil-fuel companies for exploration.[18]

Globally, the fossil-fuel sector receives an astonishing $5.9 trillion in subsidies, with the majority coming from just five nations—the US, China, Russia, India, and Japan.[19] Many of the big oil companies also received vast sums from the Federal Reserve as part of the COVID-19 bailouts. Bailout Watch reports that the big fossil-fuel companies received $8.2 billion, while cutting tens of thousands of jobs and ratcheting up executive pay.[20] Apparently not satisfied with this outcome, six of these companies spent nearly $15 million in 2021 on lobbying the US government in an attempt to maintain their tax breaks.[21]

What makes this situation so bizarre is that Biden built his campaign around policies to tackle climate breakdown in part because many businesspeople close to the Democratic Party (including Larry Fink) are intimately aware that their returns could be jeopardized by a warming world. What has emerged from the hodgepodge of lobbying efforts in the White House is a set of contradictory climate policies that simultaneously provide large amounts of funding for companies working to stop climate breakdown, alongside continuing subsidies and tax breaks for those aiding and abetting it.

Such a situation looks contradictory on the surface but is, in fact, a logical result of the way political power works. State institutions are not independent entities that decide which action to take based on an objective assessment of the evidence. Instead, their actions result from political battles waged within them. Who wins these fights is shaped by the balance of power within wider society, as well as which groups are best organized within political parties and the state. It is not a coincidence that an economy dominated by fossil-fuel companies is also one in which action against climate breakdown has been slow and patchy: big businesses use their power within the state to make sure the system benefits them.

Many on both left and right argue that the melding of corporate and political power shows that our economy has been corrupted. But capitalism is and always has been a system in which public and private power are fused in service of capital. Most of the time, that means subjecting people to ruthless free-market competition while providing massive government bailouts to large corporations. Businesses choosing profits over safety and governments bailing out bosses while letting people starve do not represent a perversion of capitalism. These things *are* capitalism.

So why is state power wielded so consistently in the interests of capital? And why has this coordination become even deeper in the era of "free-market" neoliberalism? As any student of politics could tell you, states have the power to plan. Politicians' control over money, taxes, the military, and other public institutions allows them to bend other actors to their will. States are understood as completely different from businesses and banks, which have to operate in a world created for them by states.

But, as we've seen, states, corporations, and financial institutions aren't as separate as you might think. Most of the time these institutions aren't working against each other, they're working with, and through each other. As we heard from Wendy Brown in chapter 4, modern states increasingly see their priorities as similar to those of corporations; and, as Joshua Barkan has argued, modern corporations are vested with the same kind of sovereignty ordinarily thought of as restricted to states.[22] These similarities—forged through neoliberal rule—are the foundations of state-corporate cooperation, and are reinforced through this cooperation.

How does the cooperation between states and capitalists work? In lots of different, complicated, and sometimes contradictory ways. The state isn't just a fixed set of institutions, it's a "social relationship."[23] What happens within the state tends to reflect the balance of power in wider society. When workers are strong and able to organize within state institutions, state policy tends to benefit them more. But when, as is most often the case, bosses are stronger than workers, they're better able to organize within state institutions to get their way. The transition to neoliberalism has involved a reassertion of the power of capital over labor, and state policy has come to reflect that shift.

All capitalist economies—whether neoliberal, statist, laissez-faire, or anything else—rely on some form of centralized planning. When neoliberal thinkers claim to reject centralized planning in favor of free-market competition, they are in fact rejecting only certain kinds of planning—generally those that tend to benefit workers. But whether providing handouts to big businesses, breaking up unions, or "nudging" people into adopting the "right" behaviors, neoliberals are only too happy with state planning that benefits capital. To paraphrase the political economist Karl Polanyi, neoliberalism was planned.[24] And in this chapter, we're going to look at all the ways in which that planning takes place.

The Highway Code

One of the first ideas to which you'll be introduced as a political science student is *social contract theory*. Social contract theory is all about determining precisely how states maintain their legitimacy over those they govern. Why do we do what state institutions tell us to? Why don't we rebel?

The idea that underlies most social contract theory is that state power rests on an imagined "contract" that has been drawn up between groups of individuals in a theoretical "state of nature"—a world without states, or any institutions able to centralize political and social power. For Thomas Hobbes, one of the founders of modern political philosophy, life in the state of nature would be so nasty, brutish, and short that people would have little option other than to band together and give up all their individual freedom to an all-powerful sovereign.[25] Writing in the mid-seventeenth century, Hobbes depicted the entity that emerged from the social contract as a towering monster—the Leviathan—composed of the bodies of the parties to the contract.

It's not that surprising that Hobbes viewed life in such violent terms given the violence that he witnessed throughout his life. His mother, upon hearing the news that the Spanish Armada was sailing to England, reportedly had such a fright that she went into premature labor. Hobbes later quipped that "fear and I were born twins together."[26]

He traveled around Europe during the early seventeenth century, before returning to England just in time to experience the early rumblings of what would become the Civil War. As a royalist, Hobbes was forced to flee the country before war broke out, and he found himself in Paris observing the turmoil that overtook his country from afar.[27] While hosting other royalists in France, Hobbes came to see the violence that gripped the English nation in the 1640s as the inevitable result of attempts to constrain the power of the king.

Hobbes came to believe that any attempt to limit the power of the sovereign would result in disaster. Sovereigns should instead secure their legitimacy by protecting "their" people, both from one another and from external threats. To retain their right to rule, modern sovereigns simply needed to prevent society from collapsing into the kind of chaos that had prevailed when European states were being formed.

But this justification for state power wasn't good enough for the liberals who came after Hobbes. They were concerned that his view could legitimize all sorts of abuses of power on the part of sovereigns. A state could protect people while still engaging in all kinds of undesirable activities—from taxing people too much to expropriating private property. And it was through this intellectual struggle to define the limits of state power that liberalism (understood in the classical European sense, not the modern American sense) was born.

John Locke—often referred to as the father of liberalism—argued that the power of the state was limited by the rights of the citizens it governed, including the right to property.[28] For Locke, all people were born with a set of natural rights that everyone else has to respect, on pain of damnation. For a sovereign to retain its legitimacy, it had to uphold these rights. He famously conceptualized these rights as the rights to "life, liberty, and property"—words that were eventually paraphrased in the Declaration of Independence.[29]

Of these, perhaps the most important was property. Locke viewed private property as a relationship that emerged when a man "mixed" his labor with the earth through, for example, plowing the land or making tools.[30] If I found some apple seeds, planted them, and cared for the resulting tree over the course of its life, then its fruits were, by virtue of my natural rights, mine. Once private property had emerged, it was only natural that people began to exchange the things they owned to meet their needs. And this, Locke argued, is how markets were born.

Locke's theory allowed him to part with Hobbes's rather extreme argument for an all-powerful sovereign. Rather than simply protecting people, the role of the state was to protect private property and facilitate exchange. States existed to make people's lives better by helping them produce and trade things—not just to stop them from killing one another. They could achieve these aims through, for example, the enforcement of contracts, the establishment of a stable currency, and the provision of basic infrastructure.

Adam Smith, one of the founders of the discipline that came to be known as political economy, drew on many areas of Locke's thought to write his well-known work *The Wealth of Nations*, which remains a foundational text in mainstream economics.[31] If Locke was the father of liberalism, then Smith was the "father of capitalism."[32]

The role of government, in Smith's view, was to protect free markets and private property—at home and abroad. Smith believed the best way for the state to protect free trade was to limit government intervention in the market, attacking mercantilists (a group we will meet in the next chapter) who sought state protection. Monopolies, tariffs, quotas, and subsidies were all enemies of Smith's invisible hand. He railed against the "special interests"—from bankers, to landowners, to trade unions—that attempted to capture state policy and bend it to their ends.

Locke's political philosophy and Smith's political economy both rest on two common assumptions: the idea that states and markets are separate entities, and that it's up to the state to ensure the market functions most effectively.

In this view, markets are "natural"—they arise wherever human beings interact with one another. States, on the other hand, must be created by some foundational act—such as the social contract. States can adjust the conditions in which market exchange takes place, but they do not create markets as such. And these two spheres of human activity are governed by different logics: the rules of the market are the object of economics, while those of statecraft are the object of politics.

Political economy, for early liberal theorists like Locke and Smith, consisted in elaborating the rules and standards according to which this statecraft should be judged: the central consideration being whether the state was maximizing general prosperity by upholding the natural "rules" of market exchange, without infringing upon citizens' natural rights.[33] The art of government is therefore to maximize the total happiness of society—to promote the "national interest"—without intervening too much in "the economy" or "civil society."

Traditionally, many economists argued that this respect for the natural frontiers between state and market was central to the early success of economies like those of the US and the UK. By adhering to "laissez-faire" policies that gave sufficient space to early capitalists, these economies saw rates of growth unparalleled in the history of the world. In fact, as Ha-Joon Chang points out in his book *Kicking Away the Ladder,* the British and American states provided immense amounts of support to industry during the earliest stages of their development.[34] It was only once these states had grown powerful enough to dominate international markets that they began to preach the benefits of free trade as laid out by Adam Smith and David Ricardo.

Despite the fact that it was never really adhered to, the free-trade ideology proved a powerful legitimizing narrative for early capitalist nations. Neoliberals like Ludwig von Mises, and his student Hayek, whom we met in the introduction, picked up where the liberals left off. But they were writing in a very different world from that occupied by theorists like Locke and Smith. Hayek couldn't argue that the state's power should be limited by a set of divinely granted natural rights; nor could he claim that markets were self-regulating. The experience of the Great Depression had put paid to the idea that states could leave markets alone.

Rather than arguing that the law should reflect some metaphysical natural or divine law, the neoliberals believed that law was a man-made construction that should be designed to maximize the efficiency of market exchange. In contrast to the early liberals, the neoliberals were quite content to argue that there was no such thing as a natural "free market." Instead, markets had to be constructed—market forces had to be "set free."[35] And this was a process that would be undertaken with reference to the "science" of economics.[36]

It is not too much of an exaggeration to say that "economics" for the neoliberals came to occupy the role played by God in Locke's social contract theory.[37] For Locke, private property had to be respected because it was God-given—this was the natural, ethical order of things. For the neoliberals, private property had to be respected because doing so was the only way to ensure the proper functioning of the economy.

There was just one problem: democracy. Early liberals often considered democracy and capitalism to be incompatible, because the masses simply wouldn't respect the institution of private property.[38] How could the neoliberals appear to abide by the democratic process while respecting the science of economics? How might they create "a state under the supervision of the market, rather than a market under the supervision of the state"?[39]

Neoliberals are generally thought of as anti-statist. They can often be found arguing that the state needs to spend less, tax less, regulate less, and generally do less. But seeing neoliberalism as anti-statist is a very one-sided understanding of the ideology—and one that its advocates have worked hard to promote.[40]

When neoliberals say they want to shrink "the state," what they really mean is that they want to do away with politics—the arena in which we find "deliberation about justice and other common goods, contestation over values and purposes, struggles over power, pursuit of visions for the good of the whole."[41] Rather than different groups fighting to realize their particular vision of the good, we have hollowed-out—literally economized—politics within which the role of the state is reduced to "problem solving and program implementation."[42]

Meanwhile, individuals' lives are reduced to a game in which each is attempting to maximize their own "human capital" on a fundamentally uneven playing field.[43] "Human capitals" don't organize in groups to fight for their collective interests—they compete with one another to maximize their self-interest. The destruction of the labor movement combined with reforms like the introduction of tuition fees, pension privatization, and the removal of restrictions on consumer borrowing were meant to create a class of "investor-capitalists" who saw their lives as a balance sheet of assets and liabilities, and their interests as tied to those of the capitalist class as a whole.[44]

The neoliberal subject is also supposed to act as an individualized "consumer" with regard to the state. Debate over policy is reduced to a sterile debate about "what works" in which all considerations of distribution and power are sacrificed. Genuine participation in political processes is replaced by "stakeholder engagement" and "citizen consultation."[45] Citizens are replaced with subjects.

The end result is that all forms of freedom apart from "economic freedom" are radically curtailed (and, as we saw in the last two chapters, even economic freedom can't be guaranteed under neoliberalism). In other words, the neoliberal economization of politics involves the hollowing out of democracy: "[m]anagement, law and technocracy, in place of deliberation, contestation and power sharing."[46] The threat of expropriation by the masses is extinguished. Capital is safe.

But the erasure of politics, understood as a struggle between different interest groups, does not mean any reduction in the size of the state. Neoliberals know that the state must play an important and active role in constructing and maintaining market competition, while setting out a clear and rigid distinction between state intervention *in* markets, and interventions to construct the architecture of markets: between the state as an allocator of resources and the state as an enforcer of the "rules of the game."[47] The former, the neoliberals argue, constitutes planning, which is political; the latter is simply effective economic governance. Hayek, whose neoliberal economic thinking we examined in the introduction, argues that "the rule of law . . . is the opposite of a plan."[48]

To explain the distinction between the state as a rule-setter and the state as a planner, Hayek uses the metaphor of the "Highway Code": the neoliberal state can lay down the rules of the road, but it cannot tell people where to go once it has done so.[49] The most important thing about the Highway Code is that, prior to the playing of the game, outcomes are equally uncertain for everyone: no one can know beforehand who is going to win or lose. In this sense, outcomes cannot be planned. Instead, the market reveals winners and losers, showing us the route to maximum efficiency without any guidance from a centralized authority.

As Hayek points out, the idea of justice as "blind" is one of the foundations of liberalism—the law should apply to everyone in the same way, and the idea of law as a highway code does meet this standard. This idea of justice does not, of course, satisfy all definitions of fairness. One could object that people don't all drive the same vehicles, so accommodations may need to be made for some. Hayek recognizes the validity of certain legislation designed to promote equity, as long as it is made in advance of the game's commencing and doesn't unduly limit competition. One could also point out that a state is required to build the roads in the first place—an activity that Hayek allows that the state might undertake. Some people, it might be worth noting, don't even have a car to begin with—they don't have the equipment needed to compete in the race. The neoliberals may or may not condone certain measures to provide such unfortunates with access to education, health care, and other necessities—such considerations are the legitimate subject of debate among economists.

There are, then, limitations to the highway code analogy. The state must do quite a lot of proactive things to get the race started; there is a line to be drawn somewhere between proactive planning and setting the rules of the game. Hayek has his own views about precisely where that line should be drawn. Even Keynes, often portrayed as Hayek's greatest adversary, wrote that he was "deeply moved" by Hayek's arguments, simply pointing out in a letter to Hayek that the most important question was where to "draw the line" between state and market.[50]

But there's a deeper problem with the Highway Code that the neoliberals never touched upon. In the neoliberal universe, it's not entirely clear what "the state" *is*, or how "it" is supposed to make decisions.

This might seem like a silly question. We all know what the state is—we experience its power all the time. In any case, liberals had already provided a generally accepted definition of a nation-state as a territorially bounded political organization that claims a monopoly over the legitimate use of force.[51]

If this "political organization" is entirely separate from the rest of society, then the neoliberal approach makes sense. After all, what neoliberals like Hayek were trying to do was provide policymakers with a set of rules and principles against which they could assess their policies. If a particular policy aligned with the logic of the free market, then it was permissible and should be implemented—if not, it shouldn't. They were trying to tell the people who currently held the state "tool" in their hands precisely how it should be used.

But what if the state isn't autonomous? What if the state is embedded within a wider set of social relationships? What if you can't just pick it up and use it to do the things you want? Neoliberals give us a fascinating framework to understand how the state *could* function as a rule-making entity. But they don't tell us anything about what the state is, how it works, or who makes the rules. And it turns out, this matters quite a lot for the kinds of rules we get.

Take competition law. Competition is, as we have seen, the central regulating force of the free market—so it's pretty important for neoliberal theory. German neoliberals like Wilhelm Röpke believed the state had to implement a strict approach to ensuring competitive markets and policing anticompetitive behavior.[52] It was up to competition authorities proactively to monitor markets to ensure that no company had too much market power. And this stricter approach to enforcing competition policy did initially become a central part of the architecture of the postwar German state.

But in the US, policymakers were far more concerned with "government failure" than they were "market failure," influenced by the "Chicago school" of neoliberalism.[53] They claimed that state action to promote competition was permissible only where there was likely to be a clear and lasting impact on prices. In fact, competition authorities have consistently failed to act to prevent mergers—even where there is clear evidence that the merger would lead to higher prices.[54] Milton Friedman went so far as to argue that antitrust laws tend to undermine competition, and that "we would be better off if we didn't have it at all."[55] Ultimately, the Chicago school became a "mouthpiece for pro-monopoly interests."[56]

When it came to the labor market, however, more flexible nostrums are adopted. Breaking up unions on the basis that they promote anti-competitive practices in the labor market is Neoliberalism 101. Even Adam Smith would likely have balked at the "right to work" laws used to prevent workers from unionizing in the US.[57] And millions of workers across the US are made to sign astonishingly restrictive "noncompete clauses" that dramatically curtail their freedom.[58] Competition policy is strong for some and very weak for others. Why?

These different attitudes toward competition reflect the different balance of class power within each society. US lawmakers, under the influence of powerful lobbyists, have given free rein to their large multi-national companies, often approving mergers and acquisitions that have a clear chilling effect on competition and intervening only when abso-lutely necessary. But in Germany, which is host to fewer international monopolies and where organized labor is more politically influential, bat-tles over competition policy were historically less uneven. What's more, US multinationals dominate the world economy across many sectors, so policymakers in other countries often considered it beneficial to "their" capitalists to take a stricter approach to competition policy.

But, as we have seen, competition breeds corporate power, and Ger-many was no exception. Over time, the power of German multination-als grew and the balance of power within Germany—and Europe as a whole—came to resemble much more closely that in the US.[59] What's more, the imperial power of the US—wielded through its own multina-tionals as well as the state's dominance over the laws that govern the world economy—was used to discourage restrictive approaches to com-petition policy.[60] Everywhere, backed up by the power of the US state and corporations, the Chicago school view came to dominate.

The law is not some neutral apparatus that is shaped by technocratic considerations. The kinds of laws a society passes reflect the balance of power within that society, which reflects the dynamics of global capital-ism.[61] This poses a real problem to neoliberal theory, which purports to decry the influence of "vested interests" over public policy (particularly where these interests are those of organized labor). If the state is not autonomous from civil society, then it is impossible for it to act as a neutral enforcer of the "rules of the game." Instead, every state is doomed to plan predominantly in the interests of the best-organized and most powerful groups.

Neoliberal economists have occasionally acknowledged this problem—after all, they are aware that politics and economics are not as separate as their liberal forebears might have believed. But they seem to bring it up only when attacking the undue influence of workers, or "populists," over the policymaking process. The influence of massive multinational corporations and financial institutions seems to be a less pressing issue to the neoliberal—even though it is objectively a far larger one. Neoliberalism is "[deformed] by what it ignores."[62] As we saw in chapter 2, the legitimacy of neoliberalism depends upon "double truths" like this—many neoliberals will say one thing in public, and something entirely different in private.

The result of this "double truth" has been the creation of a "monstrous form of political life," which lacks the limitations on state power that the neoliberals claimed to support.[63] As we will see in the next section, the neoliberal state is a state dominated by the interests of capital in which the law is weaponized for the powerful. Far from operating as a neutral highway code, neoliberal law has led to an "assault" upon "every level of organized popular power" in the rest of society: from workers, to consumers, to activists.[64]

At the same time, the claim that the state is simply a neutral enforcer of the rules of the game prevents these groups from fighting back. When states claim to govern in the interests of supporting "the economy," resisting the exercise of state power is often seen as resisting progress and prosperity itself.

The insight that the capitalist state is not a neutral tool would not have come as a surprise to the Marx of the *Communist Manifesto*, who wrote that the state was nothing but a committee for managing the affairs of the bourgeoisie.[65] The idea that capitalist states are nothing but the pawns of powerful vested interests would obviously represent a direct challenge to liberal theory, which sees these as entirely separate from, and governed by entirely different logics to, markets.

It would, however, also present some challenges: If the state is purely an instrument of capital, then how have working people ever won victories within the state? Why can workers vote? Why does the state exist at all?

Shilling for Greensill

Lex Greensill was born in 1976 to a family of Australian farmers. He has claimed that his parents were unable to send him to university due to the financial difficulties they faced as a result of one bad harvest, so he was forced to study for his law degree via correspondence.[66] He spent the following years selling his parents' produce by the side of the road while trying to continue his legal studies. Greensill later told an interviewer that watching his parents struggle while waiting for outstanding payments was what kindled his interest in finance.[67]

Eventually he traveled to London and started working for Morgan Stanley, where he spent most of his time trying to "turbocharge" the boring business of "supply chain financing."[68] A few years later he founded Greensill Capital, which specialized in this apparently mundane activity.

So what, exactly, is "supply chain financing"? In a world where the production of even a single commodity takes place within multiple firms across different countries, there are always lots of invoices to collect and pay. Traditionally, banks would provide financing for firms when they paid invoices, or while they waited for invoices to be paid. But in the postcrisis world of low interest rates and tight regulation, supply chain financing was no longer profitable for traditional banks. That's where Greensill Capital came in. Greensill would step in to pay a company's outstanding invoices before collecting payment, plus interest, from the company in the future.

But Greensill wasn't a bank, so where did all its money come from? As it turned out, the company was sitting on an unsustainable mountain of debt. Greensill issued debt, backed by the debts owed to it by its own clients, and this debt was purchased by large investment funds. One of Greensill's most enthusiastic backers was Credit Suisse, which set up a few private investment funds that had purchased billions of dollars' worth of Greensill's debt, apparently without looking too closely at the company's balance sheet.[69]

It was not long before signs of strain began to show. When the world economy was plunged into uncertainty in March 2020, many of Greensill's clients found themselves struggling to repay their loans. Greensill had lent billions to the GFG Alliance, run by the steel magnate Sanjeev

Gupta, which was not exactly in rude health before the pandemic hit.[70] When global production collapsed during the Great Lockdown, GFG found itself struggling to survive. At the same time, the pandemic led to a dash for cash, and investors started pulling their money out of Credit Suisse's funds. Credit Suisse was ultimately forced to close the four funds lending to Greensill, which collectively contained about $10 billion of Greensill's debt, leaving investors unable to access their money.

Masayoshi Son, the owner of the investment firm SoftBank, whom we first encountered in chapter 5, rode to Credit Suisse's rescue, injecting $1.5 billion into one of the funds.[71] In return, Son demanded that the fund lend only to Greensill Capital. SoftBank pumped hundreds of millions of dollars into Credit Suisse's specialist supply chain finance fund, which went straight into Greensill's coffers. In return for Son's generosity, Greensill lent generously to many of the firms in which Soft-Bank had a stake. This arrangement allowed SoftBank to lend to Credit Suisse, which lent to Greensill, which lent to SoftBank-owned firms. It was, in essence, a giant house of cards.

It wasn't long before investors and regulators realized what was going on, and several investigations and lawsuits commenced—many of which remained open at the time of writing. The scandals threw several of Lex Greensill's close associates into the spotlight, including David Cameron. Cameron is the former UK prime minister infamous for implementing a ruthless austerity agenda and plunging the country into chaos by agreeing to demands made by extremists in his party for a referendum on the UK's membership in the European Union.

In 2016, Lex Greensill had been handing out business cards claiming to be David Cameron's "senior adviser," and the businessman was reportedly a very familiar face throughout many government departments.[72] Greensill was made a CBE (Commander of the Order of the British Empire) for "services to business" at the 2017 Birthday Honours for the Queen. It wasn't long before Greensill returned the favor, providing Cameron with a lucrative advisory role at Greensill after he stepped down as prime minister. A BBC *Panorama* investigation later revealed that the former PM had earned $10 million from his work at Greensill.[73]

Of course, Greensill was not really paying Cameron all this money for his "advice"; Cameron was being paid to put Greensill in a room with ministers who could provide him with government contracts. The strategy worked. Cameron arranged for a private meeting between Lex Greensill and Matt Hancock, then the UK's bumbling health secretary, during which the two discussed an app that Greensill had acquired called Earnd.[74] Earnd was supposed to allow NHS workers to access their salaries ahead of payday by taking out loans against their future pay—in much the same way as the company was offering businesses loans against future invoices.

Hancock reportedly responded positively to Greensill's advances. This is the same Matt Hancock who was later chastised by the High Court of Justice for dishing out PPE contracts without due process, £30 million of which went to a company owned by his former neighbor.[75] Cameron also worked with Lord David Prior, a former minister in Cameron's government, to set up meetings between Greensill and former NHS trust leader Sir David Dalton, and Dido Harding—the former McKinsey executive and head of the UK's disastrous Test and Trace program.[76] Harding became a household name during the UK's pandemic for spending millions of pounds in taxpayer money on consultants, including McKinsey. The High Court later ruled that the government had acted unlawfully in appointing Harding to the role.[77]

Not long after these meetings took place, Cameron emailed Matthew Gould, national director of the NHS agency responsible for digital innovation, encouraging him to use the app as part of the NHS's response to the pandemic.[78] Gould did not rebuff the request, and it wasn't long before Earnd had entered into a contract with the NHS, which allowed the company to make use of the latter's data on its staff.

By offering the app to every NHS trust, Greensill would be able to build a massive portfolio of loans, which it could then sell on financial markets to access cash. Staff would, of course, have to pay interest on the loans—interest rates may have been low initially, but once they were trapped into loan agreements secured against future pay, Greensill could quite easily have turned the screws on already financially stretched NHS employees. The company was also reportedly hoping to use the relationships it was building within the NHS to sell the institution more lucrative supply-chain-financing products.[79]

And it wasn't just David Cameron lobbying on behalf of Greensill. Former senior civil servant Bill Crothers was the head of the Crown Commercial Service (CCS), which manages how the government procures services from the private sector—allegedly to maximize "value for money." Crothers earned more than £150,000 a year determining how to spend the CCS's £15 billion budget.[80] This, apparently, was not enough for Crothers, who took on an advisory role at Greensill while still employed by the civil service.

After he left the CCS, Crothers had at least five meetings with senior members of the Cabinet Office, one of the most powerful Whitehall departments that works directly with the prime minister. He was even in attendance at the "private drink" Cameron set up between Lex Greensill and Matt Hancock. It was later revealed that Crothers had built up a substantial stake in Greensill, worth nearly $8 million in 2019.[81]

All this behind-the-scenes influencing came to light during the pandemic, when Cameron's lobbying reached fever pitch as he attempted to save the firm—and his stake in it—from collapse. Greensill applied to the Bank of England's CCCF—the emergency pandemic loan scheme through which the bank purchased the debt of several large corporations—to ease its financing troubles. But the firm's request for emergency funding was rejected on the grounds that firms that lend out money to other firms were not eligible.[82]

This was Cameron's time to shine. He fired off a number of texts to then-chancellor Rishi Sunak and several of his senior advisers, lobbying them to pressure the bank to change the rules governing the scheme.[83] Cameron sent a message to the permanent secretary to the Treasury, Sir Tom Scholar, claiming to be "baffled" at Greensill's exclusion and asking to arrange a phone call. In a message to Rishi Sunak, Cameron said it was "nuts" to leave Greensill out of the CCCF.[84] The chancellor was not convinced and did not reply to most of the former PM's texts. He did, however, send one positive reply in which he indicated that he had "pushed the team" at the Treasury to change the rules.[85]

Greensill did not get a loan through the CCCF, but that did not cut the firm off from the generosity of the British state. The British Business Bank (BBB) lent Greensill £350 million as part of the Coronavirus Large Business Interruption Loan Scheme (CLBILS) without conducting the bare minimum checks.[86] This money far exceeded the £200 million cap that was supposed to exist for any one company, and it all went straight to the Gupta's GFG Alliance.

GFG is currently under investigation by the UK's Serious Fraud Office and is facing fraud and money laundering probes in several other jurisdictions.[87] One Conservative MP accused Gupta of running a "potential Ponzi scheme"—he made the accusations in the House of Commons so as to benefit from Parliamentary defense.[88] The National Audit Office investigated the BBB's loans to GFG via Greensill, expressing concern over the "unusual" interest expressed by ministers in the firm.[89] The investigation concluded that £335 million of the £350 million lent to Greensill by the UK government is now lost permanently.

The events surrounding the rise and fall of Greensill Capital demonstrate quite clearly that the idea of a fixed boundary between public and private—state and market—has always been a fantasy. The wealthy can quite easily convert their cash into political influence, and politicians and bureaucrats are quite capable of turning their political influence into cash. In the UK—as in most other capitalist countries—the links between the public and private sectors have become so close that it is hard to know where one ends and the other begins.

But these privileges are not available to everyone. For people like Lex Greensill, the British state appears extremely porous. He can write to politicians directly, requesting help and support, as well as hiring former civil servants—and even former prime ministers—to do his dirty work for him. But to organizations like unions that lobby on behalf of workers—not to mention people trying to petition the government themselves—the British state seems impenetrable.

These different versions of state power experienced by more and less powerful actors tell us something about what the state actually is.[90] Rather than a fixed set of stable institutions, the state is a social relation, like capital itself.[91]

The exercise of state power reflects the outcome of power struggles that take place within a range of public and private institutions, which in turn reflects the balance of power in wider society. In other words, different groups, supported by different constellations of class interests, struggle over policy and legislation on a fundamentally uneven terrain—unionists fighting for minimum-wage legislation have a much harder time than corporate executives fighting for subsidies. To understand what this really means, we need to let go of the idea of the state as a united and coherent entity that acts in its own right—instead, we must focus on the forces that weigh on the exercise of political power in capitalist societies.[92]

The idea of the state as a social relation can be traced back to the Marxist theorist Antonio Gramsci, whom we met in chapter 2. For Gramsci, the struggles that take place within state institutions—whether in parliamentary chambers or presidential offices—reflect wider struggles taking place within society. Not everyone is equally able to influence these struggles: the wealthier and more powerful you are, the easier it is to get your way within state institutions. And state institutions and agents play a key role in organizing civil society itself.

Gramsci's idea of the state as a social relationship was further elaborated by Ralph Miliband, father of the Labour leader Ed Miliband and one of the great Marxist thinkers of his generation. Born in Brussels in 1924 to a family of Polish-Jewish immigrants, he was forced to flee to London just before the German invasion of Belgium during the Second World War.[93] He studied Marxist theory while at the London School of Economics, joined the Labour Party in the 1950s, and became involved in the New Left in the 1960s.

In 1969, Miliband published *The State in Capitalist Society*, in which he argued that the state is not a "thing," but a group of institutions that interact to produce what he called the "state system."[94] Miliband wanted to understand the behaviors and motivations of the elites who tended to control institutions like the military, the central bank, and the civil service. How did these elites organize themselves? And why did they always seem to act in service of capital?

State elites, Miliband contended, have common social origins, which create a "general outlook, ideological dispositions and political bias." While they may disagree on certain subjects, they all tend to hold similar views on the principles according to which society should be organized. Debates around more or less "state intervention" in this context conceal deeper commonalities between different parts of the state elite, all of whom share a belief in the state and the market—politics and economics—as separate, and governable only by them. For Miliband, the function of the capitalist state is to defend the collective interest of the ruling class.[95]

Nicos Poulantzas, the Greek-French Marxist political sociologist, held a slightly subtler view about the mechanisms through which class interests came to bear on the exercise of state power.[96] Poulantzas argued that the capitalist state is a set of institutions that helps maintain the stability of capitalism, rather than just doing what individual capitalists tell it to do.[97] In fact, it is within the state that the ruling class forms itself into a coherent group, conscious of its interests and able to enact them. To put it in Poulantzas's slightly obscure terms, the state isn't a "thing," nor is it an autonomous subject: it is a social relationship that "crystallizes" into a particular set of institutions.[98] This idea requires a little more explanation.

By working within state institutions—by lobbying or consulting, like Lex Greensill—diverse individuals from the same class can form themselves into blocs capable of making demands on behalf of their class in general. By finding others who share their interests, forming alliances, and pushing for the implementation of policies, individual capitalists can work within and around state institutions to overcome their disorganization. Corporations and individuals will, for example, often sponsor think tanks that can convene business leaders, politicians, and regulators at "roundtables" where those present discuss how to deal with a particular problem. In other words, "civil society organizations do not merely express the preexisting interests of their constituents, but are also mechanisms through which the state organizes the political power of the capitalist class."[99]

It is through this process of alliance-building and bargaining that state institutions come to protect what Miliband called the "foundations of society" within capitalism. While individual capitalists might be competing with each other over the short term, over the long run they have to figure out how to work together to protect the social relations that allow them all to exist. And the best way to do that is by working within state institutions—whether to push for lower corporate taxes, more permissive regulation, or changes to trade policy. Such associations "facilitate the systematic collaboration between state and corporate institutions that is essential for developing and implementing policy."[100]

In other words, the state has an important role to play in allowing capitalists to form and promote their *general interest* as a class, as opposed to their specific interests as individual capitalists. And it is often *only* through the state that the general interest of capital can be protected. Why? Because, as we saw in chapter 3, state institutions allow capitalists to overcome their individual interests and mount joint responses to collective action problems, from banking crises to global pandemics.

While bosses and financiers find it quite easy to organize themselves, within and outside state institutions, it is harder for the working classes to do so. The working class is larger, more diverse, and less powerful— and it therefore takes a lot more effort to consolidate working people into a coherent bloc capable of speaking with one voice and wielding power. Often, the ruling classes will use their control over the state to try to disorganize and scatter the working classes. Sometimes they will do this through force—as Thatcher did in her war with the miners— and sometimes they will do this by absorbing sections of the working class into the ruling-class power bloc.

This latter tactic often requires the ruling classes to make concessions, and the more powerful the organized working class is, the greater the concessions the ruling class will have to make. These concessions will then become institutionalized until they are reversed, often generating real costs for capitalists.[101] The welfare state, for example, is not something businesses and politicians would have agreed to had they not believed that the costs of failing to introduce it would have been even higher—costs like strikes and even political revolt.

But the difference between the victories won within the state by the ruling class and those secured by the working classes is that the former win victories for themselves, while the latter win concessions granted to them by others. The working classes can't use state institutions to generate a sense of unity and speak with a single voice. They confront the apparent—though fictitious—unity of the state as a disorganized and fractured group of individual workers and unions, and they have to play the game on terms laid down by the ruling classes.[102]

While the neoliberals framed their debate as a battle between the state and the market, it would be far more instructive to understand the neoliberal project as a battle between different social classes. Both workers and bosses were, to an uneven extent, able to penetrate and organize within state institutions during the postwar period. As we saw in chapter 2 with the example of Ford and the Tripartite Committee, the battles that took place between labor and capital within formal state institutions were often just as visible as those that were taking place outside them.

In contrast, the neoliberal state is highly porous for capital but extremely impermeable for labor: there is as little class struggle taking place within formal state institutions today as there is outside them. As we have seen, the neoliberal state is not smaller than the Keynesian state, it is simply dominated by the interests of one class.

Because the state is not run directly by capitalists, and because most advanced capitalist societies are governed based on formal democratic processes, the power of capital within state institutions is often invisible. Neoliberal governments can claim that their interventions are designed to promote free markets, efficiency, and individual choice, when in fact the legislation they are implementing is clearly weighted toward one set of class interests over another. Indeed, the enduring power of the state—and what sets it apart from other forms of organization like the corporation—is the very idea that the state is an institution that exists to promote the "general interest."[103] We're told we're being governed according to a highway code, when in fact we are being governed by a corrupt and unaccountable traffic cop.

The view of the state as an autonomous entity that sits on top of society—a view that often seems to underpin neoliberal theory[104]—is far too simplistic. States do not simply shape the "rules of the game" for economic actors based on the neutral and objective advice of professional economists; state power is shaped by the influence of the parties to that game. This doesn't just mean that the rules are written to favor some over others, it means that states will very frequently intervene *in* the game in service of capital. It is only when workers request assistance within state institutions that politicians and bureaucrats insist on the need to protect the market from the meddling influence of the state.

But state planning extends beyond legislation, regulation, and spending and into the ideologies we use to make sense of the world. Much as bosses don't simply force workers to obey their demands at work, the state doesn't just dominate its subjects using force. The very way we think about the system in which we live helps to ensure that that system can reproduce itself.[105]

In fact, successive neoliberal thinkers have actually *told* us that shaping certain kinds of subjects was their aim: from Thatcher stating that "economics are the method: the object is to change the soul," to von Mises's claim that markets should "submit the individual to a harsh social pressure." In the next section, we'll see the various and subtle ways in which neoliberal governments seek to plan without the appearance of planning—from nudging their subjects into adopting the "right" behaviors to influencing the way we think about state power.

Nudged over the Edge

In 2008, Richard Thaler and Cass Sunstein published *Nudge: Improving Decisions About Health, Wealth, and Happiness*, which rapidly became the most famous text in the field of behavioral economics.[106] The question the authors wanted to answer was "Why do people sometimes behave so irrationally?" Even those who want to live long, healthy lives drink, smoke, and eat unhealthily despite knowing that doing so is going to harm them over the long run. The authors hoped that their investigation might allow them to design a society in which it was easier for people to do things that would make them happy instead.

The authors drew on research from psychology, neuroscience, and sociology to argue that the best way to improve human decision-making is to use "nudges"—subtle cues that exploit information about human psychology to influence people's choices. Thaler and Sunstein believed that governments could use the insights about human behavior developed by behavioral economists to structure what they call the "choice architecture" of society.

Exploiting small incongruities in the way humans react to information—like changing the default option on a form—can create significant changes to the way people behave, without requiring them to change their preferences and without requiring state agents to demand a certain course of action. For example, requiring people to opt out of becoming organ donors rather than opting in increases the likelihood that someone will consent to becoming an organ donor.

The book went on to sell millions of copies. One of those copies found its way into the hands of Prime Minister David Cameron, who in 2010 announced the creation of a "nudge unit" designed to change the choice architecture of UK society and "improve economic behavior."[107] The Nudge

Unit has supervised the introduction of pension autoenrollment, introduced an "opt out" system for organ donation, and supported the government's messaging during the pandemic. The unit was so successful that the government announced plans to turn it into a private institution.[108] Those who have worked in the Nudge Unit have been hired by governments around the world to set up their own versions of the program.

But there is a darker side to the Nudge Unit. Rather than rounding people up and forcing them to leave the country, the Nudge Unit supported a cross-government effort to make life in the UK as difficult as possible for migrants—making it harder for them to access health services, housing, and employment.[109] Through this policy agenda, which is known as the "hostile environment," many migrants who had been living in the UK for decades were "nudged" into leaving through measures that were introduced to make their lives a living hell.

Michael Braithwaite moved to the UK when he was nine with his father, who took a job at the Royal Mail, and his mother, who worked as a seamstress for the NHS.[110] Braithwaite followed his parents into the public sector and went to work as a special needs teaching assistant. He took to his job so well that many of the parents asked him to work with their children after school to help them maintain the progress they were displaying in the classroom.[111]

In 2016, the school's HR department told him—incorrectly—that he would have to submit a biometric card to show he was eligible to work in the UK.[112] Braithwaite approached the Home Office, which refused to confirm his status. He was informed, after nearly sixty years of living in the UK, that he was an illegal immigrant. Soon after, he was called into a meeting with the school where he was told that he couldn't keep his job without a biometric card. Braithwaite recalls how he felt on that day: "To be told, basically, you're an illegal immigrant, you have no rights to be in that job and you have to leave the premises—on that day, Friday 3 February—you could have pulled my heart out and chucked it on the floor. They took everything out of me: my confidence, my self-esteem, who I am. It tore me apart."[113]

It was only after the Windrush scandal broke and Michael Braithwaite's story featured prominently in the news that he was finally granted the biometric pass that allowed him to work in the UK. But even this is valid for only five years. And the UK continues to struggle with a lack of qualified teachers and teaching assistants.

Desmond and Trevor Johnson arrived in the UK as unaccompanied young children, on the way to meet their parents who had moved to the country several years earlier.[114] But when Desmond returned to Jamaica to support his mother after his father's funeral, he was refused reentry. Stuck in Jamaica, he was unable to see his daughter for *fifteen years*.[115] In 2014, his brother, Trevor, a widowed father caring for two teenage daughters, was informed that he was living in the country illegally. But this was entirely untrue. Trevor describes the experience as terrifying and "very, very degrading."[116]

He later received a call from outsourcing giant Capita telling him that officers would come to his house and deport him to Jamaica, while his two daughters would be left behind.[117] His status meant that he couldn't work, but he also had his benefits cut off. The family was forced into destitution; they had to rely on food banks and even begging to survive.[118]

These disturbing examples of attempts to "nudge"—or, more accurately, shove—people out of the country show that the line between the violent power exercised by the state and its ideological and administrative power is not as clear as we might think. The state isn't just a set of institutions that can force you to do things; it is an expansive set of networks and institutions with vast power over every area of our lives—from our decisions about organ donation, to where we can work, and whether we're allowed to travel.

This fact has not been lost on Marxist theorists of the state. In 1970, Louis Althusser theorized that states have two different functions: repression and ideology.[119] What Althusser calls the "repressive state apparatus" ensures the reproduction of capitalist social relations using all the tools and strategies we would usually ascribe to the state—legislation, regulation, violence, etc. The ideological state apparatus (ISA), on the other hand, includes everything from schools to churches to media institutions that we might usually think of as being part of civil society.[120] This part of the state supports the reproduction of capitalist social relations through its power over ideas. State educational institutions, for example, construct and shape the kinds of people required for capitalist production.

Nearly a decade later, Althusser's former student Michel Foucault presented his own theory of state power in a series of lectures at the Collège de France.[121] He argued that there was an art to governing people effectively, an art that was about more than the use of force or the provision of services. There are a complicated set of ideologies and practices that maintain the relationship between government and governed—ideologies and practices that make the way in which we are ruled seem normal and just.[122] The art of maintaining this relationship is a kind of "governmental rationality," which Foucault calls "governmentality."

Received wisdom about how to govern has, Foucault argues, changed throughout the history of capitalism. In the seventeenth century, the art of government was all about how to strengthen the state—what Foucault calls "raison d'état." Statesmen were all concerned with making sure public institutions were strong, that the state's coffers were full, and that it could repel and dominate its enemies—whether internal or external.[123]

During the eighteenth century, this received wisdom began to change. Statesmen and intellectuals began to ask how the state's strength might be limited relative to other actors. Good governance became a question of "how not to govern too much." The discipline of "political economy" replaced raison d'état as the arbiter of governmental reason. Rather than prioritizing a strong state, political economists set about judging the appropriate boundaries between the state and civil society.[124] We can see this preoccupation quite clearly in the work of theorists like Locke and Smith discussed earlier in this chapter.

The shift toward neoliberalism has, Foucault argues, been associated with another shift in governmental rationality. The neoliberals sought to figure out how political power could be modeled on the idea of the market—how the principles of economics could be used to judge how a government was performing.[125] At this point the market becomes what Foucault calls "a site of truth"—we begin to judge political outcomes according to the principles of economics. For example, if GDP growth is high, we assume the government is doing well—despite the fact that most people have no idea what GDP actually is, or whether it's a good measure of social progress. (It's not.)[126]

The neoliberals were some of the first to realize that the capitalist state's challenge is not figuring out when and when not to govern, but *how to govern everything in exactly the right way.* Neoliberal states spend as much time measuring, nudging, and categorizing subjects as they do actively forcing them to do things. Regulation and law proliferate under neoliberalism as the condition for good government.[127] But the nature of government intervention changes. As well as intervening in the market, neoliberal governments are also concerned with making sure every decision conforms to the logic of the market, to the logic of economics.

For example, being able to nudge people into acting in accordance with their economic interests requires creating citizens who think of themselves and their relationships with others in terms of "interests."[128] The discipline of political economy directs itself toward producing *Homo economicus*— the rational, utility-maximizing, self-interested subject we find in mainstream economics.[129] If people aren't behaving how we would expect a rational, utility-maximizing agent to behave, then it makes sense that the state should alter the "choice architecture" of society. But no one ever really questions whether human beings actually *are* rational, utility-maximizing agents, or whose interests are served by encouraging us to think about ourselves and others in this way.

The atomized agents imagined by neoliberal policymakers also have a particular kind of orientation toward state institutions. We have already seen how the neoliberal shift was associated with increasingly frequent comparisons between the state and a corporation.[130] In the same way, citizens have been rebranded as "consumers," interacting with the state as they would with a business or service provider.[131] The citizen-consumer cares only about the effectiveness of the services with which they are provided, and the efficiency with which they are delivered. They spend little time thinking about wider considerations of social justice, let alone the class interests that shape the exercise of state power. In fact, they don't spend very much time thinking about politics at all.

The result of the transformation of the citizen into *Homo economicus* is the shrinking of political life, and the impossibility of true democracy.[132] When individuals come to think of themselves only in terms of maximizing their self-interest—understood in purely economistic terms—the possibility of collective action is drastically curtailed. This process of "demassification" involves the destruction of society itself, and its replacement with a structured competition between individ-ual human capitals—but on a fundamentally unequal playing field.[133]

In place of groups engaging in collective struggle, we find atomized indi-viduals subtly categorized into "winners" and "losers" based on how much they earn, what they own, and what they do. Changing one's lot in life re-quires using the resources at one's disposal to play the game as well as one can—through "hustling" and "entrepreneurialism"—not working with oth-ers to change the rules. The catch is, of course, that someone has to lose. And, while its architects would forcefully deny it, the game has been designed—planned—to ensure that the same people lose over and over again.

In this sense, the art of government under neoliberalism involves at least three major forms of planning: the construction of free markets, intervention within those markets, and the construction of certain kinds of subjects. As Wendy Brown puts it, the neoliberal shift has combined the introduction of an "anti-democratic culture from below" with "anti-democratic forms of state power from above."[134]

To the neoliberals, the first and last categories do not constitute plan-ning in any real sense. For thinkers like Hayek, the role of government is to create a series of games for rational individuals to play out on their own terms. As long as the state does not interfere too much in the game once it has commenced, planning has not taken place.

And yet, as we have seen in this chapter, state power can be exercised in many ways, some of which are so subtle that they are barely even notice-able. These less-noticeable forms of intervention are more effective ways for the powerful to pressure others to conform to their will. "Nudging" your subjects to obey you is far more effective than forcing them to do so at the barrel of a gun—even if a gun can occasionally be useful where a nudge fails. Changing the way your subjects think about themselves, and about the state itself, is an even more effective way to govern them. In the neoliberal era, governance is everywhere, but government is nowhere. This invisibility makes the exercise of power much harder to resist.

Ever-planned

In the midst of the pandemic, the Chinese economy was rocked by the implosion of the real estate giant Evergrande. Xu Jiayin, the company's founder, had been born to a poor family in rural China. His mother died when he was a baby, and he was raised by his grandmother.[135] Jiayin began his career working in a cement factory before studying metallurgy at the Wuhan Iron and Steel Institute and then working at Wuyang Iron and Steel Company for a decade. He founded the Evergrande Group in 1996, just as China's real estate boom got underway.[136]

In the decade following the 2008 financial crisis, Evergrande became the most valuable real estate company in the world. Shares in the company shot up 400 percent between January and August 2017.[137] In a symbol of the excesses of the Chinese real estate bubble, Jiayin, who owns more than 70 percent of the company's shares, briefly became China's richest man.[138] By 2021, the company claimed to be involved in 1,300 projects across 290 Chinese cities, directly employing two hundred thousand people and indirectly sustaining 3.8 million jobs in the wider economy.[139]

As Evergrande grew, it expanded into new sectors across mainland China, building everything from theme parks to pig farms. In 2010 the company acquired China's richest soccer club—Guangzhou FC—and ten years later started construction on the world's biggest soccer stadium in Guangzhou, at a cost of $1.7 billion.[140] It built an agribusiness venture that has invested in more than a hundred pig farms across rural China.[141] It launched a bottled water named Evergrande Spring and hired Jackie Chan in its marketing efforts.[142] It recently constructed a chain of islands in the South China Sea, which host theme parks, museums, and a variety of other entertainment complexes, and which cost $12.7 billion to construct.[143]

Many of these investments and acquisitions were financed through debt, and, in a crowded market, Evergrande quickly became China's most indebted property developer.[144] The company started to plug the gaping holes in its finances by selling wealth management products to Chinese consumers through its financial arm, promising returns of more than 11 percent.[145] Many Chinese customers, unable to invest abroad, were attracted by the high returns promised by Evergrande, though as the *Financial Times* reported in September 2021, executives later admitted that "the products were too high risk for ordinary retail investors and should not have been offered to them."[146]

In fact, Evergrande had been selling investors shares in shell companies and using the money to finance its day-to-day operations, before using cash from new investors to pay off existing ones. By the end of 2021, eighty thousand investors owned $6.2 billion in outstanding wealth management products.[147] And Evergrande had more than $330 billion in liabilities on its books right as the pandemic hit the Chinese economy.[148]

Meanwhile, the Chinese government, which had stoked the bubble by encouraging a buildup of debt to spur growth, announced new regulation of the property giant in an attempt to contain it. Property prices started to fall as lending was constrained, reducing the value of the company's existing assets and further threatening its solvency.

The Evergrande liquidity crisis hit world news when a leaked letter from the company to the Guangdong government discussing its financial difficulties began circulating online. Credit ratings agencies responded by downgrading the company's debt. Over the course of a year, the value of the company plunged from $41 billion to $3.7 billion.[149] The company was declared to be in default in 2021 but by 2022, Evergrande had restarted construction across 95 percent of its projects.[150]

How did Evergrande survive a crisis that once looked bad enough to consume the Chinese economy? While details of Evergrande's rise and fall are hard to come by, it is all but certain that the company had substantial help from the Chinese state, which exerts immense control over its domestic financial system.

State-owned banks *are* the financial system" in China; "nearly all financial risk is concentrated on their balance sheets."[151] The banks, which rely almost entirely on the huge savings of Chinese households, are "treated as basic utilities that provide unlimited capital" to state-owned enterprises and local government. While official sovereign debt stands at around 76 percent of GDP, up from 40 percent in 2014,[152] this excludes the borrowing of state-owned corporations, which receive most of their lending from China's massive state-owned banking system.

Through its control over the banking system, the Chinese state has controlled which companies default and which succeed by instructing the big banks to roll over unpayable debts ad infinitum. Various convoluted and opaque financing arrangements have been developed by several government ministries to obscure the real financial situation of the banks.[153] It is likely that Evergrande's fortunes were reversed in a similar way—even as its international investors were sure the company was on the brink of default. The Chinese state is no more above bailing out private corporations than any of its Western counterparts.

But the kind of planning pursued by the Chinese state is quite different from what we find in the West. Chinese state planning can be understood as a kind of "developmentalism": a way of legitimizing one's rule by promoting, or claiming to promote, prosperity and stability.[154] Developmentalism is a way of justifying state power that is close to what Foucault called *raison d'état*. "Support us because we'll make you richer" is the rallying cry of the developmentalist politician.

Just like its neoliberal cousin, the developmentalist approach assumes that the state can act as an autonomous force within society.[155] State planning is a matter of analyzing (and therefore constructing) "the economy" as an object before picking the "right" policies to promote economic growth. While for neoliberals this looks like tax cuts and privatization, for developmental statists it more often looks like capital controls and nationalizations.

But while developmentalism is based on a different kind of governmentality from neoliberalism, neither developmental nor neoliberal states are autonomous from the societies they govern. The developmental state is still a kind of social relationship: what happens within the state reflects the balance of power within society. As with the neoliberal state, the policies implemented by developmental states reflect a particular balance of power between class forces.[156]

Chinese planners are forced to balance a variety of different aims (like protecting financial stability and promoting economic growth) and interests (like those of workers, bosses, and bureaucrats). Divides among different groups within the Chinese state largely reflect divides between different social classes in wider society. In balancing the objectives of different social groups—not to mention their own interests—policymakers seek to maintain social stability while satisfying the powerful. The result has been the construction of an astonishingly successful model of development, which has nonetheless resulted in "the commodification, deregulation and exploitation of labour," in common with the rich world.[157] In fact, it was precisely the ability of Chinese planners to promote economic growth while suppressing the demands of workers that underpinned the Chinese "miracle."[158]

Just take the Evergrande crisis. Evergande's problems are symptomatic of a wider set of challenges faced by China's central planners: namely, there being too much money stuck at the top of the economy and not enough profitable domestic outlets for investment. China is now home to nearly five hundred billionaires whose vast wealth has caused enough embarrassment to the Chinese Communist Party (CCP) that it has launched several attacks on the country's tycoons.[159] Yet the state cannot allow wages to rise too quickly in order to facilitate domestic consumption, as doing so would augment worker power and undermine the Chinese growth model.[160]

Instead, in the wake of the financial crisis, planners tried to direct all the extra money in the Chinese economy toward productive purposes by expanding public investment.[161] The state also directed state-owned banks to lend to local governments and state-owned corporations.[162] With households also increasing their borrowing, partly to fund mortgages, Chinese debt increased sharply across the board.[163] As was the case in the rich world before 2008, the natural result has been the emergence of bubbles and other forms of financial instability—as well as rising inequality.

A few executives, like Jack Ma, the founder of Alibaba (through which Masayoshi Son made his fortune), became symbolic of the excesses of the Chinese boom. This was no small issue for the legitimacy of the government of an allegedly communist country.[164] To deal with this problem, the CCP announced a crackdown on China's major tech companies, which ended up wiping out nearly $1 trillion in equity almost overnight.[165] While these interventions obviously had a significant impact on China's economy, they also allowed the CCP to blame unscrupulous executives for the problems the country was facing.

Chinese planners have also tried to encourage international investment as an outlet for all the cash stuck at the top of the economy through the Belt and Road Initiative—a massive program of infrastructure projects across Asia, the Middle East, and parts of Europe and Africa. Through this suite of projects, China has provided billions in low-interest loans to low-income countries to allow them to invest in infrastructure linking the world to China. The

Belt and Road has been theorized as a kind of "spatial fix" that allows China to deal with its internal problems through overseas investment.[166]

The kind of developmentalist planning we find in China is not unique to nominally communist countries. Take Japan, where the state's approach to the steel industry is often seen as a successful example of industrial policy introduced by a developmental state. In fact, as academic Hajime Sato points out in his analysis of the Japanese steel industry, the way state policy was enacted actually reflected and reinforced existing class relations.[167]

Because the postwar Japanese steel industry was characterized by the presence of a small number of large firms that were capable of wielding significant influence, policy came to favor these giants.[168] Bureaucrats pushed for the industry to become more centralized to make these firms more powerful. It just so happens that, in doing so, they created highly efficient and productive steel firms that were large enough to compete internationally. The industry was also able to rely on support from the US, which helped it to thrive.[169] Japanese steel didn't succeed because state officials were autonomous from society, it succeeded because the social forces acting on them happened to push them in the right direction.[170]

Just like capital itself, the capitalist state—whether neoliberal or developmental—has to be understood as a kind of social relationship. It isn't a tool that can be picked up and used by whoever happens to win the next election, nor is it a simple extension of the power of capital. Instead, the struggles that take place within the formal state institutions reflect those that take place outside them—and the wealthy, powerful, and organized tend to dominate both.

Some states are, of course, more powerful than others. The struggle that takes place to determine policies within these states has repercussions that extend far beyond their borders. The most powerful planners, working through a network of international institutions, are able to exert the kind of imperial power that would have been the envy of emperors of old.

Money at Six Percent: How Empires Plan

The United States claims never to have had an empire. But it did—US colonialism has just been written out of history. The US colonized the Philippines, Puerto Rico, Hawaii, the US Virgin Islands, and Guam, among others. Most of these were small territories that were ultimately incorporated into the United States itself, with differing levels of autonomy. But the US occupation of the Philippines—a country of over one hundred million people—was a more typical colonial endeavor. The United States ruled over the country for more than forty years between 1899 and the Second World War. By the end of 1945, 135 million people lived under US jurisdiction "outside the mainland."[1]

As the Spanish Empire broke apart over the course of the final decades of the nineteenth century, the United States was there to pick up the pieces. Filipino independence leaders initially believed the US had come to liberate them and had already issued an independence declaration by the time US troops arrived.[2] In fact, the US and Spain had brokered a secret deal at the end of their war to ensure a peaceful handover of power, with the US paying $20 million for the territory after a peace treaty was signed in Paris. The Spanish governor-general reportedly stated that he was "willing to surrender to white people" but never to the native population.[3] When independence forces met those of the US in Manila, thousands of Filipinos were killed. The United States had succeeded in turning the Philippine war of independence into the Philippine-American War.

US rule over the Philippines was long and brutal. After defeating Spain, the US immediately set about slaughtering what remained of the Philippine independence movement. Whole towns were razed to the ground in the drive to "pacify" the US's newest colony. US troops, well practiced in the art of racism, abused the local population.[4] Rebellious townspeople were herded into "reconcentration" camps "where they could be more easily monitored."[5] The military captured and tortured those suspected of harboring nationalist sympathies. Over the course of the "pacification" campaign, as many as 750,000 Filipinos died—many from diseases that had been transported by American troops, which spread particularly quickly among malnourished Filipinos living in close quarters in US camps.[6]

One of the most striking features of the US occupation of the Philippines was "how rarely [it was] even *discussed*."[7] Initially, the Philippines was referred to as a colony, but as it became clear that such a characterization would not fit with the self-image of a democratic, postcolonial nation, the designation was changed to "territory." The greatest challenge for the US government, as with all the "territories" it colonized, was determining how millions of Black and Brown people could be incorporated into an allegedly democratic citizenry without upsetting the balance of power within the US itself. In the Philippines, the answer to this question seemed simple enough. The US had conquered the Philippines and it would rule over the local population as it had the people of Puerto Rico, Guam, American Samoa, and the US Virgin Islands, who remain disenfranchised to this day.[8]

There was one problem with this tactic. The US claimed to be a democratic and anti-imperialist nation. It had spent much of the early twentieth century encouraging other empires to grant independence to their colonies. US anti-imperialism was, of course, entirely self-interested and mostly directed toward other states. After all, how could US corporations dominate the rest of the world if whole swathes of it were guarded by imperial powers? But the Philippines still presented some stubborn problems for America's self-image. It had to be controlled without appearing to be dominated; American rule had to be planned without the appearance of planning.

In 1916, Congress passed the Jones Act, promising the Philippines independence whenever the country achieved a "stable government." Precisely what this phrase meant had been elaborated by General Leonard Wood, former governor-general of the Philippines and military governor of Cuba, who remarked: "When people ask me what I mean by stable government, I tell them 'money at six percent.'"[9] This anecdote should give an idea of the US's true aims in the Philippines. Rather than an unruly—and potentially socialistic—independent government capable of realizing economic, as well as political, sovereignty, the US wanted to create an obedient and willing recipient of US investment.

After the Second World War, during which the Philippines experienced brutal treatment at the hands of the Japanese, the US finally agreed to hand over power to a "stable government." This government just so happened to be one that allowed the US to establish military bases across the newly independent country, as well as granting unlimited access to US corporations seeking to exploit its natural resources. The idea was to "attain a degree of control over Philippine economic life unprecedented even during the colonial period."[10]

The CIA effectively ran the country after independence, engineering election victories for pro-Washington candidates. The infamous crushing of the left-wing Hukbalahap Rebellion in 1954, involving the use of napalm and psychological warfare based on stories of a fictious vampire, is counted as a major victory for the CIA.[11] And the CIA's involvement didn't stop there. One US historian later discovered that Langley had taken to writing the president's speeches and drugging his opponents. CIA secret agent Edward Lansdale—an early expert in psychological warfare, a skill he used to great effect in both the Philippines and Vietnam—reportedly physically beat one candidate when he failed to comply.[12]

Much to the delight of the United States, which had supported his campaign, Ferdinand Marcos was elected president in 1965. By the time of the election, Marcos was already a controversial figure in Filipino politics. His father, Mariano, had been drawn and quartered, his dead body left hanging in a tree, by guerrillas for alleged collaboration with the Japanese during the occupation.[13] Years earlier, Mariano had lost an election for a seat in the Philippine House of Representatives. His opponent, Julio Nalundasan, was found dead in his home from a gunshot wound the following day.[14] The young Marcos, his father, and his two uncles were accused of conspiring to commit the murder, and both the young Ferdinand and one of his uncles were given the death sentence—though this was later overturned.

Marcos fought in World War II until being taken prisoner by the Japanese, and then being released under mysterious circumstances. Evidence gathered by the *Washington Post* later revealed that Marcos's release was likely the result of his father's collaboration with the Japanese.[15] Following his release, Marcos claimed that he had been heavily decorated for his bravery during the war—though these claims were also found to be largely false.

But the greatest controversies to mire the Marcos name came when he entered office. The Marcos administration was dogged with accusations of corruption and Marcos's wife, Imelda, became a byword for venality and extravagance.[16] Both became close friends of President Ronald Reagan, and the US was able to exert extraordinary influence over the Marcos government.[17] Under pressure from President Johnson, and reversing an earlier position, Marcos agreed to send Filipino troops to support the doomed US war effort in Vietnam.

As discontent with the regime mounted, Marcos's defense secretary faked a threat on his own life to engineer a transition toward authoritarian rule.[18] He claimed that communists had tried to kill him, leaving Marcos with no choice other than to suspend the democratic process, much to Washington's delight. Thousands of people—mainly communists—were killed in the transition, their bodies dumped in public places "in order to terrorize [Marcos's] enemies."[19]

As well as using Marcos as its puppet, the US exercised its power over the Philippines via the world's latest international financial institutions, like the World Bank and the International Monetary Fund (IMF). Robert McNamara, the Ford "whiz kid" and former secretary of defense we met in chapter 2, became head of the World Bank in 1968. In this role, McNamara was centrally involved in sustaining a flow of aid to Marcos's brutal authoritarian regime with the aim of securing investment opportunities for international capital.[20] Much of this "aid" ended up in the pockets of Ferdinand and Imelda Marcos.

Walden Bello, the Filipino activist and academic, who was part of the resistance to the Marcos regime, was instrumental in proving that the US government and the World Bank were working together in the Philippines. Bello, a member of the Communist Party of the Philippines, was arrested for protesting Marcos's regime in the 1970s and was released only after a hunger strike. He and fellow researchers later broke into the World Bank headquarters to steal thousands of pages of documents relating to the lending program to the Philippines, proving beyond doubt the collaboration between the World Bank and the US state.[21] When Bello ran for vice president under Leody de Guzman in 2022, the pair were defeated by none other than Marcos's son.

The US colonization of the Philippines was brutal, but it did not end with formal independence. The Philippines has existed in a state of what Kwame Nkrumah, Ghana's independence leader, referred to as "neocolonialism": a condition in which a state is, "in theory, independent and has all the outward trappings of international sovereignty," but "in reality its economic system and thus its political policy is directed from the outside."[22] This was a familiar situation for many newly independent nations. The president of Gabon observed that "Gabon is independent, but between Gabon and France nothing has changed; everything goes on as before."[23] This observation was validated when it came to light that French politician Jacques Foccart kept letters requesting military intervention, presigned by various African presidents, in his desk drawer.[24]

Nkrumah was an intellectual and political giant who led Ghana to independence in 1957, making it the first country to receive independence from Britain in sub-Saharan Africa. A socialist and a nationalist, he spent much of his life seeking to promote unity among third-world countries, as he believed that only by working together could newly independent nations resist the influence of their former colonizers.

Unfortunately, the dream of unity proved fleeting. As we will see throughout this chapter, independence did not bring prosperity for most poor states given the ongoing neocolonial influence of the rich world, which sought to subvert cooperation between third-world countries at every turn. For decades, the development of the Philippines was hampered by collusion between the US, international institutions, domestic capitalists, and a corrupt political class, which together deprived Filipinos of basic human rights to ensure the country would remain a haven for international capital. Bello himself has referred to the situation faced by the Philippines after independence as neocolonial.[25]

We usually think of empires as violent undertakings. As Frantz Fanon observed in the 1960s, the process of conquering and governing a colony is, by definition, violent.[26] But in the context of global capitalism, empire has a more expansive meaning. Capitalist empires are not simply the states capable of winning the most wars; they are the command centers of the capitalist world system.[27] Their corporations are the largest and most powerful multinationals, extracting profits from all corners of the globe and sucking them back to the imperial core. Their financial institutions are some of the most important nodes in the networks of global finance. The priorities of their governments are forcefully communicated to—and sometimes enforced upon—less powerful states.

In fact, at the global level it is much easier to see the equivalence between economic and political power than it is domestically. The power of US businesses abroad is maintained through an international order that prioritizes the interests of US capital, promulgated by the US government and its allies.[28] The power of US finance rests on the central role played by the dollar as the global reserve currency, which is itself a function of American military, political, and economic might. American military power, meanwhile, stems from and helps to reinforce the power of a web of military contractors, weapons manufacturers, and research hubs that provide the expertise and equipment needed to maintain its supremacy. In certain parts of the world, as in Iraq after its invasion, the US government has ruled through private corporations like Halliburton.[29]

Empire is, then, about more than formal colonization—it refers to all the processes through which the world's most powerful capitalist institutions plan who gets what at the level of the world economy. Throughout history, this imperial power has often been exercised through horrendous acts of violence that have warped the development of entire societies for decades. But today, it is often exerted in far more covert ways, such as through the secretive system of international courts or international financial institutions imposing rigid conditions on countries trying to access emergency lending.

But America's adoption of the responsibilities of empire was not uncontested. Debates and struggles that took place within state institutions, of the kind outlined in the previous chapter, led to the US adopting the role of guardian of global capital. As they dealt with problems and challenges at the global level, key actors within the US state came to see American interests as defined "in terms of the extension and defence of global capitalism."[30] Ultimately, the US state took it upon itself to ensure that no part of the world could close its doors to international investment. This desire to keep the world "open" to capital, rather than overaccumulation or a struggle for resources, is what explains so many of America's imperial escapades in recent decades.[31]

This chapter will analyze the different ways in which empire has been conceptualized throughout the history of capitalism and the way in which imperial power is expressed today. We'll also look at the contradictory ways in which liberals have conceived of empire and development, before showing that the global economy is structured in such a way as to maintain the imperial power of the rich countries at the expense of poor ones. We'll also look at how this international system was designed—quite consciously—to limit democratic influence over economic policy and to neutralize any threats to the power of international capital.

Pacifying the Natives

Walter Bagehot, a nineteenth-century liberal theorist and former editor of the *Economist*, once wrote that "[the British] are pre-eminently a colonizing people. We are, beyond all comparison, the most enterprising, the most successful, and in most respects, the best colonists on the face of the earth."[32] Occasionally, consolidating the UK's great imperial power required the allegedly benevolent British to use force against "the natives." Bagehot, though he remained an ardent liberal, believed that it was appropriate for the British state to use force against these "backward" peoples wherever they stood in the way of the "civilizing" influence of the British Empire—whether in sub-Saharan Africa, Australia, or Ireland.

Liberals have always claimed to oppose imperialism and to champion freedom—especially free trade. The close links between imperialism and liberalism have therefore been written out of its intellectual history.[33] But liberals like Bagehot found it quite easy to support both free trade and imperialism—and often quite brutal imperialism at that.

In the eighteenth century, liberal advocates of free trade were writing in opposition to mercantilists, who believed that national prosperity was best protected by maximizing exports and minimizing imports. To the mercantilist, trade was a zero-sum game, and the balance of payments was the scorecard: those states with the largest current account surpluses were winning, while those with deficits were losing. Building up empires, within which trade was zealously guarded, was seen as the best way to "beat" other nations economically—as well as to promote national security.

Liberals, on the other hand, argued that the whole world would be better off under free trade. One of the greatest liberal political economists was David Ricardo, who wrote his magnum opus, *On the Principles of Political Economy and Taxation*, in 1817.[34] Ricardo was both a theorist and practitioner of capitalism—he made his fortune in the City of London by speculating on events like the Battle of Waterloo.[35] He used his wealth to support his career as a politician and a leading liberal intellectual, voting for measures to promote free trade wherever he had the chance.

With his theory of comparative advantage, Ricardo sought to prove that free trade would always benefit both participants in the exchange, rather than only the seller. He argued that it was always more efficient for countries to specialize in producing the things they were best at, rather than trying to meet all their consumption needs through domestic production. Such specialization would boost productivity all around. And higher productivity would mean that, when they can trade with each other, all countries were able to consume more than they would have if they had worked alone.[36]

When applied to the world economy, the argument has a clear implication: the whole world would be better off if each country produced the commodities for which it had a comparative advantage and traded with other states doing the same. It wouldn't matter if one country was more productive than all the others; that country—indeed, every country—would still benefit from greater levels of specialization than would be possible under autarky (a situation in which each country produces and consumes all the commodities it needs itself). Of course, such outcomes are possible only under free trade. If states impose tariffs, quotas, or other nontariff barriers to trade, then the costs of trade may increase to such an extent that they outweigh the benefits of specialization.

Ricardo's theory of comparative advantage was a weapon in the long-running battle between liberal free traders and mercantilists—a battle the free traders ultimately won. This victory was not, however, based on the superiority of the liberals' ideas. As Ha-Joon Chang has pointed out, early capitalist states provided immense amounts of support to infant industry—including, but not limited to, the use of tariffs and quotas.[37] As these industries developed under the careful tutelage of the state, trade barriers were steadily reduced so as to allow powerful new firms to enter world markets and compete at the level of the global economy. While trade barriers may have fallen, the state continued to provide many other forms of support and protection for domestic industry.

Yet newly independent states were told they would have to adhere to free trade policies if they wanted to "catch up" with the rest of the world. These countries were fed the lie that Britain and America had grown rich through free trade, and that if they only opened up their markets to international competition, they would too.[38] Instead, these states found their national economies were dominated by corporations that had been protected by imperialist nations now preaching the benefits of the free market. This was the "imperialism of free trade."[39]

One of the most ardent champion of this view of international development was Walt Rostow, who published his *Stages of Economic Growth* in 1960. Rostow was born into a family of Russian Jewish socialists, before becoming one of the most ardent anti-communists in the US government.[40] He took up a strategic role in the military during World War II, selecting targets for bombardment to inflict maximum pain on the Germans, and later joined a government department seeking to deploy political and psychological warfare against the USSR. Rostow was ultimately invited to serve in the administration of John F. Kennedy, where he campaigned for various ruthless US invasions. He believed that the US could bomb Vietnam into submission—a strategy that led to the deaths of thousands of civilians.

The Stages of Economic Growth proposed a linear and teleological model of capitalist development, in which societies progressed through several stages—from the "traditional" phase, characterized by subsistence agriculture and little technological development; through the "takeoff" phase, in which industrialization, urbanization, and capital accumulation all increase; to the age of "mass consumption," associated with high incomes and consumption, and a growing services sector.[41] The idea was that development everywhere would look exactly as it had in industrializing Britain.

According to the infamous Sachs-Warner hypothesis, countries open to international trade achieve higher long-term growth rates than those closed to trade. Sachs and Warner purported to show that "open" economies grew 2.45 percentage points faster than closed ones over the long run. But the categories of analysis used in this paper were problematic at best,[42] while more historically grounded approaches have unambiguously shown the central role played by the state throughout the history of capitalist development.[43]

Contrary to the predictions of those who argued that free trade would allow poor countries to catch up with rich ones, the structure of the world economy has remained relatively stable over the last several hundred years: there are a small number of wealthy and powerful economies that dominate the world, a larger number of very poor countries that have little power, and the rest lie somewhere in between. It is true that some countries have been able to move up the hierarchy by industrializing, but, in the same way as Britain and America, they have done so by *protecting* their economies before trying to practice free trade.[44]

So why hasn't free trade benefited the poor world as much as its advocates believed it would? One of the first answers to this question comes from (you guessed it) Karl Marx. Marx saw that the inequalities that existed between countries and regions under capitalism reflected the timing of industrialization in each. Some had been able to industrialize early and dominate surrounding areas, preventing those areas from catching up and leaving them trapped exporting agricultural commodities to industrialized areas.[45] As we have seen, the state played a central role in development in these places[46]—not only implementing policies to support infant industries, but also, as Marx noted, enclosing common land to create a poor and desperate workforce that could be forced down mines and into "dark satanic mills."[47]

From their emergence in individual nations, these inequalities eventually became visible at the level of the world economy. As Marxist theorist Nikolai Bukharin writes, "entire countries appear today as 'towns,' namely the industrial countries, whereas entire agrarian territories appear to be 'country.'"

Economic theory suggests that these differences will eventually even out, because capitalists in rich countries will invest in poor ones as investment opportunities in their home markets dry up.[48] This investment would be channeled into businesses in the Global South, allowing them to grow and ultimately challenge the dominance of established businesses in the Global North.

But mainstream theory didn't account for the growth of powerful monopolies that would be able to dominate their home markets—and eventually large parts of the world market. These multinational corporations easily outcompete smaller ones operating in the Global South, using their power over the market to price-gouge their suppliers, forcing these smaller firms to cut costs by reducing wages and worsening working conditions.[49] And they often also ally with powerful financial institutions to buy up any competitors that do emerge in order to consolidate their hold over the world market.[50] Moreover, companies headquartered in the rich world can offshore production to poor countries, taking advantage of low labor costs and reshoring the profits to their home nation.[51]

Capitalist states make sure these inequalities persist by preventing people from moving around to find better-paying jobs, and by preventing states in the Global South from accessing resources and technology that would help them to industrialize. Together, these processes facilitate the generation of "super profits"—or "imperial rents"—for capitalists in the rich world, as well as stunting industrialization in the poor world and keeping these states in a position of dependency.[52]

The fusion of economics and politics is a critical part of this model and is something early liberal theorists missed. States consistently seek to protect "their" capitalists all over the world. Whether in the form of taxation, trade policy, or foreign policy, capitalists always rely on politicians to provide them with opportunities for profit-making abroad.[53] Lenin, who in 1917 wrote that imperialism was the "highest stage" of capitalism, realized that this fusion of state and corporate power would make it even harder for poor states to catch up with rich ones.[54]

While this fusion of corporate and political power is largely hidden within modern capitalist economies, historically it was understood to be a central component of imperial power. We have already seen how early capitalist states sought to govern the world economy through corporate sovereigns like the East India Company. The Nazi Party also encouraged the creation of "trusts, combines and cartels" on the basis that doing so would support the German state's imperial power—at home and abroad.[55] Unions, and any other threats to corporate power, were destroyed, and a law was passed to "force industries to form cartels where none existed."[56] Unchecked corporate power—fused with that of the state—was a key component of Nazism.

In the 1960s, a group of economists from Latin America drew on Marxist theories of imperialism to explain why poor countries remained so poor even after the era of formal colonialism, in response to the errors of modernization theory. Dependency theorists like Raúl Prebisch argued that the world was divided into an advanced, industrialized "core" and a less advanced, predominantly agrarian "periphery."[57] The Argentine Prebisch was initially a staunch advocate of free trade, but as US multinationals began to dominate Argentine ones from the 1930s he shifted to supporting protectionism.[58] Prebisch went on to serve as the first secretary general of the United Nations Conference on Trade and Development (UNCTAD), through which he sought to promote the cause of Global South solidarity and change the unfair rules of the world economy in favor of poor countries.

Dependency theory was based on the observation that poor countries remained dependent on producing and exporting primary commodities to, and importing manufactured commodities from, rich countries.[59] As they developed, wealthy states, with large, powerful corporations and sophisticated technologies, saw increased productivity translated into higher wages and higher domestic demand. But poor states, with less powerful corporations and limited access to technology, were forced to keep wages low to remain competitive, hampering domestic development.

Over time, the terms of trade between rich and poor countries declined, and poor states were forced to export ever more primary commodities to afford the manufactured commodities they needed from the rich world. States in the periphery then found themselves at the mercy of the commodities cycle, experiencing severe economic downturns, often coupled with public debt crises, whenever commodities prices fell.[60] And because demand for commodities like food is relatively stable—people can eat only so much—falling food prices do not tend to translate into higher demand. Instead, they lead to lower revenues for producers.

Meanwhile, workers in the core are more productive than those in the periphery, as they're working with more advanced technologies and have better training. These factors also mean they have more bargaining power, so they can demand higher wages. And higher wages allow consumer markets to develop more rapidly in the rich world, creating yet more opportunities for domestic investment for capitalists in the Global North.

Dependency theorists like Prebisch realized that, because of the dynamics of the commodities cycle and the rules and norms promulgated by powerful states and international institutions, peripheral societies remain unable to industrialize in the same way as core states once were. They are trapped in a position of "dependency" relative to the core: they have no choice other than to export primary commodities to wealthy economies that need them, but they find themselves unable to convert the revenues from these exports into the resources required for industrialization.

As we've seen, the divide between the core and the periphery is not only a function of different levels of historical development; it is necessary for the functioning of modern capitalism.[61] Capitalists in the imperial core are able to generate super profits only through their hyperexploitation of cheap labor in the periphery.[62] The hyperdevelopment of the capitalist core comes at the direct expense of the periphery.

While claiming a grand civilizing mission to end poverty and promote development, rich countries have in fact *under*developed the rest of the world in order to enrich themselves. In his book *How Europe Underdeveloped Africa*, Walter Rodney argues forcefully that the wealth of the rich economies comes through the exploitation of poor ones, through "trade, colonial domination, and capitalist investment."[63] The exploitation of the Global South is a cornerstone of production in the Global North, a relationship that yields great profits for corporations headquartered in countries that used to colonize much of the planet.[64]

The dependency theorists believed that peripheral states had to focus on industrialization if they were ever to escape the low-income trap. Some leaders of newly independent nations realized this early on. They knew they would have to use the power of the state to protect their domestic industries if they wanted to develop. Often, the balance of class power in these societies actually favored the kind of developmentalist policies discussed in the last chapter, because domestic capital was smaller and weaker and therefore needed more state support. And the USSR was often willing to support independent states to pursue more statist development paths. As we'll see, many newly independent nations tried to do just this.

But, with a few carefully chosen exceptions, the US wouldn't let them. If poor states had been allowed to industrialize, they would have been harder to exploit. As a result, when peripheral countries did try to industrialize in the mid-twentieth century, powerful states, corporations, and international institutions worked together to undermine these efforts. As home to the most powerful capitalists in the world, the responsibility for protecting the system fell primarily to the United States, which worked tirelessly over subsequent decades to maintain the hierarchy of global capitalism—and its own position at the apex.

Banana Republics

One of the earliest examples of US attempts to keep down a country attempting to modernize was Guatemala—the original "banana republic." The United Fruit Company—now known as Chiquita—began harvesting bananas in the late nineteenth century. The company had been incorporated when a US businessman was invited by the Costa Rican government to construct a railway linking the capital to the coast.[65] The railway was never completed, but the bananas planted to feed the workforce on the surrounding land proved an extraordinarily profitable export. The United Fruit Company was formed in 1899; by 1900 it was the world's largest exporter of bananas.[66]

The company controlled vast tracts of land across Central America, and much like Ford in the Amazon, came to run what looked like a parallel state infrastructure. It ran the Guatemalan postal service and was granted a ninety-nine-year concession to build and run the railway line from Puerto Barrios on the Atlantic to Guatemala City.[67] Later, the Guatemalan government gave the UFC a concession to plant on 100 square kilometers of uncultivated land even as ordinary Guatemalans struggled to access land of their own.[68]

By the 1930s, the UFC was the largest single landowner, and the largest employer, in Guatemala. Much of the land it owned had been forcibly expropriated from the indigenous Maya population, with the active support of the Guatemalan state. Its workers were treated appallingly, and over the course of the 1920s and 1930s multiple strikes were organized against low wages and job cuts. Most were broken up, often with the support of the Guatemalan government.[69]

Large landowners—including the UFC—responded by supporting the candidacy of Jorge Ubico, who promised to clamp down on working-class and indigenous revolt. Ubico was a large landowner and an admirer of European fascism who had compared himself to Mussolini and Napoleon.[70] He had risen through the ranks of the Guatemalan army after studying in the US and participated in several coups before finally taking power in 1931.[71]

Ubico did not disappoint his backers, and immediately set about constructing a repressive, authoritarian regime that targeted communists and the indigenous population, while consolidating the power of landowners.[72] He handed over tracts of land to the UFC, granted it tax exemptions, and enabled the company's forced expulsions of local peasants and indigenous people.[73] Landownership was such a singularly important political issue that Ubico even passed a law that legalized execution by landowners protecting their property.[74] Also conscious of the interests of industrialists, he began construction on a number of large infrastructure projects, many of which made use of the forced labor of peasants and indigenous people.

The actions Ubico took to consolidate the power of the UFC made him a natural ally of the US, whose political leaders approved as much of his ruthless annihilation of communists and trade unionists as they did his protection of US businesses.[75] But when unrest began to mount in Guatemala during the 1940s, the US was busy dealing with the fallout of war in Europe and Japan. Cornered by the escalating power of the labor movement, and unable to rely on international support, Ubico was forced to step down. After several years of turmoil, a radical young general, Jacobo Árbenz, became the president in 1950 and quickly set about expropriating from the country's landowning elite.

Árbenz was born in 1913 to a Guatemalan mother and a Swiss German immigrant father, who became addicted to morphine a few years after Árbenz was born and later committed suicide.[76] While his early childhood had been comfortable, his father's addiction plunged the family into bankruptcy and they could not afford to send him to university.[77] But Árbenz had been an excellent student and was able to secure a military scholarship to continue his studies. His progressive ideas were formed by his experience supervising political prisoners being used as forced labor, and by his wife, who first exposed him to Marxism.[78]

While Árbenz was not a communist, he was a progressive politician and had frequent interactions with members of the Communist Party of Guatemala. When he came to power, he made it clear that his goal was not socialist revolution, but "to convert Guatemala . . . into a modern capitalist state."[79] Doing so required extensive land reform.

Under Decree 900, huge tracts of uncultivated land were transferred from Guatemala's oligarchy to landless workers and indigenous people.[80] The bill sounded radical, but only a relatively small number of plots were affected, and the owners were compensated with government bonds. The results were remarkable. One-sixth of the population received land through the redistribution process, and a state bank provided these small landowners with loans that allowed them to cultivate their land, and even to begin to invest in modern machinery.[81] Agricultural productivity—not to mention the lives of tens of thousands of people—improved dramatically.

But the reforms seriously hurt the UFC. Much of the land the company owned in Guatemala was uncultivated. The firm was sitting on thousands of hectares of idle land while peasants starved for a lack of it. The new law expropriated much of this land so it could be put to productive use. And if that wasn't bad enough, the company couldn't even access adequate compensation for its expropriated land. Compensation was tied to the official value of the land, and the UFC "had been criminally undervaluing its holdings to avoid paying taxes."[82]

The UFC responded with a coordinated campaign against the Árbenz regime in the hope of encouraging the American government to depose him.[83] The company had a number of journalists on its payroll, who set about undermining Árbenz's reputation—at home and in the US.[84] But many US congressmen were already on the company's side, as they were convinced that Árbenz was a communist and a threat to US interests in its "backyard." Many claimed Árbenz had been secretly trained in Moscow, employing a "McCarthyist logic to vilify Árbenz and his followers."[85] Within a year of his election, President Eisenhower had embarked on a plan to overthrow Árbenz, code-named PBSuccess.

The tactics used would be the same ones the CIA deployed to depose progressive leaders all over the world. They planted "boxes of rifles marked with communist hammers and sickles" as evidence of Árbenz's Soviet ties.[86] They drew up lists of government ministers and bureaucrats who would be assassinated in the wake of the coup to terrify the opposition into submission. And then they set about planning the coup itself, which they would unconvincingly try to portray as the spontaneous reaction to Arbenz's reforms.

The US found an "unimpressive" army officer[87]—Lieutenant General Carlos Castillo Armas—to front the operation, providing him with weapons and troops trained by the CIA. By June 1954, Armas and his CIA-trained men reached the Guatemalan border. At this point, Árbenz discovered the coup attempt and released the news to the Guatemalan press. But the Americans were not deterred and started to broadcast false reports of an Armas victory on US-controlled radio stations.[88] The US was using fake news as a weapon long before it hit the headlines back home.

While Armas's ragtag group of mercenaries could never hope to defeat the Guatemalan army by force, the US's clear determination to depose Árbenz led to defections within his administration and severely weakened the president. A panicked Árbenz resigned on June 27, 1954, handing power over to the head of the armed forces, convinced that the Americans would not attempt to install Armas in his place.[89] But a few days after Árbenz's resignation, the newly chosen president was informed by a local CIA representative that he was "not convenient for the requirements of American foreign policy."[90] The American ambassador later showed up at the president's house with a list of Guatemalans the US suspected of communist sympathies, informing him that these people "would need to be shot immediately."[91]

It was not long before Armas was declared president of Guatemala. The violence that his regime unleashed—with the full and active support of the United States—was unimaginable. Between three and five thousand of Árbenz's supporters were rounded up and executed.[92] Forced labor—slavery—was reinstated in parts of the country.[93] Peasants and indigenous people began organizing against the regime, and several years later these tensions exploded into a civil war, in which two hundred thousand people were killed or displaced.[94] During the war, the US-backed government also perpetrated a genocide against the indigenous Maya population that resulted in the deaths or "disappearance" of nearly thirty thousand indigenous Guatemalans.[95]

The US government wanted to send a message to poor and downtrodden people around the world: they could not hope to resist the power of American capitalism. Such a show of force was necessary because many were already trying to do so.

In 1955, at the Bandung Conference, representatives of twenty-nine peripheral states home to 55 percent of the world's population—from Indonesia, which hosted the conference, to India and China—formed what eventually became the Non-Aligned Movement.[96] The conference issued a collective statement of the right to self-determination of all states and a rejection of military, political, and economic imperialism of the kind that had been practiced in places like Guatemala.

Indonesia's president Sukarno was a key organizer of the conference. Sukarno had been born into a wealthy family—his father was an aristocrat and his mother a Balinese Brahmin Hindu—and he became involved in Indonesia's budding nationalist movement at university.[97] He was a key part of the resistance to both Dutch colonialism and the Japanese occupation of Indonesia during World War II, and after the war he became Indonesia's first president. His eclectic approach to politics, which sought to combine "Nationalism, Islam and Marxism," made him enduringly popular.[98]

Sukarno realized that resisting the US might require building links with other independence leaders to counter the power of the rich world. In this, he was aligned with Kwame Nkrumah, Ghana's charismatic independence leader and a founding member of the Non-Aligned Movement. Nkrumah's quest for independence had been based on the idea that Ghanaians must "seek ye first the political kingdom," and that all else would follow.

But he quickly discovered that political sovereignty was only half the battle. Without economic sovereignty, Ghana was condemned to be ruled by outside interests.[99] Nkrumah believed the only way to resist the power of the neocolonist was for developing nations to work together and present a united front against their former colonizers.[100]

The US knew it could not allow forceful expressions of Global South solidarity like those shown at Bandung to go unchallenged. As Vincent Bevins documents in his book *The Jakarta Method*, the US sought either to undermine or overthrow many of the leaders and regimes involved in the Non-Aligned Movement, including Indonesia's Sukarno.

Unlike Nkrumah, Sukarno was not an ideologically committed communist; he did, however, often take the same line as the Communist Party of Indonesia—then the third-largest communist party in the world—and pragmatically aligned with other peripheral socialist states in order to protect Indonesia's sovereignty.[101] All of this meant that Sukarno was seen as a threat to international capital, and therefore to the interests of the United States.

In 1967, a young Indonesian general—General Suharto—ousted Sukarno from power with the explicit support of the US. Suharto had served in a Japanese militia during the Second World War, where he became acquainted with the rigid nationalist and militaristic ideology used to indoctrinate Japanese troops.[102] As soon as he came to power, Suharto immediately set about exterminating Indonesia's communists.

The fact that the murders took place on the basis of ideology rather than race has led to disagreement about whether the conflict can be called a genocide. What is not in question is the scale of the bloodshed: "between five hundred thousand and one million people were slaughtered, and one million more were herded into concentration camps."[103] The events surrounding Suharto's seizure of power, and the murders that followed, remain shrouded in mystery. Suharto, encouraged and supported by the US, prevented journalists from reporting on the massacres. Only after his death did the true scale of the killings come to light.

The strategies used in Indonesia were replicated in socialist states all over the world, with the active or passive support of the United States. From Brazil to Chile, anti-communists began talking openly about their own "Jakarta plans." Bevins is clear about what this meant: "the state-organized extermination of civilians who opposed the construction of capitalist authoritarian regimes loyal to the United States." The next testing ground for the Jakarta Method would be Latin America, where hundreds of thousands of people would be killed or "disappeared" in the name of anti-communism over the subsequent decades.[104]

At home, the US government justified these actions—where they were revealed to the public—by claiming that it was acting to protect "freedom" by ridding the world of the communist threat. The actions taken to promote this "freedom" often involved literally exterminating communists and socialists who dared resist the power of the world's foremost empire. One historian found that the number of victims of US-backed violence in Latin America "vastly exceeded" the number of people killed in the Soviet Union and the Eastern Bloc over the same period.[105]

Why did the world's foremost imperial power find it necessary to unleash such extreme violence on some of the poorest people on the planet? To protect the structure of the capitalist world system. Had states in the Global South been allowed to band together, resist the power of the rich world, and forge their own development paths, these countries would have been far harder to exploit. The rich world needed the poor countries to remain scattered and underdeveloped—global capitalism could not function were they to unite.

And the United States has always been willing to invest in ensuring this threat never comes to fruition. In 2022, the Defense Department budget was $877 billion, or nearly 4 percent of US GDP.[106] In contrast, China, the next-largest spender, spent around $292 billion on defense in 2022, or around 1.6 percent GDP. And the US has been spending around that amount for many years now.

The fusion of public and private interests that motivates American military spending and foreign policy is often referred to as the "military-industrial complex."[107] Sprawling arms companies and private armies benefit from US imperialism and work closely within the state apparatus to start and lengthen conflicts that will allow them to win lucrative government contracts.

As private companies have become more involved in the exercise of US power abroad, it has become imperative to the US state to protect these firms, which provide most of the manpower, technology, and finance necessary to run the US's vast military. In this way, public and private corporations work together to plan US interventions, generally justifying violations of sovereignty by appealing to the need to protect "democracy" and "freedom."

Perhaps the clearest example of the planning power of the US military-industrial complex comes from Iraq. One of the first things the US government did with occupied Iraq was sell off state assets en masse.[108] In doing so, the planners of the invasion sought to share its spoils with US businesses and to introduce the disciplining hand of American capital into Iraqi society.

The next step was to introduce legislation that the *Economist* described as a "wish list that foreign investors dream of," including capping the tax rate at 15 percent and allowing investors to take unlimited sums of money out of the country.[109] Naomi Klein sees the invasion and occupation as a perfect example of the "shock doctrine" whereby crises and disasters—often caused by the parties involved—are used as a means to extract profit and embed capitalist social relations.[110]

Klein makes clear that the occupation of Iraq was planned. Iraq was chosen as a test bed for a process of imperial state-building designed to uproot an allegedly dysfunctional society and build a capitalist utopia in its place. US corporations were brought in to run the Iraqi state—including Halliburton, which had fifty thousand workers in the region, and KPMG, which was paid $240 million to build a "market-driven system" for the government.[111] Iraq's Green Zone was effectively run as a "private city-state" by Halliburton, which was charged with managing everything from building roads, to cleaning the streets, to organizing "disco nights."[112] Billions were siphoned out of the pockets of Iraqis—and Americans—to pay for this playground for corporate America.

As should be clear from the examples outlined in this chapter, the US military is the cornerstone of its power as an imperial planner. US imperialism is fundamentally about protecting the unequal structure of the capitalist world system and preventing the emergence of potential rivals to this system.[113] Private actors also benefit handsomely from America's role as the guardian of global capitalism, and this fusion of public and private interests is what makes the US military-industrial complex so enduring.

But the exercise of imperial power is about more than brute force. As we have seen, the structure of the world economy privileges the interests of capital, concentrated in the core, over workers, concentrated in the periphery. This system does not reproduce itself on its own; it must be protected and upheld by both the force of the US state and the legal and political institutions it promulgates. Where poor countries have not been subjugated to the power of capital by force, as in Guatemala, Indonesia, and Iraq, they have been given little choice other than to submit voluntarily.

The People versus Chevron

Texaco, founded in 1902 as the Texas Fuel Company, spent the 1970s and '80s dumping billions of gallons of toxic waste and crude oil into Ecuador's Amazon rainforest, creating one of the greatest ecological disasters in modern history. The spill contaminated vast swathes of the rainforest: rivers ran black, and an increase in various forms of cancer and birth defects was noted among many of the communities that populated the region.[114] The disaster has been referred to as the "Amazon Chernobyl."[115]

In 1993, thirty thousand Ecuadorians who had been affected by the disaster decided to take action against Texaco. By the time the verdict was delivered, Texaco was owned by Chevron after a merger that had created the second-largest oil company in the United States and the fourth-largest publicly traded oil company in the world. The Ecuadorians filed a class action lawsuit and, after a legal battle that lasted nearly two decades, Chevron was finally ordered to pay $9.5 billion in compensation for the disaster on behalf of Texaco.[116]

Immediately following the verdict, the company left Ecuador, selling all its assets and threatening a "lifetime of litigation" if the government ever attempted to collect the money it was owed.[117] The company had form. In 2008, it won a case against a group of plaintiffs "seeking to hold it responsible for the fatal shooting of protesters on an offshore oil platform in Nigeria."[118] When Chevron won the case, it tried to claw back legal fees from the widows and children of those who had been killed.

In 2009, Chevron launched an investor-state dispute settlement (ISDS) claim against the Ecuadorian government in the hope of reversing the outcome of the case. ISDS provisions are written into many international trade and investment treaties, providing protections for investors concerned about governments using their democratic prerogatives to tax, regulate, and prosecute corporations.[119] Under ISDS provisions, investors can take governments to court for unpredictable changes in policy that run contrary to their interests; for example, Philip Morris—the global tobacco company—launched an ISDS in a failed attempt to sue the Australian government after it introduced plain packaging on cigarettes. Most cases are resolved in favor of large multinational corporations and powerful states, while poor countries lose out.[120]

Chevron also launched a campaign of targeted intimidation against the lawyer for the Ecuadorian plaintiffs, Steven Donziger. They hired private investigators to follow him, smeared him in the press, and spent millions trying to bring him down through the legal system.[121] The company argued that the initial verdict had been obtained through fraud and accused Donziger of racketeering under legislation initially introduced to target mobsters.[122] Shortly before the suit went to trial, Chevron dropped the demand for monetary damages, thus denying Donziger the right to a jury trial.[123]

Instead, Chevron accused Donziger of fraud, relying on the findings of a single judge who frequently ruled in favor of large corporations and has been accused of "implacable hostility" toward Donziger.[124] In a highly unusual move, the judge, Lewis Kaplan, allowed Chevron to bring anonymous witnesses, violating "basic legal principles."[125] He even barred the defense from mentioning "pollution in Ecuador" on the grounds that it was not relevant to the case.[126] Ultimately, Kaplan accepted a disgraced Ecuadorian judge who had received more than $2 million in cash and gifts from Chevron as a witness.[127] It was this judge—Antonio Guerra—who confirmed Chevron's accusations of fraud and bribery.

But Guerra later admitted that he had lied and recanted his story.[128] In response, Kaplan said he would have come to the same verdict without the judge's evidence.[129] Later investigations revealed that "there [was] no evidence to corroborate allegations of a bribe or a ghostwritten judgment, and that large parts of his sworn testimony . . . were exaggerated and, in other cases, simply not true."[130] The entire case was full of irregularities and breaches of normal legal proceedings. As one Harvard Law School professor put it, "[Donziger] has effectively been convicted of bribery by the finding of a single judge in a case in which bribery wasn't even the charge."

In another strange set of legal proceedings, Kaplan ordered Donziger to hand over his phone and laptop, which Donziger argued would violate attorney-client privilege.[131] As a result, Kaplan charged Donziger with contempt of court and placed him in "forced confinement," which left him trapped in his house indefinitely. The US attorney had refused to follow through on Kaplan's contempt of court proceedings, so he appointed a private firm to bring the case instead—a firm that had previously represented Chevron.[132]

The trial destroyed Donziger's life. He spent two and a half years under house arrest; his bank accounts were frozen and he was prohibited from earning money; his passport was seized and he faces huge legal fines.[133] When Donziger lost the case, he also lost his law license and was sentenced to six months in prison: a powerful warning to anyone who dared to stand up to the might of the fossil-fuel companies and their protectors within the state.

The ISDS case launched by Chevron in 2009 was ultimately resolved in the company's favor in 2018.[134] The tribunal ordered the Ecuadorian government to prevent the courts from enforcing the earlier judgment. Chevron has also pushed for the Ecuadorian government to be forced to pay $800 million of the company's legal costs.[135] The campaigning organization War on Want called the case "unprecedented" in "directly overturning a democratically accountable national court judgement."[136]

ISDSs are part of a growing body of international law that, with the active support of powerful states, has helped to routinize corporate crime on a mass scale.[137] The international system contains a "massive, powerful, and still largely hidden body of international rules that companies are using to chill government action, coerce policy outcomes, oppose enforcement of legitimate policy measure, and ultimately sue governments if their demands aren't satisfied."[138] ISDSs are included in thousands of bilateral trade and investment treaties, creating a "parallel system of justice" that is "heavily biased" toward large corporations, and in which ordinary citizens foot the bill for lengthy legal battles.[139]

Even the capitalist journal *The Economist* balked at the introduction of ISDS provisions, writing, "If you wanted to convince the public that international trade agreements are a way to let multinational companies get rich at the expense of ordinary people, this is what you would do: give foreign firms a special right to apply to a secretive tribunal of highly paid corporate lawyers for compensation whenever a government passes a law to, say, discourage smoking, protect the environment or prevent a nuclear catastrophe. Yet that is precisely what thousands of trade and investment treaties over the past half century have done."[140]

Over the last several decades, ISDS provisions have been used successfully to defeat the democratic process in a number of cases:

- Ethyl Corp sued the Canadian government when it attempted to introduce a law banning toxic chemical methylcyclopentadienyl. The government withdrew the ban and paid $13 million to the corporation.
- Metalclad Corp sued the government of Mexico after it refused to issue the company with a permit to build a waste disposal facility as a result of health and environmental concerns. The government was forced to pay $16.79 million.
- Vattenfall sued the German government for the introduction of legislation designed to protect rivers from the impact of the company's coal-fired power plants. The government was forced to water down the legislation.[141]

In one case, documented in the incredible book *The Water Defenders*, campaigners battling to prevent gold mining in El Salvador defeated an international mining giant in an ISDS case.[142] In other areas, similar operations had led to the introduction of toxic chemicals into local water supplies, leading to severe health issues—from kidney failure, to cancer, to nervous system disorders. The campaign succeeded, and the government called a halt to gold mining in the country. But the mining company that stood to lose most from this decision, Pacific Rim, took the Salvadorean government to court in response. The book describes the terrifying and bloody ordeal that took place over the course of subsequent years as Pacific Rim, armies of corporate lawyers, and hired thugs sought to terrorize the water defenders into submission. In a rare victory, the campaigners won—in part due to their concerted campaign, but in part simply due to luck.

The international courts system has allowed democracies to become "encased" in a system of treaties and laws that severely limits the power of national governments to impose any legislation that will harm the interests of international capital.[143] Neoliberals justified the construction of this system on the basis that it would protect "free markets." But this apolitical language disguised what was in fact a deeply political project to maintain the dominance of the world's most powerful countries, and the capitalists based in these countries, over the vast majority of people on the planet. International law is, in the final instance, made by and for international capital.[144]

ISDSs are just one part of the system of rules and norms developed at the international level to keep poor countries poor, and rich countries rich.[145] The so-called international rules-based system was designed to promote the power and wealth of rich countries at the expense of poor ones.[146] And this system was constructed through the politics of the shock doctrine.

In June 1981, the chairman of the US Federal Reserve, Paul Volcker, hiked interest rates to an astonishing 20 percent. The Volcker shock—described by Leo Panitch and Sam Gindin as a "founding moment" in the history of neoliberalism[147]—was initially not especially popular with anyone outside Wall Street. Unemployment shot up to 10.8 percent by 1982, and the ensuing recession harmed profits, as well as pushing up the deficit.[148]

But Volcker had a plan. His goal was to convince financial markets that the Fed had the power—and the courage—to tame inflation for good by destroying the unions demanding higher wages. Volcker is remembered as a hero among neoliberals for bringing down inflation by engineering a recession that helped permanently to curb the power of the US labor movement. The Volcker shock is an excellent example of neoliberal planning: Volcker created a recession that institutionalized the power of capital over labor while claiming to be following the laws of the free market.[149]

But the Volcker shock didn't just change the US economy; it had repercussions all over the world. With interest rates so much higher in the US than elsewhere, money flooded into US financial markets to take advantage of higher returns, leaving many other countries in deep debt distress.[150] This trend was, in itself, an example of imperialism—the US was using its power over the global economy to solve its own domestic class conflicts, forcing other states into debt distress. The same process is taking place all across the world economy today. As the Federal Reserve raises interest rates to engineer a slowdown that will prevent workers from demanding higher wages, money is being sucked out of poor countries to take advantage of these higher rates, pushing many nations to the brink of bankruptcy.

In the era following the Volcker shock, the US also sought to dominate poor countries in more overt ways as well. The international financial institutions set up in the wake of the Second World War, like the IMF and the World Bank, were mobilized to provide debt relief for poor countries in crisis in the 1980s. But the US used its sway within these institutions to influence the nature of the "support" being offered to these countries, forcing them to adopt policies that would align with US interests in exchange for emergency financial assistance.[151] In this way, "the international debt crisis was methodically leveraged to advance the Chicago School agenda."[152]

The World Bank and the IMF, with US support, offered loans to poor countries on the condition that these struggling states remove capital and exchange controls, privatize state-owned industries, and remove subsidies for necessities like fuel and food, among other things. Neoliberal economists claimed that these "structural adjustment programs" (SAPs) would encourage growth by replacing inefficient import-substituting industrialization programs with a strategy of "export-led growth."[153] Many believed that shifting from protectionism to free trade, while liberalizing domestic markets, would allow low-income countries to achieve the kind of "takeoff" predicted by Walt Rostow.

But as dependency theorists like Prebisch would have predicted, these measures failed, deepening inequalities between rich and poor countries.[154] Trade liberalization simply made it easier for predatory multinational corporations to enter the economies of the Global South and displace domestic capitalists before reshoring profits to the Global North. Meanwhile, domestic producers faced large barriers to exporting their goods on a global market weighted toward core countries, in part due to the protectionism of the rich world.[155]

Financial liberalization gave rise to immense financial instability, and austerity increased poverty and inequality.[156] The plans also made it easier for elites to siphon their cash out of their countries into tax havens, undermining democracy.[157] The financialization of the world economy "facilitated the outward flow of capital from developing countries."[158] One IMF economist later admitted that "everything we did from 1983 onward was based on our new sense of mission to have the south 'privatized' or die; toward this end we ignominiously created economic bedlam in Latin America and Africa."[159]

For most of the world's poorest states, the results were disastrous, especially in Nkrumah's home in sub-Saharan Africa.[160] The poor world did not have the productive base to withstand the overwhelming power of foreign capital. Multinational corporations entered these countries, bought up national assets, and reshored profits back to the Global North. By 2004, per capita GDP across sub-Saharan Africa was less than half of what it was in 1974.[161] As a result, the size of these nations' debts only increased relative to their GDP. The programs also sharply increased inequality, as well as pushing millions of people further into poverty.[162]

In East Asia, in the wake of a financial crisis that had had devastating consequences for both economic and human development, structural adjustment added insult to injury. The Asian financial crisis of 1997 was the direct result of financial globalization, pushed by Western states and the international financial institutions they dominated, yet the blame was placed on the governments of the Asian countries themselves.[163] Many of these states had managed to achieve impressive rates of growth and poverty reduction, in part through the support that had been provided by the state to certain industrial sectors.[164] As Joseph Stiglitz points out, these countries had succeeded precisely because they defied many Washington Consensus policies pushed by the IMF.[165]

Yet the crisis was used by the international financial institutions as a stick with which to beat these economies into submission. Bailouts were provided, but most of the benefit accrued to the foreign banks that had been lending to these governments.[166] Meanwhile, extremely harsh austerity programs were imposed and were associated with a dramatic increase in poverty and inequality.[167] In South Korea—one of the poster children for structural adjustment—researchers found that businesses gained most from structural adjustment while the labor force had to shoulder most of the costs.[168] The unemployment rate rose by a factor of four in Korea, a factor of three in Thailand, and a shocking factor of ten in Indonesia.[169] Urban poverty in Korea tripled, while in Indonesia it doubled.[170]

The fall of the Berlin Wall allowed the international financial institutions to expand into what had previously been known as the "second world." The results of neoliberal shock therapy there, championed by allegedly progressive economists like Jeffrey Sachs, who later stated that the reforms had been a mistake, are now well known. In Russia, swift and careless privatizations allowed the wealthy to buy up state-owned assets on the cheap and created a powerful oligarchy with a stranglehold over the nation's economy.[171] Over the long term, privatization in Russia has been disastrous: "general economic collapse, combined with the deterioration of infrastructure, the lack of credit, and the inability of the state to provide a crime-free environment, has kept foreign direct investment out and new legitimate enterprise formation to a minimum."[172]

Even in Poland, which is traditionally held up as a success story for the reforms, unemployment and inequality increased drastically under the Balcerowicz Plan. The government that had implemented the plan was pushed out of power not long after its introduction. Ukraine's economy has been devastated over the course of successive rounds of structural adjustment: even before the Russian invasion, its GDP per capita was, in purchasing-power-parity terms, 20 percent lower than it was in 1990.[173]

As Joseph Stiglitz put it: "The results of the policies enforced by Washington Consensus have not been encouraging: for most countries embracing its tenets development has been slow, and where growth has occurred, the benefits have not been shared equally; crises have been mismanaged; the transition from communism to a market economy . . . has been a disappointment."[174]

But the negative economic impact of structural adjustment should not have come as a surprise. Rather than promoting growth or development, structural adjustment was designed to signal the "predictability" of poor nations' policies to investors and creditors.[175] Much like the move to central bank independence, it was designed to insulate state policy from democratic accountability and ensure that "economic populism" did not undermine capital accumulation. In other words, the Western development agenda became a kind of "anti-politics machine," in which the whims of "experts" substituted for democratic deliberation.[176] Whether this new regime promoted development was, at best, a secondary consideration.

One thing that structural adjustment did not do was reduce the power of the state.[177] The astonishing acceleration of globalization that took place over the course of the second half of the twentieth century was not, as some have argued, based on the triumph of global markets *over* nation-states. It rather represented the extension of an American imperialism, in which the US state acted as the major champion and protector of capitalist interests in the US and around the world.[178]

The neoliberals have always portrayed their proposals as attempts to embed freedom and liberal democracy. And yet, when people have not chosen the right outcome, neoliberal policies have been forced upon them anyway. The divide between authoritarian statist societies and democratic market ones, which was emphasized by thinkers like Hayek, turns out not to be much of a divide at all. Whether by frustrating democracy, or by supporting authoritarianism, capital tends to find a way to bend the state—and the market—to its will.

In fact, all over the world, neoliberal thinkers have supported authoritarian regimes in the name of "freedom." As we'll see in the next section, the neoliberals have often rallied behind ruthless autocrats in the hope of insulating national economic policy from democratic pressures. The neoliberal project, at the global level, has been about "encasing" the rules that protect capital—even if that means sacrificing the thing neoliberals claim to value most: freedom.

The Human Right to Capital Flight

Apartheid South Africa was a grossly unequal and racist society, within which the population was divided into four main groups, each of which comprised a separate "nation": white, Black, colored, and Indian. Marriage between different races was restricted, the right to vote was limited to "whites," and Black populations were relocated to "townships" or "locations" to enforce their separation from the rest of society. Eventually, the government sought to create several separate "homelands," or Bantustans, for Black citizens, with the aim of developing a series of separate, ethnically homogeneous nation-states.

The system of apartheid lasted until 1994 when, after years of resistance and struggle, it was slowly dismantled. That same year South Africa's first genuinely democratic elections were held and the African

National Congress (ANC) came to power. The fact that such a visible system of institutionalized racism had continued to exist so long into the twentieth century remains a source of confusion to liberals, many of whom continue to see the system as a uniquely African one—that is, one that no "civilized" person could ever have supported.

But the rewriting of the history of apartheid South Africa as an atavistic hangover from a bygone era ignores the extensive support the apartheid government enjoyed around the world right up until the moment it fell. Wilhelm Röpke, one of the founders of the neoliberal movement, whom we met in chapter 6, was "the single most high-profile champion for white South Africa."[179]

While many in liberal circles know Röpke for his championing of what is now known in Germany as the "social market economy," his views on race have been written out of his official biography. He firmly believed in the inferiority of the Black race and supported apartheid. He described the "South African Negro" as "a man of an utterly different race" who "stems from a completely different type and level of civilization."[180] Röpke also diverged from other liberals in the 1960s when he supported the unilateral declaration of independence made by apartheid Rhodesia.

But Röpke's views were not motivated by racism alone. He, along with many of his fellow neoliberals, believed that it was imperative to protect the rules governing the economy from unfettered democracy.[181] Many neoliberals believed that Black South Africans, who like many other formerly colonized peoples had not been socialized into the necessary reverence for liberal rules and norms, couldn't be trusted with the vote. Some neoliberals defended apartheid on the grounds that, as Quinn Slobodian put it, "democracy might have to be restricted for certain peoples in order to preserve stability and prosperity."[182]

As we'll see, the attitude toward democracy in South Africa was part of a wider neoliberal project to "encase" democracy around the world. The specter of decolonization hung heavy in the minds of neoliberals, who saw the attempts at international solidarity of the kind practiced in Bandung as a threat to their project.[183] How could billions of the world's poorest people be enfranchised without upsetting the delicate balance of power between capital and labor?

Far from seeking to limit the scope of state power, the neoliberals actively sought to construct a system of international rules and norms—supervised by the world's most powerful capitalist states—that would prevent the emergence of economic democracy and consolidate the power of rich countries over poor.[184] This system was meant to institutionalize a separation between economics and politics at the level of the world economy. South Africa's Bantustans were the perfect incarnation of this logic. They allowed the apartheid government superficially to accede to demands for self-government, providing some Black South African subjects with the appearance of national sovereignty.

But the boundaries of this sovereignty would be predetermined by the South African government, and, crucially, the ownership of the most valuable land and natural resources would be jealously guarded by white South Africans, who were seen as the only people disciplined and civilized enough to respect the rule of the market. Enforcing this kind of separation would require a strong state capable of resisting popular pressure, just like the one found in apartheid South Africa.

As we saw in the introduction, the neoliberals believed they were fighting a war against nationalistic economic planning. Hayek in particular seemed to have been gripped by a kind of revolutionary zeal in his battle against "serfdom." And yet even his vision of the world required its own form of planning, one that was explicitly antidemocratic in nature.

Hayek was adamant that his new world order would not be based on any "architectural design" or "blueprints"—it would instead be based on the impersonal logic of the Highway Code. Yet while he may often have discouraged active intervention in the national economy, he had no problem with powerful capitalist states, corporations, or financial institutions bending poor states to their will.[185]

One of the most powerful mechanisms through which these inequalities have been enforced is through the international financial system. The laws and norms of international finance are, as we saw in chapter 5, determined by a constellation of powerful public and private actors and enforced through both domestic and international courts.[186] During the 1980s, the neoliberals sought to construct a regulatory architecture at the international level that would institutionalize the "human right to capital flight" by ensuring that investors were always able to leave poor countries, taking their cash with them.[187]

The idea was that potentially unruly new nations could be inoculated against "economic nationalism" through capital mobility, which would allow the wealthy and large corporations to move their money out of any country that threatened property rights. The threat of capital flight has been a powerful tool used by core states and multinational corporations against poor countries. Chevron, for example, fled Ecuador in the wake of the early court ruling against it, selling all its assets and taking its cash with it. And this tactic has proved particularly easy to use on the very poorest countries in the world—countries like Zambia.

When Zambia gained independence in 1964, it was heavily dependent upon copper exports, and at the time, its copper mines were owned by foreign corporations.[188] To ensure the country benefited from its natural resource wealth, the Zambian government nationalized large sections of the industry and imposed taxes on the foreign miners.[189] These taxes ended up capturing the majority of the profits from the exploitation of the country's copper, and these new government revenues were channeled into building infrastructure, expanding public services, and subsidizing basic necessities like food and fuel.[190]

But Zambia was in a race against time, and it hadn't been able to develop its domestic industry quickly enough to insulate itself from the commodities crash when it finally came. Copper prices fell sharply over the course of the 1970s and '80s—in part a result of the economic crisis generated by the Volcker shock—and this plunged Zambia into a deep crisis.[191] Employment and output fell and taxes dried up, leading to a debt crisis: external debt rose from $814 million to $3.244 billion over the course of the 1970s, and then doubled again to $6.916 billion by the end of the 1980s.[192] As the dependency theorists had warned, if a state like Zambia couldn't diversify from a dependence on the export of volatile commodities, then it would lurch from crisis to crisis without ever building up the capital needed for sustainable development.

In exchange for emergency lending, the government was forced to cut public spending, devalue the currency, raise interest rates, and reduce subsidies on necessities.[193] Successive currency devaluations proved particularly regressive, as without much international demand for copper, they did little to stimulate export earnings. Instead, devaluations increased the price of imports, particularly food.[194]

Developmentalism was finally abandoned in the late 1980s, quashing what remained of Zambian industry. At the nadir of global copper prices, under pressure from the international financial institutions, the US-friendly president Frederick Chiluba sold off most of the Zambian copper sector on the cheap to international investors.[195] The multinationals that purchased these assets knew they were getting an excellent deal, yet the government still offered the companies generous tax breaks to ensure the negotiations were wrapped up quickly, in line with the wishes of the World Bank and the IMF.[196] By 1996, 223 state-owned companies had been privatized.[197]

Throughout the privatization process, both the Zambian government and the international investors seeking to buy its assets were being advised by large international banks and law firms based in the rich world.[198] The government was also under immense pressure from the international financial institutions from which it was borrowing, then gripped by a relentless drive for privatization. While the World Bank was holding the Zambian privatization process up as a model for the rest of the world, keener observers were criticizing the process for the "looting, deindustrialization, deepening debt and increasing poverty that would emanate from it."

The newly privatized, and now foreign-owned, corporations were—and are—able to avoid substantial amounts of tax through loopholes and deductions. This tax avoidance, combined with the low tax rates the government had imposed and financial deregulation, meant that profits were sucked out of the country and into the pockets of shareholders in the rich world.[199] What's more—and as has been the case with IMF- and World Bank–driven privatization programs all over the world—domestic elites walked away from the process with substantial kickbacks, generating visible inequalities that remain a source of resentment in Zambia to this day.

Privatization meant that most Zambians did not benefit from the rebound in copper prices seen after the 1990s.[200] Per capita GDP fell from $1,455 in 1976 to $1,037 by 1987, and the trade deficit continued to increase throughout the 1990s.[201] The percentage of the population that is undernourished increased by 5 percentage points to 50 percent between 1990 and 2001.[202] Over the same period, the country fell thirty-three places in the UN's Human Development Rankings.[203] Yet the pressure for privatization and austerity from the international financial institutions has not abated, with the IMF demanding that the government follow through with a pledge to privatize the state-owned electricity company and the public bank, under the threat of losing $1 billion in development aid.[204]

Thanks to the decimation of the rest of the economy over the course of the 1980s and '90s, by the time the 2008 financial crisis hit, copper accounted for 80 percent of Zambia's exports.[205] While the Zambian economy had very little exposure to the banks that caused the crisis, this didn't stop it from being knocked back by the crash in commodities prices that followed.[206] The country suffered from higher unemployment and inflation, lower government revenues, and a loss of foreign exchange. As money flowed out of the country, the Zambian government once again found itself unable to service its liabilities to international creditors.[207]

It was at this point that international capital began to turn the screws on Zambia. First, the pressure came from the mining companies. As the government entered negotiations with its creditors, the foreign-owned mining sector stepped up an "intense" lobbying effort to cut its tax liabilities.[208] The government caved and cut taxes on the sector, as well as giving in to numerous demands for greater allowances, which will make it even easier for the mining companies to avoid what little tax they still owe.[209]

Then the vultures swooped in. In 2007, just as Zambia was concluding an international negotiation to write down a portion of its debt, Donegal International—a vulture fund located in the British Virgin Islands—bought $3.3 million of the outstanding debt, sure that Zambia would be unable to repay.[210] The company then sued Zambia for $55 million for reneging on the loan, winning $15.5 million in compensation.[211] As one Zambian official pointed out, paying compensation to Donegal meant that "the treatment, the Medicare, the medicines that would have been available to in excess of 100,000 people in the country will not be available."[212] By 2019, many Zambians were actually worse off than they had been in the 1980s.

States like Zambia have been continuously promised that if they only follow the prescriptions of the World Bank and the IMF, they will "catch up" with the Global North. Opening up one's economy is supposed to lead to financial inflows that support development, as mainstream economic models assume that this investment flows from rich countries to poor ones.[213]

Yet since the 1980s—when capital mobility was institutionalized—the volume of investment flowing *out* of the Global South has exceeded that flowing into it.[214] In part, this is because Western financial institutions have helped elites in the Global South siphon money out of their home nations to avoid tax and expropriation.[215] Putin's henchmen, for example, kept a lot of their money in London property, confident that no British government would dare touch it. Another factor is the artificial inflation of returns in the rich world.[216] Investors have little incentive to park their cash in long-term infrastructure projects in Zambia when they can get double the return by buying up property or financial assets in London—assets that can be sold at any time.

In fact, neoliberal theorists like Röpke never much cared if poor countries "caught up" with rich ones.[217] Röpke saw it as necessary that the Global South be kept in a position of underdevelopment in order to prevent "overindustrialization and underagriculturization of the world." Capital mobility was central to this project. If international investors could not threaten to pack up and leave at the slightest hint of developmentalist economic policy, then how could "rogue" states be disciplined into adopting neoliberalism?

Röpke's arguments perfectly summarized the critique of neocolonialism leveled by thinkers like Kwame Nkrumah, who believed that the Global North actively sought to keep the Global South in a position of permanent underdevelopment. As we've seen, the institutionalization of capital mobility was, from the start, part of a strategy designed to keep states in the Global South from realizing true political and economic independence. By enforcing a "human right to capital flight," the neoliberals ensured that international investors would punish any country that failed to abide by their policy agenda.

But this kind of neoliberal planning, because it is couched in the language of law and norms, is rendered invisible to most observers. The policies advocated by neoliberals are presented as mechanisms to protect the free market from the overbearing power of the state, even as—

in private—neoliberal thinkers have described the need for strong, often highly authoritarian governments to promote the interests of capital.

The neoliberal vision for the capitalist world system should not be understood as one premised on the absence of planning, but as one premised upon a different kind of planning: invisible planning in service of capital.

This system was, of course, constructed under the watchful eye of the United States.[218] And the world's foremost imperial power has not been above exploiting its role at the center of the international financial system to promote its own interests, and those of international capital. We've already seen how the response to the 2008 financial crisis ended up entrenching unfairness and inequality in the American economy, but it also served to embed US dominance over global finance—underpinned by the immense power of the dollar.[219]

The US dollar is the world's reserve currency. Central banks around the world hold a significant portion of their reserves in dollars—today around 60 percent of all reserves are held in dollars, though this is down significantly from 71 percent in 2001.[220] Many international transactions take place in dollars; for example, since the 1970s Saudi Arabian oil exports have been priced in dollars, creating a cycle of petrodollars in which the US purchases oil from the Saudis and the Saudis use the resulting dollars to buy weapons from US companies.[221] And many non-US governments and corporations borrow in dollars because doing so insulates their lenders from currency risk.

Why is the dollar still so central to the world's financial system? Because dollars, and assets denominated in dollars like US Treasuries, are seen as some of the safest assets in the world. Until recently, few investors have worried about the ability of the US government to repay its debts, and most remain confident that the United States will do what it needs to do to ensure the proper functioning of the dollar-based international financial system. In essence, people trust the dollar because they trust the planning power of the American government—for as long as the US's economic and military power seems unassailable, so too does its currency.

The 2008 financial crisis, despite originating in the US, actually worked to strengthen the dollar's role in international finance.[222] The key mechanism through which the dollar's power was strengthened was the establishment of "swap lines" between the Federal Reserve and a select group of central banks around the world. When the crisis hit, central banks needed to access dollars to bail out their domestic banks, many of which had accrued massive dollar-denominated liabilities. But top central bankers soon realized they didn't have enough dollars to plug the hole.

In response, the United States engaged in an innovative kind of planning designed to prop up global capitalism, and the dollar's role at its center. The Federal Reserve set up swap lines with several of the world's major central banks—from the Bank of England to the Bank of Japan, to the European Central Bank (ECB). These swap lines allowed central banks to borrow dollars cheaply in order to shore up their domestic financial system. The US Federal Reserve was, as Panitch and Gindin put it, "acting as the world central bank."[223]

Such overt imperial planning directly contradicted the rhetoric of noninterventionism that underpinned the Washington Consensus policies the US had helped force on so many other states. And it showed quite clearly that global capitalism was a system "not of limited but of big government, of massive executive action, of interventionism."[224]

But only certain governments—those deemed important US allies— were able to access this funding. The Fed had "hand-picked a group of core central banks to issue dollar credits on demand."[225] In deciding which banks were able to access dollars, the Fed was able to reinforce the uneven structure of the capitalist world system. While the Bank of England and the ECB dished out billions in aid to their domestic banks, countries like Zambia were being sued in international courts by vulture funds hoping to squeeze as much money out of one of the world's poorest states as possible.

Whether through the secretive system of international courts, international institutions that exploit crises to force neoliberal policies on poor states, or a financial system designed to discipline disobedient governments into submission, the international rules-based system restricts and undermines development. This is not a problem for the businesses that profit from the exploitation of poor countries and their people. In fact, were it not for these inequalities between the rich and poor worlds, global capitalism could not exist.

Empire is, in this sense, about more than formal colonization—it refers to all the ways in which the world's most powerful countries and the international institutions they dominate plan economic activity at the level of the global economy. The international financial system was constructed and designed quite self-consciously by neoliberals who, while claiming to abhor planning of any kind, were quite happy to support planning that protected the interests of capitalists in the rich world.

But maybe the neoliberals were not being completely cynical when they claimed to champion the ideals of freedom and democracy. Maybe they just thought these things should only ever be available to people like them.

PART III

DEMOCRATIC PLANNING

8

The Architect and the Bee: How to Plan Democratically

In January 1976, workers at the Lucas Aerospace Corporation produced one of the most radical documents in Britain's economic history. The Alternative Plan for Lucas Aerospace—known as the Lucas Plan—was a bold strategy to reorient the company away from the production of weapons toward the production of socially useful commodities. Management had spent the previous decade trying to "rationalize" the sprawling enterprise, introducing successive restructuring plans, all of which included mass layoffs.[1]

By the 1970s, the company was struggling to compete with emerging aerospace giants in the US, Japan, and Europe. Some hoped for a last-minute nationalization, but the UK economy wasn't exactly in rude health either, and workers quickly realized that nationalization was not on the table.[2] The message was clear: Lucas's fate would be decided by "the market." Trade unionists from across the organization went to Tony Benn, one of the foremost democratic socialists on the British left, then the secretary of state for industry. He reaffirmed that nationalization was not in the cards, but gave the workers another suggestion: Why not come up with their own plan to save the firm?[3]

At first, the unionists wrote to academics, policymakers, and local officials seeking advice, but only three bothered to respond.[4] So, they went to the workers for ideas instead. The response was astounding. Lucas's workers came up with hundreds of ideas about how to transform the company into a viable, and socially useful, organization. More than 150 ideas for new products were brought together in the final document, which also contained detailed information about the human and technical resources the firm could draw on, market analysis, and a step-by-step plan for transitioning to the new way of working.[5]

The ideas workers proposed were divided into six categories: "medical equipment, transport vehicles, improved braking systems, energy conservation, oceanics, and telechiric [robotic arms] machines."[6] Some examples included expanding production of kidney dialysis machines, constructing wind turbines, researching solar-cell technology, and developing hybrid power for cars. These were extraordinarily radical and farsighted ideas at a time when human-induced climate change was only first being discussed.

Management was stunned, as were many ministers in the government. Workers from across the organization had banded together, overcoming the geographical, technical, and cultural barriers that divided them, to create a plan that would simultaneously save their jobs, transform Lucas Aerospace, and capture the imaginations of working people all over the world. For this reason, the plan was rejected by the firm's senior managers, who could not wrap their heads around the idea that the workers they were used to controlling could demonstrate such ingenuity. The leaders at Lucas Aerospace preferred to see their organization die rather than hand it over to the workers.

As one MP put it: "It took the shop stewards three years to meet the management to discuss the corporate plan, because they were challenging the hierarchical nature of our society, which is that the bosses shall make the decisions and the workers shall accept them, and woe betide workers who question those decisions and perhaps even produce better ones."[7]

The Lucas Plan was an extraordinarily ambitious document that challenged the foundations of capitalism. In place of an institution designed to generate profits via the domination of labor by capital, the workers at Lucas Aerospace had developed an entirely new model for the firm—one based on the democratic production of socially useful commodities. It was almost as if the workers had never needed managing at all, as though they were creative architects rather than obedient bees.

In fact, a trade union leader at Lucas, Mike Cooley, later wrote a book entitled *Architect or Bee? The Human Price of Technology*. Cooley was an Irish engineer at Lucas and one of the architects of the Lucas Plan. He was such an effective union leader that Lucas fired him in 1981 for spending too much time on union business.[8] But, as we will see later in this chapter, Cooley continued his work on socially useful production with the Greater London Enterprise Board. He is remembered as a pioneer of the "human-centered design" movement. In 2018, in the foreword to Cooley's book *Delinquent Genius: The Strange Affair of Man and His Technology*, Irish president Michael D. Higgins referred to him as "the most intelligent Irishman, the most morally engaged scientist and technologist Ireland has sent abroad."[9]

Cooley had a view of "ordinary people" that was diametrically opposed to that of thinkers like both Hayek and Keynes. In fact, he believed he had never met an "ordinary" person in his life.[10] Everyone he knew, all the people with whom he worked, had "extraordinary . . . skills, abilities and talents," as the Lucas Plan showed. For Cooley, the great crime of capitalism is that "those talents [are] never used or developed or encouraged."[11]

Cooley's democratic socialism fit with the spirit of the times of the 1970s. The new social movements, which had emerged from the protest movements of 1968, were challenging traditional hierarchies in the Labour Party, the labor movement, and society more generally.[12] Rank-and-file workers were disappointed with what little progress had been made on wages, working conditions, and the broader political demands made by the unions after a decade of successive Labour governments. Both groups were increasingly disillusioned with the top-down, bureaucratic approach to nationalization that had become characteristic of the postwar consensus.

Many on the New Left saw worker democracy as a way to bridge the gap between the protest movements of 1968 and the institutional strength of the labor movement.[13] Meanwhile, many on the "Old Left" saw the plan as a way to reinvigorate the tired postwar consensus. The peace movement saw it as an example of how to destroy the military-industrial complex without alienating workers.[14] Farsighted environmentalists saw it as a model for transitioning to a green economy without any job losses.[15] And everyone from Marxists to anarchists saw it as a fantastic example of how to build worker power and socialize production without the support of the capitalist state. Even more liberal-minded commentators conceded that the workers at Lucas Aerospace had achieved something quite remarkable.[16]

In this time of turbulence, the actions of the workers at Lucas Aerospace were like a lightning rod for radicals everywhere. While the British political class played up the threats to order and stability posed by weed-smoking hippies and striking workers with Soviet sympathies, the British Left coalesced around the Lucas Plan as a very real and practical example of what could be achieved when working people drew on their collective skills, solidarity, and creativity.

Then came 1979. In her first term, Margaret Thatcher radically re-structured the UK economy. She waged war on the UK's unions, while also privatizing whole swathes of the public sector and releasing finan-cial capital from the chains imposed by the postwar consensus.[17] The shift in government undermined the labor movement in general, and the Lucas Plan specifically.[18] Cooley was "effectively sacked" for his activi-ties in 1981 and the plan foundered.[19]

Where the workers behind the Lucas Plan had laid the foundations for the development of an economy that respected the dignity, creativity, and autonomy of workers, Thatcher used her control over the state to ruthlessly reassert the power of capital over labor. Cloaking her project in the language of freedom and autonomy, she crushed one of the most innovative and ingenious examples of democratic production the world had ever seen. The success of the neoliberal movement ensured that "in-dividualized consumerism rather than collective services and a democ-ratized state and economy became the main legacy of working-class struggles during the twentieth century."[20]

In 1996, after successive rounds of reorganization and restructuring, Lucas merged with an American company to form LucasVarity PLC, which immediately announced cost-cutting measures that led to three thousand job losses.[21] Three years later, the merger was reversed when LucasVarity was purchased by the US company TRW, which carved up and stripped the company in the shareholder value revolution of the 1990s.[22] Around the turn of the century, Lucas Aerospace was acquired by TRW Aeronautical Systems, and two years later it was sold to US man-ufacturing company Goodrich Corporation.[23] In 2012, Goodrich was ac-quired by United Technologies for $16.5 billion, which merged Goodrich with an existing subsidiary to form UTC Aerospace Systems.[24]

A few years later, United Technologies, the parent company of UTC Aerospace, had something of a shock when a plane for which it had provided many components nose-dived out of the sky. United supplied Boeing with avionics, cabin components, and mechanical systems for the 737 MAX, and one of its subsidiaries—Rosemount—had supplied Boeing with the faulty angle-of-attack sensors that had played a role in the two crashes.[25] A month after the Ethiopian Airlines crash, United announced that it could lose $80 million in earnings as a result of Boeing's decision to cut production of the 737 MAX.

In 2018, United Technologies acquired Rockwell Collins and merged UTC Aerospace Systems—the part of the company that can trace its lineage back to Lucas Aerospace—to form Collins Aerospace.[26] Collins continued to have a strong relationship with Boeing, providing inputs for its Boeing Business Jet 737 MAX—the private version of the 737 MAX.[27] In 2020, UTC merged with Raytheon Technologies, one of the largest multinational aerospace and defense conglomerates on the planet.[28]

What was once Lucas Aerospace, whose workers had been at the forefront of a movement to create a new mode of production based on democracy, sustainability, and social utility, had by the early twenty-first century become a subsidiary of Raytheon, a sprawling American conglomerate deeply enmeshed in the military-industrial complex that was supplying corporate jet parts to a company whose unbridled greed led it to manufacture planes that fell out of the sky. There is no better illustration of the two paths we faced as a planet during the 1970s: total domination by capital, or sustainable, socialized, democratic production.

The economy that produced the 737 Max disasters is no less centrally planned than that which produced the Lucas Plan; the main difference is that fifty years ago workers had an input into the planning process, which is now dominated by corporate executives, bureaucrats, politicians, and financiers. The choice we faced in the 1970s was one between democratic socially useful production and the extraction of profit at any cost. It was the choice between a society in which workers organize themselves to produce kidney dialysis machines for a public health care system, or one in which bosses direct workers to produce jets for a company that, in a just society, would have been found guilty of corporate manslaughter.

While the Lucas Plan may have failed, it provided inspiration for workers all over the world for the next few decades. When Mike Cooley was fired from Lucas after becoming a very visible spokesperson for the plan, he was hired as the Greater London Enterprise Board's technology director.[29] Cooley worked with the Greater London Council, which had set up the Board in 1982, to "make the case for socially useful production" and to support firms that engaged their workers in industrial planning.[30] Technology networks set up by the GLC sought to mobilize groups of workers, communities, and academics to produce innovative new products, and to support workers to negotiate with management over the speed and scope of automation.[31]

The GLC created a "product bank," which contained the design ideas that emerged from this process, and sold access to this bank to communities, local authorities, and private companies.[32] It also built a technology exchange that matched firms designing new technologies with those looking to solve production problems.

Groups such as LEEN (the London Energy and Employment Network) sought to make use of these new ideas to transform the public sector.[33] LEEN's Right to Warmth campaign drew attention to the energy needs of different communities and designed solutions that could be implemented by local authorities. The GLC ultimately created the Popular Planning Unit, which reached out to communities to identify their development priorities and engaged residents in the design of solutions.[34]

Thatcher dissolved the GLC in 1986, in part because its radical approach to democratic planning contravened the principles of neoliberalism. But the spirit of Lucas would not die without a fight. In 1984, workers in Barrow were informed that the Vickers shipyard would be used to build the new *Vanguard*-class submarines carrying Trident nuclear missiles.[35] Rather than concede to demands that they support the construction of new nuclear missiles—an idea many of the workers found abhorrent—the Barrow Alternative Employment Committee came up with an alternative strategy for the shipyard that would protect workers without forcing them to participate in the UK's military-industrial complex.

Like the Lucas Plan, the report the workers produced was ignored and the Trident program went ahead, running 72 percent over budget.[36] By 1989, the region in which the shipyard was located still had the highest unemployment rate in England. Ultimately, the arms manufacturer BAE Systems took over, cutting nearly two thousand jobs.[37] Once again, the choice between democratic production for social purpose and centralized production for corporate profits proved a stark one. BAE has been the subject of several corruption scandals, including the al-Yamamah arms deal between the UK and Saudi Arabia, which was marked by astonishing levels of corruption.[38] The company continues to supply weapons to the authoritarian Islamist regime in Saudi Arabia to this day, weapons that are being used to commit war crimes in Yemen.[39]

Thatcher won the fight against socialism in the UK. In repressing trade unionists and community organizers, she was able to claim that the country faced a choice between an overbearing, repressive state (which she made even more repressive) and free markets. In the decades since, political debate has failed to break out of this sterile dichotomy. Those on the left argue for higher public spending funded by taxes on the rich. Those on the right argue for cuts to both public spending and taxes.

When we accede to the idea that politics should be defined by one great battle between "the state" and "the market," we play into the hands of the right. Markets often seem unfair and ruthless, but they're also an abstract concept: no one has ever had a face-to-face encounter with "the market." But nearly everyone has had a face-to-face encounter with a representative of the state—and generally not a positive one. Whether a police officer, a tax official, or an unfriendly bureaucrat, most of the en-counters people have with state institutions are fundamentally alienating and unpleasant.[40] In fact, while levels of trust in social institutions vary considerably across time and space, one constant is that people tend to trust corporations more than they do governments.[41]

We have continued to frame our politics in such self-defeating terms simply because these are the only ones that make sense to us. Capitalism, according to common understanding, means free markets, and socialism means state central planning. If you want more social-ism, you have to add more state, and if you want more capitalism, you have to extend markets. Yet the defining feature of capitalism is not the presence or absence of "free markets," any more than the defining feature of socialism is the centralized planning of the economy. Mar-kets existed long before the emergence of capitalism, and state plan-ning existed long before the emergence of socialism.

Aside from the fact that it's wrong and it doesn't work, there's an even more fundamental reason to avoid pitching leftist politics as one of state versus market: it's disempowering. There is a big difference be-tween approaching people with an offer of protection and approaching them with an offer of empowerment. The former encourages people to alienate their sense of political agency to a group of unaccountable representatives and bureaucrats who, at best, pay attention to their needs only once every four years. When these electoral promises are broken, people fall into despair and disillusionment, often giving up on politics altogether because "politicians are all the same."

But when we frame our political project in terms of collective empowerment, we show that politics can't be reduced to elections—it's something we all do every day. Organizing with your colleagues to demand higher wages is politics, protesting climate breakdown is politics, even fighting alongside your neighbors to keep your local library open is politics. Socialism should not be based on asking people to trust politicians—it should be based on asking people to trust each other.

The significance of the Lucas Plan is that it showed in very concrete terms exactly how people could work together to build a better world. People do not need to surrender their power to state institutions that can control and protect them. Nor do they need to surrender control to a market that is dominated by the powerful. Instead, we can work together to create the kind of world we want to live in. In place of domination, we can build a society based on cocreation. In this chapter, we'll look at ten real-world examples of attempts to do just this.

Such a perspective might sound naive to those who are convinced that humans are naturally competitive beasts who need to be tamed by authoritarian social institutions. Liberal philosophy stretching all the way back to Hobbes has been grounded on the premise that without an all-powerful sovereign to control their competitive instincts, people would tear each other apart. There's just one problem with this argument: it's demonstrably untrue.

Lord of the Lies

In 1857, R. M. Ballantyne, the prolific Scottish author, published *The Coral Island: A Tale of the Pacific Ocean*, which became an instant bestseller and has not been out of print since. The book depicts the adventures of Ralph Rover, who, at fifteen, is shipwrecked on a coral reef of a remote desert island with two of his close friends. Ralph describes how the boys came together in the face of a desperate situation to survive, and even thrive, on the island.

Ralph and his friends are able to extend the benefits of civilization to the island's indigenous inhabitants. The boys witness a battle between two of the native tribes, with the victorious "savages" capturing their opponents before engaging in acts of cannibalism. The boys leap into action, preventing the atrocities and winning the admiration of the remaining tribespeople, whom they attempt to educate about their "civilized" ways.

Nearly a century later, a depressed schoolmaster read Ballantyne's boyhood adventure story and decided he could do better. Having spent a great deal of time around young British boys, he believed he could capture how they would really behave when stranded on a desert island. The resulting novel became an instant classic, selling millions of copies and finding its way into classrooms all over the world.

William Golding's *Lord of the Flies* offers a darker vision of Western civilization than the one depicted by Ballantyne. *The Coral Island* is premised on the idea that the Christian values the English schoolboys have learned remain a permanent feature of their characters, no matter where they are in the world. But Golding's novel suggests that were you to scratch the surface of this cultivated exterior, you would find a darker side to human nature.

Golding was an authoritarian, and his journals reveal a very dark side to his own nature.[42] As a young man, he reports attempting to rape a young girl,[43] and as a schoolmaster he set up a fight between boys in his care to see what would happen.[44] He had a challenging relationship with alcohol and was prone to frequent bouts of intense binge drinking.[45]

Lord of the Flies charts the descent of an apparently decent group of boys into barbarism. While Ballantyne's story sees the "savage" elements of human nature as confined to the "uncivilized" peoples of the earth, Golding seems to argue that once you strip away Western civilization, we are all savages at our core.

Here we have two competing views of human nature put forward by two very different men. Ballantyne's desert island tale purports to show that Christianity and the values of Western civilization can pull people out of conditions of savagery and shape them into ethical, compassionate, God-fearing beings. Golding, on the other hand, believed the civilizing influence of religion is nothing more than a veneer, and that as soon as the pressures of society are removed, humanity reverts to its natural state of savagery.

As it turns out, neither story provides an especially accurate portrayal of human nature. In his book *Humankind: A Hopeful History*, Rutger Bregman provides an account of what really happened when six boys were shipwrecked on a Polynesian island in the mid-1960s.[46] The boys, who were all students at a Christian boarding school, had commandeered a boat to escape the confines of their school and reach Fiji. When hit by a storm, they found themselves lost at sea and were forced to catch rainwater in coconut shells, which they shared equally between them.

After eight days, they finally spotted an island—'Ata—considered uninhabitable. According to the captain who rescued them more than a year later, the boys had "set up a small commune with a food garden, hollowed-out tree trunks to store rainwater, a gymnasium with curious weights, a badminton court, chicken pens and a permanent fire."

The boys had achieved this feat by constructing their own egalitarian social order. They worked in teams, alternating responsibilities such as tending the garden, cooking the food, and guarding against wild animals. They settled any arguments among themselves, and one of the boys even managed to build a "makeshift guitar from a piece of driftwood, half a coconut shell and six steel wires salvaged from their wrecked boat." A lack of rain made conditions extremely difficult and, to make matters worse, one of the boys broke his leg, which they set "using sticks and leaves." Local doctors were astonished at their good physical and mental health when they returned to Tonga over fifteen months later.

The story utterly repudiates Golding's cynical view of human nature. On the surface, it has more in common with Ballantyne's imperialist fantasy. Had it simply been the civilizing influence of the church that had allowed the boys to remain such good friends throughout their ordeal?

Unfortunately for Ballantyne, who had never visited any of the places he wrote about so vividly, the anthropological evidence doesn't support his view of humanity either. As David Wengrow and David Graeber demonstrate in their book *The Dawn of Everything*, far from experiencing a miraculous conversion upon meeting their European "saviors," many indigenous people were repulsed by their contact with European societies, which they saw as greedy, competitive, and thoroughly *un*civilized.[47]

Wengrow and Graeber piece together what they call "the indigenous critique" of European society from notes detailing the interactions between indigenous intellectuals and European adventurers. Among other things, indigenous societies considered Europeans to be cruel, individualistic, and highly irrational. Indigenous intellectuals who traveled to Europe frequently commented on how astonishing it was to find such wealthy nations, with plenty of available housing, allowing so many people to freeze on the streets.

These accounts are borne out by the fact that many indigenous people captured by Europeans would gratefully return home as soon as they were freed, while Europeans captured by indigenous peoples often preferred to remain with their captors. Their contact with the Christian peoples of the West, if anything, made indigenous societies more chaotic: Westerners brought disease and violence to the places they colonized, ultimately destroying these more egalitarian societies.

When you look at the evidence, it's quite clear that human beings have at least as much of a natural capacity for cooperation and compassion as they do for competition and violence. Human nature is malleable. Human beings are as disposed toward compassion and empathy as any other animal species. What differentiates us from other animals is our capacity to reimagine and re-create the world around us. As Marx wrote, human beings are architects, not bees.

Yet most people living in modern capitalist societies have a pretty dim view of human nature. And indeed, much of the evidence presented in this book so far would appear to confirm this. From the Boeing executives who built faulty planes, to the Goldman Sachs analysts who lied to their clients before being bailed out by the taxpayer, the capitalist class seems to provide the best evidence that society is made up of innately selfish individuals whose cooperative impulses extend, at best, to their immediate family and friends.

But this view is highly one-sided. As we will see in this chapter, people are capable of amazing feats of ingenuity, compassion, and cooperation—even in a social order as brutal and competitive as our own. Capitalism, of course, rewards the opposite behavior: ruthlessness, competitiveness, and self-interest. No wonder these are the behaviors we see most prominently on display at the top of our society.

And those at the top are precisely those who benefit from the belief that everyone is just like them. You don't have to look particularly hard to find the view of humanity as inherently selfish repeated by those in positions of authority. The managers at Lucas Aerospace certainly shared this view. And it is no coincidence that Golding was a schoolmaster—he was probably quite used to being disobeyed by his students, and likely saw this as an indication of man's inherent selfishness.

But disobedience to authority is not an indication of selfishness; it's an assertion of an individual's autonomy. In fact, the willingness to disobey is precisely what separates genuinely civilized societies from barbarous ones. One only has to listen to the testimony at the Nuremberg trials to see what can happen when people unquestioningly obey their superiors.

The belief that human nature is inherently selfish is, as Hobbes was well aware, the best justification for the exercise of authority by the ruling class. If human beings are so badly behaved when left to our own devices then, like children, we need to be subjected to authority; we need to be governed; we need to be ruled. The stability of capitalism relies on obedience—whether to bosses, bureaucrats, or the police.

But wherever there is power, there is resistance. People always find ways to resist attempts to control their behavior and exercise their autonomy. Time and time again throughout history, people have demonstrated their extraordinary capacities to cooperate in pursuit of a higher purpose. And it is through these examples of resistance and solidarity that we can find the springs of a new world order emerging.

People-Powered Planning

The best evidence for the human capacity to cooperate in pursuit of collective goals are the real-life examples of people doing just this. The following section contains several examples of democratic planning in corporations and communities all over the world. Choosing only a handful of thousands of examples was challenging, so I chose those with which I was most familiar, and that seemed closest and most relevant to the arguments outlined in the rest of the book.

More than anything, these examples are supposed to illustrate the incredible things people can achieve when they work together outside capitalist institutions. In a world that often seems hopeless, these springs of resistance and cooperation are an enduring source of inspiration for those seeking to build a truly democratic society.

Australia's Green Bans

Five years before the Lucas Plan was developed, residents in a small Sydney suburb were organizing against developers seeking to build luxury housing on the last patch of underdeveloped bushland in their area—Kelly's Bush.[48] Local women worked together to lobby local and regional politicians to reject the proposal, but they found themselves beaten back and ignored at every turn.

In 1968, Jack Mundey, a communist, environmentalist, and peace activist, took up the leadership of the Builders Labourers Federation (BLF), which represented 90 percent of construction workers in the state of New South Wales.[49] He was an early advocate of red-green politics and had been arrested after a sit-in protesting the war in Vietnam. He has been called an "Australian hero" for his role in defending historic parts of Sydney.[50]

With Mundey's election, workers in the BLF asserted their right "to insist their labor not be used in harmful ways." Mundey succinctly articulated the BLF's approach to local development at a rally in 1971: "There must be, in all this city, area provision for working-class people, for people of low and middle income, to be able to reside in the area. It's not much good winning a 35-hour week if we are going to choke to death in planless and polluted cities, where rents are too high, where ordinary people can't live."[51]

The activists at Kelly's Bush decided to approach the BLF, hoping they might be able to prevent construction from taking place on the site. The union agreed to put its new philosophy into practice and announced strike action to prevent the development from going ahead. The development firm, AV Jennings, retaliated by hiring nonunion workers to break the strike. BLF members working on AV Jennings building sites across the country downed tools in response. Backed into a corner, the company abandoned its plans to develop the area, and Kelly's Bush was saved.

The strategy of working with residents to protect local areas became known as the "green ban." Fifty-four bans were introduced throughout New South Wales from 1971 to 1974 to protect "workers' spaces, afford-able housing, and heritage sites."[52] The same year as the Kelly's Bush action, BLF workers refused to build over a park used by residents in a Sydney hous-ing estate. They also protected tenants living on Sydney's Victoria Street from developers trying to build more expensive housing in the area. When a project to build a freeway through Sydney threatened the tenants of eighty thousand homes with eviction, the BLF downed tools until local authorities came up with a sustainable solution to keep the tenants housed locally.

When developers attempted to turn some of Sydney's oldest buildings into luxury apartments, the BLF refused to work on the site until plans were drawn up to protect both residents and the buildings. When indige-nous activists occupied houses in Redfern to prevent a new development going ahead, the BLF stood in solidarity with the activists. The National Trust even established a relationship with the BLF to protect buildings of historical significance; the BLF refused to participate in the demolition of seventeen hundred such buildings in 1972.[53]

By strengthening workers' confidence, the success of the green bans strengthened the labor movement all over Australia. But, just as elsewhere in the world, workers' power was presented as a threat to the governabil-ity of the nation. If workers could take control of the construction pro-cess, then what was to stop them from taking control of other processes previously considered the preserve of the powerful?

Local newspapers with close relationships to big businesses started a campaign against the BLF, as did several local politicians. The *Sydney Morning Herald* published "five editorials in twelve days calling for BLF leaders to be jailed." Mundey began to receive death threats.[54] But the fight against the BLF did not stop there.

When the BLF had organized to prevent the development of Potts Point, the developer used violence against the workers and residents dis-rupting construction. The leader of the residents' action group, Arthur King, was kidnapped.[55] Two years later, campaigning journalist Juanita Nielsen was murdered as a result of her participation in the green ban movement. Her killer was never found, but investigations suggest that police corruption hindered the investigation into her death.[56]

Largely thanks to this campaign of terror, Mundey was eventually replaced with a more conservative leader. But the legacy of the green bans lived on, and many of the developments that the BLF targeted never went ahead. All told, Australia's green bans "stopped, stalled, or affected $5 billion worth of redevelopment projects."[57] Ultimately, the bans led to the transformation of New South Wales's planning system. Local authorities were forced to start accounting for historical significance, environmental impact, and the wishes of residents when considering planning applications.

And just like the Lucas Plan, the legacy of the green bans was not limited to the country in which they took place: "German politician Petra Kelly visited Australia and was inspired by Mundey and the union. She returned to Germany, incorporating the techniques of resistance learned in Australia and started the German Green Party in 1979. This is thought to be the first use of the term 'green' to describe environmentalist politics in Europe."[58]

Marinaleda

Two years after the death of Spain's fascist dictator, Francisco Franco, the Union of Farm Workers was formed in the small Andalusian village of Marinaleda. At the time, the villagers were living in "abject poverty."[59] The newly formed union, led by Juan Manuel Sánchez Gordillo, who has been described as the Spanish Robin Hood, mobilized the locals to occupy land left uncultivated by absentee landowners.[60] The occupations continued until, in 1980, hundreds of locals went on "a hunger strike against hunger" in protest against the jealous monopolization of the land by a small local elite.[61] Over subsequent years, villagers undertook dozens more occupations facing the constant threat of eviction by the Guardia Civil. Their rallying cry was "land for those who work on it."

Eventually, the villagers won, and the local government gave them twelve hundred acres from one of the local estates.[62] During the struggle, the group had formed a party—the Workers' Unity Collective—which went on to win a majority of seats in local elections, and Sánchez Gordillo was elected mayor. To this day, members of the cooperative—most people who live in the village—make decisions collectively through general assemblies.

The cooperative is profitable, and these profits are retained and reinvested in job creation. All workers in the co-op—including the mayor—earn the same wage of €47 per day, and they each work six and a half hours a day.[63] There are a few unemployed people in the town in receipt of nationally provided unemployment benefits, but they are able to survive quite easily on their €400 per month thanks to the cooperative's other investments—particularly in housing.[64] Much of the rest of the common land is used for community services, like the sports center and kindergarten, which residents can access for another €15 a month. Local schools even provide children with three free meals a day.

Part of the reason the local government has been able to dedicate so much investment to these communal facilities is that it saved money by scrapping the police force.[65] Sánchez Gordillo argued that, in a town with no unemployment and in which residents all work together to make decisions, there is no need for law enforcement. Crime rates are comparatively low, and most residents maintain that their decision to remove the police was the right one.

Sánchez Gordillo continues to sweep local elections, and the model has even spread to another nearby town, Somonte. In 2012, workers drew on lessons from Marinaleda and occupied government land before securing collective ownership and establishing a new cooperative.[66] One woman interviewed by British author Dan Hancox describes how the Marinaleda model spread to her town: "The land was some of the most fertile in Spain, but had for decades been used by the government to grow corn, to bring in European subsidies—it created next to no work, and no produce; the corn was left to rot. Those 400 wasted hectares were about to be auctioned off privately by the government when the Andalusian Workers' Union turned up in March 2012; they occupied it, were evicted by 200 riot police, and in true Marinaleda style, returned the next day to start again. The auction never took place."[67]

The People's Plan for the Royal Docks

The London Docklands was in dire straits by the 1980s as containerization transformed global shipping. Private developers saw the Docklands as a massive opportunity, and one developer, with the typical mindset of a colonizer, declared the area "a blank canvas upon which we can paint the future."[68] Thatcher saw the area in the same way. Redeveloping the Docklands would allow her to build a low-tax, low-regulation, high-profit paradise from the ground up.

The London Docklands Development Corporation (LDDC) acquired almost five thousand acres of what was once publicly owned land with the support of the Thatcher government. The idea for the LDDC was simple—relieve the congestion in the city by relocating significant portions of its financial sector to the former docks. Firms were encouraged to relocate through the creation of an enterprise zone, in which "market controls, planning permissions and taxes [were] heavily reduced or abolished to attract investment."[69]

The preferences of the area's fifty-two thousand residents were ignored by the LDDC, but they did not accept their marginalization lying down. Instead, they approached the radical Greater London Council for help. The GLC agreed, and a "People's Plan Centre" was opened in Newham. When the LDDC proposed the construction of London City Airport in 1983, residents worked with the GLC's popular planning officers to develop "the People's Plan for the Royal Docks." The plan was based on its authors' conviction that "there must be more to our working lives, and our children's, than being porters and lavatory attendants for passing businessmen."[70]

The GLC's Popular Planning officers were able to draw on the knowledge of socially useful production they had gained from studying the Lucas Plan.[71] They proposed the creation of worker cooperatives, which would use existing infrastructure to create socially useful products that could be purchased by the GLC. The plan also proposed the provision of full-time childcare for children under five, which would create employment for the thousands of unemployed women then living in the Docklands. And where the LDDC wanted to build thousands of luxury homes, the People's Plan proposed investing in the area's social housing stock.

Local people worked together to spread the word about the plan. Tenants designed posters for the PR campaign, and billboards were put up around the city.[72] People's Armadas compiled demands and delivered them to Parliament in cavalcades of a thousand or more. But Thatcher's destruction of the GLC killed the plan and cleared the way for the LDDC. Just like the story of Lucas Aerospace, the People's Plan clearly shows the choice British society was faced with during the 1980s: a world designed by and for the people, or one designed by and for powerful private actors supported by the British state.

Participatory Budgeting

In 1989, the Brazilian city of Porto Alegre embarked on a radical new experiment in local democracy. When the Brazilian Workers' Party (PT) took control of the city in municipal elections, they introduced the idea of "participatory budgeting" (PB)—a process through which citizens worked with local authorities to develop economic and financial plans for their area.[73] Every year, citizens of Porto Alegre come together to debate how to spend their city's budget in a series of meetings that take place at the neighborhood level.

The Porto Alegre model is widely considered to be one of the most successful examples of democratic local planning anywhere in the world. At its peak in 2002, over seventeen thousand citizens were involved in the participatory process, responsible for distributing a budget of $160 million.[74] Low-income citizens, women, and ethnic minorities were particularly well represented at the meetings, which allowed for a transfer of funding to more deprived neighborhoods.[75] Over a period of several years, the PB agenda "brought those usually excluded from the political process into the heart of decision making, significantly increasing the power and influence of civil society and improving local people's lives through the more effective allocation of resources."[76]

Ultimately, more than 250 Brazilian cities adopted participatory budgeting.[77] The model has been studied comprehensively. Where successful, it has been found to result in greater levels of participation in government; improved outcomes for low-income residents, women, and other marginalized communities; increased transparency and accountability in political institutions; and more progressive distributions of municipal budgets.[78]

The model spread to fifteen hundred cities all over the world. In Canada, participatory budgeting has been trialed successfully in at least three cities—Guelph, Toronto, and Vancouver.[79] As in Porto Alegre, these experiments have been particularly beneficial for disadvantaged communities, allowing many marginalized groups to engage in democratic processes for the first time. In Toronto, for example, social housing tenants have been involved in decision-making through the Toronto Community Housing Corporation (THTC), allowing them to deliver key infrastructure and improve common spaces.[80] A participatory budgeting process was also started in

New York in 2011, when residents were given the power to allocate some of the city's capital budget.[81] Millions of dollars have since been invested in everything from parks, to libraries, to public housing.

People's Planning, Kerala

Seven years after Porto Alegre, another experiment in decentralized planning began in Kerala, India. In 1996, the Left Democratic Front won Kerala's regional elections and introduced "the People's Plan Campaign," with the ambition of bringing government closer to the people.[82] As in Brazil, communities throughout Kerala were involved directly in the decisions being made by local government. But in India, the link to planning was clearer. The national government was in the process of drawing up its ninth Five-Year Plan, which aimed to modernize and develop India, and each state was expected to feed ideas into the State Planning Board (SPB).[83]

Part of what made Kerala's planning process so successful was the links that were forged between local and national planning processes. A large amount of the cash at the SPB's disposal was reserved for projects developed within the framework of the People's Plan, based on a pledge made by the board that 35 to 40 percent of India's ninth plan would consist of schemes formulated at the local government level. Through a series of meetings and seminars attended by a diverse range of residents, local governments were able to "design and implement their own plans . . . through direct public participation."[84] Through this process, the ideas developed by local communities found their way into the regional government's submissions to the national Five-Year Plan.

The results were astounding. In 1991, 28 percent of the population was using public health facilities, and this increased to 48 percent by 2018—despite retrenchment in the public finances at the national level.[85] More than six hundred thousand Keralan students moved from private schools to public ones.[86] Kerala achieved its Sustainable Development Goal for infant mortality reduction ahead of the rest of India in 2020. More than one hundred thousand kilometers of roads were constructed across a remote and rural region.[87] The proportion of Keralans living below the poverty line fell from 25 percent in 1993–94 to 6 percent in 2011–12.[88] What's more, as in Brazil, the campaign boosted civil society, leading to the formation of self-help groups such as Kudumbashree, "the world's largest network of women with more than 4,100,000 members [whose mission is] to eradicate extreme poverty through community action."[89]

Ciudad Futura, Argentina

As the birthplace of Che Guevara, Rosario, Argentina, has a proud revolutionary history.[90] So, when the municipal government tried to sell tracts of public land to luxury housing developers that would have resulted in the eviction of 250 families, its people fought back. A group of local people launched a grassroots campaign to resist the sale—and they won. The city government made a U-turn, banning the construction of gated communities and allowing the grassroots movement to determine how the land would be used. Members of the movement consulted the locals, and together they decided to use the land to start a dairy cooperative.

The Resistance Dairy created jobs, boosted the local economy, and provided residents with cheap and healthy food.[91] Today, the co-op produces nine hundred liters of milk a day, as well as cheese and dulce de leche.[92] Families can form "consumer circles" of three to five households and, in exchange for a small monthly fee, receive a basket of food from the co-op. The co-op also has a food-share program—known as the Anti-Inflationary Mission—which helps local people to access food in the context of Argentina's constantly rising prices.[93]

The co-op also set up two secondary schools and a preschool to support the hundreds of poor children in the area who lacked access to education.[94] It launched a social health initiative aimed at supporting those with drug and alcohol problems. The group even branched out into entertainment, setting up a cooperative social club and cinema called Distrito Sie7e (District Seven), which holds parties and live music in the evenings and assembly-style meetings to discuss the movement's priorities during the day.

In 2012, the organizers decided to take their movement into mainstream politics, forming Ciudad Futura, which is now a thriving local political party. Funding came from the profits of all the local businesses the movement had set up, and by 2018 membership had grown threefold. Ciudad Futura candidates—all of whom were women—won four seats in the municipal government in 2019, gaining 11 percent of the vote, despite the party facing a legal challenge for "excluding men" from their selection process.[95] One of the party's councilors outlined its philosophy in an interview: "What's the use of going on about how bad everything is? It serves for nothing. If you have the ability to show that the city can be different, based on concrete practices, that's where the potential of your project is. Everything else is incidental. Our only unique characteristic is this idea of demonstrating, right now, that there are alternatives, and doing so on an increasing scale."[96]

Better Reykjavik

Iceland was one of the major success stories of the pre-2008 boom. Having successfully transformed its economy from one based primarily on fishing to one based on the export of financial services, the country's banking system ballooned in the run-up to the crisis.[97] Yet when the global financial system collapsed in 2008, it threatened to destroy Iceland's economy.

The countries most exposed to Iceland's banks—the highly financialized economies of the UK and the Netherlands—offered Iceland a loan to allow it to provide bailouts for international depositors, but the country's citizens would have had to repay the loan over the long run. In what has been described as "the only known direct democratic votes on sovereign debt resettlement in history," Iceland's citizens were offered a vote on the proposal and roundly rejected it.[98]

While foreign governments were threatening to ostracize Iceland from the international financial system and ratings agencies were downgrading its debt, the Icelandic people set about the long and painful process of rebuilding from the crash. When local elections were held in 2010, the Best Party developed a new democratic policy platform as part of their campaign. The party began asking citizens to pitch policy ideas using the online platform Better Reykjavik. Over the course of just two weeks, forty thousand people participated in the process and over a thousand ideas were discussed, many of which were included in the party's platform.[99] When the Best Party won power in 2010, Better Reykjavik became an official part of the city's political infrastructure.

Two years later, a participatory budgeting process called My Neighborhood was introduced so that citizens could have a say in how their local budget was spent. Participants in the program have control over 300 million ISK of the city's budget.[100] Over 150 ideas have been approved, including a proposal to provide shelters for the homeless and another to turn the city's main commercial street into a pedestrian-only corridor.[101] As well as being able to determine funding for public services, residents are able to allocate 6 percent of the local government capital investment budget to shape the city's infrastructure spending.

Similar platforms have now spread across Europe. Estonia established its Your Priorities platform at a national level, based on the Icelandic model, in the wake of a political scandal in 2012 that compromised the government's legitimacy.[102] More recently, Barcelona developed its Decidim ("we decide") platform, which allows citizens to determine how 5 percent of the municipal budget—around €75 million—is spent over three years.[103]

Cooperation Jackson

In 2014, Kali Akuno helped to found Cooperation Jackson, which he envisioned as an umbrella organization for cooperatives and community enterprises in the city of Jackson, Mississippi. The aim was to "build a base of autonomous power in Mississippi" that could serve as a catalyst for the democratization of the economy.[104] The plan, known as the Jackson-Kush Plan, was based on three pillars: people's assemblies, a network of progressive political candidates, and a broad-based solidarity economy.

Akuno and his comrades started out by setting up a network of people's assemblies that would feed into a People's Task Force, which would initiate the proposals decided on by the assemblies.[105] In 2009, the group helped elect Chokwe Lumumba to the local council, as well as leading successful campaigns to elect the first-ever Black sheriff of Hinds County, to resist cuts to the public transport budget, and pass antiracist legislation in the city.[106] In 2017, Chokwe Antar Lumumba—Lumumba's son—stood as the Democratic Party's candidate for mayor of Jackson and won with 90 percent of the vote.[107]

The final pillar of the Jackson-Kush Plan—building a solidarity economy—relied on the construction of cooperative and community organizations from the ground up.[108] Akuno's vision included plans for housing cooperatives, credit unions, urban farms, agricultural cooperatives, land conservation trusts, and an expansion of public services. The organization occupied unused land to start a network of urban farms and farmers' markets, which worked together to "promote a healthy diet, affordable produce, and food sovereignty in the city." It also developed a campaign to expand worker organizing in the city with the aim of overturning anti-union legislation.

Since then, the city's co-op networks have blossomed. The Freedom Farms Cooperative grows and sells fresh produce in the local area; the Green Team Landscaping Co-op provides lawn services to clients and the organizations within the co-op network; and the Community Production Cooperative hosts skills training and events for members and residents, as well as supporting local artists. The group has plans to develop several other cooperatives, in areas from waste management to health care, to construction, to auto repair. They have also worked with their allies in local government to develop a cooperative incubator and to provide financing support for local co-ops.

Cooperation Jackson has also created a community land trust, through which they have purchased large tracts of land with a plan to build sustainable, affordable housing and prevent gentrification. They've developed a "fab lab" to train workers in new high-tech skills, developed a People's Grocery Initiative and community kitchens, and established a new cultural arts cooperative.[109] They've also worked with government to re-municipalize public utilities, create a "human rights charter" to future policy, and roll out a participatory budgeting platform.[110] The group even sprang into action during the pandemic, distributing PPE equipment and setting up an eviction support hotline.

Preston, UK

With its finances stretched and the main street in terrible condition, Preston's city council's hopes for redevelopment lay with a partnership with John Lewis to redevelop the town's shopping center. But when John Lewis pulled out of the project in 2011, council leader Matthew Brown realized he needed a new strategy. Rather than outsourcing public services to private contractors, or relying on big corporations to rescue the town, Brown developed a plan to bring community wealth building (CWB) to Preston.

Community wealth building is an approach to economic development that "redirects wealth back into the local economy, and places control and benefits into the hands of local people."[111] The council would use its procurement budget to boost local businesses and "anchor institutions"—institutions that can't move, like universities and hospitals.[112] In doing so, it would help create jobs, support local businesses, and keep wealth in the area.

Writing in the *Tribune* in January 2022, Brown listed some of the successes of the Preston Model, which saw Preston become the UK's most improved town in the first few years of its implementation:

> In the last three months, we have brought forward the Real Living Wage increase, benefitting over ten percent of our staff. We are making solid progress with our partners in developing North West Mutual, our regional community bank. . . . We are delivering a £70 million regeneration of our city center, primarily in municipal ownership, including a new £42 million city-owned cinema and leisure development and a cooperative housing project. . . . We currently have five new worker-owned firms registered. . . . One newly registered worker cooperative, the Preston Cooperative Education Centre (PCEC), has been founded by members of Preston Trades Council, and is being tasked to work with unions to support new cooperative businesses that their members will own and control.[113]

These successes have been pushed through even in the context of a deep economic crisis, following years of stagnation and rising inequality—both of which had a disproportionate impact on the North of England. And local people have noticed. While Labour performed badly across the country in local elections in 2021, Preston Labour bucked the trend, and easily retained control of the council with an impressive share of the vote.

Blaenau Ffestiniog[114]

Blaenau Ffestiniog is often seen as a classic example of a town that has been left behind by globalization. Most of the villages in Bro Ffestiniog—of which Blaenau is one—can trace their history back to slate mining, which dominated the Welsh economy for much of the nineteenth century. With the collapse of the slate industry, Blaenau became one of the poorest places in the UK. Slate, which does not provide especially good insulation, has also left another legacy—Blaenau has the highest rate of fuel poverty in Wales.

In the early 2000s, the Welsh government began to distribute funding to disadvantaged communities through its Communities First program. A local Blaenau resident—Ceri Cunnington, who had returned to Bro after traveling the world with his Welsh-language ska band Anweledig—used the funding to set up a social enterprise called Antur Stiniog, a mountain biking center that would create jobs and bring investment back into the community. Then he set up a local charity—Y Dref Werdd—that focused on maintaining the natural environment and supporting local clean-energy projects. Not long after, his bandmate Rhys Ifans purchased the old police station with the inheritance his dad had left him. With the help of some enthusiastic local teenagers, he converted it into a youth and arts center.

Before long, social enterprises were springing up all over Bro. About a mile down the road in Llan Ffestiniog, two hundred residents came together with support from the Welsh government to purchase their local pub, Y Pengwern. A few minutes from Y Pengwern lies Cwmni Gwesti Seren, a hotel run by and for disabled people. Ceri set up Cwmni Bro to organize all the local cooperatives and social enterprises and help them obtain funding—his office sits directly above that of Y Dref Werdd, which is now a multipurpose community hub that helps people struggling with food and fuel poverty.

And just like that, Blaenau Ffestiniog became the town in Wales with the most social enterprises per capita. Fifteen of them employed nearly two hundred people before COVID, and politicians have come from all over the country to learn the key to their success.

It wasn't long before the model began to spread across North Wales. Fifteen miles away in Bethesda, a group of volunteers set up Partneriaeth Ogwen, which purchased unused properties on the main street, offering the commercial spaces to local businesses and the apartments above to residents at affordable rents. Then they started their own energy cooperative—Ynni Ogwen, a hydroelectricity plant offering green, affordable power before feeding profits back into the community. A similar model was developed in Penygroes, where Yr Orsaf, a community enterprise, has, with help from the government, raised £1 million to purchase local assets and put them to use for the community.

The amount that this small community has achieved over a relatively short period is remarkable, and academics and politicians have taken to studying Blaenau to draw some lessons from this success. But, as Ceri told me when I interviewed him in 2021, there's no secret to what he and his fellow residents have achieved: "It's not rocket science—it's just community."

....

Experiments in local democratic planning and community organizing like those outlined in this chapter are happening right now all over the world. But they remain small and often isolated islands of resistance to capitalism in a sea of exploitation and oppression. Some argue that this kind of planning can only ever succeed on a small scale. The global economy is simply too large and complex to be subjected to any conscious control.

Yet, as we have seen, capitalist economies are subjected to conscious control all the time—just not *democratic* conscious control. Powerful corporations, financial institutions, states, and empires use their influence to plan who gets what within capitalist societies—and most of the time, their decisions are skewed toward the interests of capital. When people argue that democratic planning at scale is impossible, they are really arguing that it is impossible to challenge capital's power. As we will see in the next chapter, this is patently untrue.

The local-level examples of democratic planning outlined here provide the foundations on which the shift to a democratic economy will be based. Not only do they show what is possible, they also help to engage and politicize people in a project of collective social transformation. But without reforms to the structure of capitalist societies, such innovations are bound to remain small. Unless we socialize and democratize the ownership of society's most important resources—unless we dissolve the class divide between capital and labor itself—there can be no true democracy.

9

Taking Back Control:
Democratic Planning at Scale

On September 4, 1970, socialist candidate Salvador Allende was elected president of Chile by a narrow margin. President Nixon was reportedly furious when he heard the result. US businesses with operations in Chile had spent vast sums trying to bring Allende down, many out of fear that their Chilean operations would be nationalized if he won. The CIA spent nearly half a million dollars on anti-Allende propaganda during the campaign, and they poured even more money into opposition groups running a "scare campaign" attempting to link Allende's victory with the imposition of Soviet-style repression.[1]

Allende was, however, intimately familiar with the failings of Soviet-style socialism. The last thing he wanted was to reconstruct the rigid model of centralized planning that was creating so many problems in the USSR. Instead, he sought to pave his own "Chilean path to socialism," involving a thorough democratization of the economy.[2]

As soon as he was elected, Allende announced plans to build tens of thousands of new homes, introduce rent controls, improve and expand the pension system, introduce free and universal medical care, provide new mothers and young children with free milk and free school meals, and greatly expand the social security net.[3] Public works programs were introduced to create employment and boost wages. Allende also cut top salaries, clamped down on government corruption, and substantially reduced taxes for low- and middle-income Chileans.

Rural society was also transformed. Large landowners were expropriated, peasants' councils were formed to organize rural workers, and measures were introduced to support Chile's indigenous population.[4]

Women were encouraged to work together to set up cooperatives to facilitate collective, democratic management of services like cleaning, cooking, and childcare.

Allende, who had spearheaded the legislation that introduced the Chilean national health service, also significantly improved health outcomes.[5] Health care services were expanded and democratized, with hospital councils and neighborhood health councils introduced to engage citizens in decisions about health care provision.[6] Infant mortality and various other mortality indicators fell under Allende as a result.[7] Enrollment in public schools increased sharply between 1971 and 1973, and the illiteracy rate fell two percentage points in two years.[8] Tuition fees were removed, and university admissions increased commensurately, particularly for working-class young people due to the "democratization" of universities.[9] Millions of books—from classic works of literature to accessible texts on political economy—were published and distributed to workers across the country. Overall, public spending on social services rose from 20 percent to 26 percent of GDP.[10]

The government also decided to nationalize US-owned copper companies "in effect without compensation because of deduction for excess profits."[11] Allende even went so far as to nationalize 90 percent of the banking system and he undertook an administrative takeover of over three hundred factories.[12] But Allende was not attempting to introduce the top-down state management of old. Corporate governance in private and state-owned firms was democratized, with workers being elected to key management and board positions.[13]

Within a few years, Allende had introduced a national minimum wage, brought in measures to expand workers' representation in the government's Social Planning Ministry, and introduced centralized collective bargaining between workers and bosses, mediated by the government. Workers across the economy experienced "sharp and fast" increases in real wages, even as income inequality fell.[14] Price controls were also set up to control inflation, which were monitored by distribution networks controlled by the state. The wage share of national income increased from 54.9 percent in 1970 to 65.8 percent in 1971.[15]

Naturally, President Nixon was not going to let Allende build a successful experiment in democratic socialism in America's "backyard." He stated outright that he wanted to make the Chilean economy "scream."[16] The US immediately cut foreign aid to Chile and used all the resources at its disposal to prevent the country from accessing international investment and credit. US businesses refused to trade with Chile, severely restricting the economy's access to many consumer goods and manufacturing inputs. The US discouraged financial institutions from lending to the Chilean state and its firms. In 1972, the US's Export-Import Bank (EXIM) reduced Chile's credit rating to the lowest possible grade while cutting tens of millions of dollars in credit to the nation.[17]

Unable to access international credit, the government had to rely on export earnings and foreign exchange reserves to purchase imports. But a sudden and dramatic decline in the price of one of Chile's main exports—copper—led to a severe balance of payments crisis and further compromised the government's access to foreign currency.[18] US pressure made it harder for the government to secure imports of food and consumer goods from abroad, leading to shortages and making it harder to maintain price controls. Allende was forced to rely on expansionary monetary policy to keep the economy going, and by February 1972, consumer prices were 34 percent higher than they had been twelve months earlier.[19] Eventually the Allende government committed the cardinal sin of announcing that it would be reneging on many of its international debts.

It was in this extraordinarily difficult context that Chile embarked upon a unique experiment in democratic, decentralized planning. Allende had come to power intent upon creating what he considered to be a genuinely socialist economy based on principles of democratic control over industry, agriculture, public services, and macroeconomic management. But such a system had never been tried on a mass scale before, and no one was quite sure how it would work.

How would workers' control of industry connect to the planning processes being undertaken by the national government? How would information be exchanged in a timely manner between different state institutions, industrial and rural workers, and the people? How could different social groups be mobilized to fight for the reforms the government was introducing in the face of a coordinated foreign campaign to undermine them? Having handed power to workers in many industries, the Allende government faced the challenge of coordinating production to ensure a balance between supply and demand at the macroeconomic level. Essentially, this was a challenge of creating a self-organizing and adaptive economic system.

Scientists in the Soviet Union had sought to overcome similar challenges several years before Allende came to power.[20] They had proposed that the suite of computers that were then being used for military purposes could be repurposed for "real-time economic planning." Automating the processes through which production data was gathered and analyzed could create a more adaptive and efficient process of economic planning—as opposed to the implementation of a new plan every five years. But the Soviet model was never implemented, as it presented a challenge to the power and authority of the government departments that dominated the planning process.

Meanwhile, US military scientists were working on ARPANET—the predecessor to the internet. While the network was initially constructed as a platform through which scientists could share resources, those involved in the project quickly realized it would be far more useful as a communication network. Real-time communication allowed scientists to collaborate more effectively and promoted innovation and information sharing.

Given resource constraints, it would not have been feasible for Allende's government to try to build its own version of the internet. But by combining insights from the US and the USSR, Allende's government managed to create something that was, in some ways, more radical.

The solution that emerged was the brainchild of two men from quite different backgrounds, but who shared a deep interest in the field that came to be known as systems theory.[21] Stafford Beer, a British consultant and specialist in systems theory, was the father of what is now known as management cybernetics. While sympathetic to the socialist cause, Beer spent much of his life as a consultant for private executives struggling with the challenges of planning and coordination that were becoming increasingly prevalent within the sprawling modern corporation.

Fernando Flores was a minister in the State Development Corporation (CORFO), with a background in engineering.[22] While working in the Chilean railway sector, Flores had come across one of Beer's books and quickly became enthralled by the man's ideas. Flores realized that Beer's work could be useful in helping the Allende government to construct a genuinely decentralized network with the few resources available to it. He commissioned Beer to build a network that could be used to coordinate the process of economic planning while leaving as much power as possible in the hands of the workers.

Beer proposed the creation of a network that would allow the government to exchange information with state-owned factories in a timely manner.[23] By facilitating real-time data exchange between factories and the government, the network would allow the former to alert the latter of blockages and the latter to instruct the former to alter production quickly in response to emergencies. The long-term aim would be to use the network to predict future economic behavior, as well as directing production today.

There was just one problem: Chile didn't have nearly enough computers to build the kind of network that Beer envisaged. But the team developed a hack to solve this problem too. An army major informed the team that the National Telecommunications Enterprise had four hundred Telex machines in a storage facility. These rudimentary machines allowed operators to input information, which could be transmitted between machines quickly and efficiently.[24] Project Cybersyn was born.

The system was far from perfect. The network was too centralized to be considered properly democratic—most of the information exchange took the form of instructions that were passed down from the central government to workers in state-owned enterprises. It relied on fairly rudimentary technology and programs that were infinitely more simplistic than those found in the smartphones we carry around in our pockets. And technological solutions could only go some way toward alleviating the material challenges that the Chilean economy had begun to experience.

Nevertheless, under these extraordinary circumstances, the program achieved some remarkable successes—particularly when the US began to tighten the screws on the Chilean economy. In 1972, sections of the workforce, including truckers, small businesspeople, and professional workers, went on strike in protest against food shortages and rampant inflation.[25] The government managed to survive the twenty-four-day strike only by using the communication network that had been established through Project Cybersyn to rapidly shift production.

Allende managed to hold out for so long, in spite of these challenges, because Project Cybersyn allowed him to keep production going and keep workers engaged in the planning process. Imagine what he could have achieved under more propitious economic conditions and with a few laptops at his disposal. In the end, Allende shot himself when US-sponsored troops stormed the presidential palace and installed the murderous dictator Augusto Pinochet, famous for "disappearing" those who dared to oppose his regime by throwing them out of planes into the ocean below.

All the examples of democratic planning we've seen so far have been small-scale experiments taking place on a community or a firm level. These experiments have all relied on capitalist organizational structures and political institutions, as well as wider markets in which they could buy and sell goods and services. Without these wider supports, it would be easy to argue that these attempts would have failed. Perhaps we simply have to accept that small-scale challenges to the dominance of capitalism will remain small—that there is no good way to democratize society at scale.

The Chilean experience shows that it is possible to begin building democratic institutions at scale. There are, however, several prerequisites. First, any attempt to democratize an economy will encounter massive resistance from capital—especially if undertaken in the Global South. The only route to a democratic economy will therefore run through struggle. The sine qua non of democratizing society is building a movement capable of resisting the vested interests that would seek to prevent us from reaching this point.

Second, control over the state is important for achieving democracy at scale. If capitalists want to disrupt a political movement, they can stop investing (capital strike) or move their business elsewhere (capital flight). Even where resistance does not come from capital itself, the capitalist state is generally both willing and able to act on its behalf. Reactionary governments have frequently unleashed extraordinary violence on movements seeking to challenge the status quo.

The way in which state power is exercised is, as we know, dependent on the balance of class power in society. Were an organized working class capable of resisting these strategies, workers could organize within state institutions both to limit the direct use of state power against labor and to undermine capital's power to strike or flee. The potential effectiveness of these strategies is precisely why vested interests fight so hard to undermine worker organizing and prevent left-wing governments from coming to power.

It's also why thinkers like Ralph Miliband argued that there was no route to what he called "parliamentary socialism"—that is, the transformation of state institutions using democratic processes.[26] Yet the examples outlined in the case studies in the last chapter show that powerful political movements can elect progressive candidates, and those candidates can achieve meaningful reforms while in office—whether that's Mayor Chokwe Lumumba in Jackson, the Workers' Party leadership in Porto Alegre, council leader Matthew Brown in Preston, or MP Tony Benn supporting the Lucas Plan while part of a Labour government.

Socialists must struggle within and outside *all* social institutions—including those of the state—to shift the balance of power in society in favor of workers. Developing policy proposals is therefore as critical as laying out democratic alternatives to the status quo that can be built in our communities today.

Finally, as Allende discovered, technology is a critical variable in shaping what kinds of social organization are possible. In our world, the research and development of new technologies is monopolized by powerful corporations and the capitalist states that sponsor them. Most new technologies are therefore developed either to maximize profits or to strengthen a state's military power.

For as long as capital controls the means of production, it will also control the technological development of society. And as long as capital controls the development of technology, it will constrain our ability to imagine new ways of organizing society. It is quite possible that, had Chilean and Soviet scientists been able to continue with their experiments, they would have created the kind of technology required for democratic planning at scale by now. We will never know. What we do know is that truly democratic societies require democratic technology. And democratic technology requires wresting control of the means of production away from capital.

Making Capital Scream

If capitalism is not defined by the presence or absence of markets, but by the domination of society by capital, then socialism is not defined by the presence or absence of planning, but by the democratization of society. Rather than a system of top-down control, true democratic socialism would be a project of collective liberation, which would allow workers to take control over production and citizens to take control over government.

This shift will not, however, happen on its own. Working people must organize to fight for it. Traditionally, this fight has been organized in the main by the labor movement. Working people came together in unions to fight for better wages and conditions, and successive victories made them steadily more confident in articulating wider political demands. The workers who organized to take control of Lucas Aerospace are a fantastic example of how the labor movement plays a dual role, both protecting workers in the economy today and supporting them to build a better world for tomorrow.

Unionists have been central players in many of the experiments in democratic planning seen in the previous chapter, and they remain critical to articulating the policy demands required for building a fairer society. In Germany, for example, the largest union has been campaigning for the introduction of a four-day workweek, based on evidence that doing so would boost productivity and employment while improving living standards. In both the US and the UK, a network of unions mobilized behind proposals for the Green New Deal, working tirelessly against fossil-fuel lobbyists attempting to convince workers that the green transition could cost them their jobs.

But unions are just one part of the broad and deep coalition that we'll need to win a more democratic economy. Community organizing will also be critical. The examples of community-led democratic planning in the previous chapter are important not only because they provide a different way of organizing the economy but also because they help inspire people to become active in wider politics. In an individualistic society, it can be difficult even to imagine what it might be like to work with others to fight for social change. People often find it a little easier to join a campaign to save their local library or clean up their local park than they do to join a union or go along to a protest.

But these small, local acts of support can have a powerful effect on people's sense of solidarity. Organizing with others to change the world around you can give you a sense of the possibilities of collective action. Many of the experiments outlined in the previous chapter will have started with communities coming together to solve small, local problems before realizing they had the power to change their entire community, not just one aspect of it.

This is not to say that all local campaigns are inherently revolutionary. The nature of a community campaign will always depend on the class background of its participants: a campaign to prevent a new wind turbine led by executives concerned about house prices will be very different from a campaign to protect a local library led by working-class residents. But working people who have watched their communities be torn apart by decades of neoliberalism and austerity are increasingly coming together to build new kinds of communities—as they have done all over the world, from Jackson, Mississippi, to Porto Alegre, to Blaenau Ffestiniog.

Building working-class power also requires people to engage in protest and direct action—both as means to fight regressive policies and to draw public attention to them. Protest is often framed in purely negative terms—as preventing something bad from happening. But resistance can be creative as well as reactive. Whether it is workers fighting to resist pay cuts, debtors organizing to resist unpayable debts, tenants organizing to resist rent hikes, or environmentalists organizing to resist the degradation of our environment, protest campaigns can shift the public conversation and win victories.

The networks, resources, and relationships developed through campaigns to resist the domination of capital often provide the foundations for the emergence of more constructive projects. For example, in the wake of the financial crisis, the Occupy movement sprang up in cities around the globe demanding justice for the 99 percent who were being forced to pay for a crisis caused by the 1 percent. Despite the media attention they generated, most of these movements did not achieve much at the time, but they did create networks that led to the emergence of other successful campaigns, such as Strike Debt.[27]

In 2012, Strike Debt campaigners launched Rolling Jubilee, in which they crowdfunded to purchase thousands of dollars in risky debt on secondary markets in order to cancel it.[28] The campaign managed to raise hundreds of thousands of dollars, which was used to write off $13.5 million in medical debt, $1.2 million in personal debt, and $3.8 million in student loans.

Some criticized Rolling Jubilee for failing to engage the debtors who benefited from the action in a political movement, but they could not level the same criticism at the Debt Collective, which also emerged out of networks created during the Occupy movement.[29] The Debt Collective sees itself as a kind of union for debtors, encouraging them to come together and resist their creditors where their debts are unjustified or unpayable.

The Debt Collective helped thousands of students file debt forgiveness claims following the bankruptcy of their university, and during the pandemic they organized sixteen hundred debtors to strike and defer their student loan payments as part of a broader political movement fighting for the write-off of student debt. These groups aren't only helping working-class people resist their oppression today; they're also demonstrating the feasibility of a debt jubilee: a critical measure to democratize our financialized economy.

The networks that emerged out of the Occupy movement also provided the foundation for the revival of the Democratic Socialists of America (DSA), and for Bernie Sanders's bid for the presidency. Those involved in the UK's smaller Occupy movement were also involved in the anti-austerity movement from 2010, out of which emerged a network of activists who became involved in the campaign for Jeremy Corbyn's campaign for leadership of the Labour Party. These bids for state power did, of course, end in failure—both as a result of issues with their internal organization and due to coordinated campaigns to crush them.

Yet both these campaigns, and the movements that emerged from them, shifted the conversation on issues ranging from inequality to climate breakdown, as well as leading to new organizations that endure to this day. Several organizations that have survived Corbynism—from the World Transformed festival that takes place alongside the Labour conference every year, to Novara Media and *Tribune* magazine, for which I am a columnist, to the New Economy Organisers Network (NEON), which provided me with my media training—can trace some part of their organizational history back to networks formed during these years. Resistance can always be creative, even if it is framed in purely negative terms.

As we enter a world of pervasive ecological breakdown, direct action will become even more important to resist projects that would further compromise the environment upon which we all depend. All around the world, climate protestors have organized to halt polluting projects and draw attention to the need to decarbonize. Campaigners against the Keystone XL pipeline staged sit-ins across the proposed route and even formed a human chain around the White House.[30] Despite hundreds of arrests—including that of Green Party presidential candidate Jill Stein—Obama was forced to back down and put the pipeline on hold.

And even less targeted actions have had a substantial impact.[31] Throughout 2018 and 2019, movements like Extinction Rebellion and Fridays for Future focused public attention on the question of climate breakdown and forced a public conversation on the issue. In September 2019, millions of people in nearly every country on earth marched for climate justice in the largest mass-climate protest in history.[32] As soon as journalists and commentators were forced to start asking questions about climate breakdown—even hostile ones—public opinion began to shift.[33]

In the Global South, where millions rely on the natural world to provide daily sustenance as well as a livable environment, resistance to climate breakdown has proved equally fierce. When the Bolsonaro regime moved to weaken environmental protections over the Amazon to open up the area for mining and logging, deforestation rates increased 22 percent between 2020 and 2021.[34] Much of this activity was based on illegal land grabbing, often involving violence against the indigenous groups who still live in the Amazon.

But indigenous people, with the support of the environmental movement, have resisted these incursions with some notable successes. Thousands poured into the streets to protest the government's new laws, and in October 2022 Bolsonaro was defeated by the left-wing candidate Luiz Inácio Lula da Silva, whose campaign highlighted his previous groundbreaking reforms designed to protect the rainforest.[35]

In each of these examples, activists have sought ways to work within party and state institutions to achieve their goals. Too often, socialists have seen efforts to build power at the grassroots level and efforts to work within political parties as competing—rather than complementary—strategies. But any movement to build a democratic economy will have to be a movement that works "within and against" the state.[36]

In the Jackson-Kush Plan, for example, Kali Akuno laid out his strategy for building "dual power" in Mississippi by creating powerful popular institutions outside the federal and local state and working to transform existing political parties and democratic institutions.[37] Building power at the grassroots allowed Akuno and others to elect a mayor who was sympathetic to their aims and who put in place strategies to support the movement. This positive reinforcement between activist and party power is exactly the strategy socialists will need to pursue if we want to challenge the power of capital and build a truly democratic economy.

In the world of organizing there exists a creative tension between building from the ground up and shifting institutional structures from the top down. Policy demands can be of as much help in creating a sense of organizational solidarity as a campaign to build a new community enterprise or a strike against an exploitative employer. When movements—or a network of movements—can allow both to take place at the same time, finding suitable roles for the different people who compose them, they can become very powerful indeed.

By mobilizing to implement policies to democratize the state, the firm, finance, and international institutions, we can both encourage the experiments in democratic decision-making that are already taking place and negate the repressive power of capital. In the next few sections, I'll provide a schematic summary of proposals to do just this.

Democratizing Work and the Corporation

As we've seen, corporations are political institutions with power over both workers and wider society, privileges granted to them by capitalist states. The capitalist corporation is defined by the class division between those who own and manage these corporations on the one hand, and those who produce their output on the other. Democratizing the corporation means eliminating this distinction and giving workers and citizens power to control the engines of production.

First and foremost, achieving this aim requires leveling the playing field between workers and bosses. The anti-union laws imposed by neoliberal governments all over the world[38] should be removed and sectoral collective bargaining introduced—and this must be viewed from a transnational perspective, including workers throughout the value chain.[39] Unions must also take measures to democratize their internal structures and give greater voice to rank-and-file workers, as well as supporting those working to unionize precarious workers.[40, 41] And if you're not already in one, then join a union! Ask your union rep about how to get involved, and if you're not sure if your workplace is unionized, your national network of trade unions—such as the TUC for readers in the UK, or the AFL-CIO for those in the US—should have information about the unions that represent workers in your sector.

Policies to free up workers' time and increase their pay are also critical to shifting the balance of power between workers and bosses.[42] Those struggling to survive are less able to participate in social institutions or engage in resistance or collective action. And giving workers more control over their time is a way to provide them with a sense of dignity and autonomy that can boost their confidence in making demands of employers and the government.

Moving to a four-day workweek with no loss of pay is an important first step toward democratizing work, which would also increase employment and allow people more time to participate in collective activities of the kind outlined in the previous section.[43] Other critical policy changes in this area include closing the gap between regulation of the gig economy and formal employment, and introducing a living wage.

We must also ensure that workers have the right to refuse work. No worker should be forced to take a poorly paid, dangerous job simply because they have to survive. Some argue this is a case for a universal basic income (UBI), but most UBIs are proposed at a level that would not allow workers to survive without work.[44] And handing out cash does little to democratize the economy and could instead reinforce neoliberal individualism and consumerism.

A far better proposal would be to decommodify everything people need to survive by providing a program of universal basic services, whereby all essential services like health care, education (including higher education), social care, and even food, housing, and transport are provided for free or at subsidized prices.[45] And ensuring that these services are governed democratically would also help build social solidarity at the local level—something that a UBI would be unlikely to achieve.

Expanding public ownership of firms—whether at a local or national level—is another key element in the democratization of the economy, because it challenges capital's power over investment.[46] Capitalists will often threaten to stop investing or move abroad if socialist governments come to power or if socialist movements become too strong. But democratic public ownership makes these threats less credible by fixing investments in place. What's more, truly democratic publicly owned corporations can facilitate production at scale in a way that is harder to achieve in an economy built solely on cooperative and mutual enterprises.

But transferring a firm from private to public ownership will go only so far. The fact that public ownership is not in itself threatening to capital should be clear from the fact that it remains common in capitalist societies. It is not enough to nationalize corporations; we must democratize decision-making within them as well.

The UK think tank We Own It has outlined some proposals to show how this might be achieved in practice: creating a collective organization to represent citizens on the boards of publicly owned corporations, allowing them to vote on corporate governance procedures; formalizing trade union and civil society representation in publicly owned corporations, both on boards and throughout the organization; and establishing participatory budgeting and e-democracy processes to set budgets and develop new ideas for production and services provision.[47]

Collective ownership comes in many forms, from worker cooperatives, to producer cooperatives, to mutuals.[48] Like public ownership, collective ownership is not always genuinely democratic—there are plenty of cooperative enterprises within which workers lack voice and power, and some cooperatives (for example, consumer cooperatives) continue to rely on exploitative labor practices. But building the cooperative economy can have positive effects when combined with other measures.

One particularly exciting new model comes from the gig economy, where workers are organizing to build alternatives to the extractive, monopolistic platforms that currently dominate the sector.[49] Cooperatively owned apps, such as the Driver's Co-Operative and cleaning business Up & Go, give workers an ownership stake and allow them to participate in decision-making. The Platform Cooperative Consortium has information about platform co-ops across different sectors all over the world.[50]

Supporting co-ops as part of a community wealth-building agenda can help to tackle the power of the outsourcing giants as well as allowing local people a greater say in how their public services are owned and run, while providing good employment for worker-owners—as in Preston and Jackson, Mississippi.[51] Agricultural cooperatives can play a key role in protecting the environment and the rights of those who live in it—as we saw in Ciudad Futura, Argentina. The UK-based New Economics Foundation has several policy proposals for supporting the cooperative economy, including developing an appropriate legal framework for cooperatives, providing public financing to allow cooperatives to emerge and scale, and accelerating the community wealth-building agenda to allow local government to support the emergence of local cooperatives.[52]

Worker ownership is an even more radical option. One of the best-known historic attempts to expand worker ownership is Sweden's Meidner Plan.[53] In the 1970s, trade union economists developed an initiative to steadily socialize ownership in the Swedish economy by requiring all companies above a certain size annually to issue new shares that would be transferred to a worker fund. In this way, workers would become owners of the firms in which they worked. Worker representatives, selected through the unions, would then take seats on corporate boards on behalf of the company's worker-owners.

In the UK, the Labour Party developed a similar proposal through which large companies would have to place a certain portion of their shares each year into a worker fund that would confer some decision-making power and distribute dividends.[54] While it is true that worker ownership doesn't inherently challenge the imperative to maximize profits—even at the expense of society as a whole—the policy is a promising way both to empower workers and challenge the power of capital, as should be evident by the ferocity with which both the Meidner Plan and Labour's employee ownership funds were resisted.[55] Another proposal is to establish a "European directive on minimum standards for the right to information, consultation, and worker representation on boards of directors."[56] This approach could also be extended to bankruptcy proceedings to support workers to buy out a company themselves through the bankruptcy process.[57]

Democratizing Finance

As we saw in chapter 5, decisions about investment are currently the closely guarded prerogatives of capital. Financial institutions, which finance and mediate these decisions, therefore have significant power to control which businesses succeed, which individuals thrive, and which states grow. Yet they wield this power with a view to maximizing profits, even at the expense of people and planet. Democratizing the financial system—that is, handing power over investment decisions to the workers and communities that will be affected by those decisions—will be a cornerstone of democratizing society.[58]

Introducing public, democratically governed retail banking could help break the stranglehold of the big banks over this critical public service, allowing for lower fees and interest rates for consumers and curbing the power of financial capital over our democratic institutions. One proposal, outlined by the UK Labour Party in 2019, would be to set up a network of Post Banks through the postal system.[59] This public bank would be capitalized by the central government and run as a subsidiary of the Post Office, with governance decentralized to local and regional levels—a model that should be simple to replicate in other national contexts.

The banks could provide standard retail services such as current accounts, savings accounts, insurance services, and small loans at low interest rates. The banks could also be used to achieve other public policy goals such as helping those with unsustainable debts refinance their borrowing—or even writing off debt for households in poverty. And subjecting the institution to democratic decision-making processes—by, for example, providing it with a democratically elected board—would further boost worker and citizen power.

Public investment banks are already important actors within the world economy. Many capitalist states use public banks, sovereign wealth funds, and public pension funds to direct investment within their economies.[60] Clearly, setting up public investment banks does not inherently promote democratization or threaten the power of capital.

But these institutions will have a key role in democratizing the economy, because they help to socialize investment decisions, challenging capital's ability to threaten strike or flight. And they could play an important role in supporting the democratization of the economy through, for instance, lending to cooperative enterprises or decarbonization programs.[61] Subjecting these institutions to genuinely democratic decision-making processes, like those outlined for other public companies in the previous section, would be an even more radical proposal.

Democratizing the financial system is also a critical prerequisite to democratizing ownership throughout the economy. Asset managers like BlackRock control vast quantities of other people's money and use it to prop up the status quo. A public, democratic asset manager could challenge the power of these behemoths and help democratize investment decisions, as well as socializing ownership in the economy. In my first book, *Stolen*, I outlined a proposal for a People's Asset Manager (PAM)—a public, democratic BlackRock that could democratize investment and socialize ownership throughout the economy.[62]

The PAM would contain several "pots" of cash, some of which it would manage on behalf of society as a whole (such as a citizens wealth fund) and some of which it would manage on behalf of individuals (such as public sector pensions). The former fund could invest based on collectively determined public goals, while the latter would have to be determined by pension holders themselves with a view to securing returns as well as promoting other social objectives. The PAM could work with the national investment bank proposed earlier in this section, investing in companies to which the bank had lent—in the same way that many investment banks also have asset management arms that allow them to take advantage of investment opportunities that arise from their lending activities.

Democratizing the State

The kind of democracy that exists in capitalist societies is inherently limited. Participation is limited to elections, and most people have little to no say in the manifestos of the parties vying for their votes. The close links between "cartelized" political parties, capital, and the state mean that policy is generally limited to small reforms that will not fundamentally threaten the status quo.[63] And even where progressive parties do come close to winning power, there are vast swathes of the state apparatus that have deliberately been placed outside democratic control.[64]

Aware that the system is stacked against them, working-class voters in much of the rich world have been leaving the electorate en masse.[65]

Trust in democracy is at all-time lows.[66] Many allegedly democratic countries are becoming ever more authoritarian in the face of fierce resistance from those suffering most from the economic and political turmoil currently engulfing our politics.[67]

In the midst of this onslaught, it is critical that socialists fight to defend the hard-won democratic rights that many of us have come to enjoy. But defending liberal democracy is not enough; it must be deepened. The kinds of democratic reforms required to strengthen democracy will differ from place to place. There is a great deal more variation in political institutions than there is across economic ones—in part because the latter have been subject to the pressures of imperialism. But there are some common demands around which socialists can rally.

In many countries, the liberal revolutions that began in the eighteenth century have not yet been completed. The UK, for example, still has a monarchy, an upper chamber (the House of Lords), and a local authority (the City of London Corporation, a private organization that governs one of the world's largest financial centers, including having power over local taxation and policing) that are all insulated from democratic accountability. Socialists must fight alongside genuine liberals to remove these undemocratic feudal hangovers. And in authoritarian regimes, the introduction of democratic reforms is—alongside building unions and community institutions to protect people's livelihoods—of the highest priority.

Democratizing central banking will be another essential part of democratizing both the state and the economy.[68] As I argue in *Stolen*, the makeup of central bank committees should be changed to include representation from the government, labor and social movements, and other stakeholders, as well as containing a majority of directly elected members. Their decisions should be scrutinized frequently by an independent panel of citizens, including some experts, who would report to the government and, if necessary, directly challenge the bank's decisions.

Participatory budgeting and policymaking should also be introduced at every level of government. Citizens should be offered a chance to have a say in policymaking and spending in municipal, regional, and national government. As outlined in the previous chapter, participatory budgeting is already widespread and currently practiced in hundreds of cities around the world. Innovations like Better Reykjavik and Decidim in Spain show how the democratic process can be deepened even further by allowing citizens a chance to vote on the policies that will be in a party's manifesto.

Social democratic parties should commit to promoting subsidiarity—that is, ensuring that decisions are undertaken as close as feasible to those affected. This does not mean that all decisions should be made at the local level. It would not be feasible to conduct, say, macroeconomic or climate policy locally. But where it is possible for a decision to be made closer to a community without dampening its effectiveness, decentralization should be encouraged—not because localism is inherently progressive, but because it is easier for organized workers and communities to apply pressure to local government than it is to national government, and smaller local victories provide momentum that can support movements to transform national politics too.

Equalizing the balance of power between capital and labor also requires imposing strict limits on political donations and lobbying. In the US, where the money directed into politics has reached eye-watering levels, vested interests are able to raise and donate millions to their preferred candidates, allowing them to exert significant influence over policy. Corporations are now also legally considered people, which means restrictions on corporate donations have been outlawed in the name of free speech. And a powerful network of right-wing think tanks, lobbyists, and media organizations dominates the wider political landscape.

In the US, reactionary interpretations of the constitutional right to free speech make reforming campaign finance difficult—but there are plenty of proposals to limit the influence of money in politics that would bypass these problems.[69] Campaign finance reform must also consider ways to ensure progressive parties are able to access funding. In Germany, all political parties that surpass a certain voting threshold receive a stipend from the state that they can use to support allied movements and institutions.

Introducing any of these reforms will require democratizing political parties. Many social democratic parties have become "cartelized": they have developed such close relationships with state institutions that they no longer feel they need to nurture links with their activist bases.[70] In fact, many of these parties have focused far more on ridding themselves of socialists than on winning elections. If social democratic parties continue to spend all their energy fighting the surge in support for socialism among their base, they will guarantee their ongoing electoral marginalization. But for many politicians, electoral marginalization is a small price to pay for maintaining their control over a dying institution—which is why it is necessary to democratize political parties and ensure they are accountable to their members and the wider political movements that support them.

The strategies required to achieve this will vary from place to place. In majoritarian electoral systems like those in the US and the UK, activists have little choice other than to work within existing social democratic parties. Doing so successfully will, however, require a strong focus on building power outside these parties as well—in communities, within the labor movement, and on the streets.

These electoral systems themselves must also be the focus of reform. Systems like first-past-the-post privilege the two largest parties, as well as parties with significant regional support, over smaller parties that nevertheless command extensive popular support. Moving toward more proportional systems, which nevertheless contain an element of local accountability for representatives,[71] would be a step forward for democratic politics in countries like the US and the UK.

In more pluralistic electoral systems, progressives have had more success in building new political parties from the ground up. The idea of the "movement party" championed by activists and politicians in countries like Spain provides an interesting model.[72] Democratic accountability between leaders and the wider movement is the central requirement for a movement party—and measures like the democratic selection of candidates and policies (including through e-democracy) are critical in this regard.

Another central factor in ensuring Left political parties retain democratic legitimacy is through the promotion of working-class candidates. As Ralph Miliband observed, in most countries, politics is dominated by an insular elite that permits entry to few outsiders.[73] Historically, labor movements provided another route for working-class leaders to emerge and enter mainstream politics, but as the unions have declined, so too has working-class representation. In any case, this route was often foreclosed to marginalized groups within the working class. Ensuring truly democratic candidate-selection processes is key to ensuring these political parties are able to win the trust of electorates.

Democratizing International Institutions

Neoliberal hegemony is perhaps strongest, and hardest to challenge, at the level of the world economy. As we have seen, neoliberal academics and policymakers spent decades constructing an architecture for the global economy that has insulated capital from democratic pressure. The result has been the ongoing exploitation and underdevelopment of the poor world by the rich. But, as geopolitical power begins to shift, there are opportunities to challenge imperialism and build a genuinely democratic world order.

The principles outlined at the Bandung Conference, and those of the subsequent New International Economic Order (NIEO), remain critical to shifting the balance of power within the world economy. The spirit of Bandung centers on demands that powerful nations respect the sovereignty and territorial integrity of all others as well as the settlement of all disputes through peaceful means. Imperial powers have consistently engaged in both illegal wars of aggression cloaked in the language of freedom and democracy and "humanitarian intervention," flooding already tense regions with weapons only to leave as soon as they realize the conflicts are unwinnable. These endless wars must be opposed.

The NIEO focused on the reform of international trade, investment, and finance—as well as promoting solidarity among states in the Global South. Reviving the NIEO requires states in the Global North to end unfair tariffs and quotas—particularly those on agricultural commodities and steel—as these undermine development in the South. Tariffs, quotas, and subsidies should, however, be permitted for poor countries seeking to build up domestic industries by protecting them against unfair international competition. The infrastructure that underpins global trade must also be governed democratically, based on public good, not private profit—the regulation of sectors like shipping and tech requires a substantial overhaul in this regard.

Trade agreements must also be democratized. Rather than depending on regional agreements like NAFTA and the TPP, within which one powerful country is able to dominate others, the international trading system should be governed by multilateral agreements based on the principle of one country, one vote. Trade deals should never be used to bludgeon smaller states into adopting policies that favor capital in the North.

Regressive rules governing intellectual property rights must be re-scinded, as these prevent states in the South from accessing the technol-ogies needed to industrialize—as well as denying lifesaving drugs and life-giving seeds to billions of people. And the deeply undemocratic investor-state dispute settlements included in many bilateral and multilat-eral investment treaties must be totally abandoned.

The Global South is in the midst of a deep debt crisis, in part because of the excessive integration with international financial markets. Even before the most recent crisis, sub-Saharan Africa was losing three times more in capital flight each year than it gained in development aid.[74] Laws surrounding international trade and investment should permit all coun-tries to implement credit and exchange controls, as well as allowing them to direct credit within their own economies using both fiscal policy and arm's-length institutions like national investment banks.

Dealing with the debt crisis requires changes to the mechanisms gov-erning disputes between debtors and creditors. There is no reason why creditors should constantly be protected from the consequences of their lending decisions at the expense of generally poorer debtor nations. Kevin Gallagher and Richard Kozul-Wright argue cogently for some much-needed reforms to this system, including introducing new allocations of IMF special drawing rights, which poor countries can exchange for cash in emergencies; establishing a multilateral swap facility at the IMF like the swap lines currently offered by the US central bank; and establishing a global debt authority with the power to determine how debts are restruc-tured.[75] Most importantly, unpayable debts must be canceled. In the wake of the pandemic, and with the climate crisis looming, a new debt jubilee for the global south is the sine qua non of development and poverty reduction.

None of these reforms are likely to happen on their own. It is there-fore imperative that states in the Global South build strong links with one another—as they did at Bandung—and use their combined weight to shift the balance of power within the world economy. This power can be used to push for reform within existing institutions, but also to build new, democratic trade and investment institutions like regional development banks that can support development today. It is also perfectly legitimate for states in the Global South to build strategic alliances and economic relationships with other powerful actors within the world economy to boost their negotiating power with Western institutions.

Global South nations must work together to protect themselves from the consequences of climate breakdown caused largely by the rich world. A new international climate bank is required to provide the funding required for states in the poor world to protect their people from the effects of climate breakdown today and support decarbonization over the long run.[76] Like the domestic national investment banks proposed above, the climate bank should be both democratic and representative, with every state being given an equal vote. Decarbonizing the world economy will require new funding as well as additional finance. We need a new Marshall Plan for decarbonization, whereby rich states transfer funds, as well as skills and technologies, to states in the Global South to facilitate the transition to net zero.

Climate breakdown will inevitably mean more people are forced to move from the places most affected by global warming to those that caused it. Governments in the Global North must get real on migration. Instead of spending billions on measures designed to keep migrants out or expel or punish them once they arrive (like the astonishingly inefficient UK government plan to commandeer planes to deport people to Rwanda, and some US governors' similar strategy to fly migrants to cities like New York and Washington, DC), funds should be redirected to facilitating the training and integration of migrants and refugees.

Such measures will be of substantial benefit to rich countries, which, due to demographic aging, declining population health, and reactionary migration policies, are suffering from a severe dearth of workers in sectors like health and social care. What's more, migrant workers from parts of the world with a stronger tradition of worker organizing often bring these skills with them to the rich world, making it easier for workers in traditionally disorganized sectors to unionize.[77] As long as workers are well organized, the purported link between inward migration and lower wages will not materialize. The most important factor determining wage growth is workers' bargaining power, as demonstrated by the fact that historically high rates of employment have not led to higher wages in poorly unionized economies.

Critical precursors to achieving any of these reforms include ending tax avoidance, preventing a race to the bottom on tax rates, and shutting down tax havens. There is an urgent need to end legal forms of tax avoidance like profit shifting and introduce minimum requirements around transparency on tax reporting and financial flows. The wealthy states that act as conduits for tax avoidance—and that tend to govern or oversee most of the world's tax havens—must take the lead in this reform agenda.

Democratizing the Future

The measures outlined thus far are all reforms—some quite radical— that could make capitalist economies more democratic and socialistic. But they would still be capitalist societies. And, for as long as capital controls society's power over investment, that society will never be fully democratized. Building a truly democratic society requires eliminating the distinction between those who own and control all the means of production and everyone else. It requires allowing everyone to have some say in how our society's resources are used, at every level of social organization—from the town to the nation to the world.

Achieving this requires thinking seriously about how democratic planning might take place at scale. Socialists have shown throughout history that efficient planning at scale is at least theoretically possible. And as Leigh Phillips and Michal Rozworski show using the example of Walmart, it is already being executed in practice. Huge capitalist firms like Walmart are already deploying new technologies to facilitate efficient economic planning within their operations. Could these technologies be put to use by democratic socialist planners?

The problem with attempting to develop technologies that could facilitate a move to democratic planning at scale is one that Marx identified over a century ago. As has been shown throughout this book, technological and scientific progress are planned—and they are planned in the interests of the powerful. In the collection of writings he left unpublished at his death, the *Grundrisse*, Marx shows both that technological innovation is central to the development of capitalism and that the nature of this innovation is not neutral—it is designed to serve capital.[78]

The dynamics of economic and political competition encourage firms and states to plow money into the research and development of new technologies that augment their wealth and power. As Marx pointed out with remarkable but not unusual prescience, innovation eventually becomes so important to the development of capitalism that it becomes a business in itself.[79] Entire firms—even entire countries—specialize in coming up with new technological discoveries, not out of a need to solve a particular problem or improve a particular process, but simply out of the desire to drive innovation for innovation's sake. Come up with the ideas, and applications will follow.

While innovation has been a constant feature of human life, it is only under capitalism that it becomes the driving force of social development. In fact, technology becomes so critical to production that it appears to overpower the worker operating it. Knowledge and skill that were once deployed by the worker are taken over by the machine and, in this way, the worker becomes "a mere appendage" of the machine. This process of displacement can be a profoundly alienating and disempowering experience.

We are used to thinking of technology as a tool—something that can be used for good or ill depending on who controls it. But Marx saw that the path of technological development is influenced by social relations—capitalist firms and states develop technologies that benefit capital, not workers. This bias in capitalist technology shapes the conditions of our existence. The trade-offs of using scarce resources to produce more efficient profit-producing machines—as opposed to technologies that can solve social problems—are significant.

While he may have been one of its harshest critics, Marx believed that the technological progress made under capitalism was a precondition for the transition to socialism. Yet the technologies that might be put to use under a new social order contain inherent biases that limit their possible applications. Allende and his team were forced to use outdated technologies to construct a decentralized planning network from scratch, and the limitations of these technologies made the final product more centralized than its architects might have liked. And the planning technology developed by Walmart is designed to maximize profit, at the expense of its workers and the planet.

It seems obvious that, at this stage of scientific and technological development, we are *capable* of producing the kind of technology that could facilitate genuinely democratic planning at scale. Unfortunately, such technology, which is a precondition for the transition to democratic socialism, will never be developed within our current social order.

Yet this problem is not a reason for despair. As the late David Graeber used to say, "Capitalism dominates, but it doesn't pervade." New social orders do not spring up fully formed, and old ones collapse only after fissures and cracks slowly begin to emerge. The birth of capitalism required the development of technologies, knowledge, and social relations that did not exist under feudalism; yet a few pioneering individuals were able to identify the seeds of a new world emerging from the ashes of the old and nurtured those shoots with the resources they had available to them.

The foundations of capitalism had to be built carefully, from within the old system. Ideological and material battles had to be fought, pamphlets written, legislation passed, wars fought. Capitalism's midwives had to be smart, bold, and tenacious as they struggled to break through the cracks that had emerged within the feudal order. For them, the rewards were obvious: wealth and power beyond anything they could have imagined within the society into which they were born.

Similarly, the technologies, knowledge, and social relations we need to build a truly democratic world economy may not exist today, but their forerunners do. The work of a revolutionary is more like that of a gardener than a builder. The new world will not be brought about overnight—its seeds have to be planted, nurtured, and protected.

As we have seen, there already exist plenty of spaces in which people are working to build alternatives to the current system—despite resistance from those who benefit from the status quo. Even though both failed, the Lucas Plan and Project Cybersyn were two of the most ambitious examples of such work. Both took place during a period when it had begun to seem as though capitalist social relations might not last forever—when working people began to realize that the only thing standing between them and self-governance, between them and real freedom, was capital itself.

It is up to us to continue the legacy of those projects, to peer through the fissures that exist within the current system and work together to prize them open, to let the light in. For us, the rewards are less concrete than those won by the early capitalists. They are rewards that accrue to all, not just to a privileged few: the protection of the planet we rely on to survive, an end to the psychic trauma of living in a world marked by such deep and pervasive suffering and alienation, and a world in which every human being has the chance to flourish into their fullest selves.

Conclusion

We live in capitalism. Its power seems inescapable. So did the divine right
of kings. Any human power can be resisted and changed by human beings.

—Ursula K. Le Guin

I t's easy to look at the state of the world and feel hopeless. We live in
an age marked by war, climate breakdown, political polarization, economic inequality, and widespread poverty. Most of us feel deeply dis-
turbed by the knowledge that our world seems so profoundly damaged,
yet we often feel powerless to do anything in response.

Big corporations make a fortune from this guilt by selling us products
and services designed to placate our conscience, often with significant
unintended consequences. Financial institutions lend us money to allow
us to purchase these products, even when doing so will simply drive us
deeper into debt. Politicians tell us that all our problems could disappear
through the simple act of ticking the right box in the voting booth, yet
they consistently fail to deliver on their promises. And we're supposed to
leave global challenges to international institutions, yet these institutions
consistently seem to side with those who want to protect the status quo.

All those living under capitalism are, to a greater or lesser extent,
unfree. We are unfree because, as isolated individuals, we lack collective power to shape the conditions of our existence. If you don't like
your job, you can try to get a new one, but your wages, conditions,
and relationships with your superiors are shaped by factors far outside
your control. If you're unhappy with the political policies pursued in

your nation, you have two choices: vote for a party leader chosen by someone else, or leave. And the second of those is often available only to those with the means to do so.

It would be one thing if this sense of powerlessness was caused by the impersonal and anonymous "free market." No one can control or organize the market, it just is. "If you feel powerless in the face of the political and economic systems that govern life under capitalism," the neoliberal might respond, "welcome to the club—that's how the free market works."

The idea that capitalism is a free-market system, in which no one has any real control over the production and allocation of resources, is the foundation of the lie that society cannot change. The magic of the free market, as outlined by thinkers like Hayek, is supposed to be so profound that any attempt to control and direct it will end in failure. Even Keynes believed that the task of managing the market should be left to technocrats rather than the masses. It seems that, whatever your politics, there is no space for democracy in our world anymore.

But as we have seen throughout the course of this book, capitalism is not really a free-market system. Instead, the power of all capitalist institutions—from corporations to financial institutions, states to international organizations—is based on a certain amount of centralized planning. These institutions, and those who lead them, are able to shape the conditions of life for everyone else. And they are able to wield this power with little or no democratic accountability.

These inequalities of power do not result from conspiratorial networks created by evil elites, they're the inevitable result of the class division of society that is an inherent feature of capitalism. Capitalism hasn't been "corrupted"; it's functioning exactly as it's supposed to. As long as our society is divided into two groups—those who own everything we need to produce things, and those forced to sell their labor power for a living—some people will always have more power over the way the system works than others. Some people will always be in control, while others will remain unfree.

The problems created by capitalism seem so deeply intractable that responding to them feels like a lost cause. Yet it is precisely this sense of powerlessness that underpins the stability of the status quo. The powerful have a vested interest in making us believe the world is the way it is because it could not be any different—that any other way of organizing the world would require us to sacrifice the basic freedoms we all rightly hold so dear.

In this context, neoliberals and Keynesians have spent decades bickering over whether we should build an economy with more or less state intervention. The neoliberals have claimed that people face a choice between unaccountable and overbearing state planners and the freedom and justice ensured by the free market. Keynesians have claimed that we face a choice between ruthless free-market capitalism and stable, organized planned capitalism. Both sides have a point, and both sides get the terms of the debate completely wrong.

The choice isn't "free markets" or "planning." Planning and markets exist alongside each other in capitalist societies—indeed, in any society. The choice is whether the planning that inevitably does take place in any complex social system is democratic or oligarchic. Do we allow a few institutions to make decisions that affect everyone else, considering only their own interests, or do we move toward a system in which *everyone* has the power to shape the conditions of their existence?

We must stop talking about "free-market capitalism" and instead accept that capitalism is a hybrid system based on a fusion between markets and planning. Rather than seeing the world in which we live as emerging from mystical market forces beyond our control, we must realize that capitalism results from the conscious choices of those operating within it. When we are able to view it in these terms, the space for conscious, democratic design of our world expands.

If, after reading this book, you still believe such a system to be entirely unworkable, it might be worth asking yourself why you are so sure this is the case. Imagine for a moment that you are a medieval peasant working the land of a lord in exchange for a meager subsistence and some vague promises of protection. Your entire worldview is defined by unchanging, divinely sanctioned hierarchies over which you have little control. You were born a serf, and you will die a serf.

You don't waste much time thinking about why the world is the way it is—it just is. If you do bother to consider why you've been assigned such a rough lot in life, you're provided with ample justification for this state of affairs by people who, it seems, know far more than you about the ways of the world. If you just sit down, do as you're told, and work hard, then you'll be rewarded—perhaps not in this life, but certainly in the next.

When we look back on the world of feudal lords, bishops, and peasants, the whole system seems destined for the ash heap of history. It was so grossly unfair and unjust that it's a wonder it survived for as long as it did. And yet today, like the peasants of the past, millions of us willingly submit to our own oppression and exploitation. In fact, just like those peasants, we may not even realize that is what we are doing. We may think the world in which we live is unchangeable, and therefore believe it makes more sense to submit than to fight back. Free-market capitalism might not be the best system in the world, but it's better than all the others we've ever tried.

Such thinking is based on the arrogant and implausible assumption that all possible ways of organizing society have—at this particular point in time—already been put to the test. When you look at the history of the world, it becomes quite clear that the ideals of democracy and socialism—as articulated by liberals and socialists—have never really been put into practice. True political and economic democracy has always and consistently been thwarted by those in charge.

You might be extremely sure that human beings are, by nature, selfish creatures who could never hope to organize their own affairs. Many medieval peasants would have been quite sure that neither they nor their fellow men could be trusted with the vote. And they were, of course, assured that they were correct in this assumption by plenty of very intelligent members of the clergy. Despite their protestations to the contrary, sophists like Jordan Peterson who insist that society is inherently hierarchical play precisely the same role as those clerics. It's their job to claim superior knowledge of the way the world works to foreclose alternatives to the status quo.

But there have always been those with imaginations powerful enough to find the cracks in the current system and work to build a different world. As the feudal system began to crumble, intellectuals struggled against the dominance of the church to develop new scientific theories and technological innovations. Capitalists struggled against the conservativism of the aristocracy to assert the right to produce and trade commodities among themselves, and eventually all over the globe. Less well remembered, workers—and even peasants—fought to defend their rights in the context of the profound changes that were then underway.

In the UK, as early as the 1640s, the Levellers were arguing for reforms to the grossly unfair and unequal political system—from extended suffrage to equal rights for all. The Diggers were an even more radical group fighting at the same time for common ownership of land, as well as political reform. While the church sought to monopolize the interpretation of the gospels to legitimate the current social order, the Diggers—like many before and since—saw the revolutionary implications of Christian teaching, pointing to the communistic living style of the early Christians.

Today, there are plenty of examples of working people coming together to build real democracy from the ground up—often in extraordinarily difficult conditions and facing extremely powerful vested interests. The fact that many of these experiments have succeeded should provide some evidence that we have not exhausted all possible forms of social organization. And the fact that the powerful were so intent upon crushing movements like those led by Salvador Allende should be proof enough that, when undertaken at scale, they have the power to subvert and even uproot capitalism itself.

The greatest barrier to the emergence and spread of these movements is not the overwhelming power of capital. It is the conviction, held by millions of people, that change is impossible. The moment we let go of our collective belief in the inevitability of the current system is the moment we start to build a new one.

We do not have to live in a society defined by such extreme inequalities of wealth and power. We do not have to spend the rest of our lives dealing with feelings of hopelessness and despair. We do not have to live in a world that is so unfree. We have only to peer through the cracks already emerging within capitalism to catch a glimpse of the real freedom that awaits on the other side.

Notes

INTRODUCTION

1. Katie Brigham, "How Conflict Minerals Make It into Our Phones," CNBC, February 15, 2023, https://www.cnbc.com/2023/02/15/how-conflict-minerals-make-it-into-our-phones.html.

2. Brandy Zadrozny, " 'Carol's Journey': What Facebook Knew about How It Radicalized Users," NBC News, October 22, 2021, https://www.nbcnews.com/tech/tech-news/facebook-knew-radicalized-users-rcna3581.

3. John Smith, *Imperialism in the Twenty-First Century: Globalization, Super-Exploitation and Capitalism* (New York: Monthly Review Press, 2016); Sarah Butler and Thaslima Begum, "Abuses 'Still Rife': 10 Years on from Bangladesh's Rana Plaza Disaster," *The Guardian*, April 24, 2023, https://www.theguardian.com/world/2023/apr/24/10-years-on-bangladesh-rana-plaza-disaster-safety-garment-workers-rights-pay.

4. Viola Wohlgemuth, "How Fast Fashion Is Using the Global South as a Dumping Ground for Textile Waste," Greenpeace, April 22, 2022, https://www.greenpeace.org/international/story/53333/how-fast-fashion-is-using-global-south-as-dumping-ground-for-textile-waste/.

5. Harriet Agerholm and Colletta Smith, "Growing Share of Under-30s Pay Unaffordable Rent," BBC News, August 19, 2022, https://www.bbc.com/news/business-62525269.

6. Jack Ewing, *Faster, Higher, Farther: How One of the World's Largest Automakers Committed a Massive and Stunning Fraud* (New York: W. W. Norton, 2018).

7. Ashitha Nagesh, "How Debt Kills—Jerome Rogers: 1995–2016," BBC News, May 29, 2018, https://www.bbc.co.uk/news/resources/idt-sh/How_debt_kills.

8. Juliet Ye, "Foxconn Installs Antijumping Nets at Hebei Plants," *Wall Street Journal*, August 3, 2010, https://www.wsj.com/articles/BL-CJB-9896.

9. As Marx put it, capitalist production "rests on the fact that material conditions of production are in the hands of non-workers in the form of property in capital and land, while the masses are only owners of the personal conditions of production, of labour power." Karl Marx, Critique of the Gotha Programme, Marxist Internet

Archive, accessed August 21, 2023, https://www.marxists.org/archive/marx/works/1875/gotha/.

10. Friedrich A. Von Hayek, *The Road to Serfdom: Text and Documents—The Definitive Edition* (Chicago: University of Chicago Press, 2007).

11. John Maynard Keynes, *The General Theory of Employment, Interest, and Money* (New York: Springer, 2018).

12. Philip Mirowski, *Never Let a Serious Crisis Go to Waste: How Neoliberalism Survived the Financial Meltdown* (London: Verso Books, 2014).

13. Hayek, *Road to Serfdom*.

14. Philip Mirowski and Dieter Plehwe, *The Road from Mont Pèlerin: The Making of the Neoliberal Thought Collective* (Cambridge, MA: Harvard University Press, 2015).

15. William Davies, "The Neoliberal State: Power against 'Politics,'" in Damien Cahill, Melinda Cooper, Martijn Konings, and David Primrose (eds.), *SAGE Handbook of Neoliberalism* (Thousand Oaks, CA: SAGE Publications Ltd., 2018), 273–83, https://doi.org/10.4135/9781526416001.n22; Mirowski, *Never Let a Serious Crisis Go to Waste*.

16. Phil Harvey and Lisa Conyers, *Welfare for the Rich: How Your Tax Dollars End Up in Millionaires' Pockets—And What You Can Do About It* (New York: Post Hill Press, 2020).

17. Barry C. Lynn, *Cornered: The New Monopoly Capitalism and the Economics of Destruction* (New York: Trade Paper Press, 2009); Matt Stoller, *Goliath: The 100-Year War Between Monopoly Power and Democracy* (New York: Simon & Schuster, 2019); David Dayen, *Monopolized: Life in the Age of Corporate Power* (New York: The New Press, 2020).

18. Ernest Mandel, *Late Capitalism* (London: Verso, 1999); Leigh Phillips and Michal Rozworski, *People's Republic of Walmart: How the World's Biggest Corporations Are Laying the Foundation for Socialism* (London: Verso, 2019).

19. Isabelle Ferreras, *Firms as Political Entities: Saving Democracy through Economic Bicameralism* (Cambridge: Cambridge University Press, 2017).

20. Jonathan Tepper and Denise Hearn, *The Myth of Capitalism: Monopolies and the Death of Competition* (New York: Wiley, 2019); Dayen, *Monopolized*.

21. Ferreras, *Firms as Political Entities*.

22. Joshua Barkan, *Corporate Sovereignty: Law and Government under Capitalism* (Minneapolis: University of Minnesota Press, 2013).

23. See, for example, Michael Hudson, *Killing the Host: How Financial Parasites and Debt Bondage Destroy the Global Economy* (NP: ISLET, 2015); Katharina Pistor, *The Code of Capital: How the Law Creates Wealth and Inequality* (Princeton, NJ: Princeton University Press, 2020).

24. Ferreras, *Firms as Political Entities*.

25. Michael Hudson and Ahmet Oncu, *Absentee Ownership and Its Discontents: Critical Essays on the Legacy of Thorstein Veblen* (NP: ISLET, 2016).

26. Martin Beddeleem, "Recoding Liberalism: Philosophy and Sociology of Science against Planning," in Quinn Slobodian, Dieter Plehwe, and Philip Mirowski (eds.), *Nine Lives of Neoliberalism* (London: Verso, 2020).

27. See Geoff Mann, *In the Long Run We Are All Dead: Keynesianism, Political Economy, and Revolution* (London: Verso, 2017).

28. Slobodian et al., *Nine Lives of Neoliberalism*.

29. Karl Marx, *Capital: A Critique of Political Economy, Volume I* (London: Penguin UK, 2004).

30. Ellen Meiksins Wood, *Democracy Against Capitalism: Renewing Historical Materialism* (London: Verso, 2016).

31. Ferreras, *Firms as Political Entities*.

32. Nicos Poulantzas, *State, Power, Socialism* (London: Verso Books, 2014).

33. Meiksins Wood, *Democracy Against Capitalism: Renewing Historical Materialism*.

34. Grace Blakeley, "Public Spending Isn't Socialism," *Tribune*, August 11, 2021, https://tribunemag.co.uk/2021/11/public-spending-socialism-covid-pandemic-austerity-trade-unions-workers-rights.

CHAPTER 1: HOW TO GET AWAY WITH MURDER

1. The following account is a highly abridged version of the events surrounding the Boeing 737 MAX disasters. I have had to exclude a great deal of pertinent, and often shocking, information for the sake of brevity. I would highly recommend consulting these sources for a fuller understanding of the events surrounding the disasters: Maureen Tkacik, "Crash Course," *New Republic*, September 18, 2019, https://newrepublic.com/article/154944/boeing-737-max-investigation-indonesia-lion-air-ethiopian-airlines-managerial-revolution; Alec MacGillis, "The Case against Boeing," *The New Yorker*, November 11, 2019, https://www.newyorker.com/magazine/2019/11/18/the-case-against-boeing; Peter Robison, *Flying Blind: The 737 MAX Tragedy and the Fall of Boeing* (London: Penguin UK, 2021); Gregory Travis, "How the Boeing 737 Max Disaster Looks to a Software Developer," *IEEE Spectrum*, April 18, 2019, https://spectrum.ieee.org/how-the-boeing-737-max-disaster-looks-to-a-software-developer.

2. Sinéad Baker, "This Timeline Shows Exactly What Happened on Board the Lion Air Boeing 737 Max that Crashed in Less than 13 Minutes, Killing 189 People," *Insider*, October 29, 2019, https://www.businessinsider.com/lion-air-crash-timeline-boeing-737-max-disaster-killed-189-2019-10.

3. Ibid.

4. Tkacik, "Crash Course."

5. Ibid.

6. Jeff Wise, "6 Minutes of Terror: What Passengers and Crew Experienced Aboard Ethiopian Airlines Flight 302," *Intelligencer*, April 9, 2019, https://nymag.com/intelligencer/2019/04/what-passengers-experienced-on-the-ethiopian-airlines-flight.html.

7. Ibid.

8. Ibid.

9. Ibid.

10. Ibid.

11. Ibid.

12. The Federal Democratic Republic of Ethiopia, Ministry of Transport, Aircraft

Accident Investigation Bureau, "Interim Investigation Report on Accident to the B737-8 (MAX) Registered ET-AVJ Operated by Ethiopian Airlines" (Addis Ababa, March 9, 2020), https://reports.aviation-safety.net/2019/20190310-0_B38M_ET -AVJ_Interim.pdf.

13. MacGillis, "The Case against Boeing."

14. Tkacik, "Crash Course."

15. Ibid.; John A. Byrne, "How Jack Welsh Runs GE," *BusinessWeek*, May 28, 1998, http://www.businessweek.com/1998/23/b3581001.htm.

16. Micheline Maynard, "Wife of Ousted Boeing Chief Seeks Divorce After 50 Years," *New York Times*, March 14, 2005, https://www.nytimes.com/2005/03/14/business /wife-of-ousted-boeing-chief-seeks-divorce-after-50-years.html.

17. Tkacik, "Crash Course."

18. Robison, *Flying Blind*.

19. Ibid.

20. Ibid.

21. John Cassidy, "How Boeing and the F.A.A. Created the 737 MAX Catastrophe," *The New Yorker*, September 17, 2020, https://www.newyorker.com/news/our -columnists/how-boeing-and-the-faa-created-the-737-max-catastrophe.

22. Travis, "How the Boeing 737 Max Disaster Looks to a Software Developer."

23. "The GE-manufactured LEAP engines had a 40% larger diameter than the original 737s and weighed twice as much." Ibid.

24. Gregory Travis, a former pilot and software engineer, explains: "The angle of attack is the angle between the wings and the airflow over the wings. Think of sticking your hand out of a car window on the highway. If your hand is level, you have a low angle of attack; if your hand is pitched up, you have a high angle of attack. When the angle of attack is great enough, the wing enters what's called an aerodynamic stall. You can feel the same thing with your hand out the window: As you rotate your hand, your arm wants to move up like a wing more and more until you stall your hand, at which point your arm wants to flop down on the car door. This propensity to pitch up with power application . . . increased the risk that the airplane could stall . . . Worse still, because the [engines] were so far in front of the wing and so large, a power increase will cause them to actually produce lift, particularly at high angles of attack . . . And the lift they produce is well ahead of the wing's center of lift, meaning the [engines] will cause the 737 Max at a high angle of attack to go to a higher angle of attack." Ibid.

25. Ibid.

26. Ibid.

27. As Travis puts it, "*The* major selling point of the 737 Max is that it is just a 737— any pilot who could fly a 737 could fly a 737 Max with no new training." Ibid.

28. Tkacik, "Crash Course."

29. Ibid.

30. Robison, *Flying Blind*; Tkacik, "Crash Course."

31. Dominic Gates, "Why Boeing's Emergency Directions May Have Failed to Save 737 MAX," *Seattle Times*, April 8, 2019, https://www.seattletimes.com/business

/boeing-aerospace/boeings-emergency-procedure-for-737-max-may-have-failed-on
-ethiopian-flight/.

32. Tkacik, "Crash Course."

33. Cassidy, "How Boeing and the F.A.A. Created the 737 MAX Catastrophe."

34. Tkacik, "Crash Course."

35. Clare Bushey, "Boeing investors could wait 'years' for dividend to return," *Financial Times*, April 27, 2020, https://www.ft.com/content/842082c4-543b-4c0e -b826-2437a409db1f.

36. Robison, *Flying Blind*.

37. Ibid.

38. Ibid.

39. Ibid.

40. Ibid.

41. Cassidy, "How Boeing and the F.A.A. Created the 737 MAX Catastrophe."

42. Michael Laris, "With Its Ties in Washington, Boeing Has Taken over More and More of the FAA's Job," *Washington Post*, March 24, 2019, https://www .washingtonpost.com/local/trafficandcommuting/with-its-ties-in-washington -boeing-has-taken-over-more-and-more-of-the-faas-job/2019/03/24/6e5ef2c6-4be8 -11e9-9663-00ac73f49662_story.html.

43. Ibid.

44. BBC News, "Boeing Admits Knowing of 737 Max Problem," May 6, 2019, https:// www.bbc.co.uk/news/business-48174797.

45. US Department of Justice, Office of Public Affairs, "Press Release: Boeing Charged with 737 Max Fraud Conspiracy and Agrees to Pay over $2.5 Billion," January 7, 2021, https://www.justice.gov/opa/pr/boeing-charged-737-max-fraud-conspiracy -and-agrees-pay-over-25-billion.

46. Paul Constant, "It's Time to End Corporate Welfare. Boeing Is Exhibit A for Why," *Insider*, January 23, 2020, https://www.businessinsider.com/its-time-to-end -corporate-welfare-boeing-is-exhibit-a-2020-1?r=US&IR=T.

47. Good Jobs First, "Good Jobs First Submits Comments to SEC on Disclosure Rules," July 21, 2016, https://goodjobsfirst.org/good-jobs-first-submits-comments-sec -disclosure-rules/.

48. Danny Westneat, "Tax Breaks for Boeing: We're No. 1," *Seattle Times*, November 12, 2013, updated August 25, 2017, https://www.seattletimes.com /seattle-news/tax-breaks-for-boeing-wersquore-no-1/.

49. Michael Hiltzik, "Boeing Got a Record Tax Break from Washington State and Cut Jobs Anyway. Now the State Wants to Strike Back," *Los Angeles Times*, May 3, 2017, https://www.latimes.com/business/hiltzik/la-fi-hiltzik-boeing-washington -20170503-story.html.

50. Sabrina Siddiqui, "Trump to Nominate Former Boeing Executive as Defense Secretary," *The Guardian*, May 9, 2019, https://www.theguardian.com/us -news/2019/may/09/trump-defense-secretary-boeing-patrick-shanahan.

51. Mark Katkov, "Acting Defense Secretary Shanahan Investigated over Ties to Boeing," NPR, March 21, 2019, https://www.npr.org/2019/03/21/705440896 /acting-defense-secretary-shanahan-investigated-for-boeing-ties.

52. David Shepardson and Jeff Mason, "Ties between Boeing and Trump Run Deep," Reuters, March 12, 2019, https://www.reuters.com/article/us-ethiopia-airlines -trump-idUSKBN1QT2MQ.

53. Ibid.

54. Ibid.

55. Tkacik, "Crash Course."

56. Ibid.

57. Robison, *Flying Blind*.

58. Aaron Gregg, Jeff Stein, and Josh Dawsey, "Senate Aid Package Quietly Carves Out Billions Intended for Boeing, Officials Say," *Washington Post*, March 25, 2020, https://www.washingtonpost.com/business/2020/03/25/boeing-bailout -coronavirus/.

59. Public Citizen, "Corporations that Received Billions During the Pandemic Cut Thousands of Jobs and Gave CEOs Millions," April 26, 2021, https://www.citizen .org/news/corporations-that-received-billions-during-the-pandemic-laid-off -thousands-of-workers-and-gave-ceos-millions/.

60. Davide Scigliuzzo and Julie Johnsson, "Boeing's Bailout: Saved by the Fed Without Paying a Dime," Bloomberg, May 2, 2020, https://www.bloomberg.com /news/articles/2020-05-02/the-non-bailout-how-the-fed-saved-boeing-without -paying-a-dime.

61. Aaron Gregg, "How a $17 Billion Bailout Fund Intended for Boeing Ended Up in Very Different Hands," *Seattle Times*, February 23, 2021, https://www.seattletimes .com/business/how-a-17-billion-bailout-fund-intended-for-boeing-ended-up-in-very -different-hands/.

62. Ibid.

63. Ibid.

64. See the Cambridge capital controversy, which refers to a debate that took place between mainstream and heterodox economists regarding theorization of "capital" within the neoclassical model. See also, Marc Lavoie and Mario Seccareccia, "What Even Famous Mainstream Economists Miss About the Cambridge Capital Controversies," Institute for New Economic Thinking, June 15, 2015.

65. Marx, *Capital, Volume I*.

66. Marx, Critique of the Gotha Programme.

67. Marx, *Capital*.

68. Ferreras, *Firms as Political Entities*; Chamayou, *The Ungovernable Society*.

69. Barkan, *Corporate Sovereignty*; Grietje Baars, *The Corporation, Law and Capitalism: A Radical Perspective on the Role of Law in the Global Political Economy* (Leiden: Brill Academic Publishers, 2020); Gregg Barak, *Unchecked Corporate Power: Why the Crimes of Multinational Corporations Are Routinized Away and What We Can Do about It* (Oxford: Routledge, 2017).

70. Hudson and Oncu, *Absentee Ownership and Its Discontents*.

71. Phillips and Rozworski, *People's Republic of Walmart*.

72. Ibid.

73. Søren Mau, *Mute Compulsion: A Marxist Theory of the Economic Power of Capital* (London: Verso Books, 2023).

74. Tess Riley, "Just 100 Companies Responsible for 71% of Global Emissions, Study Says," *The Guardian*, July 10, 2017.

75. Marxist theorist Ernest Mandel writes: "What makes planning possible is the actual control that the capitalist has over the means of production and the labourers in his enterprise, and over the capital which in the event may be accumulated outside the enterprise." *Late Capitalism* (London: Verso, 1999).

76. Frederic Jameson, *Postmodernism, or The Cultural Logic of Late Capitalism* (London: Verso, 1982).

77. Hudson and Oncu, *Absentee Ownership and Its Discontents*.

78. Ferreras, *Firms as Political Entities*.

CHAPTER 2: THE UNITED STATES OF FORDLÂNDIA

1. Antonio Gramsci, *Prison Notebooks* (New York: Columbia University Press, 2011).

2. Max Wallace, *The American Axis: Henry Ford, Charles Lindbergh, and the Rise of the Third Reich* (New York: St. Martin's Press, 2003).

3. Ken Silverstein, "Ford and the Führer," *The Nation*, January 6, 2000, https://www.thenation.com/article/archive/ford-and-fuhrer/.

4. Wallace, *The American Axis*.

5. Gramsci, *Prison Notebooks*.

6. Joseph A. Buttigieg, "Introduction," in Gramsci, *Prison Notebooks*.

7. Ibid.

8. Ibid.

9. Ibid.

10. Gramsci traced the emergence of Prohibition in the US back to precisely this kind of logic. The importance of "peace in the factories" increased under Fordism: a system in which individual laborers were "welded into a human-machine." Gramsci, *Prison Notebooks*.

11. Daniel M. G. Raff and Lawrence H. Summers, "Did Henry Ford Pay Efficiency Wages?," *Journal of Labor Economics* 5, no. 4 (October 1987): S57–S86, https://www.jstor.org/stable/2534911.

12. Panitch and Gindin, *The Making of Global Capitalism*.

13. Stephen Meyer III, *The Five Dollar Day: Labor Management and Social Control in the Ford Motor Company, 1908–1921* (New York: State University of New York Press, 1981).

14. Ford R. Bryan, *Henry's Lieutenants* (Detroit, MI: Wayne State University Press, 2003).

15. Tim Worstall, "The Story of Henry Ford's $5 a Day Wages: It's Not What You Think," *Forbes*, March 4, 2012, https://www.forbes.com/sites/timworstall/2012/03/04/the-story-of-henry-fords-5-a-day-wages-its-not-what-you-think/?sh=5e8eef68766d.

16. Ibid.

17. Meagher, *Competition Is Killing Us*.

18. Lynn, *Cornered*.

19. Panitch and Gindin, *The Making of Global Capitalism*.

20. Greg Grandin, *Fordlandia: The Rise and Fall of Henry Ford's Forgotten Jungle City* (New York: Metropolitan Books, 2009).

21. Ibid.

22. Barkan, *Corporate Sovereignty.*

23. Grandin, *Fordlandia.*

24. Ibid.

25. Ibid.

26. Ibid.

27. Ibid.

28. Drew Reed, "Lost Cities #10: Fordlandia—the Failure of Henry Ford's Utopian City in the Amazon," *The Guardian*, August 19, 2016, https://www.theguardian.com /cities/2016/aug/19/lost-cities-10-fordlandia-failure-henry-ford-amazon.

29. Ibid.

30. Tomé Morrissy-Swan, "Fordlândia, Henry Ford's Abandoned Utopian Dream in the Middle of the Amazon Rainforest," *The Telegraph*, September 12, 2019, https:// www.telegraph.co.uk/travel/destinations/south-america/brazil/galleries/fordlandia -utopian-dream-in-the-amazon-rainforest/.

31. Tim Trainor, "How Ford's Willow Run Assembly Plant Helped Win World War II," *Assembly*, January 3, 2019, https://www.assemblymag.com/articles/94614-how -fords-willow-run-assembly-plant-helped-win-world-war-ii.

32. "Willow Run," Detroit Historical Society, Encylopaedia of Detroit, accessed July 7, 2023, https://detroithistorical.org/learn/encyclopedia-of-detroit/willow-run.

33. Silverstein, "Ford and the Führer."

34. Ibid.

35. Ibid.

36. Gramsci, *Prison Notebooks.*

37. "They represent simply the most recent phase of a long process which began with industrialism itself." Gramsci, *Prison Notebooks.*

38. Scott Lash and John Urry, *The End of Organized Capitalism* (London: Polity Press, 1987).

39. Michael Kalecki, "The Political Aspects of Full Employment," *Political Quarterly* 14, no. 4 (October 1943): 322–30, https://delong.typepad.com/kalecki43.pdf.

40. Chamayou, *The Ungovernable Society.*

41. Ibid.

42. Allan Nevins and Frank Ernest Hill, *Ford: Decline and Rebirth, 1933–1962* (ACLS Humanities E-Book, 2008).

43. Ibid.

44. Ibid.

45. Ibid.

46. Yongwoo Jeung, "A U.S. Tripartite Experiment in the Kennedy Administration," *Polity* 52, no. 1 (January 2020): 116–55, https://doi.org/10.1086/707026.

47. Garry Emmons, "One-on-One with Robert McNamara," Harvard Business School, September 1, 2004, https://www.alumni.hbs.edu/stories/Pages/story-bulletin .aspx?num=2355.

48. Phil Rosenzweig, "Robert S. McNamara and the Evolution of Modern Management," *Harvard Business Review*, December 2010, https://hbr.org/2010/12 /robert-s-mcnamara-and-the-evolution-of-modern-management.

49. Ibid.

50. Negotiations within the Tripartite Committee centered on the development of proposals that would encourage "responsible collective bargaining, industrial peace . . . higher standards of living and increased productivity." Jeung, "A U.S. Tripartite Experiment in the Kennedy Administration."

51. Ibid.

52. Panitch and Gindin, *The Making of Global Capitalism*.

53. Jeung, "A U.S. Tripartite Experiment in the Kennedy Administration."

54. Ibid.

55. Ibid.

56. Isabel Studer-Noguez, *Ford and the Global Strategies of Multinationals: The North American Auto Industry* (Oxford: Routledge, 2002).

57. Harry C. Katz, John Paul MacDuffie, and Frits K. Pil, "Crisis and Recovery in the U.S. Auto Industry: Tumultuous Times for a Collective Bargaining Pacesetter," in Howard R. Stanger, Ann C. Frost, and Paul F. Clark (eds.), *Collective Bargaining Under Duress: Case Studies of Major US Industries* (New York: Cornell University Press, 2014).

58. Studer-Noguez, *Ford and the Global Strategies of Multinationals*.

59. Julie Froud, Colin Haslam, Sukhdev Johal, and Karel Williams, "Cars after Financialisation: A Case Study in Financial Under-Performance, Constraints and Consequences," *Competition & Change* 6, no. 1 (January 1, 2002): 13–41, https://doi.org/10.1080/10245290212675.

60. Keith Bradsher, "Ford Motor to Pay $10 Billion Dividend and Ensure Family Control," *New York Times*, April 15, 2000, https://www.nytimes.com/2000/04/15/business/ford-motor-to-pay-10-billion-dividend-and-ensure-family-control.html.

61. Marcelo José do Carmo, Mário Sacomano Neto, and Julio Cesar Donadone, "Multiple Dynamics of Financialization in the Automotive Sector: Ford and Hyundai Cases," *Gestão & Produção* 27, no. 4 (January 2020), https://doi.org/10.1590/0104-530x5173-20.

62. Ibid.

63. Ibid.

64. Mitchell Hartman, "What Did America Buy with the Auto Bailout, and Was It Worth It?," *Marketplace*, November 13, 2018, https://www.marketplace.org/2018/11/13/what-did-america-buy-auto-bailout-and-was-it-worth-it/.

65. Phoebe Wall Howard, "Ford Took $6B Government Loan in 2009—and Debt Still Haunts Company," *Detroit Free Press*, July 29, 2020, https://eu.freep.com/story/money/cars/ford/2020/07/29/ford-government-loan-department-energy-debt/5526413002/.

66. Carmo, Neto, and Donadone, "Multiple Dynamics of Financialization in the Automotive Sector."

67. Alan Mulally quoted in Lynn, *Cornered*.

68. Ibid.

69. Chamayou, *The Ungovernable Society*.

70. Ibid.

71. Ibid.

72. Ibid.

73. Ibid.

74. "Governability is indeed a compound capacity, one which presupposes, on the side of the object, a disposition to be governed but also, on the other side, on the subject's side, an aptitude to govern." Ibid.

75. Panitch and Gindin, *The Making of Global Capitalism*.

76. Grace Blakeley, *Stolen: How to Save the World from Financialisation* (London: Repeater, 2019).

77. Ibid.

78. Wendy Brown, *Undoing the Demos: Neoliberalism's Stealth Revolutions* (New York: Zone Books, 2011); Colin Crouch, *The Strange Non-Death of Neoliberalism* (London: Wiley, 2011).

79. Davies, "The Neoliberal State: Power against 'Politics'"; Mirowski, *Never Let a Serious Crisis Go to Waste*.

80. James O'Connor, *The Fiscal Crisis of the State* (New York: St Martin's Press, 1973).

81. Panitch and Gindin, *The Making of Global Capitalism*; Frederic Durand, *Fictitious Capital: How Finance Is Appropriating Our Future* (London: Verso, 2014).

82. Panitch and Gindin, *The Making of Global Capitalism*.

83. Crouch, *The Strange Non-Death of Neoliberalism*.

84. Jamie Peck, "Preface," in *Constructions of Neoliberal Reason* (Oxford: Oxford University Press, 2010).

85. Andrew Gamble, "The Free Economy and the Strong State: The Rise of the Social Market Economy," in Ralph Miliband and John Saville (eds.), *The Socialist Register 1979: A Survey of Movements and Ideas* (London: Socialist Register, 1979).

86. Steve Maher, *Corporate Capitalism and the Integral State* (Basingstoke, UK: Palgrave Macmillan, 2022).

87. For a discussion of the benefits provided to big businesses by the American state, see Dayen, *Monopolized*; Tepper and Hearn, *The Myth of Capitalism*.

88. Crouch, *The Strange Non-Death of Neoliberalism*.

89. Ibid.

90. Brown, *Undoing the Demos*.

91. Wendy Brown, *In the Ruins of Neoliberalism: The Rise of Antidemocratic Politics in the West* (New York: Columbia University Press, 2019).

92. Brown, *Undoing the Demos*.

93. Ibid.

94. Blakeley, *Stolen*.

95. Lynn, *Cornered*.

96. Mirowski, *Never Let a Serious Crisis Go to Waste*.

97. Barkan, *Corporate Sovereignty*; Baars, *The Corporation, Law and Capitalism*.

98. Baars, *The Corporation, Law and Capitalism*.

99. Brown, *In the Ruins of Neoliberalism*.

100. Hayek, *Road to Serfdom*.

101. Chamayou, *The Ungovernable Society*.

102. Peter Triantafillou, *Neoliberal Power and Public Management Reforms* (Manchester: Manchester University Press, 2017).

103. Chamayou, *The Ungovernable Society.*

104. David Graeber, *Utopia of Rules: On Technology, Stupidity, and the Secret Joys of Bureaucracy* (New York: Melville House, 2015).

105. Samuel Knafo, Sahil Jai Dutta, Richard Lane, and Steffan Wyn-Jones, "The Managerial Lineages of Neoliberalism," *New Political Economy* 24, no. 2 (2018): 245–51, https://doi.org/10.1080/13563467.2018.1431621.

106. As Wendy Brown puts it: "deliberation about justice and other common goods, contestation over values and purposes, struggles over power, pursuit of visions for the good of the whole [do not appear in neoliberal accounts of the public realm]. Rather, public life is reduced to problem solving and program implementation, a casting that brackets or eliminates politics, conflict and deliberation about common values or ends." Brown, *Undoing the Demos.*

107. Gamble, "The Free Economy and the Strong State."

108. James Ferguson, *The Anti-Politics Machine: Development, Depoliticization, and Bureaucratic Power in Lesotho* (Minneapolis: University of Minnesota Press, 1979).

109. Triantafillou, *Neoliberal Power and Public Management Reforms.*

110. Jamie Peck, *Constructions of Neoliberal Reason.*

111. Brown, *In the Ruins of Neoliberalism.*

112. Mirowski, *Never Let a Serious Crisis Go to Waste.*

113. See Peck, "Preface," in *Constructions of Neoliberal Reason.*

114. Mirowski, *Never Let a Serious Crisis Go to Waste.*

115. Wolfgang Streek, *Buying Time: The Delayed Crisis of Democratic Capitalism* (London: Verso, 2014).

116. Galbraith, *The New Industrial State.*

117. Lash and Urry, *The End of Organized Capitalism.*

118. As Chamayou argues, the neoliberal state "must continuously save capitalism from its self-destructive tendencies, but without ever affecting the fundamental economic relationships that determine them." Chamayou, *The Ungovernable Society.*

119. Panitch and Gindin, *The Making of Global Capitalism.*

120. Chamayou, *The Ungovernable Society.*

121. Panitch and Gindin, *The Making of Global Capitalism.*

122. Naomi Klein, *The Shock Doctrine: The Rise of Disaster Capitalism* (London: Penguin UK, 2008).

CHAPTER 3: DISASTER CAPITALISM

1. Drew Dahl and William R. Emmons, "Was the Paycheck Protection Program Effective?," Federal Reserve Bank of St. Louis, July 6, 2022, https://www.stlouisfed .org/en/publications/regional-economist/2022/jul/was-paycheck-protection -program-effective.

2. Ibid.

3. Alana Abramson, "'No Lessons Have Been Learned.' Why the Trillion-Dollar Coronavirus Bailout Benefited the Rich," *Time*, June 18, 2020, https://time .com/5845116/coronavirus-bailout-rich-richer/.

4. David Yaffe-Bellany, "'The Big Guys Get Bailed Out': Restaurants Vie for Relief Funds," *New York Times*, April 20, 2020, https://www.nytimes.com/2020/04/20/business/shake-shack-returning-loan-ppp-coronavirus.html.

5. Nancy Luna, "Shake Shack Gets $10 Million Paycheck Protection Loan, Cuts 1,000 Workers," *Nation's Restaurant News*, April 17, 2020, https://www.nrn.com/fast-casual/shake-shack-gets-10-million-paycheck-protection-loan-cuts-1000-workers.

6. Yaffe-Bellany, "'The Big Guys Get Bailed Out': Restaurants Vie for Relief Funds."

7. Joe Kukura, "Which Big Companies Returned PPP Loans—and Which Didn't," Lendio, June 15, 2020, https://www.lendio.com/blog/companies-returned-ppp-loans/, Lydia DePillis, "The Government Gave Free PPP Money to Public Companies Despite Warning Them Not to Apply," ProPublica, September 23, 2021, https://www.propublica.org/article/the-government-gave-free-ppp-money-to-public-companies-despite-warning-them-not-to-apply.

8. The other three included a subcontractor for the US Postal Service called Evo Transportation and Energy Services, a $69 million steel manufacturer called Universal Steel & Alloy Products Inc., and $143 million streaming service Quantum Corporation. Joe Kukura, "Which Big Companies Returned PPP Loans—and Which Didn't," Lendio, June 15, 2020, https://www.lendio.com/blog/companies-returned-ppp-loans/.

9. Ibid.

10. Ibid.

11. Tom Bergin and Lawrence Delevingne, "Exclusive: U.S. Taxpayers' Virus Relief Went to Firms That Avoided U.S. Taxes," Reuters, May 28, 2020, https://www.reuters.com/article/us-health-coronavirus-companies-tax-excl-idUSKBN2341ZE.

12. Tom Benning, "In Texas, Federal PPP Loans Went to a U.S. House Campaign, Senate Hopeful's Law Firm and Lieutenant Gov's Radio Stations," *Dallas Morning News*, July 13, 2020, https://www.dallasnews.com/news/politics/2020/07/07/how-much-small-business-aid-did-companies-owned-by-rep-roger-williams-and-other-texas-politicos-get/.

13. Office of Congressional Ethics, "OCE Referral Regarding Rep. Roger Williams," Office of Congressional Ethics, August 11, 2016, https://oce.house.gov/reports/investigations/oce-referral-regarding-rep-roger-williams.

14. Associated Press, "Congress Created PPP Loans—Then at Least 12 Members Reaped Their Benefits," *Fortune*, July 8, 2020, https://fortune.com/2020/07/08/ppp-loan-recipients-members-of-congress/.

15. Ibid.

16. Karl Evers-Hillstrom, "Political Donors Whose Businesses Got PPP Loans Injected $52 Million into 2020 Election," OpenSecrets, July 23, 2020, https://www.opensecrets.org/news/2020/07/ppp-loans-donors-52m.

17. Nick Schwellenbach and David Szakonyi, "Large Political Donations Came After Paycheck Protection Program Loans," Project on Government Oversight (POGO), November 17, 2020, https://www.pogo.org/investigation/2020/11/large-political-donations-came-after-paycheck-protection-program-loans.

18. Peter Dreier, "Trump Mega-Donor Geoff Palmer Is Also LA's Most Controversial

Developer," *American Prospect*, September 19, 2016, https://prospect.org /power/trump-mega-donor-geoff-palmer-also-la-s-controversial-developer/.

19. Ed Pilkington and Jon Swaine, "The Seven Republican Super-Donors Who Keep Money in Tax Havens," *The Guardian*, November 7, 2017, https://www.theguardian .com/news/2017/nov/07/us-republican-donors-offshore-paradise-papers.

20. Schwellenbach and Szakonyi, "Large Political Donations Came After Paycheck Protection Program Loans."

21. Ibid.

22. Ibid.

23. David Gilbert, "Here's Every Disturbing Conspiracy Marjorie Taylor Greene Believes In," *VICE News*, January 29, 2021, https://www.vice.com/en/ article/3an47j/heres-every-disturbing-conspiracy-marjorie-taylor-greene-believes-in; Martin Pengelly and Joan E. Greve, "Fury as Marjorie Taylor Greene Likens Covid Rules to Nazi Treatment of Jews," *The Guardian*, May 25, 2021, https:// www.theguardian.com/us-news/2021/may/25/marjorie-taylor-greene-nazi-jews -condemnation.

24. Em Steck and Andrew Kaczynski, "Marjorie Taylor Greene Indicated Support for Executing Prominent Democrats in 2018 and 2019 Before Running for Congress," CNN Politics, January 26, 2021, https://edition.cnn.com/2021/01/26/politics /marjorie-taylor-greene-democrats-violence/index.html.

25. Lauren Fedor, "Pro-Putin Republicans Break Ranks by Heaping Praise on Kremlin," *Financial Times*, March 26, 2022, https://www.ft.com/content /fd870fa9-007a-4cd4-bffc-d72aa2a35767.

26. Schwellenbach and Szakonyi, "Large Political Donations Came After Paycheck Protection Program Loans."

27. Ibid.

28. Hettie O'Brien, "The Blackstone Rebellion: How One Country Took on the World's Biggest Commercial Landlord," *The Guardian*, September 29, 2022, https://www .theguardian.com/business/2022/sep/29/blackstone-rebellion-how-one-country -worlds-biggest-commercial-landlord-denmark.

29. Select Subcommittee on the Coronavirus Crisis, "Examining Pandemic Evictions: A Report on Abuses by Four Corporate Landlords During the Coronavirus Crisis," Staff Report, July 2022, https://www.8newsnow.com/wp-content/uploads /sites/59/2022/07/SSCC-Staff-Report-Examining-Pandemic-Evictions.pdf.

30. Ibid.

31. Ben Charlie Smoke, "Corporations Receiving Bailout Billions Have Laid Off Staff and Paid Investors," *VICE News*, August 4, 2020, https://www.vice.com/en /article/m7jxvn/corporations-receiving-bailout-billions-have-laid-off-staff-and-paid -investors; Ben Charlie Smoke, "The UK Government Has Bailed Out Companies Complicit in Human Rights Abuses and Environmental Destruction," VICE News, August 17, 2020, https://www.vice.com/en/article/ep4k7k/uk-government-ccff -human-rights-environment.

32. Ibid.

33. Ibid.

34. Olivier Petitjean and Maxime Combes, "Corporate Welfare in a Time of

Pandemic," Rosa-Luxemburg-Stiftung Brussels Office, December 14, 2020, https://www.rosalux.eu/en/article/1848.corporate-welfare-in-a-time-of-pandemic.html#.

35. Ibid.

36. Ibid.

37. Anthony Klan, "Profitable Australian companies urged to repay government Covid support," *Financial Times*, September 7, 2021, https://www.ft.com/content/b26ae089-18a0-4860-9a5a-8e4b198b1a17.

38. Jonathan Montpetit, Simon Nakonechny, and Marie-Hélène Hétu, "Why Millions of Dollars in Pandemic Aid Is Going to Corporations Making Healthy Profits," CBC News, December 11, 2020, https://www.cbc.ca/news/canada/montreal/cews-wage-subsidy-jobs-covid-1.5834790.

39. Reuters Staff, "Volkswagen Says Diesel Scandal Has Cost It 31.3 Billion Euros," Reuters, March 17, 2020, https://www.reuters.com/article/us-volkswagen-results-diesel-idUSKBN2141JB.

40. Panitch and Gindin, *The Making of Global Capitalism*.

41. Hudson, *Killing the Host*.

42. Ibid.

43. Porter Stansberry, "This is One of the Biggest Wall Street Frauds Ever . . . ," *Information Clearing House*, February 26, 2010. Quoted in Hudson, *Killing the Host*.

44. Hudson, *Killing the Host*.

45. Edmund L. Andrews, "Fed Rescues AIG with $85 Billion Loan for 80% Stake," *New York Times*, September 17, 2008, https://www.nytimes.com/2008/09/17/business/worldbusiness/17iht-17insure.16217125.html.

46. Tepper and Hearn, *The Myth of Capitalism*.

47. Andrews, "Fed Rescues AIG with $85 Billion Loan for 80% Stake."

48. Rick Rothacker and Rachelle Younglai, "U.S. to Sell Rest of AIG Stock, Ending $182bn Rescue," Reuters, December 10, 2012, https://www.reuters.com/article/us-usa-treasury-aig/u-s-to-sell-rest-of-aig-stock-ending-182-billion-rescue-idUSBRE8B919020121211.

49. Hudson, *Killing the Host*.

50. Dominic Rushe, "How Goldman Sachs Gained from Bailout of AIG," *The Guardian*, January 27, 2017, https://www.theguardian.com/business/2011/jan/27/goldman-sachs-received-aig-bailout-cash.

51. Hudson, *Killing the Host*.

52. Ibid.

53. Ibid., 229.

54. Ibid., 233.

55. Nassim Nicholas Taleb, "Why Did the 2008 Crisis Happen?," *New Political Economy*, October 2010, https://www.fooledbyrandomness.com/crisis.pdf.

56. "The decisive role of American state agencies in encouraging the development of mortgage-backed securities figured prominently in their spread throughout global financial markets." Panitch and Gindin, *The Making of Global Capitalism*.

57. Tepper and Hearn, *The Myth of Capitalism*.

58. Ibid.

59. Ibid.

60. "The worry about cross-border capital flow," *The Economist*, January 13, 2022, https://www.economist.com/leaders/2022/01/13/the-worry-about-cross-border -capital-flows#:~:text=Since%20the%20global%20financial%20crisis,just%20 before%20Lehman%20Brothers%20collapsed.

61. Panitch and Gindin, *The Making of Global Capitalism*.

62. Eric Helleiner, *States and the Reemergence of Global Finance: From Bretton Woods to the 1990s* (New York: Cornell University Press, 1994).

63. Ibid. As Helleiner argues, the three most important policy decisions were: "1) to grant more freedom to market operators through liberalization initiatives, 2) to refrain from imposing more effective controls on capital movements, and 3) to prevent major international financial crises."

64. Panitch and Gindin, *The Making of Global Capitalism*.

65. Dani Rodrik, *The Globalization Paradox: Why Global Markets, States and Democracy Can't Coexist* (Oxford: Oxford University Press, 2011).

66. Joseph Stiglitz, *Globalization and Its Discontents* (London: Penguin UK, 2015).

67. Ibid.

68. Jesse Eisinger, "Why Only One Top Banker Went to Jail for the Financial Crisis," *New York Times*, April 30, 2014, https://www.nytimes.com/2014/05/04/magazine /only-one-top-banker-jail-financial-crisis.html.

69. Ibid.

70. Ibid.

71. William D. Cohan, "How Wall Street's Bankers Stayed Out of Jail," *The Atlantic*, August 11, 2015, https://www.theatlantic.com/magazine/archive/2015/09/how -wall-streets-bankers-stayed-out-of-jail/399368/.

72. The decision not to prosecute any bankers appears to have been the result of a conscious choice on the part of the Department of Justice not to bring cases against systemically important financial institutions (read: big banks) for fear of destabilizing the financial system. The bankers had managed to convince some of the most senior leaders in the DOJ that if they tried to punish their executives for wrongdoing then the banks would throw a tantrum, potentially jeopardizing the US economy. After leaving the DOJ, the man who developed this doctrine (Eric Holder)—known as the Holder Doctrine—returned to the law firm he worked at before becoming attorney general under President Obama. This firm's clients included Bank of America, Citigroup, and Wells Fargo. The partners were reportedly so convinced he would return that they kept his old office open for him. The banks were quite happy with the minimal settlements they ended up paying, but the US recovery from the crisis was extremely slow. Ibid.

73. Colleen Shalby, "The Financial Crisis Hit 10 Years Ago. For Some, It Feels like Yesterday," *Los Angeles Times*, September 15, 2018, https://www.latimes.com /business/la-fi-financial-crisis-experiences-20180915-htmlstory.html.

74. Ibid.

75. Karl Marx, *The Communist Manifesto* (New York: Oxford University Press, 2008).

76. José-Luis Peydró, Ozlem Akin, Christian Fons-Rosen, "Government-connected bankers made unusually large gains during the 2008 financial crisis," Imperial College Business School, March 1, 2021, https://www.imperial.ac.uk/business

-school/ib-knowledge/finance/government-connected-bankers-made-unusually-large
-gains-during-the-2008.

77. Stoller, *Goliath.*

78. "How Goldman Sachs Came Roaring Back," *Jewish Chronicle*, July 30, 2009,
https://www.thejc.com/news/world/how-goldman-sachs-came-roaring-back
-1.10565?reloadTime=1675814400011.

79. Simon Johnson quoted in Lynn, *Cornered.*

80. Tabby Kinder, "McKinsey Earnt £560,000 for Giving 'Vision' to New English
Pandemic Body," *Financial Times*, August 19, 2020, https://www.ft.com
/content/3cc76ad4-4d75-4e07-9f6d-476611fbb28f.

81. Gareth Iacobucci, "Dido Harding: the Former Business Leader Now Heading
Up England's Covid-19 Response," *British Medical Journal*, September 2, 2020,
https://www.bmj.com/content/370/bmj.m3332.

82. Ibid.

83. Patrick Daly, "NHS Test and Trace Boss Dido Harding Defends Paying Consultants
£1,000-a-Day," *Independent*, January 18, 2021, https://www.independent.co.uk
/news/health/nhs-test-and-trace-dido-harding-b1789098.html.

84. Andrea Downey, "McKinsey Bags £560k Deciding 'Vision' for New NHS Test
and Trace Body," Digital Health, August 26, 2020, https://www.digitalhealth
.net/2020/08/mckinsey-bags-560k-deciding-vision-for-new-nhs-test-and-trace-body/.

85. Sheelah Kolhatkar, "McKinsey's Work for Saudi Arabia Highlights Its History
of Unsavory Entanglements," *The New Yorker*, November 1, 2018, https://www
.newyorker.com/news/news-desk/mckinseys-work-for-saudi-arabia-highlights-its
-history-of-unsavory-entanglements.

86. Walt Bogdanich and Michael Forsythe, *When McKinsey Comes to Town: The
Hidden Influence of the World's Most Powerful Consulting Firm* (New York:
Doubleday, 2022).

87. Michelle Celarier, "The Story McKinsey Didn't Want Written," Institutional Investor,
July 8, 2019, https://www.institutionalinvestor.com/article/2bsw5rr7qqvzy3eprn08w
/corner-office/the-story-mckinsey-didnt-want-written.

88. Peter Wells, "McKinsey Agrees to $15m Settlement over Bankruptcy Disclosures,"
Financial Times, February 19, 2019, https://www.ft.com/content/dd3b119a-3476
-11e9-bb0c-42459962a812.

89. Michael Forsythe, Walt Bogdanich, and Bridget Hickey, "As McKinsey Sells Advice,
Its Hedge Fund May Have a Stake in the Outcome," *New York Times*, February 19,
2019, https://www.nytimes.com/2019/02/19/business/mckinsey-hedge-fund.html.

90. Andrew Edgecliffe-Johnson, "McKinsey Investment Fund Fined $18m by SEC for
Compliance Lapses," *Financial Times*, November 19, 2021, https://www.ft.com
/content/3d6aa8f6-00c7-42b8-b7ed-2f6626358154.

91. Bogdanich and Forsythe, *When McKinsey Comes to Town.*

92. Michael Forsythe and Walt Bogdanich, "McKinsey Advised Purdue Pharma How
to 'Turbocharge' Opioid Sales, Lawsuit Says," *New York Times*, February 1,
2019, https://www.nytimes.com/2019/02/01/business/purdue-pharma-mckinsey
-oxycontin-opioids.html.

93. Ibid.

94. Ian MacDougall, "How McKinsey Is Making $100 Million (and Counting) Advising on the Government's Bumbling Coronavirus Response," ProPublica, July 15, 2020, https://www.propublica.org/article/how-mckinsey-is-making-100-million-and-counting-advising-on-the-governments-bumbling-coronavirus-response.

95. Ibid.

96. Ibid.

97. Ibid.

98. Ibid.

99. As ProPublica put it: "McKinsey's data was one of the factors cited by VA officials to justify hiring the firm within 24 hours. As a contracting document explained: The firm 'already possessed an immense amount of both global and community epidemiological data on COVID-19' the VA didn't otherwise have access to. McKinsey customers pay not only in cash but by adding new data that the firm will be able to sell to the next customer." Ibid.

100. Observing the descent into fascism in Europe, Walter Benjamin wrote in 1940 that "[t]he tradition of the oppressed teaches us that the 'state of emergency' in which we live is not the exception but the rule." Walter Benjamin, "On the Concept of History," Marxist Internet Archive, accessed July 8, 2023, https://www.marxists.org/reference/archive/benjamin/1940/history.htm.

101. Luke Kemp, "The 'Stomp Reflex': When Governments Abuse Emergency Powers," BBC Future, April 28, 2021, https://www.bbc.com/future/article/20210427-the-stomp-reflex-when-governments-abuse-emergency-powers.

102. Ibid.

103. Ibid.

104. Ibid.

105. Nicola Habersetzer, "Moscow Silently Expands Surveillance of Citizens," Human Rights Watch, March 25, 2020, https://www.hrw.org/news/2020/03/25/moscow-silently-expands-surveillance-citizens.

106. "Bahrain, Kuwait and Norway Contact Tracing Apps Among Most Dangerous for Privacy," Amnesty International, June 16, 2020, https://www.amnesty.org/en/latest/news/2020/06/bahrain-kuwait-norway-contact-tracing-apps-danger-for-privacy/.

107. "France to Use CCTV to Monitor Mask-Wearing on Public Transport," Privacy International, March 16, 2021, https://privacyinternational.org/examples/4463/france-use-cctv-monitor-mask-wearing-public-transport.

108. Tehilla Shwartz Altshuler and Rachel Aridor Hershkowitz, "How Israel's COVID-19 Mass Surveillance Operation Works," Brookings Institute, July 6, 2020, https://www.brookings.edu/articles/how-israels-covid-19-mass-surveillance-operation-works/.

109. Deborah Brown and Amos Toh, "Technology Is Enabling Surveillance, Inequality During the Pandemic," Human Rights Watch, March 4, 2021, https://www.hrw.org/news/2021/03/04/technology-enabling-surveillance-inequality-during-pandemic.

110. "Hangzhou Considers Expansion Options for Coronavirus Surveillance App," Privacy International, May 26, 2020, https://privacyinternational.org/examples/3888/hangzhou-considers-expansion-options-coronavirus-surveillance-app.

111. Mariana Mazzucato and Rosie Collington, *The Big Con: How the Consulting*

Industry Weakens Our Businesses, Infantilizes Our Governments and Warps Our Economies (London: Allen Lane, 2023).

112. Ibid.

113. Patrick Watson, "Coronavirus Socialism," *Forbes*, April 13, 2020, https://www.forbes.com/sites/patrickwwatson/2020/04/13/coronavirus-socialism/?sh=19f7aab45225.

114. Emil W. Henry Jr., "Will Coronavirus Launch the Second Wave of Socialism?," *The Hill*, March 26, 2020, https://thehill.com/opinion/campaign/489612-will-coronavirus-launch-the-second-wave-of-socialism/.

115. John Horgan, "Will COVID-19 Make Us More Socialist?," *Scientific American*, April 20, 2020, https://blogs.scientificamerican.com/cross-check/will-covid-19-make-us-more-socialist/.

116. Chris Hughes, "The Free Market Is Dead: What Will Replace It?," *Time*, April 26, 2021, https://time.com/5956255/free-market-is-dead/.

117. Vladimir Lenin, *"The State and Revolution,"* Lenin Internet Archive, 1993, accessed July 8, 2023, https://www.marxists.org/ebooks/lenin/state-and-revolution.pdf.

118. James Connolly, "The New Evangel: State Monopoly Versus Socialism," Marxist Internet Archive, accessed July 8, 2023, https://www.marxists.org/archive/connolly/1901/evangel/stmonsoc.htm.

119. S&P Global Press Release, "S&P 500 Buybacks Set Quarterly and Annual Record," S&P Global, March 15, 2022, https://press.spglobal.com/2022-03-15-S-P-500-Buybacks-Set-Quarterly-and-Annual-Record.

120. Patrick Temple-West and Victoria Guida, "'Eye-popping' Payouts for CEOs Follow Trump's Tax Cuts," *Politico*, July 30, 2018, https://www.politico.com/story/2018/07/30/eye-popping-payouts-for-ceos-follow-trumps-tax-cuts-747649.

121. Niket Nishant, "Global M&A Volumes Hit Record High in 2021, Breach $5 Trillion for First Time," Reuters, December 31, 2021, https://www.reuters.com/markets/us/global-ma-volumes-hit-record-high-2021-breach-5-trillion-first-time-2021-12-31/.

122. Richard Partington, "Covid-19 Has Cost Global Workers $3.7tn in Lost Earnings, Says ILO," *The Guardian*, January 25, 2021, https://www.theguardian.com/business/2021/jan/25/covid-19-workers-lost-earnings-ilo-job-losses.

123. Peter Beaumont, "Decades of Progress on Extreme Poverty Now in Reverse Due to Covid," *The Guardian*, February 3, 2021, https://www.theguardian.com/global-development/2021/feb/03/decades-of-progress-on-extreme-poverty-now-in-reverse-due-to-covid.

124. Alexandre Tanzi and Catarina Saraiva, "U.S. Suffers Sharpest Rise in Poverty Rate in More Than 50 Years," Bloomberg, January 25, 2021, https://www.bloomberg.com/news/articles/2021-01-25/u-s-suffers-sharpest-rise-in-poverty-rate-in-more-than-50-years.

125. Ibid.

126. "Lowest Paid Are Most Likely to Have Lost Income and Increased Debt in Pandemic—TUC Research," Trades Union Congress, February 1, 2021, https://www.tuc.org.uk/news/lowest-paid-are-most-likely-have-lost-income-and-increased-debt-pandemic-tuc-research.

127. Joe Rennison, "How the Fed's Fine Intentions Feed US Wealth Inequality," *Financial Times*, July 26, 2021, https://www.ft.com/content/57730688-aa49-4549 -a127-4b2d625260a4.

128. Robert Frank, "The Wealthiest 10% of Americans Own a Record 89% of All U.S. Stocks," CNBC, October 18, 2021, https://www.cnbc.com/2021/10/18/the -wealthiest-10percent-of-americans-own-a-record-89percent-of-all-us-stocks.html.

129. Luke Savage, "US Billionaires Got 70% More Wealth Under COVID. They Didn't Deserve Any of It," Jacobin, October 20, 2021, https://jacobin.com/2021/10 /billionaire-wealth-pandemic-covid-elon-musk-bezos-gates.

130. Ben Steverman and Alexandre Tanzi, "Top 50 Richest People in the US Are Worth as Much as Poorest 165 Million," Bloomberg, October 8, 2020, https://www .bloomberg.com/news/articles/2020-10-08/top-50-richest-people-in-the-us-are -worth-as-much-as-poorest-165-million.

131. Jasper Jolly, "Number of Billionaires in UK Reached New Record During Covid Crisis," *The Guardian*, May 21, 2021, https://www.theguardian.com /business/2021/may/21/number-of-billionaires-in-uk-reached-new-record-during -covid-pandemic.

132. Larry Elliott, "UK Wealth Gap Widens in Pandemic as Richest Get £50,000 Windfall," *The Guardian*, July 12, 2021, https://www.theguardian.com/busi ness/2021/jul/12/uk-wealth-gap-widens-in-pandemic-as-richest-get-50000-windfall.

133. David Dawkins, "Europe's Billionaires Are $1 Trillion Richer Than a Year Ago," *Forbes*, April 6, 2021, https://www.forbes.com/sites/daviddawkins/2021/04/06 /europes-billionaires-are-1-trillion-richer-than-a-year-ago/?sh=3b24f35b76e5.

134. Anshool Deshmukh, "This Simple Chart Reveals the Distribution of Global Wealth," Visual Capitalist, September 20, 2021, https://www.visualcapitalist.com /distribution-of-global-wealth-chart/.

135. "The Suez Canal," The History Channel, February 16, 2018, updated March 30, 2021, https://www.history.com/topics/africa/suez-canal.

136. Panitch and Gindin, *The Making of Global Capitalism*.

137. Mary-Ann Russon, "The Cost of the Suez Canal Blockage," BBC News, March 29, 2021, https://www.bbc.co.uk/news/business-56559073.

138. Grace Blakeley, "Shipping Chaos Is the Latest Sign That Capitalism Is Eating Itself," *Tribune*, May 31, 2022, https://tribunemag.co.uk/2022/05/globalisation -shipping-global-trade.

139. Greg Miller, "Top 10 Liners Control 85% of Market—and They're Not Done Yet," FreightWaves, June 9, 2021, https://www.freightwaves.com/news/top-10-liners -control-85-of-market-and-theyre-not-done-yet.

140. "Is It Time for Investors to Exit the Container Shipping Space?," Drewry, December 23, 2021, https://www.drewry.co.uk/news/news/is-it-time-for-investors -to-exit-the-container-shipping-space.

141. Laurie Havelock, "How Shipping Firms Are Making Record Profits, and Making Ordinary People Pay the Price," iNews, June 21, 2022, https://inews.co.uk/news /shipping-firms-record-profits-ordinary-people-pay-1698145.

142. K. Oanh Ha, Jack Wittels, Khine Lin Kyaw, and Krystal Chia, "Worst Shipping

Crisis in Decades Puts Lives and Trade at Risk," Bloomberg, September 17, 2020, https://www.bloomberg.com/features/2020-pandemic-shipping-labor-violations/.

143. Ibid.

144. Justin Jacobs, "Exxon Registers Highest Profit Since 2014 after Boost from Oil and Gas Prices," *Financial Times*, February 1, 2022, https://www.ft.com /content/6a62453f-5cfb-42c4-bc57-902d673b8b93.

145. Ibid.

146. Nick Edser, "Shell Reports Stronger than Expected Profits," BBC News, May 4, 2023, https://www.bbc.co.uk/news/business-65478978.

147. Alex Lawson, "BP Scales Back Climate Goals as Profits More Than Double to £23bn," *The Guardian*, February 7, 2023, https://www.theguardian.com /business/2023/feb/07/bp-profits-windfall-tax-gas-prices-ukraine-war.

148. "How Energy Company Profits Have Surged," *New Statesman*, February 8, 2022, https://www.newstatesman.com/chart-of-the-day/2022/02/how-energy-company -profits-have-surged.

149. Mark Sweney, "Workers Asking for Pay Rises Risk Embedding Inflation, Says Bank Boss," *The Guardian*, August 5, 2022, https://www.theguardian.com /business/2022/aug/05/workers-asking-for-pay-rises-risk-embedding-inflation-says -bank-boss-andrew-bailey.

150. Miles Brignall, "2022 the UK's Worst Year for Real Wage Growth Since 1977, TUC Says," *The Guardian*, December 11, 2022, https://www.theguardian.com /uk-news/2022/dec/12/2022-the-uks-worst-year-for-real-wage-growth-since -1977-tuc-says.

151. Isabella M. Weber and Evan Wasner, "Sellers' Inflation, Profits and Conflict: Why Can Large Firms Hike Prices in an Emergency?," University of Massachusetts Amhurst Economics Department Working Paper Series, Working Paper Number 2023-2, page 343, accessed: July 8, 2023, https://scholarworks.umass.edu/econ _workingpaper/343.

152. Zachary Carter, "What If We're Thinking About Inflation All Wrong?," *The New Yorker*, June 6, 2023, https://www.newyorker.com/news/persons-of-interest/what -if-were-thinking-about-inflation-all-wrong.

153. Weber and Wasner, "Sellers' Inflation, Profits and Conflict."

154. Rupert Russell, *Price Wars: How the Commodities Markets Made Our Chaotic World* (New York: Doubleday, 2022).

155. Max Krahé, "For Sustainable Finance to Work, We Will Need Central Planning," *Financial Times*, July 11, 2021, https://www.ft.com/content/54237547-4e83-471c -8dd1-8a8dcebc0382.

156. "The Economics of the Climate," *The Economist*, October 27, 2021, https://www .economist.com/special-report/2021/10/27/the-economics-of-the-climate.

157. See Alexander Zevin, *Liberalism at Large: The World According to the Economist* (London: Verso Books, 2021).

158. "2020 Tied for Warmest Year on Record, NASA Analysis Shows," NASA press release, January 14, 2021, accessed July 8, 2023, https://www.nasa.gov/press -release/2020-tied-for-warmest-year-on-record-nasa-analysis-shows.

159. "Earth Had Its Seventh-Warmest January on Record; Global Sea Ice Extent Hit

Record Low," Assessing the Global Climate in January 2023, National Centers for Environmental Information, February 14, 2023, accessed July 8, 2023, https://www .ncei.noaa.gov/news/global-climate-202301.

160. David Stanway, "World Hits Record Land, Sea Temperatures as Climate Change Fuels 2023 Extremes," Reuters, July 3, 2023, https://www.reuters.com/business /environment/climate-nears-point-no-return-land-sea-temperatures-break -records-experts-2023-06-30/.

161. Ibid.

162. Peter Frankopan, *The Earth Transformed: An Untold History* (London: Bloomsbury, 2023).

163. Jan Willem Erisman, James N. Galloway, Sybil Seitzinger, Albert Bleeker, Nancy B. Dise, A. M. Roxana Petrescu, Allison M. Leach, and Wim de Vries, "Consequences of Human Modification of the Global Nitrogen Cycle," *Philosophical Transactions of the Royal Society B: Biological Sciences* 368, no. 1621 (July 2013), https://doi .org/10.1098/rstb.2013.0116.

164. Damian Carrington, "Global Pollinator Losses Causing 500,000 Early Deaths a Year—Study," *The Guardian*, January 9, 2023, https://www.theguardian.com /environment/2023/jan/09/global-pollinator-losses-causing-500000-early-deaths -a-year-study.

165. United Nations Convention to Combat Desertification, *Global Land Outlook 2*, United Nations, https://www.unccd.int/resources/global-land-outlook/glo2.

166. Karl Marx, *Capital: A Critique of Political Economy, Volume III* (London: Penguin, 1992).

167. Mike Davis, *The Monster at Our Door: The Global Threat of Avian Flu* (New York: The New Press, 20105).

168. Friends of the Earth Europe, "The EU Emissions Trading System: Failing to Deliver," October 2010, accessed July 8, 2023, https://www.foeeurope.org/sites /default/files/publications/foee_ets_failing_to_deliver_1010.pdf.

169. Sandra Laville, "Fossil Fuel Big Five 'Spent €251m Lobbying EU' Since 2010," *The Guardian*, October 24, 2019, https://www.theguardian.com/business/2019/oct/24 /fossil-fuel-big-five-spent-251m-lobbying-european-union-2010-climate-crisis.

170. John Greenwood, "BlackRock 'Undermining Objectives of Climate Coalition It Just Joined'—Majority Action," Corporate Adviser, December 14, 2020, https:// corporate-adviser.com/blackrock-undermining-objectives-of-climate-coalition-it -just-joined-majority-action/.

171. Geoff Mann, *Climate Leviathan: A Political Theory of Our Planetary Future* (London: Verso Books, 2018).

172. See chapter 4 for an explanation of these terms.

173. Craig Paton, "World Leaders Urged to Try Harder to Avoid Climate Change 'Death Sentence,'" *Evening Standard*, November 1, 2021, https://www .standard.co.uk/news/uk/vladimir-putin-xi-jinping-glasgow-united-nations -cop26-b963703.html.

174. As my friend and mentor the late Leo Panitch told me in an interview in 2020: "As Marx told the insurrectionists in 1851, we're involved in a ten, fifteen, twenty-year process—he really should have said 150–200 years! I realize that runs against

the time horizon posed by the ecological crisis, but any proposed solution to that crisis is implausible without building up the necessary political capacity; the degree of planning and collective consciousness involved that needs to be built for an adequate response to the climate crisis is huge."

175. Neil Smith, *Uneven Development: Nature, Capital, and the Production of Space* (New York: Verso, 2010).

CHAPTER 4: AMERICAN-MADE SWEATSHOPS: HOW BIG BUSINESS PLANS

1. Catherine Clifford, "Jeff Bezos' Single Teen Mom Brought Him to Night School with Her When He Was a Baby," CNBC, June 14, 2019, https://www.cnbc .com/2019/06/14/jeff-bezoss-single-teen-mom-brought-him-to-night-school-with -her.html.

2. "Amazon's Jeff Bezos Wins ITUC's World's Worst Boss Poll," International Trades Union Congress, May 22, 2014, accessed July 8, 2023, https://www.ituc-csi.org /amazon-s-jeff-bezos-wins-ituc-s.

3. Sara Lebow, "Amazon Holds on to 80% of the Books, Music, and Video Market Online," Insider Intelligence, December 15, 2022, https://www.insiderintelligence .com/content/amazon-holds-books-music-video-market-online.

4. PYMNTS, "Amazon's Share of US eCommerce Sales Hits All-Time High of 56.7% in 2021," PYMNTS, March 14, 2022, accessed July 8, 2023, https://www.pymnts .com/news/retail/2022/amazons-share-of-us-ecommerce-sales-hits-all-time-high-of -56-7-in-2021/.

5. Lebow, "Amazon Holds on to 80% of the Books, Music, and Video Market Online."

6. Aran Ali, "AWS: Powering the Internet and Amazon's Profits," Visual Capitalist, July 10, 2022, https://www.visualcapitalist.com/aws-powering-the-internet-and -amazons-profits/.

7. Brad Stone, *The Everything Store: Jeff Bezos and the Age of Amazon* (New York: Little, Brown, 2013).

8. Meagher, *Competition Is Killing Us.*

9. Emily Guendelsberger, *On the Clock: What Low-Wage Work Did to Me and How It Drives America Insane* (New York: Little, Brown, 2019).

10. Michael Sainato, "'They're More Concerned about Profit': Osha, DoJ Take on Amazon's Grueling Working Conditions," *The Guardian*, March 2, 2023, https:// www.theguardian.com/technology/2023/mar/02/amazon-safety-citations-osha -department-of-justice.

11. Michael Sainato, "'Go Back to Work': Outcry Over Deaths on Amazon's Warehouse Floor," *The Guardian*, October 18, 2009, https://www.theguardian .com/technology/2019/oct/17/amazon-warehouse-worker-deaths.

12. Ariel Zilber, "Amazon Employees Rage over Being Forced to Work after Colleague Died from Heart Attack," *New York Post*, January 10, 2023, https:// nypost.com/2023/01/10/amazon-employees-rage-over-treatment-of-coworker -who-died-in-warehouse/.

13. Ibid.

14. Ibid.

15. Dayen, *Monopolized.*

16. Ibid.

17. Ibid.

18. Ibid.

19. Louie Smith and Alexa Phillips, "Amazon Workers 'Treated Like Slaves and Robots' as Ambulances Called to Centers 971 Times," *Mirror*, November 23, 2021, https://www.mirror.co.uk/news/uk-news/amazon-workers-treated-like-slaves-25531239.

20. Janet Burns, "Report: Amazon's Anti-Union Training Is Revealed in Leaked Video," *Forbes*, September 27, 2018, https://www.forbes.com/sites/janetwburns/2018/09/27/amazons-anti-union-training-strategy-revealed-in-leaked-video/?sh=7ad240e46068.

21. Michael Sainato, "US Judge Orders Amazon to 'Cease and Desist' Anti-Union Retaliation," *The Guardian*, November 28, 2022, https://www.theguardian.com/technology/2022/nov/28/amazon-staten-island-new-york-retaliation.

22. Steven Greenhouse, "'Old-School Union Busting': How US Corporations Are Quashing the New Wave of Organizing," *The Guardian*, February 26, 2023, https://www.theguardian.com/us-news/2023/feb/26/amazon-trader-joes-starbucks-anti-union-measures.

23. David Streitfeld, "How Amazon Crushes Unions," *New York Times*, October 21, 2021, https://www.nytimes.com/2021/03/16/technology/amazon-unions-virginia.html.

24. "Amazon Profits Triple Amid Reports of Union Busting and Poor Treatment," Unite the Union, April 30, 2021, https://www.unitetheunion.org/news-events/news/2021/april/amazon-profits-triple-amid-reports-of-union-busting-and-poor-treatment/.

25. Josh Taylor, "Police Called to Remove Union Officials from Amazon Warehouse in Sydney," *The Guardian*, November 26, 2021, https://www.theguardian.com/australia-news/2021/nov/26/police-called-to-remove-union-officials-from-amazon-warehouse-in-sydney.

26. Mark Kelley, Linda Guerriero, and Lisa Ellenwood, "Workers Pushing to Unionize Amazon Say They Faced Retaliation and Unfair Tactics," CBC News, October 21, 2021, https://www.cbc.ca/news/canada/amazon-workers-delivery-drivers-unionize-1.6215475.

27. "Amazon Workers in Leipzig Start 48-Hour Strike for Higher Wages," Reuters, June 26, 2023, https://www.reuters.com/markets/europe/german-union-calls-amazon-workers-leipzig-strike-48-hours-2023-06-26/.

28. "Amazon Workers in Barcelona Strike over Warehouse Closure," Reuters, February 2, 2023, https://www.reuters.com/technology/amazon-workers-barcelona-strike-over-warehouse-closure-2023-02-02/.

29. Alex N. Press, "In Poland, Amazon Workers Are Organizing," *Jacobin*, July 27, 2021, https://jacobin.com/2021/07/poland-amazon-warehouse-workers-union-grassroots-resistance-organizing.

30. Annie Palmer, "Amazon Workers Go on Strike in Italy over Labor Conditions," CNBC, March 22, 2021, https://www.cnbc.com/2021/03/22/amazon-workers-go-on-strike-in-italy-over-labor-conditions-.html.

31. Hayley Cuccinello, "Amazon Workers Strike in the US and 30 Other Countries on Black Friday in Global 'Make Amazon Pay' Campaign," *Insider*,

November 25, 2022, https://www.businessinsider.com/make-amazon-pay
-warehouse-strike-protest-black-friday-2022-11?r=US&IR=T.

32. Sarah Butler, "Amazon's Main UK Division Pays No Corporation Tax for Second
Year in a Row," *The Guardian*, May 31, 2023, https://www.theguardian.com
/technology/2023/jun/01/amazon-uk-services-main-division-pay-no-corporation
-tax-for-second-year-in-row-tax-credit-government-super-deduction-scheme.

33. Matthew Gardner, "Amazon Avoids More Than $5 Billion in Corporate Income
Taxes, Reports 6 Percent Tax Rate on $35 Billion of US Income," Institute on
Taxation and Economic Policy, February 7, 2022 https://itep.org/amazon-avoids
-more-than-5-billion-in-corporate-income-taxes-reports-6-percent-tax-rate-on-35
-billion-of-us-income/.

34. Rupert Neate, "Amazon Had Sales Income of €44bn in Europe in 2020 but Paid
No Corporation Tax," *The Guardian*, May 4, 2021, https://www.theguardian
.com/technology/2021/may/04/amazon-sales-income-europe-corporation-tax
-luxembourg.

35. Matt Reynolds, "Jeff Bezos Wants to Fix Climate Change. He Can Start with
Amazon," *WIRED*, October 2, 2020, https://www.wired.co.uk/article/jeff-bezos
-climate-change-amazon.

36. "Historical GHG Emissions (1990–2020)," Climate Watch, accessed July 8, 2023,
https://climatewatchdata.org/ghg-emissions.

37. Will Evans, "Amazon Drastically Underestimates Its Carbon Footprint," *Mother
Jones*, March 1, 2022, https://www.motherjones.com/environment/2022/03
/amazon-drastically-undercounts-its-carbon-disclosure-project/.

38. Richard Pallot, "Amazon Destroying Millions of Items of Unsold Stock in One of Its
UK Warehouses Every Year, ITV News Investigation Finds," ITV News, June 22,
2021, https://www.itv.com/news/2021-06-21/amazon-destroying-millions-of-items
-of-unsold-stock-in-one-of-its-uk-warehouses-every-year-itv-news-investigation-finds.

39. Nat Levy, "Amazon Gives $350K to Group Supporting Jenny Durkan for Seattle
Mayor, Its Biggest Local Political Contribution Ever," *GeekWire*, October 19,
2017, https://www.geekwire.com/2017/amazon-gives-350k-group-supporting-jenny
-durkan-seattle-mayor-biggest-local-political-contribution-ever/.

40. Dayen, *Monopolized*.

41. Monica Nickelsburg, "Amazon's $1.45M Fails to Upend Seattle City Council, but
Tech Giant Wins Small Victories," *GeekWire*, November 5, 2019, https://www
.geekwire.com/2019/amazons-1-45m-effort-upend-seattle-city-council-yields
-mixed-results-early-reporting/.

42. Moon lost, but Sawant won, and the makeup of the city council did not change
substantially, dealing a major blow to Amazon's political maneuvers. Amazon's
loss came in part thanks to interventions from democratic socialist politicians like
Bernie Sanders, and came just a few years after Amazon was forced to cancel the
construction of a new second headquarters in Queens, New York, after democratic
socialist congresswoman Alexandria Ocasio-Cortez pushed back against the plans.

43. Stephanie Denning, "Why Jeff Bezos Bought the *Washington Post*," *Forbes*,
September 1920, 2018, https://www.forbes.com/sites/stephaniedenning/2018/09/19
/why-jeff-bezos-bought-the-washington-post/.

44. Andrew Perez and David Sirota, "Jeff Bezos Weaponizes the *Washington Post* Homepage," *Jacobin*, May 27, 2021, https://www.jacobinmag.com/2021/05 /washington-post-jeff-bezos-amazon-minimum-wage-native-advertising.

45. Ali Breland, "How Amazon Bullies, Manipulates, and Lies to Reporters," *Mother Jones*, June 25, 2021, https://www.motherjones.com/politics/2021/06/amazon -journalists-pr-tactics/.

46. Stone, *The Everything Store*.

47. Dayen, *Monopolized*.

48. Lynn, *Cornered*.

49. See Paul Walker, *The Theory of the Firm: An Overview of the Economic Mainstream* (London: Routledge, 2016), for a discussion.

50. Arrow and Hahn, for example, write that "Adam Smith's 'invisible hand' is a poetic expression of the most fundamental of economic balance relations, the equalization of rates of return, as enforced by the tendency of factors to move from low to high returns." Anything that gets in the way of this tendency of factors to move from low to high returns represents an impediment to the functioning of the free market. Kenneth J. Arrow and Frank H. Hahn, *General Competitive Analysis* (San Francisco: Holden-Day, 1971), 1.

51. Ronald Coase, "The Nature of the Firm," *Economica* 4, no. 16 (1937).

52. Ferreras, *Firms as Political Entities*; Chamayou, *The Ungovernable Society*.

53. Walker, *The Theory of the Firm*.

54. Marx, *Capital, Volume I*.

55. Ferreras, *Firms as Political Entities*.

56. The Sveriges Riksbank Prize in Economic Sciences in Memory of Alfred Nobel 1991, "Ronald H. Coase: Biographical," The Nobel Prize, accessed July 8, 2023, https://www.nobelprize.org/prizes/economic-sciences/1991/coase/biographical/.

57. Ronald H. Coase, "Law and Economics and A. W. Brian Simpson," *Journal of Legal Studies* 25, no. 1 (January 1996): 103–19, https://www.jstor.org/stable/724523.

58. Ibid.

59. Ronald Coase, *The Nature of the Firm: Origins, Evolution, and Development* (New York: Oxford University Press, 1993).

60. Grant M. Hayden and Matthew T. Bodie, *Reconstructing the Corporation: From Shareholder Primacy to Shared Governance* (Cambridge: Cambridge University Press, 2020).

61. Walker, *The Theory of the Firm*.

62. As Walker notes, "The use of authority to supersede the price mechanism is, in Coase's view, the distinguishing mark of the firm." In Coase's own words: "the operation of a market costs something and by forming an organisation and allowing some authority (an "entrepreneur") to direct the resources, certain marketing costs are saved." Ibid.

63. Chamayou, *The Ungovernable Society*

64. Triantafillou, *Neoliberal Power and Public Management Reforms*.

65. Ferreras, *Firms as Political Entities*.

66. Baars, *The Corporation, Law and Capitalism*.

67. Chamayou, *The Ungovernable Society*.

68. Ferreras, *Firms as Political Entities.*

69. In fact, it seems as though Coase himself was both aware of this issue as well as relatively dismissive of its implications. In *The Nature of the Firm*, he writes about the central features of the employer-employee relationship using quite striking—if not historically unusual—language: 1) The servant must be under the duty of rendering personal services to the master or to others on behalf of the master, otherwise the contract is a contract for sale of goods or the like. 2) The master must have the right to control the servant's work, either personally or by another servant or agent. It is this right of control or interference, of being entitled to tell the servant when to work (within the hours of service) and when not to work, and what work to do and how to do it (within the terms of such service) which is the dominant characteristic in this relation and marks off the servant from an independent contractor, or from one employed merely to give to his employer the fruits of his labor.

70. Joseph A. Schumpeter, *Capitalism, Socialism and Democracy* (London: Routledge, 2006).

71. Tepper and Hearn, *The Myth of Capitalism.*

72. Meagher, *Competition Is Killing Us.*

73. Ibid.

74. Ibid.

75. Thomas Philippon, *The Great Reversal: How America Gave Up on Free Markets* (Cambridge, MA: Belknap Press, 2019).

76. Meagher, *Competition Is Killing Us.*

77. In a review of Philippon's book, Jan Eeckhout argues that "there is no evidence that bestows a different experience in the evolution of market power in Europe compared to the United States." Jan Eeckhout, "Book Review: *The Great Reversal* by Thomas Philippon," *Journal of Economic Literature* 59, no. 4 (December 2021): 1340–60, https://www.janeeckhout.com/wp-content/uploads/Commentary_03.pdf.

78. Jan Eeckhout, *The Profit Paradox: How Thriving Firms Threaten the Future of Work* (Princeton, NJ: Princeton University Press, 2021).

79. Meagher, *Competition Is Killing Us.*

80. Phillips and Rozworski, *People's Republic of Walmart.*

81. Ibid.

82. Ferreras, *Firms as Political Entities.*

83. Lynn, *Cornered*; Dayen, *Monopolized.*

84. Crouch, *The Strange Non-Death of Neoliberalism.*

85. Elsadig Elsheikh and Hossein Ayazi, "The Era of Corporate Consolidation and the End of Competition: Bayer-Monsanto, Dow-DuPont, and ChemChina-Syngenta," Haas Institute for a Fair and Inclusive Society at the University of California, Berkeley, Research Brief, October 2018, accessed July 8, 2023, https://belonging .berkeley.edu/era-corporate-consolidation-and-end-competition.

86. Alan Taylor, "Bhopal: The World's Worst Industrial Disaster, 30 Years Later," *The Atlantic*, December 2, 2014, https://www.theatlantic.com/photo/2014/12/bhopal -the-worlds-worst-industrial-disaster-30-years-later/100864/.

87. Carey Gillam, "'Disturbing': Weedkiller Ingredient Tied to Cancer Found in 80% of US Urine Samples," *The Guardian*, July 9, 2022, https://www.theguardian.com /us-news/2022/jul/09/weedkiller-glyphosate-cdc-study-urine-samples.

88. Patricia Cohen, "Roundup Maker to Pay $10 Billion to Settle Cancer Suits," *New York Times*, June 24, 2020, https://www.nytimes.com/2020/06/24/business /roundup-settlement-lawsuits.html.

89. Silvia Ribeiro, "Syngenta: Murder and Private Militias in Brazil," Via Campesina, November 24, 2007, https://viacampesina.org/en/syngenta-murder-and-private -militias-in-brazil/.

90. TeleSUR, "Brazil Court Rules against Syngenta for Murder of MST Activist," December 1, 2018, accessed July 8, 2023, https://www.telesurenglish.net /news/Brazil-Court-Rules-Against-Syngenta-for-Murder-of-MST-Activist -20181201-0021.html.

91. Gretchen Morgenson, "How DuPont May Avoid Paying to Clean Up a Toxic 'Forever Chemical,'" NBC News, March 1, 2020, https://www.nbcnews .com/health/cancer/how-dupont-may-avoid-paying-clean-toxic-forever -chemical-n1138766.

92. Elsheikh and Ayazi, "The Era of Corporate Consolidation and the End of Competition."

93. Crispin Dowler, "Revealed: The Pesticide Giants Making Billions on Toxic and Bee-Harming Chemicals," *Unearthed*, February 20, 2020, https://unearthed.greenpeace .org/2020/02/20/pesticides-croplife-hazardous-bayer-syngenta-health-bees.

94. Elsheikh and Ayazi, "The Era of Corporate Consolidation and the End of Competition."

95. Lynn, *Cornered*; Meagher, *Competition Is Killing Us*; Stiglitz, *Globalization and Its Discontents Revisited* (New York: W. W. Norton, 2017); Stoller, *Goliath*; Lina Khan and Sandeep Vaheesan, "How America became uncompetitive and unequal," *Washington Post*, June 13, 2014, https://www.washingtonpost .com/opinions/how-america-became-uncompetitive-and-unequal/2014/06/13 /a690ad94-ec00-11e3-b98c-72cef4a00499_story.html.

96. Tepper and Hearn, *The Myth of Capitalism*.

97. Marx, *Capital, Volume I*.

98. "With the development of the capitalist mode of production, there is an increase in the minimum amount of individual capital necessary to carry on a business under its normal conditions," Marx, *Capital, Volume I*.

99. Marx, *Capital, Volume I*; Hadas Thier, *A People's Guide to Capitalism: An Introduction to Marxist Economics* (Chicago: Haymarket Books, 2020).

100. Lynn, *Cornered*.

101. Paul A. Braun and Paul Sweezy, *Monopoly Capital* (New York: NYU Press, 1966).

102. As Baran and Sweezy argue in *Monopoly Capital*, "[t]he abandonment of price competition does not mean the end of all competition: it takes new forms and rages on with increasing intensity." Baran and Sweezy, *Monopoly Capital*.

103. Meagher, *Competition Is Killing Us*.

104. Kumar, *Monopsony Capitalism*.

105. Ibid.

106. Nicholas Shaxson, *Treasure Islands: Tax Havens and the Men Who Stole the World* (New York: Random House, 2011); Barak, *Unchecked Corporate Power*.

107. Doug Dowd, "Some Memories of Paul Baran and Paul Sweezy," *Monthly Review*, September 29, 2012, https://mronline.org/2012/09/29/dowd290912-html/.

108. Ibid.

109. Ibid.

110. Ibid.

111. Tepper and Hearn, *The Myth of Capitalism*.

112. Karl Marx, Theories of Surplus Value, Volume II, Marxist Internet Archive, accessed July 27, 2023, https://www.marxists.org/archive/marx/works/1863/theories-surplus-value/.

113. Tepper and Hearn, *The Myth of Capitalism*; Dayen, *Monopolized*.

114. Baran and Sweezy, *Monopoly Capital*.

115. Shoshana Zuboff, *The Age of Surveillance Capitalism: The Fight for a Human Future at the Frontier of Power* (London: Profile Books, 2018).

116. Meagher, *Competition Is Killing Us.* Yanis Varoufakis, *Technofeudalism: What Killed Capitalism* (London: Allen Lane, 2023).

117. Ibid.

118. Ibid.

119. Tepper and Hearn, *The Myth of Capitalism*.

120. Meagher, *Competition Is Killing Us*.

121. Tepper and Hearn, *The Myth of Capitalism*.

122. Meagher, *Competition Is Killing Us*.

123. Tepper and Hearn, *The Myth of Capitalism*. As Baran and Sweezy pointed out (in the 1960s!), "to be bought out and absorbed is often the ultimate ambition of the small business." Baran and Sweezy, *Monopoly Capital*.

124. Baran and Sweezy, *Monopoly Capital*.

125. Zia Qureshi, "The Rise of Corporate Market Power," Brookings Institute, May 21, 2019, https://www.brookings.edu/articles/the-rise-of-corporate-market-power/.

126. Rana Foroohar, *Don't Be Evil: The Case against Big Tech* (London: Penguin UK, 2019).

127. Kenneth Rogoff, "Big Tech Is a Big Problem," Project Syndicate, July 2, 2018, https://www.project-syndicate.org/commentary/regulating-big-tech-companies-by-kenneth-rogoff-2018-07.

128. Qureshi, "The Rise of Corporate Market Power."

129. Michał Kalecki, *Collected Works*, vol. 1 (Oxford: Oxford University Press, 1990).

130. Galbraith, *The New Industrial State*.

131. For an outline of Marx's theory of centralization, see Thier, *A People's Guide to Capitalism*.

132. Peter Walker, "Call Centre Staff to Be Monitored via Webcam for Home-Working 'Infractions,'" *The Guardian*, March 26, 2021, https://www.theguardian.com/business/2021/mar/26/teleperformance-call-centre-staff-monitored-via-webcam-home-working-infractions.

133. Thodoris Chondrogiannos and Nikolas Leontopoulos, "How a Global Call Centre Giant (Mis)managed the Pandemic," Investigate Europe, May 7, 2020, https://www.investigate-europe.eu/en/2020/how-one-of-the-worlds-biggest-call-centre-companies-mismanaged-the-pandemic-crisis/.

134. Olivia Solon, "Big Tech Call Center Workers Face Pressure to Accept Home Surveillance," NBC News, August 8, 2021, https://www.nbcnews.com/tech/tech-news/big-tech-call-center-workers-face-pressure-accept-home-surveillance-n1276227.

135. Frank W. Elwell, "Harry Braverman and the Working Class," Rogers State University, accessed July 9, 2023, http://faculty.rsu.edu/users/f/felwell/www/Theorists/Braverman/Presentation/Braverman.pdf.

136. Ibid.

137. Harry Braverman, *Labor and Monopoly Capital: The Degradation of Work in the Twentieth Century* (New York: Monthly Review Press, 1998).

138. The challenge of more efficiently controlling the worker's labor "presents itself as the challenge of management." Braverman, *Labor and Monopoly Capital*.

139. Braverman argued that capitalism "completely transforms technology."

140. G4S, "Our History," accessed July 9, 2023, https://www.g4s.com/who-we-are/our-history.

141. Adam Taylor, "How the Plan to Privatize London's Olympic Security Turned into a Disaster," *Insider*, July 18, 2012, https://www.businessinsider.com/g4s-olympic-security-disaster-2012-7?r=US&IR=T.

142. Matthew Taylor and Robert Booth, "G4S Guards Found Not Guilty of Manslaughter of Jimmy Mubenga," *The Guardian*, December 16, 2014, https://www.theguardian.com/uk-news/2014/dec/16/g4s-guards-found-not-guilty-manslaughter-jimmy-mubenga.

143. "Jimmy Mubenga," 4Front Project, accessed July 9, 2023, https://www.4frontproject.org/jimmy-mubenga.

144. Ibid.

145. Paul Lewis and Matthew Taylor, "Jimmy Mubenga Death: G4S Guards Will Not Face Charges," *The Guardian*, July 17, 2012, https://www.theguardian.com/uk/2012/jul/17/jimmy-mubenga-guards-no-charges.

146. Ibid.

147. Robert Booth, "Jimmy Mubenga: Judge Refused to Allow Jury to Hear about Guards' Racist Texts," *The Guardian*, December 17, 2014, https://www.theguardian.com/uk-news/2014/dec/17/jimmy-mubenga-racist-texts-not-heard-case.

148. Ibid.

149. "Jimmy Mubenga," 4Front Project.

150. Alison Holt, "What I Saw When I Went Undercover," BBC News, September 4, 2017, https://www.bbc.co.uk/news/resources/idt-sh/g4s_brook_house_immigration_removal_centre_undercover.

151. Mattha Busby, "G4S to Leave Immigration Sector after Brook House Scandal," *The Guardian*, September 24, 2019, https://www.theguardian.com/business/2019/sep/24/g4s-to-leave-immigration-sector-after-brook-house-scandal.

152. Tom Sanderson, "G4S Uses 'Unacceptable' Force on Pregnant Detainee at UK

Family Detention Centre," openDemocracy, October 24, 2012, https://www
.opendemocracy.net/en/shine-a-light/g4s-uses-unacceptable-force-on-pregnant
-detainee-at-uk-family-detention-ce/.

153. Ruth Hopkins, "South African Prisoners Sue G4S over Torture Claims," *The Guardian*, February 13, 2015, https://www.theguardian.com/world/2015/feb/13
/south-african-prisoners-sue-g4s-over-torture-claims.

154. Kevin Rawlinson, "Private Firms 'Are Using Detained Immigrants as Cheap Labour,'" *The Guardian*, August 22, 2014, https://www.theguardian.com/uk
-news/2014/aug/22/immigrants-cheap-labour-detention-centres-g4s-serco.

155. Yeganeh Torbati and Mica Rosenberg, "Orlando Shooter Was Employee of Global Security Firm G4S," Reuters, June 14, 2016, https://www.reuters.com/article/us
-florida-shooting-g4s-idUSKCN0Z02QS.

156. Crouch, *The Strange Non-Death of Neoliberalism*.

157. As Joshua Barkan argues in *Corporate Sovereignty*, "Corporate power should be rethought as a mode of political sovereignty."

158. Hobbes, quoted in Philip J. Stern, *The Company-State: Corporate Sovereignty and the Early Modern Foundations of the British Empire in India* (Oxford: Oxford University Press, 2012).

159. Stern, *The Company-State*.

160. Ibid.

161. Ibid.

162. Baars, *The Corporation, Law and Capitalism*.

163. Ferreras, *Firms as Political Entities: Saving Democracy through Economic Bicameralism*.

164. They are an "imaginary relationship of individuals to their real conditions of existence." Barkan, *Corporate Sovereignty*.

165. Baars, *The Corporation, Law and Capitalism*.

166. Ibid.

167. Ibid.

168. Michel Foucault, *The Birth of Biopolitics: Lectures at the Collège de France, 1978–1979* (Basingstoke, UK: Palgrave Macmillan, 2010).

169. "WHO Coronavirus Dashboard," WHO, accessed July 9, 2023, https://covid19
.who.int/table.

170. Michel Foucault, *The Birth of Biopolitics: Lectures at the Collège de France, 1978–1979* (Basingstoke, UK: Palgrave Macmillan, 2010).

171. This idea of the sovereign "ban" is critical to Barkan's conception of corporate sovereignty because it shows that sovereignty is not simply a way of using force to control territory; instead, it shows that sovereignty is a set of practices that allow for the governance of life "by establishing and transgressing the boundaries of law." The corporation plays a particularly interesting role in this schema because it is not only a legal construction but a social fact that stems from the organization of capitalist society and therefore delineates the boundaries of law. Understanding this relationship allows us to see that corporate and state power are not different

types of power, engaged in conflict over the control of people and things, but complementary—if sometimes conflicting—ways of organizing life itself. Barkan, *Corporate Sovereignty.*

172. As Barkan argues, "Corporations govern life through the extension of law as well as through legally authorized suspensions, privileges and immunities from law." Barkan, *Corporate Sovereignty.*

173. Taylor Giorno, "Federal Lobbying Spending Reaches $4.1 Billion in 2022—the Highest since 2010," OpenSecrets, January 26, 2023, https://www.opensecrets.org /news/2023/01/federal-lobbying-spending-reaches-4-1-billion-in-2022-the-highest -since-2010.

174. Tepper and Hearn, *The Myth of Capitalism.*

175. Ibid.

176. Ibid.

177. Jessica Huseman, "Filing Taxes Could Be Free and Simple. But H&R Block and Intuit Are Still Lobbying against It," ProPublica, March 20, 2017, https://www .propublica.org/article/filing-taxes-could-be-free-simple-hr-block-intuit-lobbying -against-it.

178. Barak, *Unchecked Corporate Power.*

179. Meagher, *Competition Is Killing Us.*

180. Barak, *Unchecked Corporate Power.*

181. Ibid.

182. Baars, *The Corporation, Law and Capitalism.*

183. Barak, *Unchecked Corporate Power.*

184. Ibid.

185. Baars, *The Corporation, Law and Capitalism.*

186. Ibid.

187. Ibid.

CHAPTER 5: BUYING TIME: HOW BIG BANKS PLAN

1. J. W. Mason, "Socialize Finance," *Jacobin*, November 28, 2016, https://jacobin .com/2016/11/finance-banks-capitalism-markets-socialism-planning.

2. Gabriel Sherman, "'You Don't Bring Bad News to the Cult Leader': Inside the Fall of WeWork," *Vanity Fair*, November 21, 2019, https://www.vanityfair.com /news/2019/11/inside-the-fall-of-wework.

3. Britney Nguyen, "The Career Rise, Fall, and Return of Adam Neumann, the Controversial WeWork Cofounder Who Is Back with Another Real-Estate Startup," *Insider*, August 16, 2022, https://www.businessinsider.com/wework-ceo-adam -neumann-bio-life-career-2019-8?r=US&IR=T.

4. "The Unicorn List: 13: WeWork," *Fortune*, accessed July 9, 2023, https://fortune .com/ranking/unicorns/2016/wework/.

5. Sheryl Wudunn, "MEDIA; An Entrepreneurial Exception Rides the Internet in Japan," *New York Times*, July 26, 1999, https://www.nytimes.com/1999/07/26 /business/media-an-entrepreneurial-exception-rides-the-internet-in-japan.html.

6. Ibid.

7. Alan M. Webber, "Japanese-Style Entrepreneurship: An Interview with Softbank's CEO, Masayoshi Son," *Harvard Business Review*, January–February 1992, https://hbr.org/1992/01/japanese-style-entrepreneurship-an-interview-with-softbanks-ceo-masayoshi-son.

8. "Who Has Lost the Most Money in Human History?," *The Spectator*, November 19, 2022, https://www.spectator.co.uk/article/who-has-lost-the-most-money-in-human-history/.

9. Alex Konrad, "WeWork Confirms Massive $4.4 Billion Investment From SoftBank and Its Vision Fund," *Forbes*, August 24, 2017, https://www.forbes.com/sites/alexkonrad/2017/08/24/wework-confirms-massive-4-4-billion-investment-from-softbank-and-its-vision-fund/.

10. Amy Chozick, "Adam Neumann and the Art of Failing Up," *New York Times*, November 2, 2019, updated May 18, 2020, https://www.nytimes.com/2019/11/02/business/adam-neumann-wework-exit-package.html.

11. Ibid.

12. Julie Bort and Meghan Morris, "Former Employees from WeWork Share Stories about Adam Neumann Running around Barefoot, Yelling at Employees, and Demanding Cases of Tequila," *Insider*, September 30, 2019, https://www.businessinsider.com/wework-employees-share-stories-about-barefoot-adam-neumann-2019-9?r=US&IR=T.

13. Taylor Telford, "Adam Neumann's Chaotic Energy Built WeWork. Now It Might Cost Him His Job as CEO," *Washington Post*, September 23, 2019, https://www.washingtonpost.com/business/2019/09/23/adam-neumanns-chaotic-energy-built-wework-now-it-might-cost-him-his-job-ceo/.

14. Nguyen, "The Career Rise, Fall, and Return of Adam Neumann, the Controversial WeWork Cofounder Who Is Back with Another Real-Estate Startup."

15. David Trainer, "WeWork Is the Most Ridiculous IPO of 2019," *Forbes*, August 27, 2019, https://www.forbes.com/sites/greatspeculations/2019/08/27/wework-is-the-most-ridiculous-ipo-of-2019/?sh=294fb4111ad6.

16. Chozick, "Adam Neumann and the Art of Failing Up."

17. Ellen Huet, "WeWork Gave Founder Loans as It Paid Him Rent, IPO Filing Shows," *Bloomberg*, August 14, 2019, https://www.bloomberg.com/news/articles/2019-08-14/wework-gave-founder-loans-as-it-paid-him-rent-ipo-filing-shows.

18. Chozick, "Adam Neumann and the Art of Failing Up."

19. Eliot Brown, Maureen Farrell, and Anupreeta Das, "WeWork Co-Founder Has Cashed Out at Least $700 Million Via Sales, Loans," *Wall Street Journal*, July 18, 2019, https://www.wsj.com/articles/wework-co-founder-has-cashed-out-at-least-700-million-from-the-company-11563481395.

20. Peter Eavis and Michael J. de la Merced, "WeWork I.P.O. Is Withdrawn as Investors Grow Wary," *New York Times*, October 1, 2019, updated October 21, 2021, https://www.nytimes.com/2019/09/30/business/wework-ipo.html.

21. Eric Platt, "Adam Neumann's $1.6bn WeWork Exit Package Could Get Sweeter," *Financial Times*, December 24, 2019, https://www.ft.com/content/eecf1f22-2332-11ea-b8a1-584213ee7b2b.

22. George Hammond and Andrew Edgecliffe-Johnson, "SoftBank and WeWork Co-Founder Adam Neumann Agree Divorce Deal," *Financial Times*, May 27, 2021, https://www.ft.com/content/b0c047d0-6e7e-42c1-89c8-ee5f96d01a12.

23. Sergei Klebnikov, "WeWork Lays Off 2,400 Employees in Latest Round of Cost-Cutting," *Forbes*, November 21, 2019, https://www.forbes.com/sites/sergeiklebnikov/2019/11/21/wework-lays-off-2400-employees-in-latest-round-of-cost-cutting/?sh=7bf6550c6b3b.

24. Ortenca Aliaj and George Hammond, "WeWork to Make Belated Arrival on Stock Market after Spac Merger," *Financial Times*, October 19, 2021, https://www.ft.com/content/258121b8-299e-4993-91d9-cb2a18d387f4.

25. Pavel Alpeyev, "SoftBank's Vision Fund Loses $17.7 Billion on WeWork, Uber," Bloomberg, May 18, 2020, https://www.bloomberg.com/news/articles/2020-05-18/softbank-vision-fund-books-17-7-billion-loss-on-wework-uber.

26. Hyman P. Minsky, *Induced Investment and Business Cycles* (New York: Levy Economics Institute of Bard College, 2004); Karl Polanyi, *The Great Transformation: The Political and Economic Origins of Our Time* (Boston: Beacon Press, 2001).

27. Ann Pettifor, *The Production of Money: How to Break the Power of Bankers* (London: Verso, 2017).

28. Dayen, *Monopolized*.

29. Heather Stewart, "This Is How We Let the Credit Crunch Happen, Ma'am . . . ," *The Guardian*, July 25, 2009, https://www.theguardian.com/uk/2009/jul/26/monarchy-credit-crunch.

30. Stephen Mihm, "Dr. Doom—Profile—Nouriel Roubini—Predicting Crisis in the United States Economy," *New York Times*, August 15, 2008, https://www.nytimes.com/2008/08/17/magazine/17pessimist-t.html.

31. Cameron Cooper, "6 economists who predicted the global financial crisis," CPA Australia, July 7, 2015, https://intheblack.cpaaustralia.com.au/economy/6-economists-who-predicted-the-global-financial-crisis-and-why-we-should-listen-to-them-from-now-on.

32. Ibid.

33. Steve Keen, "I Predicted the Last Financial Crisis—Now Soaring Global Debt Levels Pose Risk of Another," *The Conversation*, September 15, 2017, https://theconversation.com/i-predicted-the-last-financial-crisis-now-soaring-global-debt-levels-pose-risk-of-another-84136.

34. See, for example, N. Gregory Mankiw, *Macroeconomics* (New York: Worth Publishers, 2018).

35. "[I]t must keep some reserves on hand so that reserves are available whenever depositors want to make withdrawals." Mankiw, *Macroeconomics*.

36. Proponents of the loanable funds model may argue that the theory has developed beyond its classical roots and is now able to incorporate a more expansive view of lending—it remains the case, however, that "the conceptual and modeling framework that is almost universally used in this literature . . . adopts a shortcut that describes banks as intermediaries of physical resources akin to warehouses." Zoltan Jakab and Michael Kumhof, "Staff Working Paper No. 761: Banks Are Not Intermediaries of Loanable Funds—Facts,

Theory and Evidence," Bank of England, October 26, 2018, updated June 2019, https://www.bankofengland.co.uk/-/media/boe/files/working-paper/2018 /banks-are-not-intermediaries-of-loanable-funds-facts-theory-and-evidence .pdf?la=en&hash=5FCDED87A783AA0483319CD4351170DB94C8A771.

37. Ibid.

38. Pettifor, *The Production of Money.*

39. Ibid.

40. Neoclassical theory rests on the assumption that business investment is determined by the cost of that investment, measured against the expected returns that will be derived from that investment, subject to risk and inflation. But Keynes argued that the two elements of the neoclassical investment equation—costs and expected returns—are governed by different price systems. Investment costs are determined by the state of the economy today—for example, the cost of building a new factory will be determined by land costs, construction costs, etc. But the returns from an investment are determined by what will happen in the economy in the future, like future rates of economic growth. See Blakeley, *Stolen,* for a discussion of Keynes's "two price theory."

41. This distinction comes down to Frank Knight's typology of risk and uncertainty. Risk is quantifiable. Assessing risk involves mining past experience to attach a likelihood to a future event: a bank might estimate that the risk of bankruptcy for a particular company in a particular industry over the next five years is 25 percent based on an analysis of previous data. The bank's estimate of risk will affect the interest rate it charges: if a quarter of firms in an industry are likely to default, then the bank will want to make sure that it's charging a rate of interest on loans made to firms in that industry that will allow it to recoup the losses made on those firms that do default. Uncertainty, on the other hand, is not quantifiable. When an outcome is uncertain, there is no way of predicting its likelihood based on previous observations. While I can know that there is a risk that any one firm within an industry will default, I cannot know for certain whether the firm to which I'm lending will default. Frank Knight, *Risk, Uncertainty, and Profit* (Kissimmee, FL: Signalman, 2009).

42. As Martijn Konings writes, "All economic choices and investments were speculative in the sense that their value would only be determined in a future that is unknowable because it will be shaped by events that we cannot predict." Martijn Konings, "The Time of Finance," *Los Angeles Review of Books,* December 28, 2017.

43. As Frederic Durand has observed, the growing power of finance in our economies amounts to "a growing pre-emption of future production." Durand, *Fictitious Capital.*

44. Crouch, *The Strange Non-Death of Neoliberalism.*

45. It was also, as Wolfgang Streek argues, part of a broader shift in the terrain of distributional conflict "to ever more abstract spheres of action and ever further from the human experience and the scope of democratic politics." Streek, *Buying Time.*

46. Blakeley, *Stolen.*

47. Aled Davies, James Freeman, and Hugh Pemberton, "'Everyman a capitalist?' or 'Free to Choose'? Exploring the tensions within Thatcherite individualism,"

Historical Journal 61, no. 2 (2018): 477–501, https://doi.org/10.1017
/S0018246X17000103.

48. Crouch, *The Strange Non-Death of Neoliberalism.*

49. Peter Behr and Ben White, "J.P. Morgan Had Many Ties with Enron,"
Washington Post, February 23, 2002, https://www.washingtonpost.com/archive
/business/2002/02/23/jp-morgan-had-many-ties-with-enron/0e21292e-fa20-4a97
-9a11-de698ebd50e9/.

50. Ibid.

51. Ibid.

52. David Teather, "JP Morgan Pays $1bn to Settle Enron Claim," *The Guardian*,
August 17, 2005, https://www.theguardian.com/business/2005/aug/17
/corporatefraud.enron.

53. Patrick Oster and Bloomberg, "Ex-WorldCom CEO Bernard Ebbers, 'Telecom
Cowboy' Sentenced to 25 Years in Accounting Fraud, Dies at 78," *Fortune*,
February 3, 2020, https://fortune.com/2020/02/03/worldcom-ceo-bernard-ebbers
-telecom-cowboy-dies.

54. Ibid.

55. Ibid.

56. Gretchen Morgenson, "When Citigroup Met WorldCom," *New York Times*,
May 16, 2004, https://www.nytimes.com/2004/05/16/business/when-citigroup-met
-worldcom.html.

57. Ibid.

58. David Teather, "JP Morgan Pays $2bn over WorldCom," *The Guardian*, March 17,
2005, https://www.theguardian.com/business/2005/mar/17/corporatefraud.

59. Paul Toscano, "Portfolio's Worst American CEOs of All Time," CNBC, April 30,
2009, https://www.cnbc.com/2009/04/30/Portfolios-Worst-American-CEOs-of-All
-Time.html.

60. Diana B. Henriques, "Bernie Madoff, Architect of Largest Ponzi Scheme in
History, Is Dead at 82," *New York Times*, April 15, 2021, https://www.nytimes
.com/2021/04/14/business/bernie-madoff-dead.html.

61. "The Madoff Files: Bernie's Billions," *Independent*, January 29, 2009, https://www
.independent.co.uk/news/business/analysis-and-features/the-madoff-files-bernie-s
-billions-1518939.html.

62. Ethan Sacks, "Bernie Madoff, Mastermind of Largest Ponzi Scheme in History,
Dies at 82," NBC News, April 14, 2021, https://www.nbcnews.com/news
/us-news/bernie-madoff-mastermind-behind-largest-ponzi-scheme-history-dies
-82-n1139831.

63. Laurence Kotlikoff, "A Look at JPMorgan Chase's 20 Years of Watching Madoff
Commit Crimes," *Forbes*, September 26, 2014, https://www.forbes.com/sites
/kotlikoff/2014/09/26/jpmorgan-chases-20-years-of-watching-madoff-commit
-crimes-read-chapter-2-at-jpmadoff-com/?sh=2df5ceaf3b89.

64. MJ Lee, "Madoff: 'JPMorgan Knew,'" *Politico*, March 21, 2014, https://www
.politico.com/story/2014/03/bernie-madoff-jpmorgan-104887.

65. Nathan Vardi, "JPMorgan Chase to Pay $1.7 Billion in Largest Bank Forfeiture in
History Settles Criminal Madoff Charges," *Forbes*, January 7, 2014, https://www

.forbes.com/sites/nathanvardi/2014/01/07/jpmorgan-chase-to-pay-1-7-billion-in
-largest-bank-forfeiture-in-history-settles-criminal-madoff-charges/.

66. Costas Lapavitsas, *Profiting Without Producing: How Finance Exploits Us All* (London: Verso Books, 2014).

67. Rudolf Hilferding, *Finance Capital: A Study in the Latest Phase of Capitalist Development* (London: Routledge, 2007).

68. Holocaust Encyclopedia, "Rudolf Hilferding," US Holocaust Memorial Museum, accessed July 9, 2023, https://encyclopedia.ushmm.org/content/en/article/rudolf-hilferding.

69. William Smaldone, *Rudolf Hilferding: The Tragedy of a German Social Democrat* (DeKalb: Northern Illinois University Press, 2015), 41.

70. Smaldone, *Rudolf Hilferding*.

71. Holocaust Encyclopedia, "Rudolf Hilferding."

72. Smaldone, *Rudolf Hilferding*.

73. The development of the stock market extends this process of financialization. Banks gain a "promoter's profit" by supporting firms to float on the stock market. Capital gains derived from speculation over the "fictitious capital" created in financial markets is made possible through the transformation of capitalist property rights: "ownership of the actual means of production is transferred from individuals to a legal entity." This transformation renders the production process increasingly independent from individual ownership of means of production. Hilferding, *Finance Capital*.

74. The increasing involvement of financial institutions in the financing of firm investment "liberates" the industrial capitalist from his role as "industrial entrepreneur." Hilferding, *Finance Capital*.

75. Panitch and Gindin, *The Making of Global Capitalism*.

76. As Costas Lapavitsas argues in *Profiting Without Producing*, "Finance capital—an amalgam of industrial and banking capital . . . 'organizes' the economy to suit its own interests."

77. Bob Bryan, "Wall Street Banks Could Make Close to $700 Million from the Bayer-Monsanto Deal," *Insider*, September 14, 2016, https://www.businessinsider.com/bayer-monsanto-wall-street-financial-advisors-payday-2016-9?r=US&IR=T.

78. Ibid.

79. Ibid.

80. Ruth Bender, "How Bayer-Monsanto Became One of the Worst Corporate Deals—in 12 Charts," *Wall Street Journal*, August 28, 2019, https://www.wsj.com/articles/how-bayer-monsanto-became-one-of-the-worst-corporate-dealsin-12-charts-11567001577.

81. Mike Stone, "Dow CEO Rewards Former Citi Banker Klein with $130 Billion Deal Prize," Reuters, December 11, 2015, https://www.reuters.com/article/us-dow-m-a-klein-idUSKBN0TU2UF20151211.

82. Anjuli Davies, "Advisors Could Reap $166 mln in Fees from Chemchina's Syngenta Deal," Reuters, February 3, 2016, https://www.reuters.com/article/syngenta-ag-ma-fees-idUSL8N15I3KD.

83. Which was famously neither holy, nor Roman, nor an empire.

84. David Graeber, *Debt: The First 5,000 Years* (New York: Melville House, 2014).

85. Marx, *Capital, Volume I.*

86. Robert Z. Aliber and Charles P. Kindleberger, *Manias, Panics, and Crashes: A History of Financial Crises, Seventh Edition* (New York: Palgrave Macmillan, 2015).

87. Robert J. Shiller, *Irrational Exuberance: Revised and Expanded Third Edition* (Princeton, NJ: Princeton University Press, 2016).

88. J. M. Keynes quoted in Durand, *Fictitious Capital.*

89. William Fleckenstein with Frederick Sheehan, *Greenspan's Bubbles: The Age of Ignorance at the Federal Reserve* (New York: McGraw-Hill, 2008).

90. Durand, *Fictitious Capital.*

91. Fleckenstein and Sheehan, *Greenspan's Bubbles*; Jeannine Aversa, "Alan Greenspan enjoys rock star renown," Associated Press, March 5, 2005, https://www.chron.com/business/article/alan-greenspan-enjoys-rock-star-renown-1914177.php.

92. Streek, *Buying Time.*

93. Richard C. Koo, *The Other Half of Macroeconomics and the Fate of Globalization* (Hoboken, NJ: John Wiley & Sons, 2018).

94. Durand, *Fictitious Capital.*

95. Ibid.

96. Ibid.

97. Benjamin S. Braun, "Speaking to the People? Money, Trust, and Central Bank Legitimacy in the Age of Quantitative Easing," *Review of International Political Economy* 23, no. 6 (November 2016): 1064–92, https://doi.org/10.1080/09692290.2016.1252415.

98. They have, in Braun's words, "made the long-term interest rate a policy variable." Benjamin S. Braun, "Central Bank Planning: Unconventional Monetary Policy and the Price of Bending the Yield Curve," in Jens Beckert and Richard Bronk (eds.), *Uncertain Futures: Imaginaries, Narratives, and Calculation in the Economy* (Oxford: Oxford University Press, 2018).

99. To be fair to the central bankers, they had been given an almost impossible task of maintaining growth and reducing inflation while government fiscal policy often works in the opposite direction and inflation rose dramatically, driven by cost pressures largely outside policymakers' control. Clearly, they cannot be expected to manage these pressures on their own. But recognizing this fact simply highlights severe problems with the macroeconomic orthodoxy—involving the separation of monetary and fiscal policy—of the last few decades.

100. Their predictions no longer carry "epistemic authority" and "commitment credibility" because they are seen less as objective predictions of likely future outcomes and more as tools for influencing the market's behavior. Braun, "Central Bank Planning."

101. "Once a barometer of the decentralized beliefs and actions of myriad market actors, the long-term interest rate has become a policy variable, manipulated by central banks to reduce the 'perceived downside risk' for investors." Braun, "Central Bank Planning."

102. Corporate Europe Observatory, "Lobbying to Kill off Robin Hood," Corporate

Europe Observatory, accessed August 24, 2023, https://corporateeurope.org/en/financial-lobby/2012/03/lobbying-kill-robin-hood.

103. Pistor, *The Code of Capital*.

104. Baars, *The Corporation, Law and Capitalism*.

105. Ibid.

106. Pistor, *The Code of Capital*.

107. Ibid.

108. This is especially the case in common law systems where the law developed through precedent and, as Pistor explains, most international financial law is governed by common law systems. Pistor, *The Code of Capital*.

109. Nicholas Shaxson, *Treasure Islands*.

110. Ibid.

111. Meagher, *Competition Is Killing Us*.

112. Barak, *Unchecked Corporate Power*.

113. Durand, *Fictitious Capital*.

114. Robin Wigglesworth, "The Ten Trillion Dollar Man: How Larry Fink Became King of Wall St.," *Financial Times*, October 6, 2021, https://www.ft.com/content/7dfd1e3d-e256-4656-a96d-1204538d75cd.

115. Ibid.

116. Ibid.

117. Ibid.

118. Jacob Greenspon, "How Big a Problem Is It That a Few Shareholders Own Stock in So Many Competing Companies?," *Harvard Business Review*, February 19, 2019, https://hbr.org/2019/02/how-big-a-problem-is-it-that-a-few-shareholders-own-stock-in-so-many-competing-companies.

119. Farhad Manjoo, "What BlackRock, Vanguard and State Street Are Doing to the Economy," *New York Times*, May 12, 2022, https://www.nytimes.com/2022/05/12/opinion/vanguard-power-blackrock-state-street.html; Lucian A. Bebchuk and Scott Hurst, "Big Three Power, and Why It Matters," Harvard Law School Forum on Corporate Governance, December 13, 2022, https://corpgov.law.harvard.edu/2022/12/13/big-three-power-and-why-it-matters/.

120. For a discussion see Brett Christophers, *Our Lives in Their Portfolios: Why Asset Managers Own the World* (London: Verso, 2023).

121. Harvard Law School Forum on Corporate Governance, "Big Three Power, and Why It Matters."

122. "How to Think about the Unstoppable Rise of Index Funds," *The Economist*, October 16, 2021, https://www.economist.com/finance-and-economics/2021/10/16/how-to-think-about-the-unstoppable-rise-of-index-funds.

123. As one *Forbes* contributor argued in 2017, "Passive investing substitutes diligence with diversification and can create a 'rising tide lifts all boats' effect on the valuation of both high *and* low quality stocks within an index." David Trainer, "Hidden Trigger For Another (Flash) Crash: Passive Investing," *Forbes*, July 20, 2017, https://www.forbes.com/sites/greatspeculations/2017/07/20/hidden-trigger-for-another-flash-crash-passive-investing/?sh=3e5ef7b577a2.

124. "The Rise of BlackRock," *The Economist*, December 5, 2013, https://www
.economist.com/leaders/2013/12/05/the-rise-of-blackrock.

125. Azar, Schmalz, and Tecu (2018) find empirical evidence for "the anticompetitive
incentives implied by common ownership concentration," including an impact on
prices. José Azar, Martin C. Schmalz, and Isabel Tecu, "Anticompetitive Effects
of Common Ownership," *Journal of Finance* 73, no. 4 (August 2018): 1513–65,
https://onlinelibrary.wiley.com/doi/abs/10.1111/jofi.12698.

126. The role of the Big Three asset managers is undermining the long-held distinction
between more coordinated economies, in which banks and states play a more
significant role in allocating capital than financial markets, and liberal market
economies, in which financial markets play a much bigger role and shareholder
value is therefore enforced much more ruthlessly. A shortcoming of the latter model,
it has often been argued, is a rigid focus on short-term returns and lack of patient
capital that can undermine the long-term stability of a firm. James Hawley and
Andrew Williams, "The Emergence of Universal Owners: Some Implications of
Institutional Equity Ownership," *Challenge* 43, no. 4 (July–August 2000): 43–61,
https://www.jstor.org/stable/40722019.

127. Klaus Schwab, *Stakeholder Capitalism: A Global Economy That Works for
Progress, People and Planet* (Hoboken, NJ: John Wiley & Sons, 2021).

128. Grant Hayden and Matthew Bodie argue that this is equivalent to arguing that
there exist certain "superheroes" who will be able to "rise above their own
self-interests . . . to make decisions that respond to the interests of all corporate
constituents." Hayden and Bodie, *Reconstructing the Corporation*.

129. Jasper Jolly, "World's Biggest Investor Accused of Dragging Feet on Climate
Crisis," *The Guardian*, May 21, 2019, https://www.theguardian.com/business/2019
/may/21/blackrock-investor-climate-crisis-blackrock-assets.

130. Jan Fichtner, Eelke M. Heemskerk, and Javier Garcia-Bernardo, "Hidden Power of
the Big Three? Passive Index Funds, Re-concentration of Corporate Ownership, and
New Financial Risk," *Business and Politics* 19, no. 2 (April 2017): 298–326, https://
doi.org/10.1017/bap.2017.6.

131. Eamon Barrett, "Republicans Accused BlackRock of Being Too 'Woke'
on Climate Change. Activists Say the Firm Isn't Woke Enough," *Fortune*,
September 14, 2022, https://fortune.com/2022/09/14/blackrock-republicans
-letter-woke-capitalism-esg-investing/.

132. As Bailey argues, the "stakeholder capitalism" agenda has "sought to 'square the circle'
of (global) capital accumulation and (national) political legitimation . . . Rather than a
genuine alternative to neoliberalism, this shift within the neoliberal policy regime seeks
to relegitimise capitalist globalisation in crisis, while deepening and extending its 'post-
democratic' political economic logic in both the private and public spheres." Kyle Bailey,
"Stakeholder Capitalism against Democracy: Relegitimising Global Neoliberalism,"
Journal of Australian Political Economy, no. 86 (Summer 2020/2021): 85–121, https://
www.ppesydney.net/jape-issues/issue-86-summer-2020-2021/.

133. Annie Massa and Caleb Melby, "In Fink We Trust: BlackRock Is Now 'Fourth
Branch of Government,'" Bloomberg, May 21, 2020, https://www.bloomberg

.com/news/articles/2020-05-21/how-larry-fink-s-blackrock-is-helping-the-fed
-with-bond-buying.

134. Sridhar Natarajan and Eric Martin, "Biden Ties to BlackRock Deepen with
Latest Treasury Hire," Bloomberg, August 11, 2022, https://www.bloomberg
.com/news/articles/2022-08-11/biden-ties-to-blackrock-deepen-with-latest
-treasury-hire.

135. Cezary Podkul and Dawn Lim, "Fed Hires BlackRock to Help Calm Markets. Its
ETF Business Wins Big," *Wall Street Journal*, September 18, 2020, https://www
.wsj.com/articles/fed-hires-blackrock-to-help-calm-markets-its-etf-business-wins
-big-11600450267.

136. Liz Rappaport and Susanne Craig, "BlackRock Wears Multiple Hats," *Wall Street
Journal*, May 19, 2009, https://www.wsj.com/articles/SB124269131342732625.

137. Cal Turner and Sara van Horn, "Asset Managers Like BlackRock Are
Controlling More and More of Our Lives," *Jacobin*, May 2, 2023, https://jacobin
.com/2023/05/our-lives-in-their-portfolios-interview-asset-management-society
-infrastructure.

138. As one observer put it, "BlackRock has become a key player in the market with
a clear conflict of interest." Ramaa Vasudevan, "How Big Finance Is Making a
Killing from the Pandemic," *Jacobin*, June 11, 2020, https://jacobin.com/2020/06
/federal-reserve-fed-coronavirus-covid-junk-bonds.

139. Christophers, *Our Lives in Their Portfolios*.

140. Jan Fichtner and Eelke M. Heemskerk, "The New Permanent Universal Owners:
Index Funds, Patient Capital, and the Distinction between Feeble and Forceful
Stewardship," *Economy and Society* 49, no. 4 (November 2020): 493–515, https://
doi.org/10.1080/03085147.2020.1781417.

141. Daniel Haberly and Dariusz Wójcik, "Earth Incorporated: Centralization and
Variegation in the Global Company Network," *Economic Geography* 93, no. 3
(2016): 241–66, http://sro.sussex.ac.uk/id/eprint/66532/1/Haberly%20and%20
Wojcik%202016%20Earth%20Incorporated%20-%20Archive%20Dec%2022
.pdf.

CHAPTER 6: CAPITAL'S CRONIES: HOW STATES PLAN

1. Niamh Lynch, "Exxon Predicted Global Warming in 1970s Despite Publicly
Dismissing Climate Change, Research Finds," Sky News, January 13, 2023, https://
news.sky.com/story/exxon-predicted-global-warming-in-1970s-despite-publicly
-dismissing-climate-change-research-finds-12785585.

2. "Exxon's Climate Denial History: A Timeline," Greenpeace, https://www
.greenpeace.org/usa/fighting-climate-chaos/exxon-and-the-oil-industry-knew
-about-climate-crisis/exxons-climate-denial-history-a-timeline/.

3. Ibid.

4. Ibid.

5. Thaddeus Herrick, "Exxon CEO Lee Raymond's Stance on Global Warming
Causes a Stir," *Wall Street Journal*, August 29, 2001, https://www.wsj.com/articles
/SB999035936679805198.

6. Jad Mouawad, "Exxon Chairman Got Retirement Package Worth at Least $398 Million," *New York Times*, April 13, 2006, https://www.nytimes .com/2006/04/13/business/exxon-chairman-got-retirement-package-worth-at-least -398-million.html#:~:text=The%20total%20sum%20for%20Mr,of%20Walt%20 Disney%2C%20in%201997.

7. "Client Profile: Exxon Corp,"OpenSecrets, accessed July 9, 2023, https://www .opensecrets.org/federal-lobbying/clients/summary?cycle=1998&id=d000000129.

8. "An Investor Enquiry: How Much Big Oil Spends on Obstructive Climate Lobbying," InfluenceMap, April 2016, https://senate.ucsd.edu/media/206150 /lobby_spend_report__april.pdf.

9. Greenpeace, "Exxon's Climate Denial History: A Timeline."

10. Roman Goncharenko, "Rex Tillerson's Cozy Ties with Russia," DW, December 14, 2016, https://www.dw.com/en/exxonmobil-ceo-rex-tillersons-close-ties-with -russia/a-36764933.

11. John Schwartz, "Exxon Mobil Lends Its Support to a Carbon Tax Proposal," *New York Times*, June 20, 2017, https://www.nytimes.com/2017/06/20/science/exxon -carbon-tax.html.

12. Dan L. Wagner, Alan Zibel, Christopher Kuveke, and Lukas Ross, "Bailed Out & Propped Up," Bailout Watch, Public Citizen, and Friends of the Earth, November 2020, https://report.bailoutwatch.org/.

13. Lawrence Carter, "Inside Exxon's Playbook: How America's Biggest Oil Company Continues to Oppose Action on Climate Change," Unearthed, June 30, 2021, https://unearthed.greenpeace.org/2021/06/30/exxon-climate-change -undercover/.

14. Ibid.

15. Niall Stanage, "Five Times Joe Manchin Has Bucked the Democrats," *The Hill*, July 16, 2022, https://thehill.com/homenews/senate/3561908-five-times-joe -manchin-has-bucked-the-democrats/.

16. Bryan Metzger, "Joe Manchin, Who Is Holding Up Crucial Climate Change Initiatives in Biden's Reconciliation Bill, Collects $500,000 a Year from Coal Stocks Dividends: Report," *Insider*, September 30, 2021, https://www.businessinsider .com/senator-joe-manchin-half-million-year-coal-stocks-climate-crisis-2021 -9?r=US&IR=T.

17. Alexander C. Kaufman, "Exxon Lobbyists Paid the 6 Democrats Named in Sting Video Nearly $333,000," *Grist*, July 16, 2021, https://grist.org/politics/exxon -lobbyists-paid-the-6-democrats-named-in-sting-video-nearly-333000/.

18. Sam Tabahriti, "US to Expand Offshore Drilling after Reviewing IPCC Climate Change Report," Offshore Technology, September 20, 2021, https://www.offshore -technology.com/news/us-offshore-drilling-gulf-of-mexico/.

19. Ian W.H. Parry, Simon Black, and Nate Vernon, "Still Not Getting Energy Prices Right: A Global and Country Update of Fossil Fuel Subsidies," IMF Working Papers, International Monetary Fund, September 24, 2021, https://www.imf.org /en/Publications/WP/Issues/2021/09/23/Still-Not-Getting-Energy-Prices-Right-A -Global-and-Country-Update-of-Fossil-Fuel-Subsidies-466004.

20. "Fossil Fuel Firms Slashed Nearly 60,000 Jobs in 2020 while Pocketing $8.2 Billion Tax Bailout," Bailout Watch, April 2, 2021, https://bailoutwatch.org/analysis/fossil -fuel-firmsslashed-nearly-60000-jobs-in-2020.

21. "6 Bailed-Out Polluters Already Spent $15M This Year Lobbying for Subsidies and against Climate Action," Bailout Watch, August 20, 2021, https://bailoutwatch.org /analysis/6-bailed-out-polluters-already-spent-15m-lobbying-this-year.

22. Brown, *Undoing the Demos*; Barkan, *Corporate Sovereignty*.

23. Bob Jessop, "The State as a Social Relation," in John L. Brooke, Julia C. Strauss, and Greg Anderson (eds.), *State Formations: Global Histories and Cultures of Statehood* (Cambridge: Cambridge University Press, 2018), https://www.cambridge .org/core/books/abs/state-formations/state-as-a-social-relation/4B73F4E00A29C8B 32B4F6248BA162746.

24. Polanyi, *The Great Transformation*.

25. Thomas Hobbes, *Leviathan* (London: Penguin Classics, 2017).

26. Alistair MacFarlane, "Brief Lives: Thomas Hobbes (1588–1679)," *Philosophy Now*, Issue 124 (February/March 2018), https://philosophynow.org/issues/124/Thomas _Hobbes_1588-1679.

27. Ibid.

28. John Locke, *The Second Treatise on Government* (London: Aegitus, 2017).

29. Locke, *The Second Treatise on Government*.

30. The authority that supported this relationship was God: God had given us ownership over our own bodies, and we could therefore mix this ownership with the earth to augment our property. Leaving potentially useful resources unused was an affront to God so anyone who thinks to make use of these resources gains the right to count them among his property. Locke, *The Second Treatise on Government*.

31. Adam Smith, *The Wealth of Nations* (London: Heritage Illustrated Publishing, 2014).

32. "Adam Smith: Father of Capitalism," BBC Forum, BBC World Service, November 21, 2017, https://www.bbc.co.uk/programmes/w3csvsfb.

33. Foucault, *The Birth of Biopolitics*.

34. Ha-Joon Chang, *Kicking Away the Ladder: Development Strategy in Historical Perspective* (London: Anthem Press, 2021).

35. Quinn Slobodian and Dieter Plehwe, "Introduction" in Quinn Slobodian, Dieter Plehwe and Philip Mirowski, *Nine Lives of Neoliberalism* (London: Verso, 2020).

36. Ibid.

37. Harvard professor Harvey Cox makes a similar point in his article "The Market as God," in which he observes that "the lexicon of the Wall Street Journal . . . turned out to bear striking resemblance to Genesis, the Epistle, to the Romans and Saint Augustine's City of God." Harvey Cox, "The Market as God: Living in the new dispensation," *The Atlantic*, March 1999, https://www.theatlantic.com/magazine /archive/1999/03/the-market-as-god/306397/.

38. Goran Therborn, *Inequality and the Labyrinth of Democracy* (London: Verso, 2020).

39. Ibid.

40. Fran Tonkiss, "Markets against States: Neo-Liberalism," in Kate Nash and Alan Scott (eds.), *The Blackwell Companion to Political Sociology* (Oxford: Blackwell,

2004), https://doi.org/10.1002/9780470696071.ch23; Mirowski, *Never Let a Serious Crisis Go to Waste*.

41. Brown, *Undoing the Demos*.

42. Ibid.

43. Ibid.

44. Aled Davies, James Freeman, and Hugh Pemberton, " 'Everyman a Capitalist' or 'Free to Choose'? Exploring the Tensions within Thatcherite Individualism," *Historical Journal* 61, no. 2 (June 2018): 477–501; Crouch, *The Strange Non-Death of Neoliberalism*.

45. Triantafillou, *Neoliberal Power and Public Management Reforms*.

46. Brown, *Undoing the Demos*.

47. Foucault, *The Birth of Biopolitics*.

48. Hayek, *The Road to Serfdom*.

49. Ibid.

50. Bruce Caldwell, "Introduction," in Hayek, *The Road to Serfdom*.

51. Max Weber, "Politics as a Vocation," in H. H. Gerth and C. Wright Mills, *From Max Weber: Essays in Sociology* (Oxford: Oxford University Press, 1946).

52. Foucault, *The Birth of Biopolitics*.

53. Meagher, *Competition Is Killing Us*; Milton Friedman, "Solutions to Market Failure," YouTube, October 29, 2010, https://www.youtube.com/watch?v=BPnJHfiFWJw.

54. Meagher, *Competition Is Killing Us*; Tepper and Hearn, *The Myth of Capitalism*.

55. Tepper and Hearn, *The Myth of Capitalism*.

56. Meagher, *Competition Is Killing Us*.

57. "We rarely hear, it has been said, of the combinations of masters, though frequently of those of workmen. But whoever imagines, upon this account, that masters rarely combine, is as ignorant of the world as of the subject. Masters are always and everywhere in a sort of tacit, but constant and uniform, combination, not to raise the wages of labour above their actual rate [. . .]. Masters, too, sometimes enter into particular combinations to sink the wages of labour even below this rate. These are always conducted with the utmost silence and secrecy till the moment of execution." In contrast, when workers combine, "the masters [. . .] never cease to call aloud for the assistance of the civil magistrate, and the rigorous execution of those laws which have been enacted with so much severity against the combination of servants, labourers, and journeymen." Smith, *The Wealth of Nations*.

58. Tepper and Hearn, *The Myth of Capitalism*.

59. Meagher, *Competition Is Killing Us*.

60. Ibid.

61. Baars, *The Corporation, Law and Capitalism*.

62. Brown, *In the Ruins of Neoliberalism*.

63. Ibid.

64. Brown, *Undoing the Demos*.

65. Karl Marx, *Manifesto of the Communist Party*, Marxist Internet Archive, accessed July 10, 2023, https://www.marxists.org/archive/marx/works/1848/communist-manifesto/.

66. Duncan Mavin, *Pyramid of Lies: The Prime Minister, the Banker and the Billion Pound Scandal* (London: Pan Macmillan, 2022).

67. John Arlidge, "How Did Lex Greensill Seduce the World?," *Evening Standard*, May 11, 2021, https://www.standard.co.uk/insider/how-did-lex-greensill-seduce -the-world-b934517.html.

68. Duncan Mavin, "Who Is Lex Greensill? The Billionaire Banker Tied to GAM's Crisis," *Financial News*, May 7, 2019, https://www.fnlondon.com/articles/lex -greensill-billionaire-banker-tied-to-gam-tim-haywood-20190507.

69. See Mavin, *Pyramid of Lies,* on the relationship between Greensill and Credit Suisse.

70. Ibid.

71. Julie Steinberg and Duncan Mavin, "Greensill Used Credit Suisse Investment Funds to Lend to Its Own Backers," *Wall Street Journal*, March 5, 2021, https://www .wsj.com/articles/greensill-used-credit-suisse-investment-funds-to-lend-to-its-own -backers-11614982505?mod=searchresults_pos12&page=1.

72. Heather Stewart and Kalyeena Makortoff, "Business Card Puts Greensill Founder at the Heart of Downing Street," *The Guardian*, March 30, 2021, https://www .theguardian.com/politics/2021/mar/30/business-card-puts-greensill-founder-at-the -heart-of-downing-street.

73. BBC Panorama Reporting Team, "Greensill: David Cameron 'Made $10m' before Company's Collapse," BBC News, August 9, 2021, https://www.bbc.co.uk/news/uk -58149765.

74. Kalyeena Makortoff, Michael Savage, and Ben Butler, "Cameron 'Lobbied Senior Downing St Aide and Matt Hancock' to Help Greensill," *The Guardian*, April 10, 2021, https://www.theguardian.com/politics/2021/apr/10/revealed-david-cameron -stood-to-gain-from-218m-greensill-trust.

75. Francesca Newton, "The 'Chumocracy' Is Just British Capitalism in Action," *Tribune*, April 23, 2021, https://tribunemag.co.uk/2021/04/britains-chumocracy.

76. Denis Campbell, "NHS England Chair Faces Demands to Explain Role in Greensill Lobbying," *The Guardian*, April 18, 2021, https://www.theguardian.com /business/2021/apr/18/nhs-england-chair-lord-prior-of-brampton-faces-demands-to -explain-greensills-lobbying-of-nhs-bosses.

77. Jane Croft, "UK Acted Unlawfully in Appointing Dido Harding to Key Covid Role, Judges Rule," *Financial Times*, February 15, 2022, https://www.ft.com/content /f13c3d34-ae79-4615-a748-a08ef00bcaba.

78. Campbell, "NHS England Chair Faces Demands to Explain Role in Greensill Lobbying."

79. Robert Smith, "Greensill Tried to Use NHS Pay 'Gift' as Lever to Sell Supply Chain Finance," *Financial Times*, April 22, 2021, https://www.ft.com/content/b76df097 -8f3c-4310-92ac-b0aaa2fa5646.

80. Kalyeena Makortoff, Ben Butler, and Joseph Smith, "Greensill Scandal: Ex-Civil Servant Had $8m Stake in Lender," *The Guardian*, April 14, 2021, https://www .theguardian.com/politics/2021/apr/13/greensill-scandal-ex-civil-servant-faces -questions-over-whitehall-meetings.

81. Ibid.

82. Kalyeena Makortoff, "Cameron Lobbied UK Government on Behalf of Greensill

Capital—Report," *The Guardian*, March 19, 2021, https://www.theguardian.com /politics/2021/mar/19/cameron-lobbied-uk-government-behalf-greensill-access -covid-loans-reports-says.

83. BBC News, "Greensill: What Is the David Cameron Lobbying Row About?," August 9, 2021, https://www.bbc.co.uk/news/uk-politics-56578838.

84. "Newly Released Texts Reveal Extent of David Cameron's Greensill Lobbying," BBC News, May 11, 2021, https://www.bbc.co.uk/news/uk-politics-57074690.

85. Peter Walker, "Rishi Sunak Told David Cameron He Had 'Pushed the Team' over Greensill," *The Guardian*, April 8, 2021, https://www.theguardian.com/politics/2021 /apr/08/rishi-sunak-told-david-cameron-he-had-pushed-the-team-over-greensill.

86. Press Association, "Greensill: British Business Bank's 'Woefully Inadequate' Checks Put £335m at Risk, Say MPs," *The Guardian*, November 20, 2021, https://www .theguardian.com/business/2021/nov/20/greensill-british-business-banks-woefully -inadequate-checks-put-335m-at-risk-say-mps.

87. Kate Beioley and Sylvia Pfeifer, "UK Fraud Agency Intensifies Probe into Sanjeev Gupta's GFG Alliance," *Financial Times*, April 27, 2022, https://www.ft.com /content/cee5f81f-1559-4d85-9e94-e1af4df85a6a.

88. Richard Fuller, "Richard comments on Serious Fraud Office investigation into Gupta Family Group Alliance," Richardfuller.co.uk, May 14, 2021, accessed October 7, 2023, https://www.richardfuller.co.uk/news/richard-comments-serious -fraud-office-investigation-gupta-family-group-alliance.

89. National Audit Office, "Investigation into the British Business Bank's Accreditation of Greensill Capital," July 7, 2021, https://www.nao.org.uk/reports/investigation -into-the-british-business-banks-accreditation-of-greensill-capital/.

90. There are, of course, plenty of challenges when it comes to talking about "the state"—a concept that covers so many different kinds of political organization throughout time and space, not to mention a range of different institutions and processes within any one society. The discussion in this section does not seek to reify "the state" as a "substantial unitary entity," but I do use the term to explore the idea of the state as a social relation. Or, to be more specific, as an "institutionally and discursively mediated condensation" or "crystallization" of a balance of social forces. For a much more detailed and nuanced exploration of the history of the concept of a state as a social relation, see Bob Jessop's *The State: Past, Present, Future* (London: Polity Press, 2018).

91. Jessop, *The State*.

92. Ibid.

93. Michael Newman, *Ralph Miliband and the Politics of the New Left* (New York: Monthly Review Press, 2003).

94. Ralph Miliband, *The State in Capitalist Society* (London: Merlin Press, 2009).

95. Jessop, *The State*.

96. Nicos Poulantzas, *State, Power, Socialism* (London: Verso Books, 2014).

97. It is the "site of the existence and reproduction of modes of production." Poulantzas, *State, Power, Socialism*.

98. This idea of the state as a "crystallization" of a social relationship is elaborated by Bob Jessop. The idea of crystallization indicates that the state is "polymorphous"— in the life sciences this refers to an organism's ability to "assume several forms,"

while in chemistry it refers to physical compounds that can "crystallize into two or more durable forms." The approach "views actually existing state formations . . . as polyvalent, polymorphous crystallizations of one or another dominant principle of societal organization that varies according to the most pressing issues in a conjuncture, general crystallizations defining long periods and specific crystallizations emerging in particular situations." Jessop, *The State*.

99. Stephen Maher, *Corporate Capitalism and the Integral State: General Electric and a Century of American Power* (Basingstoke: Palgrave Macmillan, 2023).

100. Ibid.

101. The ability of the hegemonic power bloc to impose these sacrifices in order to guarantee its hegemony is a central mechanism through which capitalist social relations reproduce themselves. Poulantzas, *State, Power, Socialism*.

102. Workers can achieve victories within the state, but they can do so only "as *dominated* classes"—and some areas of the state apparatus, like the central bank for example, are insulated from popular struggle altogether. Poulantzas, *State, Power, Socialism*.

103. Jessop, *The State*.

104. In fact, neoliberalism appears to have a dual approach to understanding state power. On the one hand, the neoliberals decry the influence of vested interests on the exercise of power within social democratic societies—they argued that the workers had too much power to advance their particular interests within state institutions. On the other hand, neoliberals expect policymakers to advance their ideas on the basis that doing so is the best way to protect "the economy," which stands in for the interests of society as a whole. In other words, neoliberal theorists expect "their" policymakers to act on behalf of the general interest while accusing "enemy" policymakers of acting on behalf of particular interests. The other explanation is, of course, that the neoliberals realized that even "their" policymakers were acting on behalf of a particular interest—that of capital—but they either believed that the interests of capital were either identical with those of society as a whole, or simply the only interests worth serving.

105. "This line of demarcation [between the state and civil society] shapes how other actors on the political scene orient their actions towards the 'state,' acting as if it existed. And struggles over dominant or hegemonic political and state imaginaries can be decisive in shaping the nature, purposes and stakes of government." Jessop, *The State*.

106. Richard H. Thaler and Cass R. Sunstein, *Nudge: Improving Decisions about Health, Wealth, and Happiness* (New Haven, CT: Yale University Press, 2008).

107. Patrick Wintour, "David Cameron's 'Nudge Unit' Aims to Improve Economic Behaviour," *The Guardian*, September 9, 2010, https://www.theguardian.com /society/2010/sep/09/cameron-nudge-unit-economic-behaviour.

108. "'Nudge Unit' Sold off to Charity and Employees," BBC News, February 5, 2014, https://www.bbc.co.uk/news/uk-politics-26030205.

109. Nick Barrett, "Hostile Environment: The Dark Side of Nudge Theory," Politics.co .uk, May 1, 2018, https://www.politics.co.uk/comment-analysis/2018/05/01/hostile -environment-the-dark-side-of-nudge-theory/.

110. Demetrios Matheou, "Surviving the Windrush Scandal," UNISON, June 6, 2018, https://www.unison.org.uk/news/magazine/2018/06/surviving-windrush-scandal/.

111. Ibid.

112. Ibid.

113. Ibid.

114. Amelia Gentleman, "'I Feel Disgusted': How Windrush Scandal Shattered Two Brothers' Lives," *The Guardian*, April 22, 2018, https://www.theguardian.com/uk-news/2018/apr/22/how-windrush-scandal-shattered-two-brothers-lives-trevor-desmond-johnson.

115. Symeon Brown, "Man Stuck in Jamaica for 15 Years," Channel 4, April 23, 2018, https://www.channel4.com/news/man-stuck-in-jamaica-for-15-years.

116. Gentleman, "'I Feel Disgusted.'"

117. Ibid.

118. Frances Webber, "The Embedding of State Hostility: A Background Paper on the Windrush Scandal," Institute of Race Relations Briefing Paper No. 11, November 19, 2018, https://irr.org.uk/app/uploads/2018/11/Embedding-State-hostility-v4.pdf.

119. Louis Althusser, *On the Reproduction of Capitalism: Ideology and Ideological State Apparatuses* (London: Verso Books, 2014).

120. Althusser's argument draws on Gramsci's formulation that the "state = civil society + political society." Althusser, *On the Reproduction of Capitalism*; Gramsci, *Prison Notebooks*.

121. Foucault, *The Birth of Biopolitics*.

122. It is a "practice that fixes the definition and respective positions of the governed and governors." Ibid.

123. To govern according to this logic is "to arrange things so that the state becomes sturdy and permanent, so that it becomes wealthy, and so that it becomes strong in the face of everything that might destroy it." Ibid.

124. Political economy therefore issues government with the challenge: "a government is never sufficiently aware that it always risks governing too much, or, a government never knows too well how to govern just enough." Ibid.

125. Or, the problem of neoliberalism is "how the overall exercise of political power can be modelled on the principles of a market economy." Ibid.

126. See, for example, Lorenzo Fioramonti, *Gross Domestic Problem: The Politics Behind the World's Most Powerful Number* (London: Zed Books Ltd., 2013).

127. Tonkiss, "Markets against States: Neoliberalism"; Davies, "The Neoliberal State: Power against 'Politics'"; Mirowski, *Never Let a Serious Crisis go to Waste*.

128. Wendy Brown argues that "homo oeconomicus is an intensely constructed and governed bit of human capital tasked with improving and leveraging its competitive positioning and with enhancing its . . . portfolio value." Brown, *Undoing the Demos*.

129. As Foucault writes, "In the liberal regime, freedom of behaviour is entailed, called for, needed, and serves as a regulator, but it also has to be produced and organised." Foucault, *The Birth of Biopolitics*.

130. Brown, *In the Ruins of Neoliberalism.*

131. Brown, *Undoing the Demos.*

132. Brown, *In the Ruins of Neoliberalism.*

133. Ibid.

134. Ibid.

135. Noriyuki Doi, "The Rise and Fall of Evergrande Founder Xu Jiayin," Nikkei Asia, October 23, 2021, https://asia.nikkei.com/Business/Markets/China-debt-crunch /The-rise-and-fall-of-Evergrande-founder-Xu-Jiayin.

136. "Meet Evergrande CEO Hui Ka-yan, the Billionaire Behind the Giant Chinese Property Developer in Danger of Defaulting on US$300 Billion in Loans," *Business Insider*, October 28, 2021, https://www.scmp.com/magazines/style/celebrity/article /3153971/meet-evergrande-ceo-hui-ka-yan-billionaire-behind-giant.

137. "Evergrande Profit Surge Brings Share-Price Gains Closer to 400%," Bloomberg News, August 29, 2017, https://www.bloomberg.com/news/articles/2017-08-29 /evergrande-profit-surge-brings-share-price-gains-closer-to-400.

138. Doi, "The Rise and Fall of Evergrande Founder Xu Jiayin."

139. Michelle Toh, "5 Things to Know about the Evergrande Crisis: A Simple Breakdown," CNN Business, September 30, 2021, https://edition.cnn.com/2021/09/24/investing /china-evergrande-group-debt-explainer-intl-hnk/index.html.

140. Rosie Perper, "China Is Building a $1.7 Billion Soccer Stadium That Is Shaped Like a Lotus and Will Seat 100,000 People Amid a Pandemic," *Insider*, April 23, 2020, https://www.businessinsider.com/photos-china-new-billion-dollar-soccer -evergrande-stadium-in-guangzhou-2020-4?r=US&IR=T.

141. Adam Minter, "Why Are China's Property Giants Buying Pig Farms?," Bloomberg, May 19, 2020, https://www.bloomberg.com/opinion/articles/2020-05-20/why-are -china-s-property-giants-buying-pig-farms.

142. Xie Yu and Elaine Yu, "How Beijing's Debt Clampdown Shook the Foundation of a Real-Estate Colossus," *Wall Street Journal*, September 18, 2021, https://www.wsj .com/articles/how-beijings-debt-clampdown-shook-the-foundation-of-a-real-estate -colossus-11631957400.

143. Xinlu Liang, "Why Ocean Flower Island—Dubbed 'Dubai of China'—Is Important to China Evergrande Group and Hainan Province," *South China Morning Post*, January 4, 2022, https://www.scmp.com/business/article/3162082/why-ocean -flower-island-dubbed-dubai-china-important-china-evergrande.

144. "Snowballing Crisis at Evergrande, World's Most Indebted Developer," Reuters, July 29, 2022, https://www.reuters.com/business/snowballing-crisis-evergrande -worlds-most-indebted-developer-2022-07-29/.

145. Ryan McMorrow, Sherry Fei Ju, and Sun Yu, "Evergrande Used Retail Financial Investments to Plug Funding Gaps," *Financial Times*, September 21, 2021, https:// www.ft.com/content/0b03d4de-1662-4d30-bcfd-c9bae24fa9cc.

146. Ibid.

147. Ibid.

148. Clay Chandler and Grady McGregor, "The World's Most-Indebted Developer Is Even Worse Off Than We Thought," *Fortune*, September 14, 2021, https://fortune .com/2021/09/14/evergrande-stock-restructuring-debt/.

149. McMorrow et al., "Evergrande Used Retail Financial Investments to Plug Funding Gaps."

150. "Construction Has Resumed at 95% of China Evergrande Projects, Unit Says," *Reuters*, April 2, 2022, https://www.reuters.com/world/china/construction-has -resumed-95-china-evergrande-projects-unit-says-2022-04-02/.

151. Carl Walter and Fraser Howie, *Red Capitalism: The Fragile Financial Foundation of China's Extraordinary Rise* (London: John Wiley & Sons, 2012).

152. "China Government Debt to GDP," Trading Economics, accessed July 10, 2023, https://tradingeconomics.com/china/government-debt-to-gdp.

153. Walter and Howie, *Red Capitalism*.

154. Adrian Leftwich, *States of Development: On the Primacy of Politics in Development* (London: Polity, 2000).

155. That it can stand "aloof from the market and the economic interests found within it." Ben Fine, Jyoti Saraswati, and Daniela Tavasci (eds.), *Beyond the Developmental State: Industrial Policy into the Twenty-First Century* (London: Pluto Press, 2013).

156. "Both the state and the market, and their interaction, are themselves determined by, if not reduced to, the economic, political and ideological interests which act upon them." Fine et al., *Beyond the Developmental State*.

157. Panitch and Gindin, *The Making of Global Capitalism*.

158. Ibid.

159. Joe Leahy, "China's Billionaires Pay the Price for Xi Jinping's Covid Crackdown," *Financial Times*, March 23, 2023, https://www.ft.com/content/b730fac4-ca65 -4ccf-805e-da1cb0043bb2.

160. Panitch and Gindin, *The Making of Global Capitalism*; Chamayou, *The Ungovernable Society*.

161. Investment—primarily public in infrastructure like high-speed rail and electric buses—became by far the largest contributor to GDP in the post-crisis years, rising to an all-time high of 48 percent of GDP in December 2011. The achievements of this infrastructure investment program have been astonishing: in "2007 there were zero miles of high-speed rail in China," but by 2015 "there were nearly 12,000 miles linking all the major cities." David Harvey, *Marx, Capital, and the Madness of Economic Reason* (Oxford: Oxford University Press, 2017).

162. Walter and Howie, *Red Capitalism*.

163. Joe Leahy, "China's Billionaires Pay the Price for Xi Jinping's Covid Crackdown."

164. Xi Jinping has stated outright that achieving "common prosperity" is "not just an economic issue, but a significant political one that matters to the party's basis to rule." Vincent Ni, "The Party's Over: China Clamps Down on Its Tech Billionaires," *The Guardian*, August 21, 2021, https://www.theguardian .com/business/2021/aug/21/the-partys-over-china-clamps-down-on-its-tech -billionaires.

165. "Xi Jinping's Crackdown on Chinese Tech Firms Will Continue," *The Economist*, November 8, 2021, https://www.economist.com/the-world-ahead/2021/11/08/xi -jinpings-crackdown-on-chinese-tech-firms-will-continue.

166. The Belt and Road Initiative represents "nothing less than an attempt to

solve China's problems of overcapacity and surplus capital, declining trade opportunities, growing debt, and falling rates of profit through a geographic expansion of China's economic activity and processes." Martin Hart-Landsberg, "A Critical Look at China's One Belt, One Road Initiative," Monthly Review Online, October 5, 2018, https://mronline.org/2018/10/05/a-critical-look-at -chinas-one-belt-one-road-initiative/.

167. Hajime Sato, "The Rise and Fall of the Developmental State? The Case of the Japanese and South Korean Steel Industries," in Fine et al., *Beyond the Developmental State*.

168. From the outset, the policy of the Japanese state was developed "in favour of large firms at the expense of small- to medium-sized firms, reflecting the changing balance among various steel firms and other agencies." Ibid.

169. The US provided "financing and other forms of support" to promote Japanese industrialization after the Second World War, and the Japanese steel industry continued to be dependent on the US for "technologies, finance, raw materials and export markets" for many years after this. Ibid.

170. "Explaining the success of the steel industry either in terms of the nature of the Japanese state or the policies introduced by it misses the point: both flow from the class structure of Japanese society and its place in the capitalist world system." Ibid.

CHAPTER 7: MONEY AT SIX PERCENT: HOW EMPIRES PLAN

1. Daniel Immerwahr, *How to Hide an Empire: A History of the Greater United States* (New York: Farrar, Straus and Giroux, 2019).

2. Ibid.

3. Ibid.

4. Ibid.

5. Ibid.

6. Ibid.

7. Ibid.

8. As one writer put it, "It is one thing to admit scattered communities of white, or nearly white men into citizenship, but quite a different matter to act in the same way with a closely packed and numerous brown people." Quoted in Ibid.

9. "The Price of Intervention," *The Economist*, May 18, 2006, https://www .economist.com/books-and-arts/2006/05/18/the-price-of-intervention.

10. Sylvia Maxfield and James Nolt, "Protectionism and Internationalism" quoted in Panitch and Gindin, *The Making of Global Capitalism*.

11. Vincent Bevins, *The Jakarta Method: Washington's Anticommunist Crusade and the Mass Murder Program That Shaped Our World* (New York: PublicAffairs, 2021).

12. Fox Butterfield, "New Book on Marcos Says U.S. Knew of His '72 Martial-Law Plans," *New York Times*, April 19, 1987, https://www.nytimes.com/1987/04/19 /world/new-book-on-marcos-says-us-knew-of-his-72-martial-law-plans.html.

13. John Sharkey, "New Doubts on Marcos' War Role," *Washington Post*, January 24,

1986, https://www.washingtonpost.com/archive/politics/1986/01/24/new-doubts-on-marcos-war-role/40076661-fe6a-4695-88ea-1ee707e1c090/.

14. Primitivo Mijares, *The Conjugal Dictatorship of Ferdinand and Imelda Marcos* (CreateSpace, 2016).

15. Sharkey, "New Doubts on Marcos' War Role."

16. See Mijares, *The Conjugal Dictatorship of Ferdinand and Imelda Marcos*, for a firsthand account of the inner workings of the Marcos dictatorship.

17. Bevins, *The Jakarta Method*.

18. Ibid.

19. Ibid.

20. Walden Bello, David Kinley, and Elaine Elinson, *Development Debacle: The World Bank in the Philippines* (Oakland, CA: Institute for Food and Development Policy, 1982).

21. You can listen to Walden Bello discussing these events on episode 3 of my podcast *A World to Win*. Grace Blakeley, "3. The Great World Bank Robbery: An Interview with Walden Bello," *Tribune*, September 2, 2020, https://tribunemag.co.uk/2020/09/3-the-great-world-bank-robbery-an-interview-with-walden-bello.

22. Kwame Nkrumah, *Neo-Colonialism: The Last Stage of Imperialism* (London: Panaf Thomas Nelson & Sons Ltd., 1965).

23. Frantz Fanon, *The Wretched of the Earth* (Paris: Presence Africaine, 1963).

24. Nicholas Shaxson, *Poisoned Wells: The Dirty Politics of African Oil* (London: St. Martin's Publishing Group, 2007).

25. Blakeley, "3. The Great World Bank Robbery: An Interview with Walden Bello."

26. Fanon, *The Wretched of the Earth*.

27. Vladimir Lenin, *Imperialism: The Highest Stage of Capitalism* (London: Penguin UK, 2010).

28. For a discussion of US imperialism see Panitch and Gindin, *The Making of Global Capitalism*.

29. Klein, *The Shock Doctrine*.

30. Panitch and Gindin, *The Making of Global Capitalism*.

31. Ibid.

32. Quoted in Alexander Zevin, *Liberalism at Large: The World According to the Economist* (London: Verso Books, 2021).

33. Zevin, *Liberalism at Large*.

34. David Ricardo, *On the Principles of Political Economy and Taxation* (London: John Murray, 1817).

35. Wilfried Parys, "David Ricardo, the Stock Exchange, and the Battle of Waterloo: Samuelsonian Legends Lack Historical Evidence," University of Antwerp Research Paper 2020-009 (December 2020), https://repository.uantwerpen.be/docman/irua/4c1fa7/rps_2020_009_pdf.pdf.

36. One textbook introduces the theory with the example of two individuals—Matt and Kim—who are stranded on a remote island with only two possible sources of food, coconuts and fish. Kim is better at both fishing and foraging for coconuts—

she can produce more of each in less time than Matt. The mercantilist philosophy would suggest that because Kim has an absolute advantage over Matt, she would be better off performing both tasks for herself and never trading with Matt. In fact, when one accounts for the idea of opportunity cost, it is possible to show that both parties would be better off specializing in the production of one commodity and trading with each other. Opportunity cost is the cost of choosing one option over another: if Kim chose only to produce coconuts, the opportunity cost of doing so would be the number of fish she would have been able to catch in the same period of time. While Kim can produce more coconuts and fish than Matt, when you account for the opportunity cost of the time she would devote to undertaking both activities and compare it to the situation in which both parties devote more of their time to the production of the good for which they have the lower opportunity cost and trade with each other, the latter scenario works out as more efficient overall. Baumol, Blinder, and Solow summarize the foundation of this argument as follows: "When every person does what they do best and then trades with others everyone can benefit because more of every commodity can be produced without increasing the amount of labor and resources used." Mankiw, *Macroeconomics*.

37. Chang, *Kicking Away the Ladder*.
38. Ibid.
39. Panitch and Gindin, *The Making of Global Capitalism*.
40. David Milne, *America's Rasputin: Walt Rostow and the Vietnam War* (New York: Hill and Wang, 2009).
41. Walt Whitman Rostow, *The Stages of Economic Growth: A Non-Communist Manifesto* (Cambridge: Cambridge University Press, 1991).
42. Dani Rodrik, *The Globalization Paradox: Democracy and the Future of the World Economy* (New York: W. W. Norton, 2011).
43. Chang, *Kicking Away the Ladder*.
44. Isabella M. Weber, *How China Escaped Shock Therapy: The Market Reform Debate* (London: Routledge, 2021).
45. Marx first wrote about this dynamic when observing the inequalities between towns and the countryside. Marx, *Capital, Volume I*.
46. Chang, *Kicking Away the Ladder*.
47. Marx, *Capital, Volume I*.
48. See, for example, the discussion of international trade in Mankiw, *Macroeconomics*.
49. Kumar, *Monopsony Capitalism*; John Smith, *Imperialism in the Twenty-First Century: Globalization, Super-Exploitation and Capitalism* (New York: Monthly Review Press, 2016).
50. See Bukharin, *Imperialism and World Economy*; Hilferding, *Finance Capital*; and Lenin, *Imperialism*.
51. See, for example, Naomi Klein, *No Logo: Taking Aim at the Brand Bullies* (Toronto: Vintage Canada, 2000).
52. Lenin, *Imperialism*.
53. Capital therefore expends ever more energy on influencing state policy, such that "the state apparatus not only embodies the interests of the ruling classes in general, but also their collectively expressed will": the government becomes "the

highest guiding force of the state capitalist trust," with the central bank as the "'golden head' of the entire state capitalist trust." Bukharin, *Imperialism and World Economy.*

54. Lenin's addition to Bukharin's arguments lies in his analysis of where the super profits generated from imperial expansion would end up. He argued that these profits could be used to sew division between the international working class by creating a "labor aristocracy" in the Global North, which could be paid higher than average wages to "bribe" them and prevent widespread social unrest. He wrote: "Capitalism has grown into a world system of colonial oppression and of the financial strangulation of the overwhelming majority of the population of the world by a handful of 'advanced' countries. And this 'booty' is shared between two or three powerful world plunderers armed to the teeth, who are drawing the whole world into their war over the division of their booty." Lenin, *Imperialism.*

55. Tepper and Hearn, *The Myth of Capitalism.*

56. Ibid.

57. Joseph L. Love, "Raul Prebisch and the Origins of the Doctrine of Unequal Exchange," *Latin American Economic Review* 15, no. 3 (1980): 45–72.

58. Edgar J. Dosman, "Raul Prebisch and the XXIst Century Development Challenges," United Nations Economic Commission for Latin America and the Caribbean, 2012, https://archivo.cepal.org/pdfs/PortalPrebisch/PrebischporDosman.pdf.

59. Raúl Prebisch, *The Economic Development of Latin America and Its Principal Problems* (New York: United Nations, 1949).

60. The Prebisch-Singer hypothesis—developed by Prebisch and Hans Singer— formalized this observation by noting that there is a systematic tendency for the price of primary commodities to decline relative to those of manufactured goods as the capitalist system develops.

61. Immanuel Wallerstein, *World-Systems Analysis: An Introduction* (Durham, NC: Duke University Press, 2004); Paul A. Baran, *Political Econ of Growth* (New York: NYU Press, 2019).

62. Wallerstein, *World-Systems Analysis.*

63. Walter Rodney, *How Europe Underdeveloped Africa* (London: Verso, 2018).

64. Smith, *Imperialism in the Twenty-First Century.*

65. Peter Chapman, *Bananas: How the United Fruit Company Shaped the World* (London: Canongate Books, 2022).

66. Richard H. Immerman, *The CIA in Guatemala: The Foreign Policy of Intervention* (Austin: University of Texas Press, 1982).

67. United Fruit Historical Society, "Chronology," accessed July 11, 2023, https://www .unitedfruit.org/chron.htm.

68. Ibid.

69. Ibid.

70. Chapman, *Bananas.*

71. Kenneth J. Grieb, "American Involvement in the Rise of Jorge Ubico," *Caribbean Studies* 10, no. 1 (April 1970): 5–21, https://www.jstor.org/stable/25612190.

72. Stephen M. Streeter, *Managing the Counterrevolution: The United States and Guatemala, 1954–1961* (Athens: Ohio University Press, 2000).

73. Ibid.

74. Ibid.

75. Bevins, *The Jakarta Method*.

76. Piero Gleijeses, *Shattered Hope: The Guatemalan Revolution and the United States, 1944–1954* (Princeton, NJ: Princeton University Press, 2021).

77. Ibid.

78. Ibid.

79. Streeter, *Managing the Counterrevolution*.

80. Gleijeses, *Shattered Hope*.

81. Ibid.

82. Bevins, *The Jakarta Method*.

83. Ibid.

84. Ibid.

85. Streeter, *Managing the Counterrevolution*.

86. Bevins, *The Jakarta Method*.

87. Bevins writes that Armas was "despised even by the conservative officers in the Guatemalan military." Bevins, *The Jakarta Method*.

88. Ibid.

89. Ibid.

90. Ibid.

91. Ibid.

92. Ibid.

93. Ibid.

94. Historical Clarification Commission, "GUATEMALA MEMORY OF SILENCE: Report of the Commission for Historical Clarification Conclusions and Recommendations," February 1999, accessed July 11, 2023, https://hrdag.org/wp -content/uploads/2013/01/CEHreport-english.pdf.

95. Ibid.

96. Christopher J. Lee (ed.), *Making a World after Empire: The Bandung Moment and Its Political Afterlives* (Athens: Ohio University Press, 2010).

97. Sukarno and Cindy Heller Adams, *Sukarno: An Autobiography, as Told to Cindy Adams* (Hong Kong: Gunung Agung, 1966).

98. Bevins, *The Jakarta Method*.

99. As Leo Panitch and Sam Gindin put it, "[t]he attempt to reconcile national self-determination and the formal equality of states with the inherently asymmetric interstate relations in a capitalist world economy . . . obscure the new realities of empire." Panitch and Gindin, *The Making of Global Capitalism*.

100. "The less developed world," Nkrumah wrote, "will not become developed through the goodwill or generosity of the developed powers. It can only become developed through a struggle against the external forces which have a vested interest in keeping it underdeveloped." Nkrumah, *Neo-Colonialism*.

101. Bevins, *The Jakarta Method*.

102. Robert E. Elson, *Suharto: A Political Biography* (Cambridge: Cambridge University Press, 2001).

103. Bevins, *The Jakarta Method*.

104. Bevins writes that a "loose network of US-backed anticommunist extermination programs . . . carried out mass murder in at least twenty-two countries": Argentina, Bolivia, Brazil, Chile, Colombia, East Timor, El Salvador, Guatemala, Honduras, Indonesia, Iraq, Mexico, Nicaragua, Paraguay, the Philippines, South Korea, Sudan, Taiwan, Thailand, Uruguay, Venezuela, and Vietnam. Bevins, *The Jakarta Method*.

105. John Coatsworth, quoted in ibid.

106. "Military spending in the United States from the fiscal year of 2000 to 2022," Statistica, accessed August 15, 2023, https://www.statista.com/statistics/272473/us -military-spending-from-2000-to-2012.

107. See Klein, *The Shock Doctrine*, for a discussion.

108. Ibid.

109. "Let's All Go to the Yard Sale," *The Economist*, September 25, 2003, https://www .economist.com/middle-east-and-africa/2003/09/25/lets-all-go-to-the-yard-sale.

110. Klein, *The Shock Doctrine*.

111. Ibid.

112. Ibid.

113. Panitch and Gindin, *The Making of Global Capitalism*.

114. "ISDS Files: Chevron v Ecuador," War on Want, April 2019, https://waronwant .org/sites/default/files/ISDSFiles_Chevron_April2019.pdf.

115. Sharon Lerner, "How the Environmental Lawyer Who Won a Massive Judgment against Chevron Lost Everything," *The Intercept*, January 29, 2020, https:// theintercept.com/2020/01/29/chevron-ecuador-lawsuit-steven-donziger/.

116. Ibid.

117. Rex Weyler, "Steven Donziger: The Man Who Stood Up to an Oil Giant, and Paid the Price," Greenpeace, February 26, 2020, https://www.greenpeace.org/international /story/28741/steven-donziger-chevron-oil-amazon-contamination-injustice/.

118. Patrick Radden Keefe, "Reversal of Fortune," *The New Yorker*, January 1, 2012, https://www.newyorker.com/magazine/2012/01/09/reversal-of-fortune-patrick -radden-keefe.

119. For a discussion, see Barak, *Unchecked Corporate Power*; T. J. Coles, *Privatized Planet: Free Trade as a Weapon against Democracy, Healthcare and the Environment* (Oxford: New Internationalist, 2019).

120. Thomas Schultz and Cedric Dupont, "Investment Arbitration: Promoting the Rule of Law or Over-empowering Investors? A Quantitative Empirical Study," *European Journal of International Law* 25, no. 4 (November 2014): 1147–68, https:// academic.oup.com/ejil/article/25/4/1147/385535.

121. Lerner, "How the Environmental Lawyer Who Won a Massive Judgment against Chevron Lost Everything."

122. Ibid.

123. Ibid.

124. Weyler, "Steven Donziger: The Man Who Stood Up to an Oil Giant, and Paid the Price."

125. Lerner, "How the Environmental Lawyer Who Won a Massive Judgment against Chevron Lost Everything."

126. Weyler, "Steven Donziger: The Man Who Stood Up to an Oil Giant, and Paid the Price."

127. Ibid.

128. Lerner, "How the Environmental Lawyer Who Won a Massive Judgment against Chevron Lost Everything."

129. Ibid.

130. Erin Brockovich, "This Lawyer Should Be World-Famous for His Battle with Chevron—but He's in Jail," *The Guardian*, February 8, 2022, https://www.theguardian.com/commentisfree/2022/feb/08/chevron-amazon-ecuador-steven-donziger-erin-brockovich.

131. Lerner, "How the Environmental Lawyer Who Won a Massive Judgment against Chevron Lost Everything."

132. Brockovich, "This Lawyer Should Be World-Famous for His Battle with Chevron—but He's in Jail."

133. Ibid.

134. Lerner, "How the Environmental Lawyer Who Won a Massive Judgment Against Chevron Lost Everything."

135. Brockovich, "This Lawyer Should Be World-Famous for His Battle with Chevron—but He's in Jail."

136. War on Want, "ISDS Files: Chevron v Ecuador."

137. Barak, *Unchecked Corporate Power.*

138. "A World Court for Corporations: How the EU Plans to Entrench and Institutionalize Investor-State Dispute Settlements," Rosa-Luxemburg-Stiftung Brussels Office, 2017.

139. Ibid.

140. "Investor-State Dispute Settlement: The Arbitration Game," *The Economist*, October 11, 2014.

141. Rosa-Luxemburg-Stiftung, "A World Court for Corporations: How the EU Plans to Entrench and Institutionalize Investor-State Dispute Settlements."

142. John Cavanagh and Robin Broad, *The Water Defenders: How Ordinary People Saved a Country from Corporate Greed* (Boston: Beacon Press, 2022)

143. Quinn Slobodian, *Globalists: The End of Empire and the Birth of Neoliberalism* (Cambridge, MA: Harvard University Press, 2018).

144. Stiglitz, *Globalization and Its Discontents.*

145. Jamie Martin, *The Meddlers: Sovereignty, Empire, and the Birth of Global Economic Governance* (Cambridge, MA: Harvard University Press, 2022).

146. Leo Panitch and Sam Gindin, "The Current Crisis: A Socialist Perspective," *Studies in Political Economy* 83, no. 1 (March 2016): 7–31, https://doi.org/10.1080/19187033.2009.11675054.

147. Dylan Matthews, "How the Fed Ended the Last Great American Inflation—and How Much It Hurt," *Vox*, July 13, 2022, https://www.vox.com/future-perfect/2022/7/13/23188455/inflation-paul-volcker-shock-recession-1970s.

148. "fundamentally, the Volcker shock was not so much about finding the right monetary policy as shifting the balance of class forces in American society." Panitch and Gindin, *The Making of Global Capitalism.*

149. Stiglitz, *Globalization and Its Discontents.*

150. Bello et al., *Development Debacle: The World Bank in the Philippines.*

151. Klein, *The Shock Doctrine.*

152. Stiglitz, *Globalization and Its Discontents.*

153. Ibid.

154. Coles, *Privatized Planet.*

155. Stiglitz, *Globalization and Its Discontents.*

156. See Shaxson, *Treasure Islands.*

157. Panitch and Gindin, *The Making of Global Capitalism.*

158. See Shaxson, *Treasure Islands.*

159. Davison Budhoo, quoted in Klein, *The Shock Doctrine.*

160. Macleans A. Geo-Jaja and Garth Mangum, "Structural Adjustment as an Inadvertant Enemy of Human Development in Africa," *Journal of Black Studies* 32, no. 1 (September 2001): 30–49, https://www.jstor.org/stable/2668013; Sarah Bracking, "Structural Adjustment: Why It Wasn't Necessary & Why It Didn't Work," *Review of African Political Economy* 26, no. 80 (June 1999): 207–26, https://www.jstor.org/stable/4006560.

161. National Bureau of Economic Research, "The Economic Decline in Africa," *The Digest*, no. 1 (January 2004), https://www.nber.org/digest/jan04/economic-decline -africa.

162. See, for example, Timon Forster, Alexander Kentikelenis, Bernhard Reinsberg, Thomas Stubbs, and Lawrence King, "How Structural Adjustment Programs Affect Inequality: A Disaggregated Analysis of IMF Conditionality, 1980–2014," *Social Science Research* 80 (May 2019): 83–113, https://doi.org/10.1016/j .ssresearch.2019.01.001.

163. Stiglitz, *Globalization and Its Discontents.*

164. Chang, *Kicking Away the Ladder.*

165. Stiglitz, *Globalization and Its Discontents.*

166. Ibid.

167. Anup Shah, "Structural Adjustment—a Major Cause of Poverty," *Global Issues*, March 24, 2013, https://www.globalissues.org/article/3/structural-adjustment-a -major-cause-of-poverty.

168. Suk-Man Hwang and Yun-Chin Lim, "The Political Economy of South Korean Structural Adjustment: Reality and Façade," *African and Asian Studies* 1, no. 2 (August 2002): 87–112, https://www.researchgate.net/publication/249600077 _The_Political_Economy_of_South Korean_Structural_Adjustment_Reality_and _Facade, DOI:10.1163/15692090260218441.

169. Stiglitz, *Globalization and its Discontents.*

170. Hwang and Lim, "The Political Economy of South Korean Structural Adjustment."

171. Stiglitz, *Globalization and Its Discontents.*

172. Lawrence King, "Shock Privatization: The Effects of Rapid Large-Scale Privatization on Enterprise Restructuring," *Politics & Society* 31, no. 1 (March 2003): 3–30, https://library.fes.de/libalt/journals/swetsfulltext/15749428.pdf.

173. Adam Tooze, "Chartbook #68 Putin's Challenge to Western Hegemony—the 2022 Edition," Chartbook, January 12, 2022, https://adamtooze.substack.com/p /chartbook-68-putins-challenge-to.

174. Stiglitz, *Globalization and Its Discontents*.

175. Panitch and Gindin, *The Making of Global Capitalism*.

176. Ferguson, *The Anti-Politics Machine*.

177. Panitch and Gindin, *The Making of Global Capitalism*.

178. Ibid.

179. See Slobodian, *Globalists*, for a discussion of Röpke's support for apartheid.

180. Ibid.

181. Ibid.

182. Perhaps the best example of the "nonracist" case for the continuation of apartheid in South Africa comes from British economist William Hutt. Hutt's book *The Economics of the Colour Bar* attacked apartheid as a form of rent seeking designed to protect the privileges of insiders against the incursions from outsiders, comparing it to the "rent seeking" practiced by trade unions. But Hutt firmly believed that moving to universal suffrage was the wrong move for South Africa and proposed instead a "weighted franchise," which "saw first in black and white and then apportioned voting rights differently to the wealthy and the poor." William H. Hutt, *The Economics of the Colour Bar* (London: The Institute for Economics, 1964).

183. As Slobodian argues, "Empires could end . . . but only if capital rights were secured and nation-states were kept from impeding the free flow of money and goods." Slobodian, *Globalists*.

184. Slobodian, *Globalists*.

185. As Slobodian puts it, "The neoliberals . . . [began] creating designs, blueprints and plans, not at the scale of the nation, but at the scale of the region and the world." Slobodian, *Globalists*.

186. Pistor, *The Code of Capital*.

187. Slobodian, *Globalists*.

188. Alastair Fraser and John Lungu, "For Whom the Windfalls? Winners & Losers in the Privatisation of Zambia's Copper Mines," Civil Society Trade Network of Zambia, accessed July 11, 2023, https://www.banktrack.org/download/for_whom _the_windfalls_/report_for_whom_the_wind_falls.pdf.

189. Ibid.

190. Ibid.

191. Ibid.

192. Lishala C. Situmbeko and Jack Jones Zulu, "Zambia: Condemned to Debt," World Development Movement, April 2004, https://www.globaljustice.org.uk/wp-content /uploads/2015/06/zambia01042004.pdf.

193. Neo Simutanyi, "Copper Mining in Zambia: The Developmental Legacy of Privatisation," Institute for Security Studies, July 1, 2008, https://issafrica .org/research/papers/copper-mining-in-zambia-the-developmental-legacy-of -privatisation.

194. Ndangwa Noyoo, "Mobilising Natural Resources for Sustainable Development: Copper Mining and Path Dependence in Zambia," *Cadernos de Estudos Africanos*, no. 41 (January–June 2021), https://journals.openedition.org/cea/6393.

195. Fraser and Lungu, "For Whom the Windfalls?"

196. Ibid.

197. Simutanyi, "Copper Mining in Zambia."

198. Fraser and Lungu, "For Whom the Windfalls?"

199. Ibid.

200. Ibid.

201. Situmbeko and Zulu, "Zambia: Condemned to Debt."

202. Ibid.

203. Ibid.

204. Ibid.

205. Duncan Green, "A Copper-Bottomed Crisis? The Impact of the Global Economic Meltdown on Zambia," Oxfam Policy & Practice Discussion Paper, December 22, 2009, https://policy-practice.oxfam.org/resources/a-copper-bottomed-crisis-the -impact-of-the-global-economic-meltdown-on-zambia-111973/.

206. Caleb M. Fundanga, "The Global Economic Crisis—Zambia's Strategy to Maintain Stability," Remarks by Mr. Caleb M. Fundanga, Governor of the Bank of Zambia, at the 4th Eastern and Southern African Management Institute (ESAMI) Summer School Event, Arusha, November 29–30, 2009, https://www.bis.org/review/r091211c.pdf.

207. Ibid.

208. Green, "A Copper-Bottomed Crisis?"

209. Ibid.

210. Ashley Seager, "Court Lets Vulture Fund Claw Back Zambian Millions," *The Guardian*, February 15, 2007, https://www.theguardian.com/business/2007/feb/16 /debt.development.

211. Ibid.

212. The Jubilee Debt Campaign, "Memorandum from the Jubilee Debt Campaign," UK Parliament House of Commons Select Committee, May 2009, https://publications .parliament.uk/pa/cm200809/cmselect/cmtreasy/615/615we12.htm.

213. Standard macroeconomic production functions tend to assume that an extra unit of capital is more valuable in a country with a lower capital stock than in one with a higher one. It therefore makes sense that profits accumulated in the rich world would be more profitably invested abroad than at home.

214. Jason Hickel, Dylan Sullivan, and Huzaifa Zoomkawala, "Plunder in the Post-Colonial Era: Quantifying Drain from the Global South Through Unequal Exchange, 1960–2018," *New Political Economy* 26, no. 6 (March 2021): 1030–47, https://doi.org/10.1080/13563467.2021.1899153.

215. Shaxson, *Treasure Islands*.

216. See Blakeley, *Stolen*, for an explanation of these dynamics.

217. Röpke argued that modernization theory exported "a fetish for industrialization that would lead to worldwide inflation, the erosion of the world food supply and the creation of a global urban proletariat." Röpke, quoted in Slobodian, *Globalists*.

218. Panitch and Gindin, *The Making of Global Capitalism*.

219. Ibid.

220. Gary Smith, "Central Banks Are Reassessing Foreign Exchange Reserves," Official Monetary and Financial Institutions Forum, January 4, 2023, https://www.omfif .org/2023/01/central-banks-are-reassessing-foreign-exchange-reserves/.

221. For a discussion of these dynamics see David E. Spiro, *The Hidden Hand of American Hegemony: Petrodollar Recycling and International Markets* (New York: Cornell University Press, 1999).

222. Adam Tooze, *Crashed: How a Decade of Financial Crises Changed the World* (London: Penguin UK, 2018).

223. Panitch and Gindin, *The Making of Global Capitalism*.

224. Tooze, Crashed: How a Decade of Financial Crises Changed the World.

225. Ibid.

CHAPTER 8: THE ARCHITECT AND THE BEE: HOW TO PLAN DEMOCRATICALLY

1. Hilary Wainwright and David Elliott, *The Lucas Plan: A New Trade Unionism in the Making?* (London: Spokesman Books, 2018).

2. Ibid.

3. Ibid.

4. Brian Salisbury, "Story of the Lucas Plan," A New Lucas Plan, accessed July 11, 2023, http://lucasplan.org.uk/story-of-the-lucas-plan/.

5. See Wainwright and Elliott, *The Lucas Plan*, for a full discussion of the plan.

6. Salisbury, "Story of the Lucas Plan."

7. Wainwright and Elliott, *The Lucas Plan*.

8. Mike Press, "Architect or Bee?," Medium, September 27, 2020, https://mikepressuk .medium.com/architect-or-bee-420de175e9c1.

9. John Palmer, "Mike Cooley Obituary," *The Guardian*, September 17, 2020, https:// www.theguardian.com/technology/2020/sep/17/mike-cooley-obituary.

10. Mike Cooley, "Acceptance Speech," Right Livelihood, 1981, accessed July 11, 2023, https://rightlivelihood.org/speech/acceptance-speech-mike-cooley/.

11. Ibid.

12. For a discussion of how the Lucas Plan fit with the spirit of the New Left, see Hilary Wainwright, *A New Politics from the Left* (London: John Wiley & Sons, 2018).

13. Adrian Smith, "Socially Useful Production," STEPS Centre Working Paper 58, https://steps-centre.org/wp-content/uploads/Socially-Useful-Production.pdf.

14. Wainwright and Elliott, *The Lucas Plan*.

15. Ibid.

16. The *Financial Times* described the plan as "one of the most radical alternative plans ever drawn up by workers for their company," and Mike Cooley as a "highly articulate far-left-wing trade unionist." Adrian Smith, "The Lucas Plan: What Can It Tell Us about Democratising Technology Today?," *The Guardian*, January 22, 2014, https://www.theguardian.com/science/political-science/2014 /jan/22/remembering-the-lucas-plan-what-can-it-tell-us-about-democratising -technology-today.

17. For a discussion, see Blakeley, *Stolen*.

18. Mike Cooley, *Architect or Bee?: The Human Price of Technology* (London: Hogarth Press, 1987).
19. Smith, "Socially Useful Production."
20. Panitch and Gindin, *The Making of Global Capitalism.*
21. "Lucas: Sad Decline of an Engineering Giant," *The Lancashire Telegraph*, March 2, 2000, https://www.lancashiretelegraph.co.uk/news/6090786.lucas-sad -decline-engineering-giant/.
22. Ibid.
23. Graham Warwick, "Goodrich to Acquire TRW Unit," FlightGlobal, June 24, 2002, https://www.flightglobal.com/goodrich-to-acquire-trw-unit/43282.article.
24. Scott Malone and Paritosh Bansal, "United Tech to Buy Goodrich for $16.5 Billion," Reuters, September 22, 2011, https://www.reuters.com/article/us -goodrich-unitedtechnologies-idUSTRE78L06X20110922.
25. Adam Samson and Patti Waldmeir, "UTC Warns of Profit Hit from Boeing Production Cuts," *Financial Times*, April 23, 2019, https://www.ft.com /content/1c426f46-65b9-11e9-a79d-04f350474d62.
26. "United Technologies Announces Intention to Separate into Three Independent Companies; Completes Acquisition of Rockwell Collins," Collins Aerospace, November 26, 2018, https://www.collinsaerospace.com/news/news/2018/11/united -technologies-announces-intention-to-separate.
27. "Boeing Business Jet (737 MAX)," Collins Aerospace, accessed July 11, 2023, https://www.collinsaerospace.com/what-we-do/industries/business-aviation /platforms/boeing/boeing-business-jet-737-max.
28. "United Technologies and Raytheon Complete Merger of Equals Transaction," RTX, April 3, 2020, accessed July 11, 2023, https://www.rtx.com/news/2020/04/03/united -technologies-and-raytheon-complete-merger-of-equals-transaction.
29. Smith, "Socially Useful Production."
30. Ibid.
31. Ibid.
32. Ibid.
33. Ibid.
34. Ibid.
35. Steven Schofield, "Oceans of Work: Arms Conversion Revisited," British American Security Information Council, January 2007, https://basicint.org/publications/dr -steven-schofield/2007/oceans-work-arms-conversion-revisited.
36. Ian Jack, "Trident: The British Question," *The Guardian*, February 11, 2016, https://www.theguardian.com/uk-news/2016/feb/11/trident-the-british-question.
37. Julia Kollewe, "BAE Systems to Cut Nearly 2,000 UK Jobs," *The Guardian*, October 10, 2017, https://www.theguardian.com/business/2017/oct/10/bae-systems -job-cuts-eurofighter-typhoon-orders.
38. David Leigh and Rob Evans, "Secrets of Al-Yamamah," *The Guardian*, February 17, 2008, https://www.theguardian.com/baefiles/page/0,,2095831,00 .html.
39. Dan Sabbagh, "BAE Systems Accused of Being Party to Alleged War Crimes,"

The Guardian, December 11, 2019, https://www.theguardian.com/uk-news/2019
/dec/11/bae-systems-accused-of-being-party-to-alleged-war-crimes.

40. Graeber, *Utopia of Rules*.
41. Edward Segal, "Public Trust Increases in Most Businesses and Industries:
    New Report," *Forbes*, January 18, 2022, https://www.forbes.com/sites
    /edwardsegal/2022/01/18/public-trust-increases-in-most-businesses-and-industries
    -new-report/?sh=6ecdd38c3dd5.
42. Rutger Bregman, *Humankind: A Hopeful History* (New York: Little, Brown,
    2020).
43. Martin Wainwright, "Author William Golding Tried to Rape Teenager, Private
    Papers Show," *The Guardian*, August 16, 2009, https://www.theguardian.com
    /books/2009/aug/16/william-golding-attempted-rape.
44. Bregman, *Humankind*.
45. Ibid.
46. Ibid.
47. David Graeber and David Wengrow, *The Dawn of Everything: A New History of
    Humanity* (New York: Farrar, Straus and Giroux, 2021).
48. For a full discussion, see Chloe Koffman, "Remembering Australia's Green
    Bans," *Tribune*, March 29, 2021, https://tribunemag.co.uk/2021/03/remembering
    -australias-green-bans.
49. Ibid.
50. Wendy Bacon, "Jack Mundey Was an Australian Hero Who Saved Sydney from the
    Bulldozers and Shaped a Generation of Activists," *The Guardian*, May 11, 2020, https://
    www.theguardian.com/commentisfree/2020/may/12/jack-mundey-was-an-australian
    -hero-who-saved-sydney-from-the-bulldozers-and-shaped-a-generation-of-activists.
51. Jack Mundey, quoted in Koffman, "Remembering Australia's Green Bans."
52. Chloe Koffman writes for *Tribune* magazine: "Labourers would stand with the
    community in objecting to high-rise developments that would damage homes and
    neighbourhoods. In case of foul play, the disputed sites were often physically defended,
    with activists frequently being arrested for squatting or resisting evictions. Protests
    in support of the bans were largely colourful affairs, with people finding new and
    creative ways to bring public attention to disputed sites, such as crane occupations,
    sit-ins, and gate-crashing the dinner parties of property developers." Ibid.
53. Ibid.
54. Lee Rhiannon, "Juanita Nielsen Was Murdered for Standing Up to Sydney's
    Developers," *Jacobin*, December 13, 2020, https://jacobin.com/2020/12/juanita
    -nielsen-murder-sydney-australia-developers.
55. Michael Dulaney, "Juanita Nielsen's Suspected Murder Brought Arthur King
    Back to Kings Cross after His Terrifying Ordeal," ABC News (Australia), July 30,
    2021, updated August 12, 2021, https://www.abc.net.au/news/2021-07-31/juanita
    -nielsen-murder-came-after-arthur-king-kidnapping/100332232.
56. Rhiannon, "Juanita Nielsen Was Murdered for Standing Up to Sydney's
    Developers."
57. Koffman, "Remembering Australia's Green Bans."
58. Ibid.

59. Dan Hancox, *The Village against the World* (London: Verso Books, 2013).

60. Ibid.

61. Ibid.

62. Ibid.

63. Dan Hancox, "Spain's Communist Model Village," *The Guardian*, October 19, 2013, https://www.theguardian.com/world/2013/oct/20/marinaleda-spanish -communist-village-utopia.

64. Hancox, *The Village against the World*.

65. Ibid.

66. Hancox, "Spain's Communist Model Village."

67. Hancox, *The Village against the World*.

68. Jade Spencer, "A Plan for a People's London," *Tribune*, May 16, 2022, https:// tribunemag.co.uk/2022/05/peoples-plan-royal-docks-london-thatcherism-glc -neoliberalism.

69. Ibid.

70. Ibid.

71. Ibid.

72. Jade Spencer, "The People's Plan for the Royal Docks," *ERA Magazine*, March 4, 2021, https://cspace.org.uk/wp-content/uploads/2021/03/The-Peoples-Plan-for-the -Royal-Docks-%E2%80%A2-ERA-Magazine.pdf.

73. "Participatory Budgeting in Porto Alegre 1989–present," Participedia, accessed July 11, 2023, https://participedia.net/case/5524.

74. "Case Study: Porto Alegre, Brazil," Local Government Association, December 12, 2016, https://www.local.gov.uk/case-studies/case-study-porto-alegre-brazil.

75. Ibid.

76. Ibid.

77. Brian Wampler, *Participatory Budgeting in Brazil: Contestation, Cooperation, and Accountability* (State College, PA: Penn State University Press, 2007).

78. Ibid.

79. Josh Lerner and Estair Van Wagner, "Participatory Budgeting in Canada: Democratic Innovations in Strategic Spaces," The Transnational Institute, February 1, 2006, https://works.bepress.com/estair-vanwagner/22/download/.

80. "Toronto Community Housing's Tenant Participation System," Participedia, accessed July 11, 2023, https://participedia.net/case/1120.

81. "Participatory Budgeting," New York City Council, accessed July 11, 2023, https:// council.nyc.gov/pb/.

82. "Kerala People's Campaign for Decentralized Planning," Participedia, accessed July 11, 2023, https://participedia.net/case/35.

83. Ibid.

84. Ibid.

85. Vyshakh T., "Bringing the State Closer to People: 25 Years of Kerala's 'People's Plan,'" *Peoples Dispatch*, September 19, 2021, https://peoplesdispatch.org/2021/09/19 /bringing-the-state-closer-to-people-25-years-of-keralas-peoples-plan/.

86. Ibid.

87. Ibid.

88. Ibid.

89. Ibid.

90. Michelle B. Switzer, "Ciudad Futura: Reimagining the Left in Argentina," NACLA, March 9, 2018, https://nacla.org/news/2018/03/09/ciudad-futura-reimagining-left-argentina.

91. Jess Scully, *Glimpses of Utopia: Real Ideas for a Fairer World* (Sydney: Pantera Press, 2020).

92. Ibid.

93. Ibid.

94. Ibid.

95. Switzer, "Ciudad Futura."

96. Kate Shea Baird, "How to Build a Movement-Party: Lessons from Rosario's Future City," openDemocracy, November 15, 2016, https://www.opendemocracy.net/en/democraciaabierta/how-to-build-movement-party-lessons-from-rosario-s-future-city/.

97. For background, see Roger Boyes, *Meltdown Iceland: How the Global Financial Crisis Bankupted an Entire Country* (New York: Bloomsbury, 2010).

98. "Better Reykjavik: Iceland's Online Participation Platform," Participedia, accessed July 11, 2023, https://participedia.net/case/5320.

99. Robert Bjarnason, "Better Reykjavik," Civil Service Policy Lab, Open Policy, October 15, 2014, https://openpolicy.blog.gov.uk/2014/10/15/better-reykjavik/.

100. Participedia, "Better Reykjavik: Iceland's Online Participation Platform."

101. Ibid.

102. Ibid.

103. "Decidim: Participatory Budgeting in Barcelona," Participedia, accessed July 11, 2023, https://participedia.net/case/7425.

104. Kali Akuno, "The Jackson-Kush Plan: The Struggle for Black Self-Determination and Economic Democracy," *Monthly Review Online*, July 2020, https://mronline.org/wp-content/uploads/2020/07/Jackson-KushPlan.pdf.

105. "The roots of our Assembly model are drawn from the spiritual or prayer circles that were organized, often clandestinely, by enslaved Africans—to express their humanity, build and sustain community, fortify their spirits and organize resistance. The vehicle gained public expression in Mississippi with the organization of 'Negro Peoples Conventions' at the start of Reconstruction to develop autonomous programs of action to realize freedom—as Blacks themselves desired it and to determine their relationship to the Union." Ibid.

106. Akuno saw it as necessary to work within and around state institutions, both to "negate the repressive power of the state" and to provide a broader platform for "the restoration of 'the commons,' [creating] more public goods utilities . . . and the democratic transformation of the economy." Ibid.

107. Renuka Rayasam, "How a 'Radical' Southern Mayor Ran Up Against Reality," *Politico*, March 31, 2021, https://www.politico.com/news/magazine/2021/03/31/chokwe-antar-lumumba-jackson-progressives-478380.

108. See Cooperation Jackson's website for more information on these organizations, https://cooperationjackson.org/.

109. Bertie Russell, "Jackson Rising," openDemocracy, September 13, 2018, https://www.opendemocracy.net/en/jackson-rising/.

110. Ibid.

111. "What Is Community Wealth Building?," Centre for Local Economic Strategies, accessed July 11, 2023, https://cles.org.uk/community-wealth-building/what-is-community-wealth-building/.

112. For more information, see Matthew Brown and Rhian Jones, *Paint Your Town Red: How Preston Took Back Control and Your Town Can Too* (London: Repeater Books, 2021); Centre for Local Economic Strategies, "What Is Community Wealth Building?"

113. Matthew Brown, "Preston Is Putting Socialist Policies into Practice," *Tribune*, January 20, 2022, https://tribunemag.co.uk/2022/01/community-wealth-building-preston-trade-unions-labour-party.

114. The following is reproduced from an article I wrote for *Tribune* in 2022, with permission. Grace Blakeley, "'It's Not Rocket Science—It's Just Community': Radical Ffestiniog," November 9, 2022.

CHAPTER 9: TAKING BACK CONTROL: DEMOCRATIC PLANNING AT SCALE

1. Seymour M. Hersh, "C.I.A. Chief Tells House of $8-Million Campaign against Allende in '70–'73," *New York Times*, September 8, 1974, https://www.nytimes.com/1974/09/08/archives/cia-chief-tells-house-of-8million-campaign-against-allende-in-7073.html.

2. Eden Medina, *Cybernetic Revolutionaries: Technology and Politics in Allende's Chile* (Cambridge, MA: MIT Press, 2014).

3. "Chile: The Popular Unity's Programme," The Róbinson Rojas Archive, accessed July 11, 2023, https://www.rrojasdatabank.info/programm.htm.

4. Ibid.

5. Sara K. Tedeschi, Theodore M. Brown, and Elizabeth Fee, "Salvador Allende: Physician, Socialist, Populist, and President," *American Journal of Public Health* 93, no. 12 (December 2003): 2014–15, https://ajph.aphapublications.org/doi/full/10.2105/AJPH.93.12.2014.

6. Ibid.

7. James W. McGuire, *Wealth, Health, and Democracy in East Asia and Latin America* (Cambridge: Cambridge University Press, 2010).

8. Ibid.

9. Ibid.

10. Ibid.

11. Peter A. Goldberg, "The Politics of the Allende Overthrow in Chile," *Political Science Quarterly* 90, no. 1 (Spring 1975): 93–116.

12. Ibid.

13. Medina, *Cybernetic Revolutionaries*.

14. Felipe Larrain and Patricio Meller, "The Socialist-Populist Chilean Experience, 1970–1973," in Rudiger Dornbusch and Sebastian Edwards (eds.), *The Macroeconomics of Populism in Latin America* (Chicago: University of Chicago Press, 1991), http://www.nber.org/chapters/c8301.

15. Markos Mamalakis, "Income Redistribution in Chile under Salvador Allende," University of Wisconsin-Milwaukee, Department of Economics, August 10, 1973, https://pdf.usaid.gov/pdf_docs/PNAAA696.pdf.

16. Medina, *Cybernetic Revolutionaries*.

17. Ibid.

18. Ibid.

19. Ibid.

20. Ibid.

21. Ibid.

22. Ibid.

23. Ibid.

24. As Eden Medina explains in his book on the subject, the system worked in the following way: "Interventors would use the telex machines at their enterprises to send production data to the telex machine located at the National Computer Corporation. Chilean computer experts would then punch the data onto cards and feed them into the mainframe. The computer ran statistical software programs that compared the new data with those collected previously, searching for significant variations. If the program encountered such a variation, it alerted the computer operators, who would send the data over the telex network to CORFO and the interventors affected. . . . CORFO would communicate with the interventors in order to better understand the situation and help resolve the problem, if one existed." Ibid.

25. Ibid.

26. Ralph Miliband, *Parliamentary Socialism: A Study in the Politics of Labour* (London: Merlin, 1972).

27. See Strike Debt!, https://strikedebt.org/.

28. See "Rolling Jubilee Student Debt Buy," Strike Debt!, https://strikedebt.org/debtbuy4/.

29. See Debt Collective, https://debtcollective.org/.

30. Suzanne Goldenberg, "Thousands Protest at the White House against Keystone XL Pipeline," *The Guardian*, November 6, 2011, https://www.theguardian.com/environment/2011/nov/07/keystone-xl-pipeline-protest-white-house.

31. Brad Plumer, "The Keystone XL Pipeline Is Dead. Here's Why Obama Rejected It," *Vox*, November 7, 2015, https://www.vox.com/2015/11/6/9681340/obama-rejects-keystone-pipeline.

32. Sandra Laville and Jonathan Watts, "Across the Globe, Millions Join Biggest Climate Protest Ever," *The Guardian*, September 20, 2019, https://www.theguardian.com/environment/2019/sep/21/across-the-globe-millions-join-biggest-climate-protest-ever.

33. Damian Carrington, "Climate Crisis Affects How Majority Will Vote in UK Election—Poll," *The Guardian*, October 30, 2019, https://www.theguardian.com/environment/2019/oct/30/climate-crisis-affects-how-majority-will-vote-in-uk-election-poll.

34. "Crisis in the Brazilian Amazon," Human Rights Watch, April 19, 2022, https://www.hrw.org/news/2022/04/19/crisis-brazilian-amazon.

35. Elizabeth Partsch, "Thousands in Brazil Protest against Anti-environmental

Laws," Impakter, March 12, 2022, https://impakter.com/brazil-deforestation-anti
-environmental-laws-indigenious/.

36. See, for example, London Edinburgh Weekend Return Group, *In and Against the State* (London: Pluto Press, 1980).

37. Akuno, "The Jackson-Kush Plan."

38. For an outine of the anti-union laws introduced across countries in the 1980s, see International Labour Organisation, *World Labour Report: 1997–98: Industrial Relations, Democracy and Social Stability* (Geneva: International Labour Organization, 1997), https://www.ilo.org/global/publications/ilo-bookstore/order
-online/books/WCMS_PUBL_9221103315_EN/lang--en/index.htm.

39. Isabelle Ferreras, Julie Battilana, and Dominique Meda, *Democratize Work: The Case for Reorganizing the Economy* (Chicago: University of Chicago Press, 2022).

40. Rebecca Gumbrell-McCormick and Richard Hyman, "Democracy in Trade Unions, Democracy through Trade Unions?," *Economic and Industrial Democracy* 40, no. 1 (August 2018), https://doi.org/10.1177/0143831X18780327.

41. Ibid.

42. Kyle Lewis and Will Stronge, *Overtime: Why We Need a Shorter Working Week* (London: Verso Books, 2021).

43. See 4 Day Week, https://www.4dayweek.co.uk/.

44. See, for example, Katharine Miller, "Radical Proposal: Universal Basic Income to Offset Job Losses Due to Automation," Stanford University Human-Centered Artificial Intelligence, October 20, 2021, https://hai.stanford.edu/news/radical
-proposal-universal-basic-income-offset-job-losses-due-automation.

45. See, for example, The Labour Party, "Universal Basic Services: The Right to a Good Life," https://labour.org.uk/wp-content/uploads/2019/09/12730_19-Universal
-Basic-Services_v5.pdf.

46. See, for example, Mathew Lawrence and Thomas Hanna, "Ownership Futures: Towards Democratic Public Ownership in the 21st Century," Common Wealth, November 2, 2020, https://www.common-wealth.co.uk/publications/ownership
-futures-towards-democratic-public-ownership-in-the-twenty-first-century.

47. "When We Own It: A Model for Public Ownership in the 21st Century," We Own It, May 2019, https://weownit.org.uk/sites/default/files/attachments/When%20
We%20Own%20It%20-%202%20page%20summary.pdf.

48. "Alternative Models of Ownership," https://labour.org.uk/wp-content
/uploads/2017/10/Alternative-Models-of-Ownership.pdf.

49. James Muldoon, *Platform Socialism: How to Reclaim Our Digital Future from Big Tech* (London: Verso, 2022).

50. See https://platform.coop.

51. Akuno, "The Jackson-Kush Plan."

52. Mathew Lawrence, Andrew Pendleton, and Sara Mahmoud, "Co-operatives Unleashed: Doubling the Size of the UK's Co-operative Sector," New Economics Foundation, July 3, 2018, https://neweconomics.org/2018/07/co-operatives
-unleashed.

53. Mio Tastas Viktorsson and Saoirse Gowan, "Revisiting the Meidner Plan," *Jacobin*,

August 22, 2017, https://jacobin.com/2017/08/sweden-social-democracy-meidner -plan-capital.

54. Mathew Lawrence and Loren King, "Examining the Inclusive Ownership Fund," Common Wealth, November 13, 2019, https://www.common-wealth.co.uk /publications/examining-the-inclusive-ownership-fund.

55. See, for example, Jim Pickard, "UK's Labour Would Seize £300bn of Company Shares," *Financial Times*, September 1, 2019, https://www.ft.com/content /dc17d7ee-ccab-11e9-b018-ca4456540ea6.

56. Isabelle Ferreras, Julie Battilana, and Dominique Meda, *Democratize Work*.

57. See, e.g., Pickard, "UK's Labour Would Seize £300bn of Company Shares."

58. Michael A. McCarthy, "The Politics of Democratizing Finance: A Radical View," *Politics & Society* 47, no. 4 (December 2019): 611–33, https:// doi.org/10.1177/0032329219878990; Fred Block and Robert Hockett, *Democratizing Finance: Restructuring Credit to Transform Society* (London: Verso, 2022).

59. Christine Berry and Laurie MacFarlane, "A New Public Banking System: A Report to the Labour Party Commissioned by the Communication Workers Union and the Democracy Collaborative," The Labour Party, https://labour.org.uk/wp-content /uploads/2019/03/Building-a-new-public-banking-ecosystem.pdf.

60. Mariana Mazzucato and Caetano Penna, "The Rise of Mission-Oriented State Investment Banks: The Cases of Germany's KfW and Brazil's BNDES," SWPS 2015-26, September 16, 2015, http://dx.doi.org/10.2139/ssrn.2744613.

61. McCarthy, "The Politics of Democratizing Finance: A Radical View."

62. Blakeley, *Stolen*. The UK think tank Common Wealth later developed this proposal in their report: Adrienne Buller, Chris Hayes, and Mathew Lawrence, "Asset Manager Capitalism: Where Next?," Common Wealth, June 21, 2022, https://www.common-wealth.co.uk/publications/asset-manager-capitalism -where-next.

63. Richard S. Katz and Peter Mair, "The Cartel Party Thesis: A Restatement," *Perspectives on Politics* 7, no. 4 (December 2009): 753–66, https://www.jstor.org /stable/40407077.

64. Peter Mair, *Ruling the Void: The Hollowing Out of Western Democracy* (London: Verso, 2013).

65. OECD (Graph), "In most OECD countries there has been a decline in electoral participation: Voter turnout in latest parliamentary election, early 1990s and late 2010s, percentage of the voting age population," in *Society at a Glance 2019: OECD Social Indicators* (OECD Publishing: Paris, 2019), https://doi .org/10.1787/907b3eb1-en.

66. Yascha Mounk and Roberto Stefan Foa, "Confidence in Democracy Is at a Low Point," *The Atlantic*, January 29, 2020, https://www.theatlantic.com/ideas /archive/2020/01/confidence-democracy-lowest-point-record/605686/.

67. "Freedom in the World 2021: Democracy under Siege," Freedom House, accessed July 11, 2023, https://freedomhouse.org/report/freedom-world/2021/democracy -under-siege.

68. David M. Woodruff, "To Democratize Finance, Democratize Central

Banking," *Politics & Society* 47, no. 4 (November 2019), https://doi
.org/10.1177/0032329219879275.

69. "Influence of Big Money," Brennan Center for Justice, accessed July 11, 2023,
https://www.brennancenter.org/issues/reform-money-politics/influence-big
-money.

70. Katz and Mair, "The Cartel Party Thesis."

71. The German system of Mixed Member Representation achieves both of these aims,
while remaining fairly proportional.

72. Cristina Flesher Forminaya, "Between Movement and Party: The Case of
Podemos," in Grace Blakeley (ed.), *Futures of Socialism: The Pandemic and the
Post-Corbyn Era* (London: Verso, 2020).

73. See, for example, James Tilley and Geoffrey Evans, *The New Politics of Class:
The Political Exclusion of the British Working Class* (Oxford: Oxford University
Press, 2017).

74. "Honest Accounts 2017—How the World Profits from Africa's Wealth," Global
Justice Now, May 24, 2017, https://www.globaljustice.org.uk/resource/honest
-accounts-2017-how-world-profits-africas-wealth/.

75. Kevin P. Gallagher and Richard Kozul-Wright, *The Case for a New Bretton Woods*
(London: Wiley, 2022).

76. Ibid.

77. For a fascinating example that looks at the centrality of Brazilian workers to
campaigns for unionization in the gig economy in the UK, see Callum Cant, *Riding
for Deliveroo: Resistance in the New Economy* (London: Wiley, 2019).

78. Karl Marx, *Grundrisse: Foundations of the Critique of Political Economy*
(London: Penguin UK, 2005).

79. For a discussion see David Harvey, "We Need a Collective Response to the
Collective Dilemma of Coronavirus," *Jacobin*, April 24, 2020, https://jacobin.
com/2020/04/david-harvey-coronavirus-pandemic-capital-economy.

Index

A

aerospace industry, 3–10, 16–19, 23, 215–22
Afghanistan, 8, 104
African National Congress (ANC), 202–3
agrochemical industry, 90–91, 123–24
Airbus, 10, 17
Akuno, Kali, 236–37, 251–52
Alibaba, 57–58, 110–11, 171
Allende, Salvador, 241–47, 265, 271
Alphabet (Google), 94, 95, 133
Alpha Natural Resources, 55
Althusser, Louis, 164–65
Amazon, 75–81, 87, 88, 95, 96
   Amazon Prime, 76
   Amazon Web Services (AWS), 75, 76, 79
   Atlas Air ("Amazon Air" subcontractor), 77
   lobbying by, 105–6
   monopoly power of, 75–77, 132–34
   New Taylorism and, 100
   Washington Post acquisition, 80
American International Group (AIG), 48–53, 136
American Samoa, US colonialism and, 174
Andalusian Workers' Union, 230
Anti-Corruption Data Collective, 43
antisemitism, 19–20, 43–44, 53
Aramco, 133
Árbenz, Jacobo, 187–89
Architect or Bee? (Cooley), 216–17
Argentina, Ciudad Futura, 234–35, 255
Armas, Carlos Castillo, 189
ARPANET, 244

Australia
   COVID-19 aid to corporations, 46
   green bans, 227–29
   Philip Morris packaging dispute, 194
   resistance to the labor movement, 78
automotive industry, 29, *see also* Ford Motor Company
AV Jennings, 227

B

BAE Systems, 220–21
Bagehot, Walter, 179
Bailey, Andrew, 64–65
Bailout Watch, 141–42
Ballantyne, R. M., 222–24
Bandung Conference (1955), 190–91, 261, 262
Bank Dyalco, 124
Bank of America, 123–24
Bank of Canada, 136
Bank of England, 64–65, 115–16, 210
   Covid Corporate Financing Facility (CCCF) and, 45–46, 155–56
   Eurodollar trading and, 131
   origins of, 125
Bank of Japan, 127–28, 210
banks and banking, *see* central banks; international finance system *and names of specific banks and institutions*
Barak, Gregg, 107
Baran, Paul, 93–94, 96, 97, 99
Barbados, climate breakdown and, 70–71
Barkan, Joshua, 143

BASF, 45
Bayer, 45, 90, 91, 106, 123–24
Bear Stearns, 136
Beer, Stafford, 244–45
behavioral economics, 162–67
Bello, Walden, 176–77
Benn, Tony, 215, 247
Bernard L. Madoff Investment Securities
    LLC, 120–21
Bevins, Vincent, 191
Bezos, Jeff, 75–77, 80–81, 132
Biden, Joe, 69, 70–71, 136, 140–42
Big Three asset managers, 133, 135, 137
biopolitics (Foucault), 105
BlackRock, 69, 132–37, 257
Blackstone Financial Management, 44, 133
"black swan" events, 50, 114
Blackwater, 104
Bodie, Matthew, 254
Boeing, 3–10, 86, 87, 96, 225
    agreements with Southwest Airlines, 5,
        10, 16
    Boeing 737 MAX, 3–9, 17, 218–19
    Boeing 787 Dreamliner, 4–5, 8
    capitalism and, 16–17
    corporate welfare and, 7–8, 29
    MCAS (Maneuvering Characteristics
        Augmentation System), 4, 5–7
    merger with McDonnell Douglas, 4,
        8–9
    shareholder distributions, 6
Bolsonaro, Jair, 251
BP, 64
Braithwaite, Michael, 163–64
Braun, Benjamin, 129–30
Braverman, Harry, 99–100
Brazil
    Amazon environmental protections,
        251
    Fordlândia in, 22–23, 186
    Porto Alegre model for participatory
        budgeting (PB), 232–33, 247
Bregman, Rutger, 224
Bretton Woods, 51
British Business Bank (BBB), 156–57
Brook House (UK), 102
Brown, Matthew, 237–38, 247
Brown, Wendy, 33, 34, 143, 167
Buffett, Warren, 95

Builders Labourers Federation (BLF,
    Australia), 227–29
Bukharin, Nikolai, 182
bureaucratization, 34–35, 147
Burke, Edmund, 103
Bush, George W., 140

C

Calhoun, David, 9
Cameron, David, 54, 154–56, 162
campaign finance reform, 259
Canada
    COVID-19 aid to corporations, 46,
        136
    Ethyl Corp. lawsuit and, 197
    resistance to the labor movement, 78
    Toronto Community Housing
        Corporation (THTC) participatory
        budgeting, 232–33
Canada Infrastructure Bank, 136
Capita, 164
Capital (Marx), vii
capitalism, 11–17
    alliances among capitalists in, 13–14
    centralization of power in, xvi–xvii, 92,
        136–37
    central vs. corporate planning and, x–xiv,
        xvi, xix–xx, 14–16
    class divisions in, x, xix, 11–14, 38–39,
        82–84, 108, 151, 158–60, 216–18,
        252, 259, 268
    democracy and, xiv–xv, 147, *see also*
        democratic planning
    dialectic/creative tension between
        markets and planning, xvi–xvii, 37, 53,
        123, 126
    distinction between capital and labor,
        30–39
    feudalism vs., 12–13, 266, 269–71
    foundations of, 264–66, 268–71
    free markets and competition and, ix,
        11–14, 15–17, 30, 36–39, 97–98, 137,
        221, 268–70
    fusion of political and economic power
        in, xviii, 10, 13–15, 33, 80, 82–84,
        95–96, 104–8, 183–85, 190, 264–65
    fusion of public and private power in,
        142–43, 159–60
    human capital and, 33, 148, 166–67

as hybrid system of competitive pressure and centralized control, ix, 16, 37, 47, 123, 269

imperialism as highest stage of, 183

international finance system as time lords of, 109, 113–14

investor-capitalists, 118, 148

Keynes and, *see* Keynes, John Maynard

Marx and, *see* Marx, Karl

means of production in, 12–13, 247, 264

"mini-capitalists" and, 33, 118, 122–23

nature of capital and, 11, 12–13

need for business firms in, 81–85

negative externalities, 88–89

new industrial capitalism (Galbraith), 37

pursuit of profit in, xiii–xiv, 25, 29

rewards for competitiveness, 225–26

as rule by capital vs. free markets, 10–11, 36–39, 137

socialism vs., 221

socialized capitalism (Galbraith), 97–98

social relationships in, 11, 13, 143, 157–59, 164, 170, 172, 265–66

stakeholder capitalism, 35–36, 135–36, 148

state vs. markets and, 220–22

surveillance capitalism, 27, 54–58, 94, 98–100, 155

see also disaster capitalism

CARES Act (2020), 9–10

Cayman Islands, as tax haven, 42, 132

central banks, 124–32

bank bailouts in the United Kingdom and, 31–32

BlackRock and, 136

democratizing, 258

emergence of central banking, 124–25

legitimacy questions, 129–32

loanable funds model and, 114–18

quantitative easing (QE) and, 127–28, 129, 136

swap lines among, 209–10

US dollar and, 178, 209–10

see also specific central banks

Central Intelligence Agency (CIA, US), 175, 189, 241

centralized planning

by Amazon, 75–81

in capitalist economies, 14–16, 24, 66–71, 98, 143, 266

collective action problem and, 47–48, 67, 70, 159–61, 166–67, 248–49, 253

corporatism/corporate planning vs., x–xiv, 14–16, 27, 30, 84

democratic, *see* democratic planning

empires and, *see* empire planning

financial crisis of 2008 and, 49–50

at Ford Motor Company, 19–24

Galbraith on, 97–98

Gramsci on, 24

Hayek on, x–xii

international finance system and, 113–14

neoliberal revolution vs., 24–26

resisting, 71–72

by states, *see* state planning

by Walmart, 88, 264, 265

Chamayou, Grégoire, 27, 30

Chan, Jackie, 168

Chang, Ha-Joon, 146, 180, 182

Chao, Elaine, 42–43

ChemChina, 90, 91, 124

Chemring Group, 46

Chevron, 64, 194–96, 205

Chicago School, 150–51, 199

Chile

democratic socialism in, 241–46

National Telecommunications Enterprise, 245

Project Cybersyn, 245–46, 247, 265, 266

State Development Corporation (CORFO), 244–45

violence of the neoliberal state in, 34

Chiluba, Frederick, 206

China

Belt and Road Initiative, 171–72, 182–83

COVID-19 surveillance and, 57–58

developmentalism and, 137, 170–72

Evergrande Group implosion, 167–69, 171

state planning in, 167–72

China CITIC Bank International, 124

Chiquita (formerly United Fruit Company, UFC), 186–89

Christophers, Brett, 136

Chrysler, 29

Citigroup, 120, 124

Civil War, 144

climate breakdown, viii, 66–71
  Amazon and, 79
  decarbonization efforts, 67, 69–71, 78, 135, 140–41, 250–51, 256, 263
  economic power of capital and, 15
  Extinction Rebellion and Fridays for Future, 251
  fossil-fuel sector and, 66, 69, 139–43
  Global North and, 263
  Global South and, 263
  Green New Deal proposal, 69, 248
  need for cooperation and, 66–71, 216, 247–52

Climate Leviathan (Wainwright and Mann), 70

Coase, Ronald, 81, 83–85

Coca-Cola, 81

Cold War, ix, xx

collective action problems, 47–48, 66–71, 159–61, 166–67, 248–49, 253, *see also* democratic planning

Collins Aerospace, 219

Colombia, surveillance of Teleperformance workers, 99

Communist Manifesto (Marx), 152

Communist Party
  of China, 171
  of Guatemala, 188
  of Indonesia, 191

community wealth building (CWB), 237–38

comparative advantage (Ricardo), 179–81

computer technology
  ARPANET, 244
  coop app platforms, 154–55, 254–55
  data protection and privacy, 27, 54–58, 94, 99, 155
  in democratizing the future, 264–66
  dot-com bubble (1997–2001), 110–11, 120, 133
  intellectual property rights and, 262
  Project Cybersyn (Chile) and, 245–46, 247, 265, 266
  surveillance capitalism and, 27, 54–58, 94, 98–100, 155
  Walmart centralized planning and, 88, 264, 265

Connolly, James, 59, 61

conspiracy theories, xvi, 38, 43–44, 53

Cooley, Mike, 216–20

Coons, Chris, 141

COP26 (UN Climate Change Conference, 2021), 70–71

Coral Island, The (Ballantyne), 222–24

Corbyn, Jeremy, 250

Cornered (Lynn), 21

corporations
  central vs. corporate planning, x–xiv
  corporate crime and, 106–7, 119–24, 156–57, 220–21
  corporate sovereignty, xiv, 22–23, 25, 80, 103–8, 143
  corporatism and, x–xiv, 14–16, 27, 30, 84
  COVID-19 pandemic programs, 9–10, 41–49, 59–60, 141–42, 155–56
  democratic planning and, *see* democratic planning
  expanding collective ownership of, 253–55, 257
  fusion of political and economic power of, xviii, 10, 13–15, 33, 80, 82–84, 95–96, 104–8, 183–85, 190, 264–65
  lobbying by, 105–6, 140, 141–42, 151, 159, 259
  managerialism and, 34–35, 84, 100, 108, 216
  profit maximization by, xiii–xiv, 25, 29
  see also taxes and taxation

COVID-19 pandemic
  airline industry and, 9
  BlackRock and, 136
  call center workers and, 98–99
  CARES Act (2020) and, 9–10
  corporate beneficiaries of, 9–10, 41–49, 59–60, 141–42, 155–56
  cost-of-living crisis, 48, 58, 63–66, 129
  Evergrande (China) implosion and, 167–69, 171
  fossil-fuel industry and, 64, 141–42
  frauds and scams in, 156–57
  housing crisis and, 43, 44–45
  inflation and, 63–66

McKinsey & Company and, 53–58, 155

mortality measures during, 105

shareholder distributions/share buybacks during, 45–47, 59–60, 64

shipping companies and, 62–63, 64

state economic programs in, 41–48

supply chain financing and, 153–54

surveillance programs, 57–58, 98–99

UK responses to, 45–46, 53–61, 155–57, 162–63

US responses to, 41–45

WeWork business model and, 112

worker loss of income and poverty, 60, 63, 98–99

zoonotic disease and, 68

creative destruction (Schumpeter), 86, 95, 96

Credit Suisse, 52, 123–24, 153–54

crony capitalism, 34

Crothers, Bill, 155–56

Crown Commercial Service (CCS, UK), 155–56

Crown Prosecution Service (CPS, UK), 102

Cunningham, Ceri, 239–40

Curaçao, as tax haven, 45

D

Dalton, David, 155

Danone, 46

Dark Waters (2019 film), 91

data protection and privacy, 27, 54–58, 94, 99, 155

Davis, Mike, 68

Dawn of Everything, The (Wengrow and Graeber), 224–25

Dayen, David, 89

Debt (Graeber), 125

Debt Collective (US), 249–50

Decree 900 (Guatemala), 188

de Guzman, Leody, 177

Delinquent Genius (Cooley), 217

democracy
capitalism and, xiv–xv, 147
democratizing the state, 257–61
planning and, *see* democratic planning
as synonymous with socialism (Meiksins Wood), xviii
"unfreedom" and, xiv–xv

Democratic Party (US)
fossil-fuel industry and, 140–41, 142
in Mississippi, 236

democratic planning, 215–66
Argentina, Ciudad Futura, 234–35, 255
Australia, green bans, 227–29
Brazil, participatory budgeting, 232–33, 247
in Chile, 241–46
for the future, 264–66
human nature and, 222–26
Iceland, Better Reykjavik program, 235–36, 258–59
India, Kerala people's planning, 233–34
international finance system and, 255–57
international institutions and, 261–64
Mississippi, Cooperation Jackson program, 236–37, 247, 251–52, 255
participatory budgeting (PB), 232–33, 235–36, 258–59
people-powered planning, 226–40, 247–52
Spain, Marinaleda workers' collective, 229–30
state-level, 241–46, 257–61
UK, Blaenau Ffestiniog program (Wales), 238–40
UK, Greater London Enterprise Board, 216–17, 219–20
UK, Lucas Plan/Lucas Aerospace Corporation, xix, 215–22, 226, 229, 231, 247, 248, 266
UK, People's Plan for the Royal Docks (London), 230–31
UK, Preston community wealth building (CWB) program, 237–38, 247, 255
for work and the corporation, 252–55

democratic socialism, 216–17, 241–48, 265

Democratic Socialists of America (DSA), 250

dependency theory, 184–86, 199, 205

deregulation, xv–xvi, 7, 31, 32, 51, 170, 206

Deutsche Bank, 49

developmentalism, 137, 170–72, 205–8

disaster capitalism, 41–71
climate breakdown and, 66–71

disaster capitalism (*cont.*)
  collective action problems and, 47–48,
    67, 70, 159–61, 248–49, 253
  corporate welfare programs and, 31–32
  COVID-19 pandemic and, *see* COVID-
    19 pandemic
  financial crisis of 1987 and, 126–27
  financial crisis of 1997 and, 51, 200
  financial crisis of 2008 and, *see* financial
    crisis of 2008 (subprime bubble)
  nature of, 38
  shock doctrine (N. Klein) and, 38, 193,
    198
  states of emergency and, 57
  Suez Canal and, 61–66
discrimination
  abuse of migrants, 101–3
  antisemitism, 19–20, 43–44, 53
  in apartheid South Africa, 202–4
  homophobic attacks, 103
  land/property seizures from indigenous
    peoples, 186–90, 228, 251
Doctor Who (television series), 109
Donegal International, 207
Donziger, Steven, 195–96
dot-com bubble (1997–2001), 110–11, 120,
  133
Dow Chemical, 90, 124
Driver's Co-Operative (cooperatively owned
  app), 254
Ducera, 123–24
DuPont, 23, 90–91, 124
Durand, Frederic, 129
Durkan, Jenny, 79
DXC, 45
Dyal, Gordon, 124
Dyalco, 124

E

Earnd (app), 154–55
East India Company (EIC), 22, 103–4,
  183
Ebbers, Bernard, 119–20
Ecuador, Chevron's "Amazon Chernobyl"
  disaster, 194–96, 205
Eeckhout, Jan, 87–88
Egg Baby, 110
Egypt, Suez Canal and, 61–66
Eisenhower, Dwight, 188–89

electoral systems, 259–61
  campaign finance reform, 259
  lobbying by corporations, 105–6, 140,
    141–42, 151, 159, 259
  political donations/contributions and,
    43–44, 80, 140, 141, 259
  working-class candidates and, 260–61
Elizabeth I (Queen of England), 103
Elizabeth II (Queen of England), 114
El Salvador, gold mining prevention in,
  197
Emissions Trading System (European
  Union), 69
empire planning, 173–211
  "banana republics" and, 186–93
  China, Belt and Road policy, 171–72,
    182–83
  comparative advantage (Ricardo) and,
    180–81
  dependency theories, 184–86
  fossil-fuel industry and, 194–97
  free trade policies and, 181–82
  imperialism and, 173–81, 183–85
  international development in, 180–81
  investor-state dispute settlement (ISDS),
    194–98
  nature of empire and, 177–79
  shock therapy, 38, 193, 198, 200–201
  structural adjustment programs (SAPs),
    198–202
  US colonialism and, 173–79, 209–10
  vulture capitalism, 202–11
employer-employee relationship, 83–85
Engels, Friedrich, 121
Enron, 55, 119
entrepreneurialism, xv–xvi, 33, 41, 85, 92,
  116–18, 167
environmental issues, *see* climate
  breakdown
Estonia, Your Priorities platform, 236
Ethiopian Airlines Flight 302 (2019), 3–4,
  219
Ethyl Corp., 197
European Central Bank (ECB), 46, 210
European Commission, 87
European Union (EU)
  Emissions Trading System (ETS), 69
  enforcement of competition law, 87
  "green" stimulus packages, 69

labor movement and, 78

United Kingdom membership in, 154

Evergrande Group (China) implosion,
167–69, 171

Everything Store, The (Stone), 80

Export-Import Bank (EXIM), 243

ExxonMobil, 64, 139–41

F

Facebook/Meta, vii, 94, 106

Fannie Mae, 50

Fanon, Frantz, 177

Ferreras, Isabelle, 83

feudalism, 12–13, 266, 269–71

Finance Capital (Kautsky), 121–22

financial crisis of 1630s (tulip bubble), 126

financial crisis of 1987 (stock market
crash), 126–27

financial crisis of 1997 (Asian crisis), 51,
200

financial crisis of 2008 (subprime bubble),
xiv, 126

American International Group (AIG)
bailout and, 48–53, 136

bond ratings agencies and, 50

as crisis of regulatory capture, 32

Evergrande (China) implosion, 167–69,
171

Ford Motor Company and, 29–30

globalization of finance and, 50–51,
209–10

Iceland, Better Reykjavik participatory
budgeting program, 235–36, 258–59

international finance system and, 207,
209–10, *see also* international finance
system

lack of prosecutions following, 38–39,
52, 131–32

McKinsey & Company and, 54–55

mortgage-backed securities and, 41,
48–50, 52, 54, 106, 127, 128–30

Occupy movement, 249–50

origins in the US, 209–10

predictions of, 114–15, 117–18

private debt creation and, 117–18

quantitative easing (QE) and, 127–28,
129, 136

Strike Debt campaign/Rolling Jubilee,
249–50

Troubled Asset Relief Program (TARP,
2008), 29, 49, 53

financial institutions, *see* central banks;
international finance system

Fink, Larry, 69, 132–37, 142

First Boston, 133

Flores, Fernando, 244–45

Florida, Pulse nightclub shooting (2016),
103

Floyd, George, 101

Flying Blind (Robison), 6

Foccart, Jacques, 177

food

agrochemical and seed industry, 90–91,
123–24

land degradation and, 68

pesticides/herbicides, 68, 90–91, 124

Ford, Henry, 19–22, 26, 28, 75, 160

Ford, Henry, II, 23, 26, 27, 28

Ford Motor Company, 19–30, 75, 86, 87,
96

corporate welfare and, 25, 29–30

Five-Dollar Day, 21, 26

Fordist production approach, 19–24

Fordlândia, 22–23, 186

Ford Motor Credit Company (FMCC),
28–29

labor movements at, 19–22, 26–29, 31,
75

shareholder distributions, 28, 29–30, 31

fossil-fuel industry, 62–64, 66, 69, 139–43,
194–97, 205, 251

Foucault, Michel, 105, 165, 170

four-day workweek proposal, 248, 253

fractional reserve banking, 114–18

France

COVID-19 aid to corporations, 46

imperialism of, 177

Franco, Francisco, 229

Freddie Mac, 50

Freedom Farms Cooperative (Mississippi),
237

free-market capitalism, ix, 11–14, 15–17,
30, 36–39, 97–98, 137, 221, 268–70

Friedman, Milton, 34, 150

G

G4S (Government 4 Sale), 46, 101–3, 104

Gabon, 177

Galbraith, J. K., 37, 97–98
Gallagher, Kevin, 262
General Electric, 4
General Motors, 27, 29
General Theory of Employment, Interest, and Money, The (Keynes), xi
Germany
  Berlin Wall removal, 200–201
  campaign finance by state and, 259
  competition policy and, 150
  COVID-19 aid to corporations in, 45, 46–47
  Ford Motor as supplier to, 23–24
  Green Party, 229
  labor movement and, 78, 248
  Nazi Party/Third Reich, 19, 23–24, 93, 122, 183–84, 226
  social market economy (Röpke) and, 203
  Vattenfall lawsuit and, 197
  Weimar Republic, 121–22
  World War II and, 158, 181
GFG Alliance, 153, 156–57
Ghana
  independence from Britain (1957), 177
  Non-Aligned Movement and, 190–91
  structural adjustment programs (SAPs) and, 200
gig economy, 92–93, 253, 254
Gindin, Sam, 31, 198, 210
Global Climate Coalition, 139
Global Intangible Low-Tax Income (GILTI), 42
Global North
  climate breakdown and, 263
  exploitation of the Global South by, 190–91, 261, 262
  Global South catching up to, 207–8
  Global South as challenge to, 182–83, 246
  Global South critique of neocolonialism and, 177, 208, 210–11
  international debt crisis, 198–202, 262
  market power and wage suppression, 93
  production by the Global South in, 185
  Washington Consensus policies, 200–201, 210

Global South
  catching up to Global North, 207–8
  as challenge to Global North, 182–83, 246
  climate breakdown and, 70–71, 263
  critique of neocolonialism of the Global North, 177, 208, 210–11
  exploitation by the Global North, 190–91, 261, 262
  international debt crisis, 198–202, 262
  market power and wage suppression by Global North, 93
  Non-Aligned Movement and, 190–92, 193
  production in the Global North and, 185
  solidarity among members of, 184–86, 192
  violence of the neoliberal state in, 34
Golding, William, 223–24, 226
Goldman Sachs, 48–49, 53, 54, 60, 123–24, 132–33, 225
Goodrich Corporation, 218
Google (Alphabet), 94, 95, 133
Gould, Matthew, 155
Graeber, David, 35, 125, 224–25, 265–66
Gramsci, Antonio, 20–22, 24, 157–58
Great Depression, 147
Greater London Council (GLC, UK), 219–20, 231
Greater London Enterprise Board (UK), 216–17, 219–20
Great Reversal, The (Philippon), 87–88
Greene, Marjorie Taylor, 43–44
Green New Deal proposal, 69, 248
Green Party (US), 251
Greenpeace, 140
Greensill, Lex, 152–59
Greensill Capital, 153–59
Greenspan, Alan, 127–29
Green Team Landscaping Co-op (Mississippi), 237
Grundrisse (Marx), 264
Guam, US colonialism and, 173, 174
Guatemala, United Fruit Company (UFC, now Chiquita) and, 186–90, 193
Guerra, Antonio, 195
Guevara, Che, 234
Gupta, Rajat, 54
Gupta, Sanjeev, 153, 156

H

Haley, Nikki, 8
Halliburton, 178, 193
Hancock, Matt, 154–56
Hancox, Dan, 230
Harding, Dido, 54, 155
Hassan, Maggie, 141
Hawaii, US colonialism and, 173
Hayden, Grant, 254
Hayek, Friedrich A., xvii–xx, 34–36, 89,
  100–101, 108, 146–47, 167, 202,
  217
  critique of centralized planning, x–xii
  Highway Code, 148–52, 165, 204
  Keynes vs., xvi, 268
  neoliberalism and, x–xii, xv–xvi
  The Road to Serfdom, vii, xi, 34, 204
Hearn, Denise, 89
Helleiner, Eric, 51
Higgins, Michael D., 217
Highway Code (Hayek), 148–52, 161,
  204
Hilferding, Rudolf, 121–23
Hitler, Adolf, 19, 23
Hobbes, Thomas, 144, 222, 226
homophobic attacks, 103
Hoover, Herbert, 22
housing crisis, viii
  Cooperation Jackson (Mississippi)
    affordable housing, 236–37, 247,
    251–52, 255
  corporate landlords and, 44–45
  COVID-19 pandemic and, 43, 44–45
  financial crisis of 2008 and, 52
How Europe Underdeveloped Africa
  (Rodney), 185
H&R Block, 106
HSBC, 124
Huffington, Arianna, 38
Humankind (Bregman), 224

I

Iceland, Better Reykjavik participatory
  budgeting program, 235–36, 258–59
ideological state apparatus (ISA), 164–65
Ifans, Rhys, 239
immigrants
  labor movements and, 263
  UK immigrant policies, 163–64, 263
India
  Bhopal, gas tragedy (2001), 90
  East India Company (EIC), 103–4, 183
  Kerala, People's Planning, 233–34
indigenous peoples
  Australian green bans and, 228
  climate breakdown and, 251
  critique of European society, 224–25
  in Guatemala, 189–90
  land/property seizures from, 186–90,
    228, 251
Indonesia
  Jakarta Method and, 190–92
  Non-Aligned Movement and, 190–91,
    193
industrial system (Galbraith), 97–98
inflation
  cost-of-living crisis, 48, 58, 63–66, 129
  Ever Given crisis (2021) and, 62–63, 64
  oil price spikes and, 62, 63
  sellers' inflation, 64–65
  Volcker shock and, 198, 205
  wage-price spiral argument and, 63–65
InfluenceMap, 140
interest rates
  inflation and, 65–66, 198, 205
  international finance system and, 115
  Volcker shock and, 198, 205
Intergovernmental Panel on Climate
  Change, 67–68
international finance system, 109–37
  Big Three institutional investors, 133,
    135, 137
  BlackRock, 69, 132–37, 257
  capital flight threat and, 93, 96, 204–5,
    208, 246, 262
  central banks and, *see* central banks
  centralization of global capitalism and,
    136–37
  confidence in, 116–18
  democratic planning and, 255–57
  developmentalism and, 137, 170–72,
    205–8
  dynamics of debt and, 114–18, 168–69,
    262
  economic nationalism vs., 204–5
  financial crisis of 2008 and, *see* financial
    crisis of 2008 (subprime bubble)
  financialization in, 121–24, 199

international finance system (*cont.*)
  fractional reserve banking, 114–18
  fraud and scandals in, 119–24, 220–21
  international debt crisis, 198–202, 262
  International Monetary Fund (IMF) and, 53, 114, 176, 198–200, 206–8, 262
  manias, panics, and crashes, 125–26
  mergers and acquisitions, 133
  planning power in, 113–14
  private law and, 130–32
  regulation of, 32, 113, 116, 130, 148, 150
  stakeholder capitalism and, 135–36
  structural adjustment programs (SAPs), 198–202
  taxes and, *see* taxes and taxation
  time lords of capitalism and, 109, 113–14
  US dollar and, 178, 209–10
  Washington Consensus policies, 200–201, 210
  WeWork/SoftBank relationship, 109–13, 117
  World Bank in, 176–77, 198–99, 206–8
International Labour Organization (ILO, UK), 60
International Monetary Fund (IMF), 53, 114, 176, 199–200, 206–8, 262
International Trade Union Confederation, 75
Intuit, 106
investor-state dispute settlement (ISDS), 194–98
Iraq, 105, 178, 192–93
Israel
  COVID-19 response, 57
  Suez crisis (1956), 61–62
Italy, labor movement and, 78

J
Jakarta Method, The (Bevins), 190–92
Jameson, Frederic, xix, 16
Japan
  developmentalism and steel industry, 172
  housing boom, 127
  quantitative easing by the Bank of Japan, 127–28
  in World War II, 175–76, 190, 191
Jassy, Andrew, 78
Jiayin, Xu, 167–69
Johnson, Boris, 70–71

Johnson, Desmond, 164
Johnson, Lyndon B., 27, 176
Johnson, Trevor, 164
Jones Act (1916, US), 174–75
JPMorgan, 52, 120–21, 123–24
JPMorgan Chase, 119

K
Kaleki, Michael, 97
Kao, Martin, 44
Kaplan, Lewis, 195
Kautsky, Karl, 121–23
Keen, Steve, 114–15
Kelly, Mark, 141
Kelly, Petra, 229
Kelly's Bush (Australia), 227–28
Kennedy, John F., 27, 181
Keynes, John Maynard, xi, xvii, xx, 126, 149, 217, 268, 269
  ambivalence toward freedom and autonomy of the masses, xvi
  centralization of power in capitalism, xvii
  Hayek vs., xvi, 268
  privatized Keynesianism, 117–18
  regulated markets and, xvi
Keystone XL pipeline, 251
Kicking Away the Ladder (Chang), 146
King, Arthur, 228
Klein, Michael, 124
Klein, Naomi, 38, 193, 198
Kozul-Wright, Richard, 262
KPMG, 193
Kushner, Jared, 33
Kyoto Protocol, 139

L
Labor and Monopoly Capital (Braverman), 99–100
labor movements
  at Amazon, 75, 77–79
  in Australia, 227–29
  "banana republics" and, 187
  conflict with capital, 37, 148, 151, 160
  democratic planning and, 247–48, 252–53
  electoral systems and, 260–61
  employer-employee relationship and, 83–85

at Ford Motor Company, 19–22, 26–29,
31, 75
four-day workweek and, 248, 253
immigrant workers and, 263
Lucas Aerospace Corporation/Lucas Plan
and, 216–17
neoliberal resistance to, 15, 31, 33–34,
62, 64–65, 77–78, 148, 160, 216–17,
218, 220, 221, 252–53
in Spain, 78, 229–30
Tripartite Committee, 27–28, 30, 160
UK resistance to, 15, 31, 33–34, 62,
64–65, 77–78, 160, 216–17, 218, 220,
221
at United Fruit Company (UFC, now
Chiquita) and, 187
US resistance to, 31, 62
Volcker shock and, 198, 205
wage-price spiral argument and, 63–65
wage suppression, 60, 63, 92–93
worker ownership and, 255
Land Rover, 28
Lansdale, Edward, 175
Lash, Scott, 37
Lazydays Holdings, 42
Lee, Susie, 42
legal issues
competition law, 87, 150, 151
corporate crime, 106–7, 119–24, 156–57,
220–21
corporation as legal construct, 105–7
international court system, 178, 194–98,
203–4, 210
investor-state dispute settlement (ISDS),
194–98
private law, 130–32
see also taxes and taxation
Le Guin, Ursula K., 267
Lehman Brothers, 38, 48
Lenin, Vladimir, 59, 61, 122, 183
Lewis, John, 237
liberalism
"blind" justice in, 149
comparative advantage and, 180–81
incomplete liberal revolutions and, 258
links with imperialism, 179–80
Lion Air Flight 610 (2018), 3–4, 7
Liveris, Andrew, 124
Locke, John, 145–47, 165

London School of Economics, 114
Lord of the Flies, The (Golding),
223–24
Lucas Aerospace Corporation/Lucas Plan,
xix, 215–22, 226, 229, 231, 247, 248,
266
Lula da Silva, Luiz Inácio, 251
Lumumba, Chokwe, 236, 247
Lumumba, Chokwe Antar, 236
Luxembourg, as tax haven, 79
Lynn, Barry, 21

M
Ma, Jack, 171
Madoff, Bernie, 120–21
managerialism, 34–35, 84, 100, 108, 216
Manchin, Joe, 141
Mann, Geoff, 70
Marcos, Ferdinand, 175–76
Marcos, Imelda, 176
Marcos, Mariano, 175–76
market power
access to financing and, 96
of Amazon, 75–77, 79–81, 88, 132–34
COVID-19 pandemic and, 59–60, 65
creative destruction (Schumpeter) and,
86, 95, 96
of Ford Motor Company, 28
free markets vs., 13
monopoly and, *see* monopoly
nature of, 16, 76–80
oligopoly and, 94, 95
over suppliers, 95
political power and, 95–96, 104–8
price markups and, 65, 76, 87, 92
Marshall Plan, 263
Marx, Karl, 52–53, 68, 82, 84, 85, 92, 94,
98, 121–25, 182, 264–65
Capital, vii
centralization of power in capitalism,
xvii–xviii
Communist Manifesto, 152
Grundrisse, 264
means of production in capitalism,
12–13, 247, 264
Mateen, Omar, 103
MCAS (Maneuvering Characteristics
Augmentation System), 4, 5–7
McConnell, Mitch, 43

McDonald's, 81
McDonnell Douglas, 4, 8–9
McKinsey & Company, 53–58, 155
McNamara, Robert, 27, 176
Meagher, Michelle, 88, 107
Meidner Plan (Sweden), 255
Meiksins Wood, Ellen, xviii
Mein Kampf (Hitler), 19
mergers and acquisitions
   in the aerospace industry, 4, 8–9, 218–19
   of agrochemical companies, 90–91,
      123–24
   of Amazon, 80
   big tech and, 95
   COVID-19 pandemic and, 59–60
   of financial institutions, 133
   of fossil fuel companies, 194–96
Merrill Lynch Investment Managers, 133
Mesopotamia, 14
Meta/Facebook, vii, 94, 106
Metalclad Corp., 197
Mexico, Metalclad Corp. lawsuit and, 197
Microsoft, 95
middle class, emergence in capitalism, 98
Miliband, Ed, 158
Miliband, Ralph, 158, 159, 247, 260
military-industrial complex (US), 9–10, 23,
      25, 191–93, 217–20, 244
Minsky, Hyman, 113, 114
MIO Partners, 54–55
Mirowski, Philip, 36
Mississippi, Cooperation Jackson/Jackson-
      Kush Plan, 236–37, 247, 251–52, 255
money laundering, 120–21, 156–57
monopoly
   Amazon and, 75–77, 132–34
   limiting investment in, 96–97
   market concentration and, 91–92, 95
   measuring monopoly power, 87–88
   monopoly capitalism, 99–100
   prices and, 92, 94–95
   problems of monopoly power, 88–89
   temporary monopoly power
      (Schumpeter), 85–88, 96
monopsony, 93, 97
Monsanto, 90, 91, 106, 123–24
Moon, Cary, 79
Morgan Stanley, 123–24, 153
Mottley, Mia, 70–71

Mubenga, Jimmy, 101–2
Muilenburg, Dennis, 7
Mulally, Alan, 29–30
Mundey, Jack, 227–29
Mussolini, Benito, 20, 187

N

Nalundasan, Julio, 175
Napoleon Bonaparte, 187
Nasser, Gamal, 61
National Association of Realtors, 106
National Labor Relations Board (NLRB),
      78
Navatek LLC, 44
neoliberalism
   bureaucratization and, 34–35, 147
   challenge of capitalist state and, 165–66
   Chicago school of, 150–51, 199
   consumer freedom of choice and, xiv,
      xv–xvi, 166–67
   corporate welfare programs and, 7–8,
      25, 29–33, 140–42, *see also* taxes and
      taxation
   crisis of governability and, 30–31
   deregulation and, xv–xvi, 7, 31, 32, 51,
      170, 206
   distinction between capital and labor,
      30–39
   "double truths" of (Hayek), 36, 152
   efficient markets as lie at heart of, 36–39,
      146–47, 268
   "encasing" democracy around the world,
      203
   Hayek and, *see* Hayek, Friedrich A.
   human capital and, 33
   international rules and norms in,
      203–4
   key stakeholders in, 35–36
   managerialism and, 34–35, 84, 100, 108,
      216
   political vs. economic influence and, 33
   post–World War II popularity of, x–xii,
      24–26
   as regime of "managerial governance,"
      34–35
   resistance to labor movements, 15, 31,
      33–34, 62, 64–65, 77–78, 148, 160,
      216–17, 218, 220, 221, 252–53
   in South Africa, 203

state as rule-setter vs. planner, 149–52, 165, 204

state role in maintaining market competition, 148

structural adjustment programs (SAPs), 198–202

as term, x

vested interests in, 10, 32, 34, 35–36, 52, 56, 119, 120, 151–52, 246, 259, 268–69

violence and coercive power of, 33–34

Neumann, Adam, 109–13

New Deal reforms, 26, 28

New Economics Foundation (UK), 255

New Economy Organisers Network (NEON), 250

New International Economic Order (NIEO), 261

New Taylorism, 100

Nielsen, Juanita, 228

Nine Years' War (1688–97), 124–25

Nixon, Richard, 241, 242–43

Nkrumah, Kwame, 177, 190, 191, 200, 208

Non-Aligned Movement, 190–92, 193

Norway

COVID-19 response, 57

developmentalism and, 137

Nudge (Thaler and Sunstein), 162–63

O

Obama, Barack, 41, 251

Occupy movement, 249–50

oligopoly, prices and, 94–95

On the Principles of Political Economy and Taxation (Ricardo), 179–80

OpenSecrets, 43

opioid epidemic, 55–56

Our Lives in Their Portfolios (Christophers), 136

OxyContin, 55–56

P

Palmer, Geoffrey H., 43

Paltrow, Gwyneth, 110

Paltrow, Rebekah, 110

Panama, as tax haven, 43, 132

Panama Papers, 43

Panitch, Leo, 31, 198, 210

parliamentary socialism (Miliband), 247

participatory budgeting (PB), 232–33, 235–36, 247, 258–59

Paulson, Henry, 49

Paycheck Protection Program (PPP, US), 41–45

Pelosi, Nancy, 42

People's Asset Manager (PAM), 257

People's Grocery Initiative (Mississippi), 237

People's Republic of Walmart, The (Phillips and Rozworski), 88

pharmaceuticals industry, 55–56

Philip Morris, 194

Philippines, US colonialism and, 173–79

Philippon, Thomas, 87–88

Phillips, Leigh, 14, 88, 264

Pinochet, Augusto, 34, 246

Pistor, Katharina, 131

Platform Cooperative Consortium, 254

Poland

Balcerowicz Plan, 201

labor movement and, 78

Polanyi, Karl, 143

Ponzi schemes, 120–21, 156–57

Poulantzas, Nicos, 158–59

Prebisch, Raúl, 184–85, 199

Prince, Erik, 104

Prior, David, 155

prison-industrial complex (US), 33–34

Prison Notebooks (Gramsci), 20

privatization, 32–33

of authority, 102–3

Global South and, 198–99, 206–8

private law and, 130–32

privatized Keynesianism, 117–18

in Russia (former Soviet Union), 201

in the United Kingdom, 218

in Zambia, 206–8

Project Cybersyn (Chile), 245–46, 247, 265, 266

Project on Government Oversight (US), 43

Protocols of the Elders of Zion, The, 19

Puerto Rico, US colonialism and, 173, 174

Pulse nightclub (Florida), 103

Purdue Pharma, 55–56

Putin, Vladimir, 44, 140, 208

Q

quantitative easing (QE), 127–28, 129, 136

R

Rajan, Raghuram, 114
Raymond, Lee, 139–40
Raytheon Technologies, 219
Reagan, Ronald, 31, 62, 176
Reconstructing the Corporation (Hayden and Bodie), 254
Republican Party (US)
  deregulation trend, 7
  fossil-fuel industry and, 140, 141
Resistance Dairy (Argentina), 234
Ricardo, David, 146, 179–81
Road to Serfdom, The (Hayek), vii, xi, 34, 204
Robison, Peter, 6
Rockwell Collins, 219
Rodney, Walter, 185
Rolling Jubilee, 249–50
Röpke, Wilhelm, 150, 203, 208
Rostow, Walt, 181, 199
Roth, Joseph F., 43
Rothschild, 123–24
Roubini, Nouriel, 114
Roundup, 90, 124
Rozworski, Michal, 14, 88, 264
Ruffalo, Mark, 91
Russia (former Soviet Union)
  centralized planning and, ix
  Cold War and, ix, xx
  COVID-19 response, 57
  dependency theory and, 185–86
  fossil-fuel industry and, 140
  Gosplan central planning agency, 109
  privatization in, 201
  Ukraine and, 44, 64, 201
  World War II and, 181
Ruth's Hospitality Group, 41

S

Sachs, Jeffrey, 201
Sachs-Warner hypothesis, 181–82
Salomon Smith Barney, 120
Sánchez Gordillo, Juan Manuel, 229–30
Sanders, Bernie, 250
Sanofi, 46
Sato, Hajime, 172

Saudi Arabia, 46, 54, 140, 209, 220–21
Sawant, Kshama, 79–80
Schlumberger, 45
Schmidt, Robert, 23–24
Scholar, Tom, 156
Schumpeter, Joseph, 85–88, 94, 95–96, 117
Serageldin, Kareem, 52
service workers, 98–99
Shake Shack, 41
Shanahan, Patrick, 8
shareholder distributions
  of Boeing, 6
  COVID-19 aid to corporations and, 45–47, 59–60, 64
  of Ford Motor Company, 28, 29–30, 31
Shaxson, Nicholas, 131–32
Shell, 64
Shock Doctrine, The (Klein), 38, 193, 198
Siegel Group, 45
Silicon Valley Bank, 65
Sinema, Kyrsten, 141
Singapore, developmentalism and, 137
Slobocian, Quinn, 203
Smith, Adam, 14, 85, 103–4, 145–47, 151, 165
Smoke, Ben, 45
social contract theory, 143–52
social democracy
  cartelization problem, 259–60
  democratizing the future and, 264–66
  neoliberalism vs., 33–34
  post–World War II, 24–25
socialism
  capitalism vs., 221
  centralized planning and, 221
  Coase and, 83, 84
  COVID-19 pandemic and, xx, 59, 61
  dangers of, x
  democracy as synonymous with (Meiksins Wood), xviii
  democratic socialism, 216–17, 241–48, 265
  expanding collective ownership of firms, 253–55, 257
  freedom in, xix
  Gramsci and, 20
  Hayek and, x–xi
  lack of class divisions in, xix
  parliamentary (Miliband), 247
  socialized capitalism (Galbraith), 97–98

state planning vs., 66
technology in transition to, 265
United Kingdom resistance to, 220, 221
Société Generale, 49
SoftBank, 110–13, 117, 154
Son, Masayoshi, 110–13, 154, 171
South Africa
    prison torture techniques, 102–3
    vulture capitalism and, 202–4
South Korea, structural adjustment
        programs (SAPs) and, 200
Southwest Airlines, 5, 10, 16
Soviet Union, see Russia (former Soviet
        Union)
Spain
    Barcelona, Decidim participatory
        budgeting program, 236, 258–59
    labor movement and, 78, 229–30
    Spanish Empire, 173
specialization, 180
Stages of Economic Growth (Rostow), 181
stakeholder capitalism, 35–36, 135–36, 148
State and Revolution, The (Lenin), 59
State in Capitalist Society, The
        (R. Miliband), 158
state planning, 139–72
    behavioral economics and, 162–67
    capitalist political economy and, 36, 65,
        145–46, 165–66, 242
    in Chile, 241–46
    in China, 167–72
    comparisons between state and
        corporation, 166
    COVID-19 pandemic and, 41–48
    developmentalism in, 137, 170–72, 205–8
    fossil-fuel sector and, 139–43
    fusion of public and private power in
        capitalism, 142–43, 159–60
    Greensill Capital and supply chain
        financing, 152–59
    Hayek and, see Hayek, Friedrich A.
    liberal definition of nation-state and,
        149–50
    in Russia (former Soviet Union), ix
    social contract theory and, 143–52
    socialism vs., 66
    state as rule-setter vs. planner, 148–52,
        165, 204
    state as social creation and, 157–62

State Street, 133, 134
Stein, Jill, 251
Stiglitz, Joseph, 51, 200, 201
Stolen (Blakeley), 257, 258
Stone, Brad, 80
Stonecipher, Harry, 4–6, 8
Streeck, Wolfgang, 36
Strike Debt campaign/Rolling Jubilee
        (2012), 249–50
structural adjustment programs (SAPs),
        198–202
Suez Canal, 61–66
    Ever Given crisis (2021), 62–63, 64
    Suez crisis (1956), 61–62
Suharto, 191
Sukarno, 190–91
Sunak, Rishi, 156
Sunstein, Cass, 162–63
supply chain financing, 152–59
surveillance capitalism, 27, 54–58, 94,
        98–100, 155
Sweden, Meidner Plan, 255
Sweezy, Paul, 93–94, 96, 97, 99
Syngenta, 90–91, 124

T

taxes and taxation
    corporate tax exemptions and tax breaks,
        7–8, 54–55, 59, 65–66, 79–80, 93,
        106, 187, 207
    international tax avoidance and evasion,
        42, 45, 79, 131–32, 199, 208, 263–64
    private law and, 131
    undervaluing assets and, 188
    in Zambia, 205, 207
Taylorism, 99–100
technology, see computer technology
Teflon, 91
Teleperformance, 98–99
temporary monopoly power (Schumpeter),
        85–88, 96
Tencent, 57–58
Tepper, Jonathan, 89
Tester, John, 141
Texaco, 194
Thaler, Richard, 162–63
Thatcher, Margaret, 15, 31, 33–34, 62,
        160, 161–62, 218, 220–21, 230–31
Tillerson, Rex, 140

Total, 46
trade agreements, 261–62
Trades Union Congress (UK), 60
trade unions, *see* labor movements
transactions cost theory of the firm (Coase), 83, 84
Travis, Gregory, 5
Treasure Islands (Shaxson), 131–32
Tripartite Committee, 27–28, 30, 160
Troubled Asset Relief Program (TARP, 2008), 29, 49, 53
Trudeau, Justin, 136
Trump, Donald, 8, 9, 33, 43, 59, 104, 140
TRW, 218
tulip bubble (1630s), 126
TurboTax, 106
Twitter/X, vii, 54

U
Uber, 111
Ubico, Jorge, 187
UBS, 124
Ukraine, 44, 64, 201
Unchecked Corporate Power (Barak), 107
Union Carbide India Limited, 90
Union of Farm Workers (Spain), 229
unions, *see* labor movements
United Auto Workers (UAW), 26–29
United Fruit Company (UFC, now Chiquita), 186–89
United Kingdom (UK)
    al-Yamamah arms deal with Saudi Arabia, 220–21
    BAE Systems, 220–21
    Barrow Alternative Employment Committee, 220
    bureaucratization and, 34–35
    collective ownership proposals, 254, 255
    corporate welfare programs and, 31–32
    COVID-19 aid to corporations, 45–46, 155–57
    COVID-19 pandemic response and, 53–61, 155–57, 162–63
    East India Company (EIC), 22, 103–4, 183
    emergence of central banks and, 124–25
    European Union membership, 154

Greater London Enterprise Board, 216–17, 219–20
Green New Deal proposal, 69, 248
immigrant policies, 163–64, 263
imperialism of, 177, 179–81, 182
Labour Party, 158, 217, 250, 255, 256
Levellers and Diggers, 271
liberal revolution and, 258
London Docklands Development Corporation (LDDC), 230–31
London Energy and Employment Network (LEEN), 220
London Olympics (2012), 101
Lucas Aerospace Corporation/Lucas Plan, xix, 215–22, 226, 229, 231, 247, 248, 266
New Economics Foundation, 255
New Economy Organisers Network (NEON), 250
Nudge Unit, 162–64
Occupy movement, 250
People's Plan for the Royal Docks, 230–31
Post Banks proposal, 256
Preston Model, community wealth building (CWB), 237–38, 247, 255
resistance to the labor movement, 15, 31, 33–34, 62, 64–65, 77–78, 160, 216–17, 218, 220, 221
UK Border Agency, 102
Wales, Blaenau Ffestiniog economic development program, 238–40
wealth inequality in, 60–61
We Own It (think tank), 254
United Nations (UN)
    Climate Change Conference (COP26, 2021), 70–71
    Conference on Trade and Development (UNCTAD), 184
    Human Development Rankings, 206
United States (US)
    Central Intelligence Agency (CIA), 175, 189, 241
    Chicago school of neoliberalism, 150–51, 199
    colonialism and, 173–79, 209–10
    COVID-19 aid to corporations, 41–45
    Export-Import Bank (EXIM), 243
    Green New Deal proposal, 69, 248

Green Party, 251
"green" stimulus packages, 69
Keystone XL pipeline, 251
military-industrial complex, 9–10, 23,
     25, 191–93, 217–20, 244
New Deal reforms, 26, 28
Non-Aligned Movement and, 190–91
Occupy movement, 249–50
power in the global economy, 151, 198,
     205
prison-industrial complex, 33–34
resistance to the labor movement, 31, 62
US dollar as global reserve currency, 178,
     209–10
wealth inequality in, 60–61
US Air Force, 8
US Central Intelligence Agency (CIA), 175,
     189, 241
US Congress, COVID-19 aid to
     corporations and, 42–44
US Department of Defense, 8, 191–93
US Department of Energy, 29
US Department of Health and Human
     Services (HHS), 56–57
US Department of Justice
   McKinsey & Company settlement, 55
   price-fixing convictions, 94
US Department of the Treasury, 141
   COVID-19 pandemic and, 9–10
   financial crisis of 2008 and, 49–50, 53
US Department of Veterans Affairs (VA), 56
US Federal Aviation Administration (FAA),
     5–7
US Federal Emergency Management
     Administration (FEMA), 56–57
US Federal Reserve, 9, 126–29, 141
   COVID-19 pandemic and, 42
   financial crisis of 1987 and, 126–27
   financial crisis of 2008 and, 49–50, 127,
     209–10
   quantitative easing (QE) and, 127–28,
     129, 136
   US dollar as global reserve currency, 178,
     209–10
   Volcker shock, 198, 205
US Occupational Safety and Health
     Administration (OSHA), 77
US Securities and Exchange Commission
     (SEC), 55

US Small Business Administration (SBA), 41
United Technologies, 218–19
universal basic income (UBI)/universal basic
     services, 253
Up & Go (cooperatively owned app), 254
Urry, John, 37
US Virgin Islands, US colonialism and, 173,
     174
UTC Aerospace Systems, 218–19
Utopia of Rules, The (Graeber), 35

V

Valeant, 55
Vanguard, 133, 134
Vattenfall, 197
Veblen, Thorstein, xv, 13
Vietnam War, 175–76, 181, 227
Vivendi, 46
Volcker, Paul, 198, 205
Volkswagen, viii, 46–47
Volvo, 28
von Mises, Ludwig, 146–47, 161–62
vulture capitalism, 202–11
   in apartheid South Africa, 202–4
   in Zambia, 205–8, 210

W

wage suppression, 60, 63, 92–93
Wainwright, Joel, 70
Wales, Blaenau Ffestiniog economic
     development program, 238–40
Wall Street crash of 1929, xi
Walmart, 88, 134, 264, 265
War on Want, 196
Washington Consensus, 200–201, 210
Washington Post, acquisition by Amazon,
     80
Water Defenders, The (Broad and
     Cavanagh), 197
wealth inequality, 60–61, 87, 89, 97, 98
Wealth of Nations, The (Smith), 145
Weber, Isabella, 65
Welch, Jack, 4
Wengrow, David, 224–25
We Own It (UK think tank), 254
WeWork, 109–13, 117
William III (King of England), 124–25
Williams, Roger, 42
Wood, Leonard, 174–75

worker ownership
  Mississippi, Cooperation Jackson
    program, 236–37, 247, 251–52, 255
  Sweden, Meidner Plan, 255
  UK, Preston community wealth building
    (CWB) program, 237–38, 247, 255
Workers' Unity Collective (Spain), 229
World Bank, 176–77, 198–99, 206–8
WorldCom, 119–20
World Economic Forum, 135
World Health Organization (WHO), 90
World Transformed festival (UK), 250
World War II, xi
  Bretton Woods institutions following,
    51
  financial institutions established after,
    198–200

Ford Motor Company and, 23–24, 25
Germany and, 158, 181
Japan and, 175–76, 190, 191
new industrial capitalism (Galbraith)
  following, 37
Philippines and, 175–76
social democratic state following, 24–25

X
X/Twitter, vii, 54

Y
Yahoo!, 110

Z
ZAGG, Inc., 42
Zambia, vulture capitalism in, 205–8, 210

About the Author

Grace Blakeley, one of the fiercest anticapitalist advocates of her generation, is an author, journalist, and commentator. She attended the University of Oxford, where she graduated with a first-class honors degree in philosophy, economics, and politics and later obtained a master's in African studies. Her writing has appeared in *Tribune* and the *New Statesman*. She is the author of *Stolen* and *The Corona Crash,* and she edited *Futures of Socialism*. Find out more at GraceBlakeley.co.uk.